# What Your Colleagues Are Saying . . .

"There was a time when a book like this would have set out to try to persuade teachers. But that's not the issue anymore. . . . Teachers everywhere are asking themselves, 'How do I teach with informational texts?' Kathy Barclay and Laura Stewart provide a rich collection of practical answers to that question. Their book can, through its practical lessons, advice, and guidance, show teachers how to make informational text a joyful reality in the lives of our youngest scholars."

—TIMOTHY SHANAHAN
Distinguished Professor Emeritus
University of Illinois at Chicago

"Kathy Barclay and Laura Stewart have done a marvelous job of providing teachers with specific suggestions for making the most of informational texts—from choosing the right texts for students, to practical and effective instructional strategies that will help students engage in close reading of these important texts, to an actual lesson format for teaching informational texts. Teaching informational texts can be a challenge for primary grade teachers. *The Everything Guide to Informational Texts* will help teachers and students meet that challenge!"

—TIMOTHY RASINSKI, PhD
Kent State University

"The book is well written, well organized, and teacher friendly. It addresses a topic— the use of informational text with younger students—that has not been sufficiently addressed in guidelines associated with the CCSS. It contains valuable lists of children's nonfiction texts, annotated and organized by grade level. The suggested lesson format is illustrated concretely with sample lesson plans based on high-quality informational texts."

—LOUISA MOATS, EdD
Contributing Writer of the Common Core State Standards

"For K–2 teachers eager to select and teach from 'informational texts of substance,' Barclay and Stewart offer much guidance. With keen insight, they also direct our pedagogical attention to the oft-overlooked, but tremendously powerful, text complexity essentials— oral language development, read-aloud, and shared reading."

—JAN MILLER BURKINS
Author of *Preventing Misguided Reading*

The **Everything** Guide

to Informational Texts, K–2

Kathy Barclay
Laura Stewart

with Deborah M. Lee

Foreword by Timothy Shanahan

# The Everything Guide

## to Informational Texts, K–2

### Best Texts, Best Practices

FOR INFORMATION:

Corwin

A SAGE Company

2455 Teller Road

Thousand Oaks, California 91320

(800) 233-9936

www.corwin.com

SAGE Publications Ltd.

1 Oliver's Yard

55 City Road

London EC1Y 1SP

United Kingdom

SAGE Publications India Pvt. Ltd.

B 1/I 1 Mohan Cooperative Industrial Area

Mathura Road, New Delhi 110 044

India

SAGE Publications Asia-Pacific Pte. Ltd.

3 Church Street

#10-04 Samsung Hub

Singapore 049483

Publisher: Lisa Luedeke

Development Editor: Wendy Murray

Editorial Development Manager: Julie Nemer

Editorial Assistant: Francesca Dutra Africano

Production Editor: Melanie Birdsall

Copy Editor: Cate Huisman

Typesetter: C&M Digitals (P) Ltd.

Proofreader: Annie Lubinsky

Indexer: Jean Casalegno

Cover Designer: Rose Storey

Interior Designer: Shawn Girsberger

Text quoted from the Common Core State Standards is copyright © 2010 National Governors Association Center for Best Practices and Council of Chief State School Officers. All rights reserved.

Chapters 1 and 3–9 opening photos by Max Conlon.

Chapter 2 opening photo © Richard Hutchings/Photo Edit.

Printed in the United States of America

*Library of Congress Cataloging-in-Publication Data*

Barclay, Kathy.

The everything guide to informational texts, K–2 : best texts, best practices / Kathy Barclay, Laura Stewart, Deborah M. Lee.

pages cm

Includes bibliographical references and index.

ISBN 978-1-4522-8310-4 (pbk.)

1. Language arts (Elementary) 2. Exposition (Rhetoric)—Study and teaching (Elementary) I. Title.

LB1576.B2955 2014

372.6—dc23          2013046209

This book is printed on acid-free paper.

14 15 16 17 18 10 9 8 7 6 5 4 3 2 1

# Contents

*Foreword*   xi
   Timothy Shanahan

*Acknowledgments*   xiii

*Publisher's Acknowledgments*   xv

**CHAPTER 1**   New Standards, Timeless Goals: How Informational
Texts Can Help Make Every Child a Reader   1

A Crash Course on the Common Core   3
The College and Career Readiness Anchor Standards for Reading   6
Naming the Skills Involved in Reading Nonfiction and Fiction   12
Where Do We Go From Here?   16

**CHAPTER 2**   Bringing Informational Texts Into Your Teaching   17

Goal 1: Expose Children to More Complex Texts   19
Goal 2: Pay More Attention to Oral Language   22
Goal 3: Be More *Intentional*   23
Goal 4: Differentiate Instruction   24
Goal 5: Explicitly Teach From the Text   26

**CHAPTER 3**   The How-To's of Selecting Stellar Texts   29

The *New* Nonfiction   30
Evaluating Format and Visual Appeal   31
Evaluating Accuracy and Authenticity   39
Evaluating Writing Style and Appropriateness for Young Children   42
Evaluating Potential Content and Curricular Connections   45

**CHAPTER 4**   The Top Ten: Focus on These
High-Impact Comprehension Strategies   49

Teaching High-Impact Skills and Strategies
   for Comprehending Informational Text   51
      *1. Use prior knowledge.*   52
      *2. Make inferences (predict, determine cause
         and effect, draw and support conclusions).*   53

3. *Visualize information.* 54

4. *Ask and answer questions.* 55

5. *Compare and contrast text and pictures.* 56

6. *Determine key ideas and details.* 57

7. *Interpret information from graphs, charts, and diagrams.* 58

8. *Use references and resources.* 59

9. *Summarize and synthesize.* 60

10. *Monitor comprehension and use fix-up tips.* 61

**CHAPTER 5**   Demystifying What Makes Lessons
Effective: The Lesson Plan Template  65

The Overarching Goal of Informational Text
  Lessons: Rigorous Text Experiences for All Students  66
The Four Lesson Steps  69
  *A Detailed Look at the Lesson Template*  69
  *Summary of the Lesson Plan Action Steps*  72
  *How the Template Addresses CCSS for Informational Text*  76
  *How the Template Helps You Model
    Text-Based Responses*  76
  *How the Template Addresses Foundational Skills*  78
  *How the Template Addresses Interdisciplinary Learning*  79

**CHAPTER 6**   Informational Text Read-Aloud Lessons in Kindergarten  81

The Common Core Standards for
  Informational Text Read-Alouds  82
Using the Lesson Plan Template for the Read-Aloud  83
  *Step 1: Prepare to Read*  83
  *Step 2: Guide Reading*  84
  *Step 3: Explicitly Teach From the Text*  84
  *Step 4: Facilitate Connections*  85
Miss Webb's Kindergarten Class: A Sample
  Informational Text Read-Aloud Lesson  85
  *Kindergarten Informational Text Standards
    Included*  97

**CHAPTER 7**   Informational Text Lessons in First Grade  101

What's Different About First Grade?  102
Mrs. Stocker's First Graders: A Sample
  Informational Text Guided Reading Lesson  102
  *First Grade Informational Text Standards Included*  118
  *Other Standards Addressed*  118

**CHAPTER 8**   Informational Text Lessons in Second Grade  121

What About Students Who Are Not Reading With Grade-Level
  Proficiency?  122
Mr. Morris's Second Graders: A Model Informational Text Guided
  Reading Lesson  124

*Second Grade Informational Text Standards Included*  138
*Other Standards Addressed*  138

CHAPTER 9  Embedding Informational Texts in Units of Study  143
An Interdisciplinary Focus  144
Planning Units of Study: Who Does What?  144
Selecting High-Quality Informational Literature for Units of Study  147
*Characteristics of Narrative and Expository Text*  156
Concluding Thoughts  158

APPENDIX A  **Checklist for Evaluating Informational Literature**  161
APPENDIX B  **Common Core State Standards (CCSS) Checklists**  163
Kindergarten CCSS Checklist  163
First Grade CCSS Checklist  165
Second Grade CCSS Checklist  167

APPENDIX C  **Lesson Plan Template**  171
APPENDIX D  **Topical List of Informational Literature**  173
APPENDIX E  **Annotated Bibliography of Children's Books**  203

*References*  255
*Index*  261

Visit **www.corwin.com/theeverythingguide** to access
downloadable versions of the Appendixes for
*The Everything Guide to Informational Texts, K–2.*

# Foreword

used to teach first grade. It was a long time ago, but my memories of it are pretty vivid. Many of the kids I worked with weren't as interested in reading as they were in knowing about their world. It wasn't that they didn't care about reading; they just didn't see it as an end in itself. They wanted to read—or, perhaps, they were *willing* to learn to read—but they really wanted to know about ventriloquism, ice skating, horses, basketball, rockets, dinosaurs, and dozens of other real-world subjects that they assumed reading would open up to them.

The problem was that the basal readers that I taught from were little more than collections of fanciful stories. Again, it wasn't that my charges didn't like stories (they loved when I read *Charlie and the Chocolate Factory* to them). It's just that they wanted more from books than that. As young as they were, they somehow grasped the potential power and value of reading . . . they were just underwhelmed by what I was serving up.

Boy, have times changed.

Publishers have upped their game when it comes to making informational texts available to young children. There are now children's magazines on science, nature, sports, and history, and there are library offerings on a wide range of topics for young kids. Reading textbooks ("anthologies") are even managing to find a place for these kinds of selections, too.

Why the big change?

One reason was that my teaching experiences weren't all that unique. Teachers everywhere were meeting six- and seven-year-olds who were more interested in the *Guinness Book of World Records* than in *Grimm's Fairy Tales*. Why not respond to their interests?

Also, there has been a growing awareness of how poorly served such children have been with regard to informational text. Studies have shown that American classrooms have offered very little informational text in the primary grades, and they have revealed that our children tend to read stories somewhat better than they read science or other informational text.

Finally, we now have the Common Core State Standards (CCSS). Previous educational standards did mention both informational and literary texts, but the relative coverage of these was left up to each teacher to decide. CCSS changed all that. It requires that teachers emphasize informational text to the same degree that they do literature—50–50—even in kindergarten, first, and second grade. And that change has opened the floodgates. Finally.

There was a time when a book like this would have set out to try to persuade teachers that they should teach with informational text. But that's not the issue anymore. Teachers are now well aware that they must teach such text, and they also usually recognize that their students are interested.

Consequently, teachers everywhere are asking themselves, "*How* do I teach with informational text?" This volume provides a rich collection of practical answers to that question. It can, through its practical lessons, advice, and guidance, show teachers how to make informational text a joyful reality in the lives of our youngest scholars.

—Timothy Shanahan
*Distinguished Professor Emeritus*
*University of Illinois at Chicago*

# Acknowledgments

The authors wish to acknowledge the publishers who gave us permission to reprint their texts of superior merit, along with excerpts of selected lesson plans: Rowland Reading Foundation, National Geographic Books, Heinemann/Raintree, Capstone Press, and Walker & Books. These books allowed our ideas to come to life.

We also recognize the contributions and suggestions of colleagues and students who informed the ideas presented in this book. Thank you for your valuable input and ideas.

To the staff, administration, and students at Perry Local School in Lima, Ohio, thank you for allowing us to showcase you and your classrooms in our book. Special thanks to teachers Mandy Kennedy, Brice Turner, and Lisa Henline, and principal Kelly Schooler. Go Commodores!

Many thanks to our photographer Max Conlon for capturing our teachers and students in action.

To our editors, we express our sincere appreciation for your valuable suggestions, assistance, and encouragement.

Finally, we gratefully acknowledge our families in supporting our efforts throughout this process.

# Publisher's Acknowledgments

Corwin gratefully acknowledges the contributions of the following reviewers:

Lisa McMahon
Kindergarten Teacher
Burley School, IL

Jane Vallin
Superkids Regional Coach
Rowland Reading Foundation
LaGrange, IL

Judy Wallis
University Adjunct, Literacy Consultant
University of Houston, TX

Suzanne Webb
Superkids Regional Coach
Rowland Reading Foundation
Houston, TX

# 1

# New Standards, Timeless Goals

## *How Informational Texts Can Help Make Every Child a Reader*

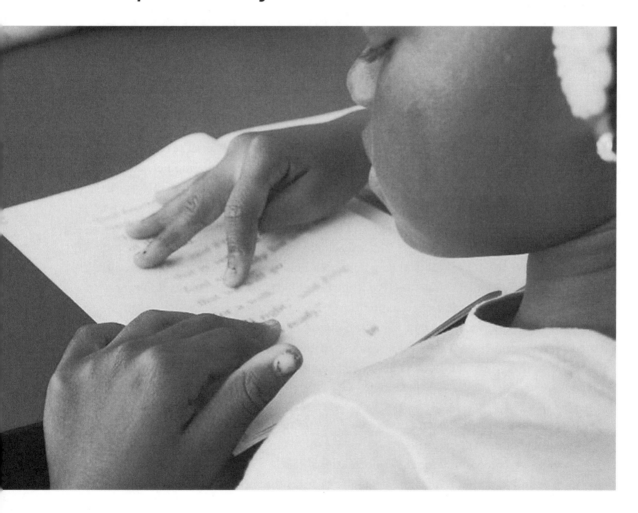

*I*t was the best of times, it was the worst of times. . . . Paraphrasing from a famous work of fiction, *A Tale of Two Cities* by Charles Dickens, might not be a predicable way to open a book on nonfiction, but we want to set a positive tone for this resource. We do think that, armed with expertise and an armful of high-quality informational texts, we teachers *are* in the best of times in education when it comes to teaching for independence and engagement. Sure, there are lots of pressures and negatives to distract us, but for the sake of our students, we need to see the positives. In our view, the Common Core State

Standards (CCSS) represent an opportunity for educators across the country to embrace the same set of academic expectations for students K–12 in order to prepare them for an ever-changing, highly competitive global society. Although the CCSS span the content areas, the standards for reading and language arts have grabbed the most headlines, and within that, informational texts seem to be stealing the limelight. Why? Part of it is due to the findings that in the last decades, K–2 curriculum has heavily favored narrative and fiction, and so it's a kind of national "correction" to bring a balance. But it's also perhaps a reflection of a collective concern in our country that America is slipping in its ranking worldwide. The content on the Internet, the content and communication of a global economy, and the smartphones and tablets we use all seem to point to the idea that we are in the Age of Information. Thus, we better make sure our students know how to navigate this vast world of information and how to operate in this "ever-changing normal."

As K–2 educators, our beliefs land smack in the center. That is, stories, fiction, narrative—all have a permanent place in developing readers and writers. Humans are wired for storytelling, our days are made up of stories, and no amount of nonfiction will change that. Ever. And yet we teachers have to get serious about developing our primary grade students' content knowledge, and there is no better way to do that than with nonfiction books.

Happily, in the last decade or so we've seen a surge in stellar, engaging nonfiction for children and adults alike, and so we have at our disposal high-quality primary-level texts appropriate for reading to students, reading with students, and reading by students. As seen within the CCSS Standard 10 (Range of Text Types), "informational text" refers to the broad category of nonfiction text, including literary nonfiction (biographies, autobiographies); history, social studies, science, the arts; technical texts, including directions, forms, and information displayed in graphs, charts, or maps; and digital sources on a range of topics. As you will note, although the term *nonfiction* refers to all factual text—both narrative/literary and expository/informational—we use the terms *nonfiction* and *informational* text interchangeably throughout this book to emphasize the CCSS's all-encompassing definition of this genre. (For a more detailed explanation of the differences between fiction and nonfiction, see Chapter 9.)

The CCSS and the renaissance of print and digital nonfiction texts for children have created terrific conditions for teachers to deepen their instructional practices around informational literature. This book is designed to help you do just that. Our goals are to help you

- become familiar with varying text structures and types of nonfiction text designed especially for developing readers.
- learn how to choose high-quality informational text.
- understand key comprehension strategies that do the most heavy lifting when it comes to understanding nonfiction.
- pump up students' exposure to nonfiction through daily read-aloud and guided reading experiences.
- understand issues surrounding text complexity and use of complex texts in grades K–2.
- engage students in big thinking around rich nonfiction text.
- differentiate instruction while utilizing a common informational text for all students.

Most important, we'll teach you to achieve these goals within a simple-to-use lesson plan template that can apply to any informational text you choose to use (see Chapter 5).

## A Crash Course on the Common Core

The following questions are ones that we are asked whenever we present at conferences, no matter where we are. In answering them here, you'll get a good overview of the CCSS and why nonfiction is such a vital part of this national initiative. Even if you happen to teach in a state that has not adopted the CCSS, the information in this section will help you set this book in important context.

- How were the CCSS developed and what are the goals they are designed to meet?
- How are the CCSS organized?
- What are the fundamental "shifts" in the CCSS and how do they apply to the primary grades?
- What are the College and Career Readiness Anchor Standards, and how do they relate to the grade-level standards?
- Do the standards specify all there is to teach?
- How are the Foundational Skills Standards and the Informational Text Standards important to K–2?
- Why is nonfiction so important? What are the benefits of using nonfiction in the primary grades?

### Consistent Expectations

A collaborative effort of the Council of Chief State School Officers (CCSSO) and the National Governors Association (NGA), the standards are an extension of a 2009 initiative led by these two organizations to identify what students should know and be able to do in a 21st-century, globally competitive society. This is reflected in the mission statement of the CCSS:

> The Common Core State Standards provide a *consistent*, clear understanding of what students are expected to learn, so teachers and parent know what they need to do to help them. The standards are designed to be *robust and relevant* to the real world, reflecting the knowledge and skills that our young people need for success in *college and careers*. With American students fully prepared for the future, our communities will be best positioned to compete successfully in the *global economy* [emphases added]. (Mission Statement of the Common Core State Standards, www.corestandards.org)

The standards were written with serious attention to research-based evidence. From the extensive data examined, the authors of the CCSS arrived at these overall goals for competence in English language arts (NGA/CCSSO 2010b, p. 7):

Students who are college and career ready in reading, writing, speaking, listening, and language:

- Demonstrate independence
- Build strong content knowledge

- Respond to the varying demands of audience, task purpose, and discipline
- Comprehend and critique
- Value evidence
- Use technology and digital media strategically and capably
- Understand other perspectives and cultures

## How the Standards Are Organized

There are three main sections of the CCSS English language arts (ELA) document (NGA/CCSSO 2010b), which is available for free online:

- English Language Arts and Literacy in History/Social Studies, Science, and Technical Subjects (K–5)
- English Language Arts (6–12)
- Literacy in History/Social Studies, Science, and Technical Subjects

English Language Arts is combined with Literacy in History/Social Studies, Science, and Technical Subjects for K–5 and separate for 6–12, reflecting the notion that most K–5 instruction is integrated and delivered by a single teacher, while in middle school and high school, English Language Arts is separate from content subjects. For the ELA and literacy standards in elementary grades (K–5), there are six strands:

- Reading Standards for Literature
- Reading Standards for Informational Text
- Reading Standards: Foundational Skills
- Writing Standards
- Speaking and Listening Standards
- Language Standards

Although the standards are organized in separate strands, their authors make clear that the most effective model for literacy is an integrated model, where all the language arts, especially reading and writing, are taught together. To that end, the ELA standards are also applicable to a wide range of subjects; teachers in all content areas must play a role in literacy development. The motivation behind this interdisciplinary approach comes from research that established the need for students to be proficient in reading complex text across disciplines. And, to address the need for these new literacy competencies, the CCSS call for media and research skills to be blended throughout ELA and subject area instruction.

*Text Complexity: Raising Rigor in Reading* by Nancy Frey, Diane Lapp, and Douglas Fisher (IRA, 2012) provides a clear explanation of the underlying rationale for exposing students to books that sufficiently engage and challenge them. It also does a great job of describing the attributes that make texts complex.

## Fundamental "Shifts" Assumed in Common Core

The Common Core State Standards are based upon strong research that informs our understanding of what students should know and be able to do by the end of each grade level. Various states have identified "shifts" in our collective educational thinking and practice that are required for implementation of the CCSS. While it is helpful to use these shifts as a way to frame our thinking when it comes to the changes brought about by the Common Core, the shifts are very broad. For the purposes of this book, we want to further refine that thinking to consider specifically what these shifts mean for beginning readers. Brief descriptions of seven of the most commonly cited shifts are listed in Figure 1.1, along with the practical considerations for K–2.

| Big Shift | What This Means | How This Plays Out for Beginning Readers With Informational Text |
|---|---|---|
| Text Complexity | Students have extensive opportunities to engage with complex texts. | Children are engaged in complex text experiences primarily through read-alouds. The complexity of the text used by students develops in sophistication commensurate with their reading abilities. |
| Increased Reading of Informational Texts | Throughout the school day, students read a balance of 50% literature and 50% informational texts by Grade 4. By Grade 12, at least 70% of texts read throughout the day should be informational texts; therefore, ELA classrooms at Grades 6–12 will focus on literary nonfiction. | Read-aloud informational text experiences gradually shift to student-read informational text, with the goal of 50/50 by fourth grade. We don't want to throw out the baby with the bathwater by giving up important narrative stories in the early grades. |
| Disciplinary Literacy | Students read, write, and speak about discipline-related topics to build content knowledge. At grades 6–12, students grapple with discipline-specific complex texts that deepen their understanding of each topic, and they demonstrate mastery by applying that knowledge when writing or speaking. | In the early grades, students read (or listen to) informational texts read aloud to prepare for the demands of reading discipline-specific texts in later grades. |
| Close Reading and Rigorous Text-Based Conversations | Students should read and reread texts of sufficient complexity to draw meaning from them. To gain deeper understanding of a text, students discuss high-quality questions about its content, structure, and language, including questions that ask students to make inferences and draw conclusions based on textual evidence. | During the read-aloud and guided reading of informational text, teachers ask questions and guide students to return to the text. Inquiries that lead students back to the text might include these: "What makes you say that?" "Show me where you found that in the text." "Read the section to us that confirms where you found that answer." |

*(Continued)*

(Continued)

| Big Shift | What This Means | How This Plays Out for Beginning Readers With Informational Text |
|---|---|---|
| **General Academic and Domain-Specific Vocabulary** | Students acquire general academic vocabulary to comprehend complex texts that cross disciplines, and domain-specific vocabulary that enables students to comprehend language specific to a discipline. Students demonstrate mastery by using both types of vocabulary when speaking and writing. | Informational text provides a rich repository of both academic and domain-specific vocabulary. Teachers capitalize on this by explicitly teaching vocabulary from the text and make efforts to use that vocabulary repeatedly and in multiple contexts to develop students' vocabulary and heighten their awareness of concepts and language. |
| **Argumentative Writing** | "An argument is a reasoned, logical way of demonstrating that the writer's position, belief, or conclusion is valid" (NGA/CCSSO 2010a, p. 23) Argument writing is important across disciplines and should compose 40% of student writing by high school. | In early grades, "argumentation" translates to "opinion" writing. In K–5, students' opinion writing should include examples, reasons, and cause and effect. The guidelines in grades K–5 are that 30% of student writing should be writing opinions. |
| **Short and Sustained Research Projects** | Students conduct short- and long-term research in which they synthesize information from many sources, construct knowledge, use technology when appropriate, and present findings in a variety of formats. | Children engage in research projects appropriate to their grade level, moving from teacher-directed projects to group research to independent research. |

FIGURE 1.1 The Fundamental Shifts in K–2 Teaching Brought on by the Common Core

## The College and Career Readiness Anchor Standards for Reading

The reading standards (literature, informational text), with the exception of the Foundational Skills Standards, are all anchored by the same College and Career Readiness (CCR) Anchor Standards. These are the broad expectations that are consistent across grades and content areas. They are the end goals to which all grade-level standards connect; the anchor standards are based on the evidence about college and workforce training expectations as outlined above. According to the CCSS, "The CCR and grade-specific standards are necessary complements—the former providing broad standards, the latter providing additional specificity—that together define the skills and understandings that all students must demonstrate" (NGA/CCSSO, 2010b, p. 10). The College and Career Readiness Anchor Standards for Reading are shown in Figure 1.2.

## Key Ideas and Details

Read closely to determine what the text says explicitly and to make logical inferences from it; cite specific textual evidence when writing or speaking to support conclusions drawn from the text.

Determine central ideas or themes of a text and analyze their development; summarize the key supporting details and ideas.

Analyze how and why individuals, events, and ideas develop and interact over the course of a text.

## Craft and Structure

Interpret words and phrases as they are used in a text, including determining technical, connotative, and figurative meanings, and analyze how specific word choices shape meaning or tone.

Analyze the structure of texts, including how specific sentences, paragraphs, and larger portions of the text (e.g. a section, chapter, scene or stanza) relate to each other and the whole.

Assess how point of view or purpose shapes the content and style of a text.

## Integration of Knowledge and Ideas

Integrate and evaluate content presented in diverse media and formats, including visually and quantitatively, as well as in words.

Delineate and evaluate the argument and specific claims in a text, including the validity of the reasoning as well as the relevance and sufficiency of the evidence.

Analyze how two or more texts address similar themes or topics in order to build knowledge or to compare the approaches the authors take.

## Range of Reading and Level of Text Complexity

Read and comprehend complex literary and informational texts independently and proficiently.

**FIGURE 1.2** College and Career Readiness Anchor Standards

*Source:* NGA/CCSSO (2010b). Copyright © 2010 National Governors Association Center for Best Practices and Council of Chief State School Officers. All rights reserved.

To clarify the range and content of student reading, the CCSS provides this explanation:

To build a foundation for college and career readiness students must read widely deeply from among a broad range of high-quality, increasingly challenging literary and informational texts. Through extensive reading of stories, dramas, poems, and myths from diverse cultures and different time periods, students gain literary and cultural knowledge as well as familiarity with various text structures and elements. By reading texts in history/social studies, science, and other disciplines, students build a foundation of knowledge in these fields that will also give them the background to be better readers in all content areas. Students can only gain this foundation when the curriculum is intentionally and coherently structured to develop rich content knowledge within and across grades. Students also acquire the habits of reading independently and closely, which are essential to their future success. (NGA/CCSSO, 2010b, p. 10)

## The Grade-Specific Standards

Anchored by the CCR standards, the grade-specific standards define "end of year expectations and a cumulative progression designed to enable students to meet college and career readiness expectations no later than the end of high school" (NGA/CCSSO, 2010b, p. 4). As children move through the grades, it is expected that they will meet each year's standards. Because of the scope of this book, we will not be examining each grade level's reading standards, but will focus on the Reading Standards for Informational Text, K–2.

## Limitations of the Standards

It is important to note that the design of the CCSS has specific limitations, which are intentional. The standards don't mandate how a teacher should teach, nor do they mandate all that can or should be taught. For example, there is no mention of advanced work beyond the core or interventions needed for those students who are performing well below grade level. Although the standards state that "all students must have the opportunity to learn and meet the same high standards" and "appropriate accommodations should be made for all students," there is nothing in the standards specific to the supports necessary for English language learners or students with special needs.

Why were these limitations intentional? The authors of the CCSS were clear that an expert teacher must use her knowledge of individual students and, by applying principles of evidenced-based research, plan and implement instruction designed to meet diverse learner needs and to move each student toward attainment of the standards.

## Taking a Closer Look at the Standards

Since the focus of this book is on selecting and using nonfiction literature, we will not be addressing all the strands of reading; however, we want to take a closer look at the expectations for students in grades K–2 with respect to the foundational skills in learning to read, and then at the Informational Text Standards.

### THE FOUNDATIONAL SKILLS OF READING

The foundational skills are particularly important to those of us who work with emerging readers, and it is important that these skills are closely attended to in K–2. The Foundational Skills Standards were designed to address the skills that must be in place for children to know *how* to read:

- Print concepts (K–1)
- Phonological awareness (K–1)
- Phonics and word recognition (K–5)
- Fluency (K–5)

The CCSS authors make clear that the foundational skills are "not an end in and of themselves," but are "necessary and important components of an effective, comprehensive reading program designed to develop proficient readers with the capacity to comprehend complex text across a range of types and disciplines" (NGA/CCSSO, 2010b, p. 15). The authors also make clear that "instruction should be differentiated; good readers will need much less practice with these concepts than struggling readers will." This requires a great deal of teacher knowledge to discern the focus of instruction within the range of abilities in the classroom. Nonetheless, the CCSS clearly calls for a mastery of the foundational skills of reading, which is particularly important in K–2.

## INFORMATIONAL TEXT STANDARDS

As we will explore in subsequent chapters, the attention on informational text may be relatively new to those of us in primary education. The specific grade-level standards all lead to the College and Career Readiness Anchor Standards; you may find it interesting to examine the Informational Text Standards for K–2 by Anchor Standard (see Figure 1.3), to see the progression within the primary grades.

### Informational Text: Key Ideas and Details

**College and Career Readiness (CCR) Anchor Standard 1:** Read closely to determine what the text says explicitly and to make logical inferences from it; cite specific textual evidence when writing or speaking to support conclusions drawn from the text.

| Grade | Grade-Specific Standard |
| --- | --- |
| Kindergarten | With prompting and support, ask and answer questions about key details in a text. |
| Grade 1 | Ask and answer questions about key details in a text. |
| Grade 2 | Ask and answer such questions as who, what, where, when, why, and how to demonstrate understanding of key details in a text. |

### Informational Text: Key Ideas and Details

**CCR Anchor Standard 2:** Determine central ideas or themes of a text and analyze their development; summarize the key supporting details and ideas.

| Grade | Grade-Specific Standard |
| --- | --- |
| Kindergarten | With prompting and support, identify the main topic and retell key details of a text. |
| Grade 1 | Identify the main topic and retell key details of a text. |
| Grade 2 | Identify the main topic of a multiparagraph text as well as the focus of specific paragraphs within the text. |

*(Continued)*

(Continued)

Informational Text: Key Ideas and Details

**CCR Anchor Standard 3:** Analyze how and why individuals, events, and ideas develop and interact over the course of a text.

| Grade | Grade-Specific Standard |
| --- | --- |
| Kindergarten | With prompting and support, describe the connection between two individuals, events, ideas, or pieces of information in a text. |
| Grade 1 | Describe the connection between two individuals, events, ideas, or pieces of information in a text. |
| Grade 2 | Describe the connection between a series of historical events, scientific ideas or concepts, or steps in technical procedures in a text. |

Informational Text: Craft and Structure

**CCR Anchor Standard 4:** Interpret words and phrases as they are used in a text, including determining technical, connotative, and figurative meanings, and analyze how specific word choices shape meaning or tone.

| Grade | Grade-Specific Standard |
| --- | --- |
| Kindergarten | With prompting and support, ask and answer questions about unknown words in a text. |
| Grade 1 | Ask and answer questions to help determine or clarify the meaning of words and phrases in a text. |
| Grade 2 | Determine the meaning of words and phrases in a text relevant to a *grade 2 topic or subject area*. |

Informational Text: Craft and Structure

**CCR Anchor Standard 5:** Analyze the structure of texts, including how specific sentences, paragraphs, and larger portions of the text (e.g., a section, chapter, scene, or stanza) relate to each other and the whole.

| Grade | Grade-Specific Standard |
| --- | --- |
| Kindergarten | Identify the front cover, back cover, and title page of a book. |
| Grade 1 | Know and use various text features (e.g., headings, tables of contents, glossaries, electronic menus, icons) to locate key facts or information in a text. |
| Grade 2 | Know and use various text features (e.g., captions, bold print, subheadings, glossaries, indexes, electronic menus, icons) to locate key facts or information in a text efficiently. |

Informational Text: Craft and Structure

**CCR Anchor Standard 6:** Assess how point of view or purpose shapes the content and style of a text.

| Grade | Grade-Specific Standard |
| --- | --- |
| Kindergarten | Name the author and illustrator of a text and define the role of each in presenting the ideas or information in a text. |
| Grade 1 | Distinguish between information provided by pictures or other illustrations and information provided by the words in a text. |
| Grade 2 | Identify the main purpose of a text, including what the author wants to answer, explain, or describe. |

## Informational Text: Integration of Knowledge and Ideas

**CCR Anchor Standard 7:** Integrate and evaluate content presented in diverse formats and media, including visually and quantitatively, as well as in words.

| Grade | Grade-Specific Standard |
|---|---|
| Kindergarten | With prompting and support, describe the relationship between illustrations and the text in which they appear (e.g., what person, place, thing, or idea in the text an illustration depicts). |
| Grade 1 | Use the illustrations and details in a text to describe its key ideas. |
| Grade 2 | Explain how specific images (e.g., a diagram showing how a machine works) contribute to and clarify a text. |

## Informational Text: Integration of Knowledge and Ideas

**CCR Anchor Standard 8:** Delineate and evaluate the argument and specific claims in a text, including the validity of the reasoning as well as the relevance and sufficiency of the evidence.

| Grade | Grade-Specific Standard |
|---|---|
| Kindergarten | With prompting and support, identify the reasons an author gives to support points in a text. |
| Grade 1 | Identify the reasons an author gives to support points in a text. |
| Grade 2 | Describe how reasons support specific points the author makes in a text. |

## Informational Text: Integration of Knowledge and Ideas

**CCR Anchor Standard 9:** Analyze how two or more texts address similar themes or topics in order to build knowledge or to compare the approaches the authors take.

| Grade | Grade-Specific Standard |
|---|---|
| Kindergarten | With prompting and support, identify basic similarities in and differences between two texts on the same topic (e.g., in illustrations, descriptions, or procedures). |
| Grade 1 | Identify basic similarities in and differences between two texts on the same topic (e.g., in illustrations, descriptions, or procedures). |
| Grade 2 | Compare and contrast the most important points presented by two texts on the same topic. |

## Informational Text: Range of Reading and Level of Text Complexity

**CCR Anchor Standard 10:** Read and comprehend complex literary and informational texts independently and proficiently.

| Grade | Grade-Specific Standard |
|---|---|
| Kindergarten | Actively engage in group reading activities with purpose and understanding. |
| Grade 1 | With prompting and support, read informational texts appropriately complex for grade 1. |
| Grade 2 | By the end of year, read and comprehend informational texts, including history/social studies, science, and technical texts, in the grades 2–3 text complexity band proficiently, with scaffolding as needed at the high end of the range. |

**FIGURE 1.3** Informational Text Standards, K–2

*Source:* NGA/CCSSO (2010b, pp. 10, 13). Copyright © 2010 National Governors Association Center for Best Practices and Council of Chief State School Officers. All rights reserved.

## Naming the Skills Involved in Reading Nonfiction and Fiction

From the earliest grades, the Common Core State Standards represent a strong and growing *across-the-curriculum* emphasis on students' ability to read and comprehend both fiction and nonfiction texts. Standard 4 in the Reading Standards for Literature calls for students in kindergarten to "recognize common types of texts (e.g., storybooks, poems)." Grade 1 students are to "explain major differences between books that tell stories and books that give information, drawing on a wide reading of a range of text types." If you examine both the Reading Standards for Literature and the Reading Standards for Informational Text, you see a strong emphasis on reading closely and critically in the same manner, that is, to determine main topics and key details, to describe connections between ideas in a text, and to compare and contrast information from two similar texts. While subtle differences exist in these two sets of standards, when the skill is identical for both literature and informational text, the standard is worded in exactly the same way. For example, in Standard 10 of the Reading Standards for Literature, we find that during the years from ages five through approximately seven, students are to progress from actively engaging "in group reading activities with purpose and understanding" (kindergarten), to "reading and comprehending stories and poetry in the grades 2–3 text complexity band proficiently, with scaffolding as needed at the high end of the range" (p. 11). In the Reading Standards for Informational Text, we find the exact same wording for the kindergarten level, yet a slightly different wording for the Grade 2 level: "By the end of the year, read and comprehend informational texts, including history/social studies, science, and technical texts, in the grades 2–3 text complexity band proficiently, with scaffolding as needed at the high end of the range" (p. 13).

In order to facilitate students' meeting of the CCSS, we have to help students know and navigate what makes fiction and nonfiction texts alike—and what makes them distinct. In a fiction selection for K–2, the structure of narrative text provides the reader with predictable elements—characters, setting, plot, and theme, all organized within a logical sequence of events. The reader expects to encounter a plot that will move the story forward and knows to read the story from beginning to end.

In a nonfiction selection, the author uses expository text structures to organize content and ideas. Unlike authors of narrative text, authors of expository text do not use dialogue, nor do they avoid use of technical vocabulary or discussion of abstract concepts. Authors of expository text typically write in present tense and often use different text structures that follow a logical order in the presentation of factual information (e.g., cause and effect, description, classification/example, problem/solution, and compare/contrast). While both narrative and expository texts may contain a table of contents, indexes and glossaries are typically included only within expository texts. Other characteristics of expository text not found in narrative text are headings, subheadings, charts, tables, and other such means of graphically portraying the information for the reader. Readers of expository text expect that what they read will be well organized, authentic, and accurate. They know the text does not have to be read from cover to cover, and that they are free to read just those portions of the text that are of interest. They also realize the need for a slower rate of reading than that used with narrative text. These are all expectations we need to explicitly teach our K–2 students to expect as well.

## The Importance of Exposure to Both Fiction and Nonfiction Texts

Research has shown that teachers' choice of read-aloud text influences students' independent reading choices (Correia, 2011; Yopp & Yopp, 2000). This is certainly one reason why researchers recommend that teachers read widely from texts that represent a variety of genres and reflect young students' diverse interests and needs. Another very compelling reason stems from trends on the National Assessment of Educational Progress indicating that fourth graders' reading achievement increases as the diversity of their reading experiences increases. Since 1990, fourth graders who reported reading a wide variety of text outperformed those students who reported reading only one type of text, underscoring the significance of both nonfiction and fiction texts for students in the early grades.

## The Ascendance of Nonfiction

Given that the Common Core State Standards are intentionally structured to develop rich content knowledge within and across grades, it's no wonder that nonfiction is emphasized. Consider what you read and write in a typical day. Our guess is that your everyday reading and writing include the types of literacy tasks and materials shown in Figure 1.4. A quick perusal of this list reveals that much of what we read and write in life is nonfiction. If this is true, then let's consider how we are preparing students for this real world.

- Text messages
- Tweets
- Blogs
- Facebook
- E-mails
- Newspapers
- Magazines
- Letters
- Advertisements
- Information
- Programs
- Charts
- Schedules
- Brochures
- Contracts
- Maps
- Articles
- Menus

FIGURE 1.4 Real World Nonfiction Reading and Writing

Researchers have long recognized that reading and listening to informational text help build children's knowledge of the world, yet, a common barrier to the use of informational text with young students is the mistaken belief that they are incapable of understanding such texts (Palmer & Stewart, 2003; Yopp & Yopp, 2000). While it is true that nonfiction text is often dense with factual information and ideas, research has revealed that the structure and concepts found within this genre can be made comprehensible to young students—even those in kindergarten (Caswell & Duke, 1998; Duthie, 1994; Martin & Kragler, 2012; Pappas, 1993; Smolkin & Donovan, 2001). In fact, kindergartners use more strategies (including picture clues) to construct meaning in nonfiction text than fiction text, and they are more likely to view themselves as "readers" when using nonfiction text (Martin & Kragler, 2012).

## Nonfiction Has a Positive Impact on Literacy Development

Researchers have demonstrated the positive impact that the use of nonfiction text in the early grades has on students' literacy development. Not only does nonfiction serve as the pathway into literacy for many emerging and experienced readers, it holds the potential for improving reluctant readers' attitudes toward reading. During the reading of nonfiction texts, both teachers and students are highly engaged and interactive in a way that differs strongly from storybook read-alouds (Smolkin & Donovan, 2001). Specifically, reading informational texts

- increases students' background knowledge in the content areas and in vocabulary.
- exposes students to the language and structure of expository texts, making them more versatile readers of nonfiction and narrative.
- sparks curiosity and desire to learn about the world.
- helps students identify with people different from themselves.
- provides print embedded within visual information and illustrations, which supports beginning readers' decoding and word recognition.
- complements fiction reading in the elementary grades, possibly helping students to promote a smoother transition between elementary school reading and intermediate-level content reading. (Duke, 2004; Snow, Burns, & Griffin, 1998)

In kindergarten through Grade 1, much of students' exposure to high-quality nonfiction text will take place through interactive read-aloud experiences. This continues in Grade 2, even as students are increasingly able to read some nonfiction texts independently. As stated in Appendix A of the CCSS document (NGA/CCSSO, 2010a),

It is particularly important that students in the earliest grades build knowledge through being read to as well as through reading, with the balance gradually shifting to reading independently. By reading a story or nonfiction selection aloud, teachers allow children to experience written language without the burden of decoding, granting them access to content that they may not be able to read and understand by themselves. Children are then free to focus their mental energy on the words and ideas presented in the text, and they will eventually be better prepared to tackle rich written content on their own. Whereas most titles selected for kindergarten and grade 1 will need to be read aloud exclusively, some titles selected for grades 2–5 may be appropriate for read-alouds as well as for reading independently. (p. 27)

Nonfiction texts provide students with a breadth and depth of information for satisfying their curiosity about the world. Through nonfiction, students build vocabulary, disciplinary knowledge, and a foundation for comprehending complex text. They also develop greater awareness of print and text features, and they enthusiastically share their knowledge through nonfiction writing, often imitating authors of informational text. Finally, not only do both boys and girls express preference for nonfiction texts, emerging, experienced, and reluctant readers find informational books highly engaging and are motivated to read books from this genre.

## Nonfiction Builds Critical Disciplinary Knowledge

In the last decade or so, science and social studies in elementary schools have been sidelined to a shocking degree. As a result, teachers and students alike are woefully unsupported in terms of the instructional time devoted to these content areas. The silver lining of the Common Core State Standards is that they have put science and social studies back on the map, making clear the importance of disciplinary knowledge and nonfiction texts that convey it. The Common Core State Standards build those goals with increasing sophistication and independence across grade levels. For example, by the end of kindergarten, students should be able, *with prompting and support,* to describe the connection between two individual events, ideas, or pieces of information in a text. By the end of first grade, the standard is exactly the same, except the students are expected to do it independently. By the end of second grade, students are expected to describe the connection between a series of historical events, scientific ideas, or concepts, or the steps in technical procedures in a text. For example, by the end of second grade, students would be expected to describe the connection between the idea that water is limited and the scientific understanding of the water cycle. (See Chapter 8 for examples of a lesson plan designed to address these concepts.)

This unparalleled attention to and demands of the reading of nonfiction literature in the lower grades found within the CCSS requires reconsideration of the way we spend our instructional time. Without reducing the time we spend in kindergarten through Grade 2 developing students' critical foundational skills of reading and writing, we must find a way to build a solid base of disciplinary content and concepts and to scaffold students' ability to learn from nonfiction texts.

## Nonfiction Lends Itself to Integrated, Inquiry-Based Units of Study

Regardless of whether the Common Core State Standards sustain over the years, we hope they will leave an indelible mark on the field in terms of establishing, once and for all, that we need to systematically provide units of study at each grade level that organize the world's content knowledge around broad, relevant themes. We know children learn best through active involvement in learning about topics that hold strong interest for them and of which they have some prior knowledge. The Common Core State Standards emphasize building broad knowledge through structured listening and learning experiences that are part of an interdisciplinary curricular approach. This attention to interdisciplinary learning and use of informational text is highly compatible with the principles of developmentally appropriate practice, which state, "Teachers integrate ideas and content from multiple domains and disciplines through themes, projects, creative opportunities, and other learning experiences so that children are able to develop an understanding of concepts and make connections across areas" (Copple & Bredekamp, 2009, p. 303).

Through engagement in meaningful, authentic learning tasks utilizing both literature and informational text, students develop important skills and strategies necessary for reading and writing. Use of an interdisciplinary approach provides ample opportunities for students to apply newly learned foundational skills in reading, and often in math, as they acquire key information and ideas. As students discuss with others texts read aloud as well as those read independently, they further their ability to read increasingly complex texts in subsequent grades. In this book we will provide a lesson plan template that can be used whenever informational text is used—during read-aloud time, the literacy block, or content area units of study.

## Where Do We Go From Here?

With this background in mind, let's move on in the next chapter to some practical application. Because of the unique needs of primary readers, it is not enough just to add more nonfiction to our day. The primary goal of these early years is to teach children *how to read.* Informational text plays an important role in supporting this goal through the development of language and content and also provides a meaningful context for application of emerging skills. Be sure to read Chapter 2 carefully, as it frames the understanding of this paradigm.

# 2

# Bringing Informational Texts Into Your Teaching

Discussing and comprehending complex text is a central expectation of the Common Core State Standards—but exactly how you do it is left to educators to design. With that in mind, in this chapter we share five goals that provide teachers in K–2 with guidance on using complex texts in appropriate ways. These goals lean heavily on a couple of longstanding instructional practices: read-alouds and guided reading/small group reading experiences. What's new in what we advocate, however, is that we think teachers ought to look for ways use the same informational text with all students in order to ensure that all students have exposure to grade-level concepts and materials and to the same academic language and content. As you can see from the graphic in Figure 2.1, we can include informational texts in a few different formats.

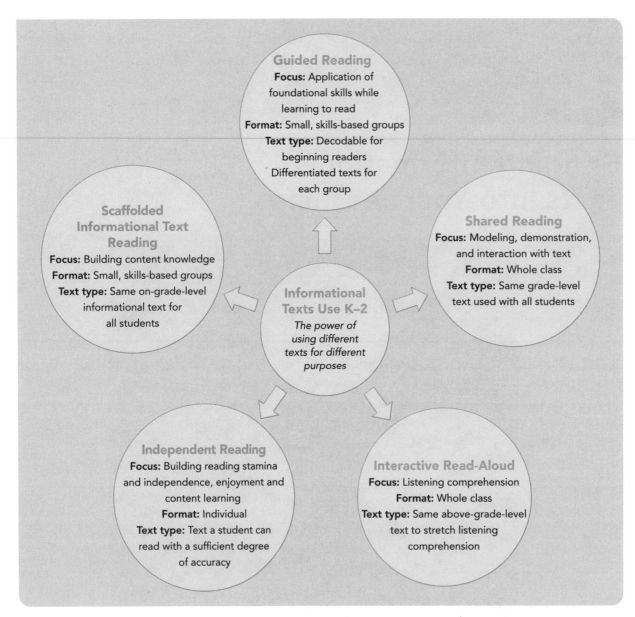

**FIGURE 2.1** Informational Text Use K–2: The Power of Using Different Texts for Different Purposes

Most of these formats are very familiar to all teachers, but you will notice that we are including two small-group guided reading formats. "Scaffolded informational text reading" is the use of one grade-level informational text for all students. We want all of our students to have access to the same high-quality, grade-level content, so we are advocating that we utilize skills-based groups with scaffolded instruction to achieve that goal. This will be explained further in this chapter and illustrated fully in Chapters 7 and 8. This scaffolded informational text reading experience is not the only instructional small-group reading opportunity taking place in the classroom! Yes, we are pushing the envelope by saying that on-grade-level texts need a bigger role instructionally, but we are *not* suggesting that guided reading and other differentiated instruction go away. In kindergarten and first grade, children must receive systematic, explicit instruction in the predictable progression of skills necessary for learning to read (phonological awareness, phonics, fluency, vocabulary, comprehension) and ample opportunities to apply their emerging skills in decodable text. Once they are independently decoding, children need core, grade-level informational text experiences as well as systematic, explicit instruction in grade-level reading skills, with application in text appropriate to their abilities. Our big message here is this: Children flourish when we expose them to and help them to read high-quality, authentic informational texts, written at their grade level, and we want to reach that goal through small group scaffolded instruction with appropriate text. Figure 2.2 (see next page) explains four of the five ways to use informational text, and the type of text to use with each one.

In this chapter and those that follow, we will show you how to embrace authentic texts in order to provide K–2 students with a firm foundation for the reading of challenging text that will be required in the later grades. (In Chapter 5 we provide a lesson template for planning virtually all types of lessons using informational text.)

Now, let's look at some at some key goals for tweaking our teaching in grades K–2 in light of the Common Core.

## Goal 1: Expose Children to More Complex Texts

Text complexity describes how difficult a text is to read and comprehend. The Common Core State Standards recommend a three-part model to determine text complexity. In the CCSS Appendix A (NGA/CCSSO, 2010a) text complexity is discussed in detail, but to summarize, it is represented in a three-part model that includes the following:

- **Qualitative factors** such as levels of meaning, structure, and language in the text, and the knowledge demands required of the reader
- **Quantitative measures** of the readability of a text based on word frequency and length, sentence length, and the text length and cohesion
- **Reader and task considerations**, such as the reader's motivation, knowledge, and experiences as well as the purpose for reading a particular text

The standards acknowledge that K–1 text is not suited to quantitative measures, given the nature of beginning reading instruction and the need for some kinds of controls on the text. In K–1, a teacher must determine if text is complex by reliance on other factors; this requires her to understand her students' background and abilities as well as have a thorough understanding of the text, its structure, and the purpose for the reading. As discussed in Chapter 6, complex text in kindergarten is provided in the form of read-alouds. In first grade, the challenge is not only to provide complex text through read-alouds but to also choose text that is "appropriately complex for Grade 1." This emphasis on grade-appropriate text is critical with the adoption of the Common Core.

## *Why Is Text Complexity Important?*

In third grade, it is expected that students will be reading on grade level. They are expected to read third-grade-level social studies, science, math, and other subject area texts, and, in many states and districts, take high-stakes third-grade tests, which are written at the third-grade level.

| Lesson Format | What This Means | Type of Informational Text |
|---|---|---|
| **Interactive Read-Aloud** (typically whole class) | The teacher chooses books/texts to read aloud to children (preferably several times a day) that are written at a higher level than that at which children are able to read on their own. The read-aloud experience is interactive, with the teacher modeling, questioning, and interacting with students. The goal is to model vocabulary, fluency, and strategies that children will eventually internalize and gradually be able to use as their burgeoning skills allow them to read more complex text independently. | Texts written above the children's current reading level, texts of sufficient depth to relay important concepts, develop strong vocabulary, and stretch children's listening comprehension level. |
| **Shared Reading** (typically whole class) | Similar to reading aloud, a shared reading experience allows the beginning reader to have a more intimate glimpse of the text as it is shared in an interactive lesson. | Same as read-aloud text, but typically shared reading text is enlarged in a big-book format or a digital format. |
| **Guided Reading (With Focus on Foundational Skills and Word Work)** (core instruction is typically whole class initially, with differentiated instruction as indicated by assessments; text reading is done in small, skills-based groups) | This is core instruction of sequential, systematic skills that all beginning readers need to be able to learn to read. | Text that has phonetic and readability controls so that students are practicing the application of their emerging skills; decodable text needs to be progressively and cumulatively decodable, matching the sequence of phonetic elements as children are learning them. |
| **Small Group Scaffolded Informational Text Reading** (small, skills-based group) | Students work in small, skills-based groups designed to provide a more focused reading experience; the teacher guides students through text with an emphasis on meaning while also providing the appropriate instruction to teach children *how to read* the text. | Text that is at grade level or above for all students; it is imperative that below-level students receive accelerated instruction of sufficient duration and intensity to bring them to grade level. |

**FIGURE 2.2** Classroom Use of Informational Text

We know when students are not reading at grade level in third grade, it is not a third-grade issue; in fact, these students have likely been struggling from the beginning. While we cannot fully make up for deficits with which some children come to school (low oral language, lack of experiences, nutritional deficits, et cetera), we can identify those who will struggle early on and provide the appropriate instructional supports to ameliorate their difficulties.

Providing students with appropriately challenging texts and appropriate teacher-guided instruction is the key to maintaining or developing a growth trajectory line to grade-level proficiency. More simply stated, students learn more when they attempt to read more challenging text with the support of a teacher who is mediating their reading (Shanahan, 2013). As Shanahan (2013) emphasizes, teachers' adaptations for challenging texts—for example, reading aloud the text for the students, having a good reader read the text to other students, using lecture and explanation to provide students with the text content, or selecting an easier text—have not been successful in helping students gain the skills they need to read and comprehend grade-level text. Rather than providing students with a steady diet of text that is matched to their "instructional level" as determined by an Informal Reading Inventory or Running Records, evidence suggests the use of more challenging, grade-level text results in greater reading gains (Morgan, Wilcox, & Eldredge, 2000). We want to get students off to a strong start in the early years, striving for grade-level proficiency *in each and every grade*, not waiting until Grade 3 to "catch them up." Not only is this inherent in the design of the Common Core State Standards, it is an absolute necessity to be able to meet the goal that all children are "college and career ready" as they leave high school.

In order to help students learn to read complex texts, we have to know texts inside and out before using them in the classroom, and have a deeper knowledge of each. (See Appendix E for an annotated bibliography of top-notch books.) Shanahan, Fisher and Frey (2012, p. 58) suggest that teachers need to answer the question: "What do we mean when we say that a text is difficult?" Some texts are difficult, or more challenging for learners, because they contain rich vocabulary; others have long, complex sentences and/or organizational structures unfamiliar to the reader. And, in many cases, the reader's own lack of prior knowledge contributes to text difficulty. As teachers, we must carefully consider the demands each text will place upon each individual learner as we plan to scaffold instruction toward comprehension of more challenging text.

## The Added Value of Informational Text

Informational text provides a teacher with opportunities to develop language, vocabulary, and concepts not usually available in fiction selections. For children who come to school with less language as well as fewer background experiences than their better prepared peers, informational text is a valuable context for filling those gaps in language and prior knowledge. According to the research supporting the CCSS (NGA/CCSSO, 2010a, pp. 3–4), there has been a general decline in the complexity of texts over the past half century, and the impact has been "too many students reading at too low a level," particularly in the area of informational or expository texts. The scarcity of informational text in primary grade classrooms is well documented (Duke, 2000; Heller, 2006; Kamberelis, 1998;

Moss & Newton, 1998; Pentimonti, Zucker, Justice, & Kaderavek, 2010; Yopp & Yopp, 2000). Another very compelling reason stems from trends on the National Assessment of Educational Progress, which indicate that fourth graders' reading achievement increases as the diversity of their reading experiences increases (National Center for Education Statistics, 2011). Since 1990, fourth graders who reported reading a wide variety of text outperformed those students who reported reading only one type of text.

## Goal 2: Pay More Attention to Oral Language

Young children come to school eager and excited to learn to read and write. They also come to school with varying degrees of readiness, specifically in the area of oral language, that impact their abilities to learn to read and write. According to research, children typically arrive in kindergarten with discrepancies in language development, and the gap between those children who are less prepared and those who are more prepared in the area of oral language may continue to widen (Biemiller, 1999; Hart & Risley, 1995; Hirsch, 2001). Students who come to school with a strong base of oral language will be more prepared to begin reading instruction than those who do not have a language-rich background. As Moats points out, "Language knowledge and language proficiency differentiate good and poor readers" (1999, p. 17). As teachers, we have to continually ask ourselves two simple questions:

1. **Have I built in enough time for children to talk before, during, and after a lesson?** Students discover what they know through oral language, build vocabulary, and learn from classmates through talk, too.

2. **Do I encourage oral language development through the use of poems, songs, rhymes, and other super-short texts young children can read aloud?** Sometimes in our push for covering the curriculum, we forget that we can take students' literacy farther when we slow down enough to include powerful, playful oral language experiences.

## The Importance of Language in Learning to Read

Why is oral language so important to reading? Oral language skills and vocabulary underlie good comprehension. The "simple view" of reading (Gough & Tunmer, 1986) is a model designed to explain the concept that reading comprehension is the product of two domains: printed word recognition and language comprehension; both are necessary to skilled reading comprehension; neither alone is sufficient. To comprehend text, children need to develop automaticity in word recognition while developing language comprehension, including vocabulary and schema, or topic-specific background knowledge.

As can be found in Appendix A of the Common Core State Standards,

The research strongly suggests that the English language arts classroom should explicitly address the link between oral and written language, exploiting the influence of oral language on a child's later ability to read by allocating instructional time to building children's listening skills, as called for in the Standards. The early grades should not focus on decoding alone, nor should the later grades pay attention only to building reading comprehension. (NGA/CCSSO, 2010a, p. 27)

Reading comprehension and vocabulary knowledge are highly correlated with one another; in fact, vocabulary is the single most important factor in reading comprehension once children have learned the alphabetic code (Stahl & Nagy, 2006). Not surprisingly, children with better vocabularies typically have higher levels of phoneme awareness and learn to read more easily than those with weaker vocabularies (Metsala, 1999).

## Why Read-Aloud Time Is Critical

For kindergarten children, especially those without a strong language or experiential background, building language comprehension needs to be deliberate and purposeful. One of the strongest ways to build language is through a routine that is beloved by teachers and students alike—the daily read-aloud time. Reading aloud with well-written children's books opens up a world of knowledge and vocabulary beyond a child's experience, and reading aloud informational text not only builds essential language skills necessary for reading but also builds concepts and academic vocabulary in content areas. The Common Core State Standards, as well as recent concerns about the imbalance between use of narrative and expository text in the early grades, have highlighted the importance of sharing informational literature with young children. In Appendix A of the CCSS we find,

> Time should be devoted to reading fiction and content-rich selections aloud to young children, just as it is to providing those same children with the skills they will need to decode and encode. (NGA/CCSSO, 2010a, p. 27)

Researchers have long recognized that reading informational text and listening to it read aloud help build children's knowledge of the world (Anderson & Guthrie, 1999; Duke & Kays, 1998; Moss, 1997). As suggested above, not only do students' syntax and vocabulary flourish, children build schemas for later disciplinary learning. Quality children's books include more uncommon and content-related words than other language children are exposed to, including language encountered through conversation and television (Hayes & Ahrens, 1988). Evidence suggests that teachers who make substantial literacy gains with low-income children have been found to use more cognitively challenging language (Taylor, Peterson, Pearson, & Rodriguez, 2002). Even more promising is the finding that teachers' use of higher cognitive language is impacted by the vocabulary diversity found in information books (Price, Bradley, & Smith, 2012). Finally, while all young children learn language from information book read-alouds, children who are learning English as a second language, in particular, reap great benefits (Freeman, Freeman, & Mercuri, 2002).

## Goal 3: Be More *Intentional*

As Epstein (2007) points out: "Intentional teaching means teachers act with specific outcomes or goals in mind for children's development and learning" (p. 1). They understand the "big ideas" of each content area and their role in helping young children develop a firm foundation for later disciplinary learning. They are also able to draw upon a solid knowledge base from which to teach children how to read, write, speak, and listen. Although reading instruction for students in the early grades must maintain a focus on the consolidation of word knowledge, this does not preclude helping students use text to acquire world knowledge (Hiebert & Pearson, 2012–2013).

Purposeful and intentional efforts to scaffold students' acquisition of the Common Core State Standards for Informational Text involves surrounding students with high-quality nonfiction texts, engaging them in a rich exchange of ideas and information, and facilitating both teacher-directed and child-initiated learning opportunities designed to help children gain important disciplinary knowledge. (See Chapter 5 for a lesson template that helps you plan any kind of lesson with nonfiction texts; see Chapters 6–8 for details on using the template for whole group interactive read-alouds and small-group guided reading instruction.)

## Goal 4: Differentiate Instruction

To ensure that all students have access to grade-level complex text, teachers need to consider specific instructional techniques that integrate the foundational skills of reading within nonfiction text. Because the foundational skills are not an end in and of themselves and are designed to be taught in differentiated ways according to the needs of the readers, specific considerations need to be made. For example, teachers must consider those primary students who are

- not yet proficient in decoding.
- decoding but not yet reading fluently.
- reading fluently from grade-level text.
- reading fluently from above grade-level text.

### Preparing for Teaching

To prepare for using a particular text with a group of readers, the teacher needs to first read the text. Only then can she begin to consider ways for structuring each group's explicit lesson, understanding and acknowledging where students are in their development as readers. Are they still mastering the alphabetic code? Do they know their letter sounds but are not blending to decode? Are they decoding but still developing fluency? Are they fluent readers but don't apply comprehension strategies to "think their way through text?" Are they strong, independent readers? Asking these kinds of questions and then forming answers based on available assessment data is an essential step in determining reading groups. From there a teacher can adapt her lesson to meet the needs of the students by supporting them with differentiated instruction. The assessment and diagnosis of individual readers goes beyond the scope of the book; some general guidelines will be provided to illustrate the concept of utilizing appropriate, grade-level text with all readers.

### Guiding the Reading of Below-Level Readers

Our emphasis with below-level readers needs to be on helping them meet the demands of reading more challenging text so they can reap the benefits of language and concepts inherent in that text, while helping them develop their skills and stamina to eventually read on grade level. *It is important to note that, in addition to grade-level informational text experience, below-level readers will continue to need explicit, systematic instruction in the necessary foundational skills. They must also continue to apply those emerging skills to appropriate text, for example, to decodable text that matches their current level of development.*

In order to utilize grade-level informational text with below-level readers, here are some tips to consider:

- Spend additional time building concepts and vocabulary before reading.
- Frontload new vocabulary and concepts through discussion, additional read-aloud experiences, or use of media to enable students to more successfully participate in the group reading experience.
- If necessary, read aloud the selection to the students, so they can hear the text read fluently and so that they can learn the concepts via their listening comprehension.
- Either after the first reading or after reading units (pages, sections) of text, pause to ask comprehension questions or guide students to comprehend concepts (keeping the big ideas in mind).
- Focusing on the needs of the students, return to the text to pull excerpts for specific teaching. For example, on a small board in your group you might list words from the text you think students may have difficulty decoding. Teach students how to blend to decode the words, and provide them with opportunities to practice that skill. If students can blend but are having difficulty with vowel patterns, choose words to reteach vowel patterns. Or, locate multisyllabic words for teaching and reinforcing structural analysis. For students who can decode but lack fluency, pull phrases or sentences or passages from the text to read aloud; then have students echo read with you, then read chorally, and finally, singly.

Below-level readers will be able to experience all the same rich, interdisciplinary connections their counterparts experience, because they have had this experience with appropriately complex text rather than text that might be watered down to meet their reading abilities. An additional opportunity that could be provided after the reading of the core grade-level text is further reading using easier text to apply their emerging skills and develop that reading mileage.

## Guiding the Reading of On-Level Readers

Our emphasis with students who are currently reading at grade level is first on assessing their needs by listening to them read aloud and working to consolidate all the foundational skills so that they are reading with accuracy. With typically developing first graders, as their decoding and word recognition skills become solid, the focus will start to shift to an emphasis on building fluency. This is because of the shift of brain energy allocation that comes when conscious energy is no longer focused on getting the text off the page and shifts to thinking through text. Tips for working with on-level readers include the following:

- Consider vocabulary carefully; although their decoding skills may be adequate, they will still likely need you to teach key vocabulary necessary for understanding the story. As you prepare for teaching, read the story carefully, and anticipate which words or concepts you may need to preteach, which you may be able to teach on the fly (as you go through the reading), and which words children will likely know.

- Be sure to give children opportunities to read aloud individually, so you can assess their decoding abilities and fluency.
- Provide ample opportunities for rereading and guided oral reading of the text to build fluency. Choral reading and partner reading are excellent strategies for building fluency.

## Guiding the Reading of Above-Level Readers

Our emphasis with above-level readers is assuring their consolidation of all of the foundational skills and developing fluency. This is important to ensure all students are solid readers. We are all too familiar with students who sometimes have very strong verbal abilities and reading behaviors but may not have those deep neural connections that allow them to "really read." Sometimes those students appear to be fluent readers in kindergarten and first grade, but as the demands of reading increase, they start to fall through the cracks. So, even with our above-level readers, it is important to allow for opportunities to read aloud so we can continually assess their decoding and comprehension skills.

A second emphasis with above-level readers is the development of independent reading. Instructionally, we help them learn how to navigate through text. This includes teaching them what to do when they hit roadblocks, how to apply fix-up strategies (see Chapter 4), and how to use self-questioning and summarizing to ensure they understand what they read. Here are some tips to consider when working with above-level readers:

- These students may have a broader base of language or experiences than other students, so concepts, vocabulary, and even the purpose for the reading may be, in large part, elicited from the students rather than built by the teacher.
- Although we still want to provide opportunities for children to read aloud to us, we may also have them read the text independently before meeting with us, and then read select passages in the group setting. Just as with the other groups, comprehension instruction will depend on the strengths and needs of the students but will still need to focus on those all-important big ideas.
- In addition to the interdisciplinary opportunities afforded all the students in the class, following up the reading of the core text with more challenging text opportunities will be important for above-level readers.

## Goal 5: Explicitly Teach From the Text

Remember the big ideas you want children to come away with after reading a particular text, and use these ideas to guide your plan for comprehension development. The lesson plan template included in Chapter 5 helps with instructional planning for *all* students and levels of reading. That said, here are some tips to keep in mind when differentiating instruction in small groups that will help keep the text's rich content and ideas central in the lesson:

- After reading units (pages, sections) of text, pause to ask comprehension questions or guide students to comprehend concepts (keeping the big ideas in mind), and then help students who need extra support to apply the types of strategies and fix-up tips (see Chapter 4) to develop fluent reading with comprehension. In other words, these group reading experiences should always leave children with the feeling that they've tackled a really interesting text—rather than give them the feeling that the time was all about cementing skills.

- Return to the text, as needed, for decoding or fluency-building instruction depending on student behaviors noticed earlier in the lesson. However, the primary focus in this part of the lesson, especially with proficient readers, is the further development and application of *previously taught* strategies. In other words, pull away from the text to think aloud for students about use of a strategy they have been introduced to that is applicable to the text. For example, if the text has cause-and-effect structures, first name it, then provide examples, and then provide opportunities for students to practice locating other causes and effects within text. The primary objective is development of the metacognitive awareness of *what we do* as readers, so we can apply those skills and strategies in our independent reading.

## In Summary

The Common Core State Standards present unique challenges and opportunities for K–2 teachers. Through intentional instruction that acknowledges the critical role of oral language, of complex text, and of differentiating instruction in learning and teaching reading, we can equip children with skills and strategies for reading in general and reading to learn. How to select and use these texts to help students apply their growing foundational reading skills while meeting the Reading Standards for Informational Text is more fully illustrated through the content, reading strategies, lesson templates, and examples provided in the subsequent chapters.

# 3

# The How-To's of Selecting Stellar Texts

Young children want to learn *everything* about *everything*. They want to know about places they haven't been, from coral reefs to outer space; they crave to know how things work, from drinking straws to thunderstorms, and about who and what lives in their world. The local firefighter fascinates them as much as a famous astronaut. As you know from your own students, young children *want* to read nonfiction, because these texts help them find answers to their many questions. Young children are scientists, discovers, tinkerers, and explorers, and in nonfiction they meet their match. Teachers with whom we work have remarked that each year they try to spot who is going to be the reader who loves the gory facts of great white sharks in book after book, and who is going to gravitate to cozier koala bears and manatees (and they are often surprised!).

In this chapter we arm you with the tools to select nonfiction with substance—texts that will provide your students with a source of facts and information as well as spark their interest in further learning. A high-quality nonfiction book is much more than a reference work; it is a means of convincing students that reading is a fun endeavor, and for teachers, nonfiction books are the ticket to in-depth information that builds important content knowledge. During the K–2 years good nonfiction text helps us model for students how to navigate, read, and learn from texts that have an array of text features, from glossaries to bar graphs.

In this chapter we'll show you what to look for in terms of the appeal, format, and accuracy of nonfiction texts, so you can choose the best books to help your students meet the Common Core State Standards for Informational Text.

In the past decade we have seen an explosion in the publication of informational literature. This may be due in part to increased emphasis on vocabulary and comprehension, and to recognition of the role that prior knowledge plays with respect to listening and reading comprehension. Through use of exemplary nonfiction texts of all types, we can provide our emergent and early readers with a strong foundation for (1) reading for key ideas and details, (2) reading for craft and structure, and (3) integrating knowledge and ideas.

And, at the risk of sounding like bossy older sisters, we implore you to fill your classroom library with lots of books. Not dozens—hundreds of titles. They are out there for the picking, and with ingenuity you can find the funds to fill your shelves. Get an independent reading program going early in the year, so children learn the routines for selecting books to read on their own.

## The New Nonfiction

Over the past few decades, no other genre has changed as significantly as has nonfiction. In fact, the nonfiction picture book has been referred to as the *new* nonfiction because it varies greatly from traditional nonfiction books (Gill, 2009). As Carter (2000) points out,

> Forty years ago, children read nonfiction books with small type and limited illustrations. . . . Today, they encounter books with carefully designed illustrations that partner with the text to contribute to their thinking. . . . Illustrations introduce core concepts necessary for understanding a topic and serve as integral portions of each book. (p. 707)

Cognizant of the needs of teachers of emergent and early readers, educational publishers (as opposed to trade book publishers) have also responded with a robust selection of nonfiction texts for interactive read-aloud experiences, big books for whole-class instruction and shared reading, and decodable text for use during scaffolded reading instruction as well as independent reading by students. Such texts, available on a wide array of topics and for readers of varying abilities, allow us to enrich and expand our content-focused units of instruction in social studies, science, and math.

Taken together, all these books serve as indispensable tools for use in modeling close reading of informational text. As teachers, we must help young readers to internalize strategies via explicit instruction, and then, through a gradual release of teacher responsibility and much practice and feedback, scaffold students' independent use of these in their own reading.

With so many books on the market, how do we choose the ones that will best meet the needs of our youngest learners? The checklist in Appendix A both combines and expands upon elements noted by Gill (2009) and Stephens (2008) and includes attention to the following four broad criteria:

1. format and visual appeal

2. accuracy and authenticity

3. writing style and appropriateness for young children

4. content and curricular connections

We begin our discussion of criteria for text selection with an examination of the overall design, style, format, and visual appeal of good nonfiction books for your classroom.

## Evaluating Format and Visual Appeal

Imagine going to the mall just to window shop. You see a new store and just have to go in. Why? What *first* grabs your attention? Is there an enticing window display? Items located near the entrance to the store that beckon you to enter? Or, perhaps the name of the store piques your curiosity, and you just have to know what treasures might lie inside? Whatever attracted your attention, once you are inside the store, chances are, you'll explore further.

Authors, illustrators, designers, and publishers of quality nonfiction have the same goal: They each use their unique talents to entice you to pick up the book and "walk inside." And they know their first shot at winning over the reader is the cover. The cover, title, illustrations, and text layout can all serve to either encourage or discourage a reader's choice, enjoyment, and even comprehension of the reading material. Think about your intended purpose for using a specific text, and then ask yourself questions, such as those in Figure 3.1, to evaluate the format and visual appeal that text may hold for your students. As you will see, questions include attention to the cover, font, type, letter size, style, illustrations, text layout, and special features of nonfiction text.

### *Is there an attractive cover?*

Publishers of many of the newer books on the market today have considered the visual appeal of both the front and back covers. Pictured in Figure 3.2 is the front and back cover of a book from National Geographic Little Kids. Photographs appear on both the front and back cover, and brief bits of interesting information on the back cover serve to further entice the reader. Notice the presence of the short, intriguing question, "Do you want to hang out with a lion?" that appears in large, bold type on the back cover. A definite attention grabber!

As you select informational texts for your students, remember that the cover serves as the child's first introduction to the text; it builds anticipation and excitement and helps to create a purpose for the reading and listening experiences to follow.

| Is the format visually appealing? | Yes | No |
| --- | :---: | :---: |
| Is there an attractive cover? | ☐ | ☐ |
| Are the font, letter size, and type large, simple, and easy to read? | ☐ | ☐ |
| Are there high-quality, appealing photographs and/or illustrations in which appropriate media have been used? | ☐ | ☐ |
| Do illustrations contribute to the visual appeal of the book? | ☐ | ☐ |
| Are the illustrations clear and large but not overly crowded? | ☐ | ☐ |
| Do the illustrations appropriately explain and enhance the content? | ☐ | ☐ |
| Do illustrations depict accurate size relationships? | ☐ | ☐ |
| Are labels and captions simple yet sufficient? | ☐ | ☐ |
| Is there a wide variety of illustrative materials (maps, charts, and graphs) that serve to clarify and extend the text? | ☐ | ☐ |
| Does the text layout (headings, sidebars, and/or other visual features, such as special fonts or letter size) serve to highlight key information for readers? | ☐ | ☐ |
| Is there an appropriate amount of text and illustrations on each page? | ☐ | ☐ |
| Is there a table of contents, index, and/or glossary? | ☐ | ☐ |

**FIGURE 3.1** Checklist for Evaluating Format and Visual Appeal

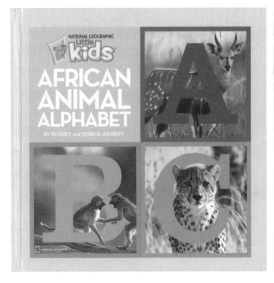

**FIGURE 3.2** Quality Texts Have Visually Appealing Covers

*Source:* Joubert & Joubert (2011)

## *Are the font, letter size, and type large, simple, and easy to read?*

While the answer to this question will not be "yes" for all informational texts used in the early grades, those that do meet this criterion and contain at least some enlarged words are especially helpful for emergent and early readers. Note the text embedded within the illustrations on the pages from *Food from Farms*, an Acorn Book from the World of Farming series (see Figure 3.3). During the read-aloud experience with emergent and beginning readers, teachers can point to and discuss words and sections of text that can be easily seen by the students.

**FIGURE 3.3** Consider Font, Letter Size, and Type

*Source:* Dickmann (2011)

A sufficiently large font makes text easier to read and helps children focus on key words and content. Whether selecting books for use during interactive read-aloud experiences, shared reading, or instructional or independent reading by individual children, consideration should be given to the font, letter size, and type.

## Are there large, clear, and well-spaced illustrations that serve to explain and enhance the content? Are labels and captions simple yet sufficient?

Illustrations are central to the effectiveness of the text in presenting new information to young readers. When evaluating illustrations in books for young children, one must look for authentic high-quality photographs and/or realistic pictures. Consider a child who has never seen a live bear. While one artist's rendering of the bears in the classic storybook *Goldilocks and the Three Bears* may provide the child with an idea of what a bear looks like, a full color photograph is going to assist the child in forming a more accurate and complete mental image. And, while elements of fantasy may appear in illustrations in fictional texts (such as mama bear wearing an apron, or papa bear putting on his hat to go for a walk in the woods), there should be no combination of realism with fantasy in illustrations found in nonfiction texts, the purpose of which is to convey true information. The front cover and two pages from *National Geographic Little Kids First Big Book of Animals* (Hughes, 2010) is shown in Figure 3.4. The large, colorful photographs and the position of the text in relation to the photographs capture the reader's interest in a way that enhances, rather than distracts from, the author's message.

While photographs and realistic drawings are important illustrative tools for use in the creation of high quality nonfiction text, this is not to say that other artistic media cannot be used to effectively portray concepts presented in nonfiction books. Award-winning illustrator Steve Jenkins constructs lifelike images through use of texture- and color-rich cut-paper collages in his science-themed informational books, such as: *Actual Size* (Jenkins, 2004), *Move!* (Page & Jenkins, 2006), and *What Do You Do With a Tail Like This?* (Jenkins & Page, 2003), a Caldecott Honor Book.

For younger children especially, illustrations in nonfiction text are a critical means of providing key information about complex topics, and they should match both the description and the action in the text. A child not yet familiar with words associated with trees might be confused upon hearing the sentence, "A trunk is covered by a hard layer of wood called bark" (Gibbons, 2002, p. 7). The positioning of the text directly below Gail Gibbons's realistic drawing of a child grasping the bark of a tree trunk serves to clarify the meaning of the words *trunk* and *bark,* both of which possess multiple meanings. Similarly, when the text in *First Big Book of Animals* (Hughes, 2010) says, "Giraffes eat leaves. Because they are so tall, giraffes can reach leaves growing high in trees" (p. 15), the reader sees a picture of giraffes eating leaves from trees.

**FIGURE 3.4** Consider Illustrations, Labels, and Captions

*Source:* Hughes (2010)

While not everything that is mentioned in the text needs to be portrayed visually, good illustrations clarify the text and serve to both support and expand the concepts being presented. Diagrams make concepts clearer, while photographs convey information, as well as beauty (Giorgis & Glazer, 2012). For example, a diagram consisting of simple labeling of objects or parts of objects is one way to present unfamiliar concepts and ideas to young children. Captions are another. Although not essential, simply stated captions can make photographs, diagrams, and other illustrations more comprehensible to readers of all ages, and they are particularly helpful for young readers.

A textbox containing a listing of simply stated facts about zebras can be found at the far right side of page 13 in *First Big Book of Animals*. Appearing top right of each page of this book is a label identifying each animal's habitat. Each of these features makes the text accessible to young children who are novices at navigating informational text, and represents elements we need to note during our evaluation and selection process.

Sometimes illustrations and brief enlarged segments of text are present in a book that is otherwise too difficult for emergent and/or early readers to understand. When this is the case, these may be the only parts of the text read directly to the children, and the more detailed text appearing in smaller font might be omitted or summarized in words younger children will understand.

## Does the text layout—headings, sidebars, and/or other visual features— serve to highlight key information for readers?

Text layout is an important consideration not only in books to be read aloud, but also in informational books designed for beginning readers. Color, bold type, varying font types and sizes, textboxes, and other visual features engage the reader by creating aesthetic appeal that builds interest. And, appropriately placed illustrations and text that are not overly crowded assist beginning readers in focusing on key content. As can be seen from the examples in Figure 3.4, bold headings and enlarged fonts catch the reader's eye, calling attention to essential ideas. In *First Big Book of Animals* additional facts about zebras appear in a circle on each page with key words in bold type. Color is used to effectively draw the reader's eye to both pictures and text, and varying fonts and type sizes serve to highlight important information. Marsh (2010) uses visual features to focus children's attention on the purposes for various physical features of the African elephant in her book, *National Geographic Kids Great Migrations: Elephants* (Figure 3.5). Arrows point from individual textboxes to the corresponding part of the elephant, making the information easily accessible to beginning readers who may have otherwise experienced difficulty reading the same information in paragraph form.

The importance of excellent visual features of text—especially those that support the young child's comprehension and enjoyment of abstract concepts and ideas outside of their prior knowledge—cannot be overemphasized. As discussed earlier in this chapter, the new nonfiction picture books are colorful and have pleasing, uncluttered designs as well as interesting information presented in a logical manner. Readers, or in the case of younger children, listeners, acquire new vocabulary and broader background knowledge. Unlike textbooks that are typically geared toward a single grade level, nonfiction picture

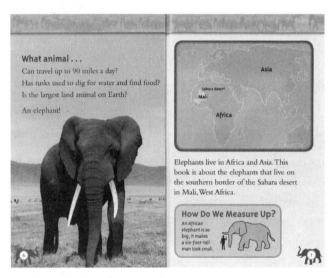

**FIGURE 3.5** Consider the Layout of the Text

*Source:* Marsh (2010)

books often include information suitable for a wider range of audiences. As teachers, we can choose to read those portions of the text we believe will be comprehensible to our listeners.

An example from Sandra Markle's *How Many Baby Pandas?* (2009) is shown in Figure 3.6. This is a unique concept book that not only reinforces counting, numerals, and recognition of number words but also introduces young children to factual information about a discipline-related topic that is both interesting and motivating. Notice the way the sidebar located at the bottom left of page 7 frames several additional facts about pandas. This information may or may not be shared during the first reading of the text, depending on the purpose for the listening experience and the ability of the listeners.

How many
baby pandas
are taking a
nap?

Baby giant pandas, like human babies, sleep a lot. Most of their energy goes toward growing bigger. They also grow their fur coat. Then they can stay warm on their own.

When baby giant pandas are about two months old, their eyes open.

7

**FIGURE 3.6**  Consider Sidebars

*Source:* Markle (2009)

## *Is there a table of contents, index, glossary, or other similar feature?*

What one learns from the reading of an informational book comes from more than just the text. In addition to headings, subheadings, and other visual characteristics, text features such as tables of contents, indexes, and glossaries provide access points into and information about the text. While not all nonfiction texts for young children must contain all of these features, teachers do need to be able to model how use of text features helps us identify the most important ideas, anticipate what the author will tell us next, understand complex ideas, and efficiently locate key information in the text. Thus, this is an important consideration when evaluating and selecting nonfiction text for young children. The good news is that more publishers are now attuned to the importance of the presence of text features in books for young children, and so an increasing number of texts containing these features are currently available. In Figure 3.7 we see examples of the table of contents and index of *National Geographic Kids Great Migration: Elephants.*

Endnotes are another feature found in more and more informational books for young children. Like glossaries, endnotes provide teachers with helpful information for use in answering children's questions and expanding upon their knowledge about the topic. For example, in the final pages of his books, Jenkins includes reduced copies of his collage animals along with interesting information about each one. The teacher can decide whether or not to read any or all of this information to the children during a first or subsequent reading of the book. Accomplished readers will be able to use these pages to find out more about specific animals of interest. Beverly and Dereck Joubert include an alphabetized listing of supplementary information at the end of *African Animal Alphabet* (see Figure 3.8). Placing the information at the end of the book allows these author/illustrators to keep the pages uncluttered and serves to focus the emergent reader's attention on the photographs and on the enlarged alphabet letter and key phrase that appear on each page (e.g., "L is for Lion"). This book also includes tips for parents and a list of related resources as well as a glossary.

The layout and visual features of nonfiction text enhance both teacher and student access to and understanding of complex information and concepts. As we evaluate texts,

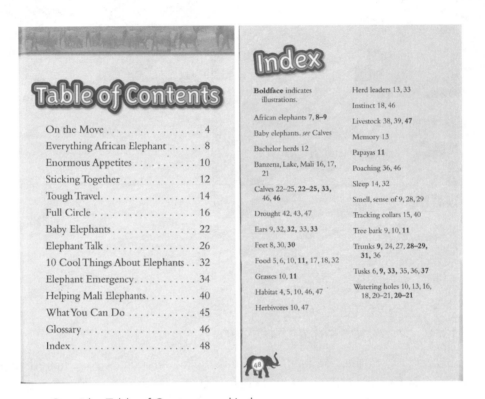

**FIGURE 3.7** Consider Table of Contents and Index

*Source:* Marsh (2010)

**FIGURE 3.8** Endnotes

*Source:* Joubert & Joubert (2011)

noting the presence of headings, sidebars, and other visual features such as those mentioned above is one way to help us locate high-quality books for use with young children.

## Evaluating Accuracy and Authenticity

Although one might assume authors, illustrators, publishers, and reviewers check carefully to ensure all content in new texts is accurate, this is not always the case. Marianne J. Dyson, a science writer and former National Aeronautics & Space Administration flight controller, states,

At MarianneDyson.com, one can find reviews of books for children and adults dealing with space, physics, astronomy, technology, and space history—all topics within Dyson's areas of expertise. Seeking sources such as Dyson's website is one way to check accuracy of books for use with young children.

> There IS gravity in space, the Moon does NOT have a dark side, and Jupiter has at least 60 moons. However, kids today might not know these things because many books are full of misleading explanations, incorrect terminology, impossible physics, old data, and confusing illustrations. (www.mariannedyson.com/spacebooks.htm)

In Figure 3.9 are additional criteria for evaluating informational literature for accuracy and authenticity. Examples of these are discussed below.

| Is the book accurate? | Yes | No |
|---|---|---|
| Is information about the authors' qualifications or process for research of the topic included? | ☐ | ☐ |
| Does the book have a recent copyright date, and/or is the information based on up-to-date research? | ☐ | ☐ |
| Do illustrations accurately depict the text? | ☐ | ☐ |
| Can facts presented in the text be verified with other authoritative sources? | ☐ | ☐ |
| Are animals depicted accurately without being given human characteristics? | ☐ | ☐ |
| Do authors refrain from making value-laden statements and/or statements of opinion, rather than fact? | ☐ | ☐ |
| Are statements of opinion clearly stated as such? | ☐ | ☐ |
| If the book is a blend of fact and fiction, is it clear which parts are fact and which are fiction? | ☐ | ☐ |

FIGURE 3.9 Evaluating Accuracy and Authenticity

Checking the accuracy of facts presented in a book against other credible sources is another way to ensure that one is providing children with correct information. For example, in one text about forest animals, the authors state that chipmunks feed in summertime because they have to sleep through winter. This is not exactly accurate, as, according to the National Geographic website:

> They feed on insects, nuts, berries, seeds, fruit, and grain which they stuff into their generous cheek pouches and carry to their burrow or nest to store. Chipmunks hibernate, but instead of storing fat, they periodically dip into their cache of

nuts and seeds throughout the winter. (http://animals.nationalgeographic.com/animals/mammals/chipmunk/)

While there are many reasons for the inaccuracies that appear in some nonfiction texts, the fact remains that incorrect information does exist, and educators must select books with care. Questions to ask when evaluating the accuracy of a text include the following:

1. Is information about the author's qualifications or process for research of the topic included?

2. Do illustrations accurately depict the text?

3. Are animals and inanimate objects depicted accurately without being given human characteristics?

4. Are statements of opinion clearly stated as such, and if the book is a blend of fact and fiction, is it clear when parts are fact and which are not?

Checking copyright dates is a good practice when selecting nonfiction books, as those with more recent copyright dates are more likely to be based on up-to-date research. This is especially important when selecting books on science and technology, as these tend to become outdated quickly; however, even in areas such as history, attitudes toward interpreting events and reporting information can change. Newer books are less likely to include stereotypes or to omit important individuals or events—both of which can be problems when using books with older copyright dates.

High-quality informational texts are based on the most up-to-date research. Bruce McMillan, author of many nonfiction books for children, says there's "no such thing as overdoing the research." In his article, "Accuracy in Books for Young Readers: From First to Last Check" (1993), he discusses the research process he uses, which consists of consulting appropriate adult books and professional research reports, working with reference librarians across the country, verifying facts using at least three reputable sources, and consulting with science checkers, such as a wildlife biologist. McMillan suggests that selection of nonfiction books for young children should include a search for "reputable writers who write with clarity and accuracy regarding factual information and who use research sources in support of their writing" (p. 2).

Authors of high-quality nonfiction books provide clearly stated information that invites discussion and leads readers to form their own opinions based on the facts presented. For example, an informational book on pets that states "cats make good pets" is misleading, as cats are not good pet choices for individuals with one or more of the five known allergies to cats. The problem occurs when the author states opinions as facts. McMillan emphasizes the need to check for value judgments and personal opinions when evaluating nonfiction text for children. Citing an example from a book on weather that shows a picture of rain and states "low pressure often brings bad weather," he illustrates the way an author might inappropriately use value-laden statements. As he points out, a farmer during a drought season would not see rain as "bad" weather.

Authors of informational books for young children have a challenging task. They must write about complex topics in just a very few words. This means, of course, that many important details must be, of necessity, excluded from the book. At that same time, authors should not include misinformation or oversimplify information to the point of inaccuracy. As consumers of these books, in addition to noting personal biases and values, we must watch for errors of omission that can lead to half-truths and misconceptions for young children who possess insufficient prior knowledge upon which to evaluate the accuracy of the information they are hearing and reading. In other words, as we review texts, we must look not only for what is included but also for what is excluded.

For example, in one book designed to acquaint children with information about animal rescue centers, the animals have human characteristics, such as the ability to speak, and the book doesn't tell how the animals rescued are cared for at the center. One animal finds another animal in distress and tells her about the animal rescue center where injured animals can receive help. He tells her he will take her there. The book doesn't, however, have any human characters. The reader is left to infer how an injured animal might get to a rescue center and what might happen there. This fictionalization of nonfiction books is problematic in that the facts are distorted to the point where they are easily misunderstood. Both the presence of anthropomorphism (the attribution of human qualities to nonhumans) and the omission of key information led to the Library of Congress's classification of the book as a work of fiction, rather than nonfiction, despite the fact that six content experts were listed as consultants.

Some books combine elements of nonfiction within a fiction story. While these books, often referred to as *faction,* are helpful for beginning readers in that they use narrative to present factual information, the authors must present accurate information and clearly convey to the reader that information which is fact and that which is fiction. Somewhat related to this is an author's assignment of human characteristics to animals—a common element found in early childhood literature. While this is fine for fiction, it is inappropriate in nonfiction. Books that may otherwise contain all factual information should not be classed as nonfiction if animals are clothed, speak, or in some way imply human emotion. In one beautifully illustrated lift-the-flap book about pets, the authors share excellent, easy-to-read, and interesting information about guinea pigs, hamsters, rabbits, and more. Unfortunately, next to the photographs of the animals are speech bubbles containing text such as, "Eweee! Have you got my lunch?" and "Carrot . . . yummy!"

While some may argue that the author's use of speech bubbles may be an acceptable way to draw young children into nonfiction text, the point here is that we need to be sure we are providing children with accurate information and appropriate understandings about the topic and about the differences between fiction and nonfiction. It's perfectly fine for animals to talk in fiction, but not in books cast as nonfiction. Having said that, cartoons, whim, and humor can be fabulous complements to accurate nonfiction.

The current emphasis on accuracy in nonfiction books for young children is both warranted and welcome. As we evaluate books for use in our classrooms, we must be cognizant of the necessity of attending to accuracy in both text and illustrations. In an attempt to prove accuracy, some books may list one or more consultants, organizations, or foundations as collaborators or reviewers. While information such as this does assist us in selecting credible books for children, ultimately, as educators it is up to us to seek out authoritative resources from qualified sources, and then, to the best of our ability, evaluate the accuracy and authenticity of each text.

# Evaluating Writing Style and Appropriateness for Young Children

Authors of excellent informational books for young children can communicate with children at their conceptual level, explaining difficult concepts and vocabulary clearly and simply. Criteria for analyzing the writing style and appropriateness for children in kindergarten through Grade 2 appear in Figure 3.10.

| Is the writing style engaging? | Yes | No |
|---|:---:|:---:|
| Does the author draw the reader in with an engaging lead? | ☐ | ☐ |
| Are ideas logically ordered? | ☐ | ☐ |
| Is the background knowledge of the reader considered? | ☐ | ☐ |
| Are new ideas presented in a way that helps children make connections to what they already know? | ☐ | ☐ |
| Is the language appropriate for the children? | ☐ | ☐ |
| Does the author explain difficult concepts clearly and simply? | ☐ | ☐ |
| Are there any interactive elements that involve the reader? | ☐ | ☐ |
| Are new terms explained, highlighted, or defined? | ☐ | ☐ |
| Do the sound and meaning devices employed by the author enhance the rhythm and flow of the language and the child's understanding of the content? | ☐ | ☐ |
| Is the author's choice of text structure appropriate for presenting the content? | ☐ | ☐ |

**FIGURE 3.10** Consider Writing Style and Appropriateness

Drawing children in with an engaging lead, good authors provide key content in an interesting manner and share conclusions that leave the children feeling satisfied or wanting to know more. Their books are well organized and present new information in creative ways. This is exactly what one can find in *Loud and Quiet: An Animal Opposites Book* by Lisa Bullard (2005). A simple introduction draws the reader into the book and sets the purpose for the listening or reading experience: "Some animals make sounds as loud as thunder. Others are so quiet they hardly make any noise at all. Let's learn about loud and quiet by looking at animals around the world" (p. 2).

On the pages that follow, high-quality color photographs of animals appear along with the word *loud* or *quiet* (see Figure 3.11). The author explains in easy-to-understand language the sounds made by each, and often includes additional interesting facts in eye-catching oval text boxes.

Another excellent example of engaging writing can be found in Laura Hulbert's *Who Has These Feet?* (2011). Illustrated by Erik Brooks, this book's simple title question immediately engages the audience and sets the purpose for the listening or reading experience. Appearing again on the first page, the question, "Who has these feet?" activates young children's prior knowledge and prompts their predictions of animals whose feet resemble

**FIGURE 3.11** Writing Style: Is It Clear, Engaging, and Informative?

*Source:* Bullard (2005)

the ones shown on the page. The answer follows on the next two pages as a polar bear—first its back and then its front—is revealed, along with text that reads, "A polar bear has these feet. A polar bear has fur on the bottom of his feet so it won't slip on the ice." The simple explanations presented by the author are easily understood by young children, and provide interesting factual information about a variety of familiar animals.

The questions posed in *Who Has These Feet?* provide an element of interactivity, as do those included in *National Geographic Little Kids Look & Learn: Match!* (2011). As can be seen in the pages shown in Figure 3.12, children are asked to locate pictures that match.

## The Author's Choice of Elements of Style

Style refers to the way the author writes the text and the voice in which he or she chooses to convey the content, as opposed to the specific content conveyed. It is always important and especially so in picture books, where creation of the mood is essential. Even in nonfiction texts, a variety of literary devices are used by authors to craft their writing—from word choice, to tone, to grammatical structure. Sound and meaning devices are two elements of style that are used by authors to make their texts more interesting to children. Sound

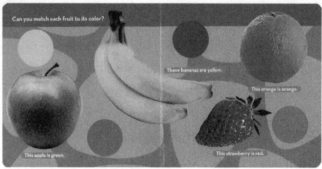

**FIGURE 3.12** Interactivity: How Well Does It Invite the Young Reader In?

*Source:* National Geographic Kids (2011)

devices, such as repetition, rhyme, alliteration, onomatopoeia, assonance, and consonance are used to bring rhythm and flow to a text. Meaning devices such as imagery, simile, and metaphor are used to convey meaning in ways that are more accessible for the audience.

In *African Animal Alphabet,* Joubert & Joubert (2011) use alliteration in the description provided for each animal. Read aloud the two excerpts that follow, noting the repetition of words that begin with the same sound as the animal's name.

- "Baby warthogs wiggle and roll in wallows of mud whenever they can. This little warthog wobbles out to whisper little grunts to its waiting mom" (p. 38).
- "A yellow-billed hornbill stands perched on a termite mound with its yellow beak glowing in the sun. Does it yap, yell, or yip? No, it makes a clucking sound" (p. 41).

The presence of alliteration is especially helpful in this text for emergent readers and writers. Since a critical foundational skill for children in this early stage of literacy development is phonological awareness, this text helps tune young ears to the sounds of language by focusing children's attention on words that sound the same at the beginning.

Steve Jenkins' purposeful choice of words make his books exceptionally fine read-alouds. Note the use of alliteration, consonance (the repetition of internal consonant sounds), and assonance (the repetition of vowel sounds) in this carefully crafted example: "A crocodile leaps to snag its meal . . . after slithering silently into the water. A snake slithers through rustling leaves. . . ." (pp. 10–12). The word *rustling* is also a nice example of onomatopoeia (words that sound like their meanings).

One cannot help but also notice the rich vocabulary words appearing in this book. Imagery—specifically the use of sensory words that evoke sight and sound, such as *leaps, snag, slithering, slithers, silently, rustling*—enables the audience to more completely and accurately visualize the action. In just this one example, not only are children presented with exact terms that further their comprehension, they are exposed to excellent models for their own writing.

A sound device frequently used in fiction texts for emergent readers is rhyme. However, this device can also be found in nonfiction texts, as in this example from Galvin's 2007 *Alphabet of Ocean Animals*: "The water bird has a giant bill that she uses like a trap. When her bill is full of fish, it closes with a snap!" (p. 19).

## The Author's Choice of Text Structure

Closely related to style is the author's choice of text structure. By organizing their text in logical ways, authors help readers read nonfiction texts differently, depending on their structure. Common text structures evident in nonfiction text include *description*, *sequence*, *comparison*, *cause and effect*, *problem/solution*, and *question/answer* (see Figure 3.13). By sharing examples of books utilizing varying text structures, and then encouraging children to create their own comparable texts through shared or independent writing, we can help provide young students with a firm foundation for informational reading and writing.

In order to provide children with the skills necessary for navigating these varying text structures, teachers must have access to representative nonfiction text, and make a conscious effort to help youngsters understand how these structures are used by authors. For example, as can be seen in Figure 3.14, "Bigger than a cantaloupe, or too small to see, hummingbirds lay the smallest bird eggs!" (p. 21), *comparison* is used by Baines (2009) in *What's in That Egg?* a uniquely presented book about life cycles.

Sandra Markle (2009) employs a very explicit *problem/solution* approach: "The biggest problem for giant pandas is that the forests where they live are being cleared. To help, the Chinese government is keeping some forests safe just for giant pandas" (p. 20). Markle's use of the phrase "the biggest problem" serves as a signal assisting beginning readers in their understanding of the rest of the paragraph in which solutions for the problem are presented.

Writing style is a conscious choice made by the author. As has been shown, a variety of styles and structures, often found within the same text, are used to enhance the rhythm and flow of language, build interest, and convey meaning. Our job, as evaluators and selectors of informational texts, is to consider the appropriateness of the author's writing style for the young children with whom the texts will be used.

## Evaluating Potential Content and Curricular Connections

Informational literature plays a key role in development of children's knowledge of the world and its people. As will be discussed in Chapter 9, texts used both within and across grade levels need to be selected around topics or themes that systematically develop the knowledge base of students. The knowledge children learn about particular topics in the early grades should then be expanded and developed in subsequent grades to ensure increasingly deeper understanding; therefore, once topics are identified, selection of an

| Text Structure | Explanation | Example |
|---|---|---|
| Description | Author describes topic through discussion of characteristics, features, attributes, and examples. | "Pumpkins are a type of squash. They can be green, red, tan, yellow, white, or even blue" (Esbaum, 2009b, pp. 6–7). |
| Sequence | Author presents information in a chronological or logical order. | "A pumpkin seed is tucked into sun-warmed earth. Spring rains soften its touch coat. Soon jagged leaves rise from twisty vines" (Esbaum, 2009b, p. 2). |
| Comparison | Author seeks to help children understand an unfamiliar object, event, concept, et cetera, by comparing it with a more familiar one. | "Not all blows are alike. Some go straight up. They can reach as high as a three-story building. Others spread out in a spray. They look like a fountain against the sky" (Berger & Berger, 1999, p. 10). "Splash! The landing sounds like an exploding firecracker" (Berger & Berger, 1999, p. 27). |
| Cause and Effect | Author presents ideas and events as causes, and the resulting effect(s) as facts that happen as the result of an idea or event. | "Deep ocean water is deep and murky. It is hard for whales to see very far. But sound travels well through water. So whales depend more on hearing than sight" (Berger & Berger, 1999, p. 11). |
| Problem/Solution | Author presents a problem and shares one or more solutions to the problem. | "The biggest problem for giant pandas is that the forests where they live are being cleared. To help, the Chinese government is keeping some forests safe just for giant pandas" (Markle, 2009, p. 20). |
| Question/Answer | Author poses a question and shares information to answer the question. | "Why are some animals striped? A zebra's stripes are like your fingerprints—completely unique" (Shields, 2011a, p. 79). |

**FIGURE 3.13** Common Expository Text Structures

adequate number of titles on each topic should be made so as to enable children to study that topic for a sustained period of time. Included in Figure 3.15 are several important points to keep in mind as texts to support content and curricular connections are selected.

Informational literature offers a breadth and depth of knowledge not often found in content textbooks. In addition to having the potential for providing children with more up-to-date information, a single book may present a way to incorporate, integrate, and reinforce skills and concepts across the content areas. Consideration of the curricular standards and the ability of the learners can assist us in choosing relevant books for establishing content and curricular connections.

## In Summary

Authors, illustrators, and publishers of today's new nonfiction are sensitive to the necessity of creating aesthetically pleasing, trustworthy, and interesting texts for today's visually oriented young learner. Evaluation and selection of high-quality informational text for children in grades K–2 involve careful attention to specific criteria related to format

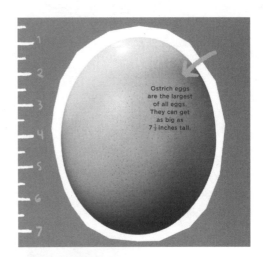

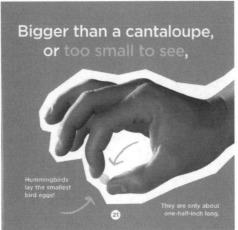

**FIGURE 3.14** *What's in That Egg?* by Becky Baines

*Source:* Baines (2009)

| Does the text lend itself to both content and curricular connections? | Yes | No |
| --- | --- | --- |
| Is the text is aligned to standards and curricular components? | ☐ | ☐ |
| Can the text be used across the curriculum in conjunction with other content areas? | ☐ | ☐ |
| Does the text relate to topics and themes that serve to build children's knowledge base? | ☐ | ☐ |

**FIGURE 3.15** Consider a Text's Content and Curricular Connections

and visual appeal, accuracy and authenticity, writing style and appropriateness for young children, and potential for content and curricular connections. Each of these factors contributes to the overall value of the text as an instructional tool. As educators, it is our responsibility to use the criteria discussed above to select the best texts for meeting the needs of the children with whom we work. Thorough evaluation leads to successful selection of informational literature, which will, in turn, lead to children's attainment of the related Common Core State Standards.

**FIGURE 3.2**

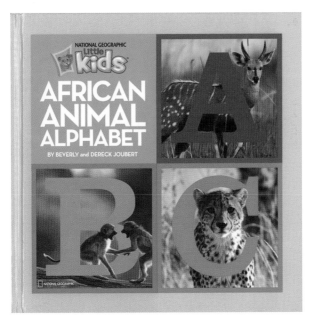

*Source:* Joubert, B., & Joubert, D. (2011). *National Geographic little kids African animal alphabet.* Washington, DC: National Geographic.

**FIGURE 3.3**

*Source:* Dickmann, N. (2011). *Food from farms.* Chicago, IL: Heinemann Library.

**FIGURE 3.4**

*Source:* Hughes, C. (2010). *National Geographic little kids first big book of animals.* Washington, DC: National Geographic.

**FIGURE 3.5**

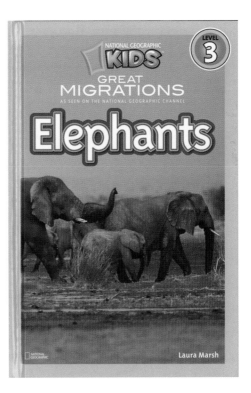

*Source:* Marsh, L. (2010). *National Geographic kids: Great migrations: Elephants.* Washington, DC: National Geographic.

FIGURE 3.11

Source: Bullard, L. (2005). *Loud and quiet: An animal opposites book.* Brookstone, MD: Capstone Press.

FIGURE 3.12

Source: National Geographic Kids. (2011). *National Geographic little kids look & learn: Match!* Washington, DC: National Geographic.

FIGURE 3.14

Source: Baines, B. (2009). *What's in that egg? A book about life cycles.* Washington, DC: National Geographic.

FIGURE 7.4

Source: Marsh, L. (2011). *National Geographic kids: Spiders.* Washington, DC: National Geographic.

# 4

# The Top Ten

*Focus on These High-Impact
Comprehension Strategies*

n the last chapter we covered how to select informational texts for your classroom that hold up under the high heat of instructional time. That is, as teachers we need to make every minute of instructional time count, so the books we read aloud and guide children to read have to be stellar. In this chapter we discuss what highly effective teachers do to help their students comprehend what they hear and read—the what, why, and how. We also show you how to explicitly teach 10 high-impact comprehension strategies supported by research to help your students comprehend informational text. Chapters 5–8 detail the instructional formats you can use to model and have students practice these strategies, but of course use your professional experience to see where they best fit, from whole class read-alouds to one-on-one conferring.

Before we begin, let's take a quick look at what we mean by strategies.

## Skills and Strategies: How They Are Different

The term *strategy* is often used to signify both deliberate and nondeliberate, or automatic, attempts to perform a task. On the other hand, *skills* are defined as automatic actions that usually occur without awareness of the components involved (Afflerback, Pearson, & Paris, 2008). As these researchers point out,

> Reading strategies are deliberate, goal-directed attempts to control and modify the reader's efforts to decode text, understand words, and construct meanings of text. . . . Reading skills are defined automatic actions that result in decoding and comprehension with speed, efficiency, and fluency. (p. 368)

It is a balance between thoughtful and deliberately applied strategies and automatic application of skills, and the ability to move effortlessly between the two, that characterizes effective readers.

## Highly Skilled Teachers Are Strategic

Strong research suggests that the key for raising student achievement is a highly skilled teacher. A strategic teacher deliberately models and then guides her students to apply a known strategy (or combination of strategies) to comprehend a specific unit (i.e., sentence, paragraph, section) of text. Then, during repeated practice opportunities, she monitors the students' ability to use the strategy on their own, systematically releasing control of each strategy to the students (Mehigan, 2005).

Whether one is using either narrative or expository text, effective strategy instruction is based on ongoing assessment of student need and close examination of the demands presented within the text to be read. We should be able to answer these questions about the strategies we are teaching (Baxter and Mehigan, 1992; Mehigan, 2005):

- Do I know WHAT the strategy is?
- Do I know how to DO the strategy?
- Do I know WHY the strategy WORKS?
- Do I know WHEN to use it?
- How will I know IF and WHEN it's working?

Much has been written about the steps teachers might use in planning strategy instruction. The questions shown in Figure 4.1 are designed to guide your thinking as you plan how best to teach and scaffold each new comprehension strategy.

## What Good Readers Do to Comprehend Text

For the past three decades, many researchers (e.g., Afflerback et al., 2008; Anderson & Pearson, 1984; Gambrell & Jawitz, 1993; Palinscar & Brown, 1984; Pearson & Fielding,

- What is the purpose for the lesson: What are the big ideas (essential information) I want my students to know after reading this text?
- What strategy or strategies present themselves in the text and will best suit the purpose of this lesson?
- How can I model (think aloud) application of the strategy for my students?
- How can I help my students understand when, why, and how they can use the strategy in their own reading?
- How can I gradually lead my students to apply the strategy in their own reading?
- How can I help my students understand how this new strategy relates to previously learned strategies?

FIGURE 4.1 Some Questions to Help You Plan Comprehension Strategy Instruction

1991; Pressley, 2000; Stanovich & Cunningham, 1993) have focused on the strategies good readers use to comprehend text, and how readers who struggle to comprehend can be helped to employ the strategies used by good readers. Through this extensive research we have learned that good readers engage in a number of practices before, during, and after reading that support comprehension. Figure 4.2 includes a list of what we refer to as "high-impact" skills and strategies necessary for reading comprehension. Although this list is not exhaustive, solid research evidence exists to support the efficacy of these skills and strategies for reading comprehension, and each plays an important role in helping students comprehend informational text.

## Teaching High-Impact Skills and Strategies for Comprehending Informational Text

Comprehension strategies are seldom used in isolation; they are used flexibly and in combination with one another. Intentional planning and implementation of comprehension instruction should include attention to scaffolding students' learning of new skills and strategies while at the same time maintaining and expanding their ability to select and apply those most appropriate for comprehending a specific piece of text. To assist you in understanding how each can be taught, in this chapter we will discuss each one singly; in Chapters 6–8 we will show how these can be applied in combination during interactive read-aloud and guided reading lessons.

Use prior knowledge.

Make inferences.

Visualize information.

Ask and answer questions.

Compare and contrast text and pictures.

Determine key ideas and details.

Interpret information from graphs, charts, and diagrams.

Use references and resources.

Summarize and synthesize.

Monitor comprehension and use fix-up tips.

FIGURE 4.2 Reading Skills and Strategies Important for Comprehending Nonfiction Text

## 1. Use prior knowledge.

It is our prior knowledge that enables us to monitor for meaning, pose questions, make predictions, draw conclusions, create mental images, synthesize, and determine importance as we read and learn. Skilled readers recall their relevant, prior knowledge (schema) before, during, and after they read in an effort both to make sense of new information and to store in memory that information with related information. Through reading and discussion with others, proficient readers adapt existing schema—deleting inaccurate information, adding new information, and connecting it to other related knowledge, opinions, and ideas. In this sense, this process builds the background knowledge we carry into readings of other texts.

## TEACHING TIPS

**Access and assess students' prior knowledge.** An important part of planning for instruction is identifying how we will determine whether students possess relevant prior knowledge for the text to be read, and how we will fill in any gaps in knowledge necessary for understanding the new text. The relevancy of the prior knowledge accessed for a particular text is critical. For example, let's say the teacher is going to read Lyon's picture book–biography, *Mother to Tigers* (2003). Asking students what they know about animals, or even specifically about tigers, will not yield the same results as asking students to think about about how to care for a baby animal separated at birth from its mother.

**Plan for times when children do not possess sufficient prior knowledge to comprehend the text.** Let's assume students will have a difficult time fully understanding and appreciating *Mother to Tigers* if they do not yet have some knowledge of how caring for a newborn animal is different from caring for an animal who is a bit older and is ready to leave its mother. We begin by posing a question: "How could we care for a baby animal separated at birth from its mother?" If children are unable to supply relevant information, we are ready to share pertinent background knowledge ourselves. For example, a quick search of the Internet reveals that the American Society for the Prevention of Cruelty to Animals (ASPCA) has information on this topic on their website (www.aspca.org/pet-care/dog-care/dog-care-newborn-puppy-care.aspx), as do other websites, such as eHOW (www.ehow.com/how_5419552_care-abandoned-newborn-puppy.html). Teachers can either share these websites with the children or use the sites to gain personal knowledge, which can then be shared with the children prior to reading the text. While these websites would likely be interesting and helpful for all children discussing this topic, those children who have insufficient prior knowledge to comprehend the text would benefit most from exposure to this information prior to, rather than after, the reading.

**Help students consolidate the new with the known.** After reading *Mother to Tigers*, ask children to discuss what they learned about caring for animals separated at birth from their mothers, and how the information in this book was different from or the same as something they already knew.

## 2. Make inferences (predict, determine cause and effect, draw and support conclusions).

Since authors to do not always explicitly state all of the information and ideas they wish for readers to gain from the text, much of what we take away from a text depends on our ability to make inferences as we read. This implies that readers are aware of the existence of implicit meaning and actively search for meaning by connecting the text with their own prior knowledge.

Proficient readers engage in a number of related mental processes as they infer, including but not limited to predicting, drawing conclusions, detecting cause-and-effect relationships, and interpreting and critically evaluating the text to construct meaning. As we model our own thought processes for inferring during reading, we can purposefully and directly demonstrate activities that support inferring, and how inferring enhances comprehension. For example, we can point out why it is important to slow one's rate while reading challenging passages, when it is helpful to pause in one's reading to clarify the author's meaning, or how rereading portions of the text can enhance our comprehension.

### TEACHING TIPS

**Ask students to share their inferences and how they inferred information not directly stated by the author.** For example, when asked to discuss what happens to baby sharks, a student might infer that baby sharks need to be taken care of after reading the following from *Life Cycles: Ocean* (Callery, 2011): "After 16 months, the shark gives birth to a litter of babies, called pups. They swim away and must take care of themselves right from the start" (p. 12). To explain this interpretation, the student might tell about caring for an abandoned newborn kitten. While the content of most informational text for young children is generally not left open to interpretation, teachers should still provide an opportunity for students to construct their own understanding of the text. Gradually, we invite students to share their own inferences *and* to defend their conclusions with references from the text. Have students ask, "I wonder?" as they read as a way of making inferences and actively seeking out understanding.

**Focus on using information from the text to support or refute prior knowledge**. In the above instance, the teacher would want to direct the student's attention to other parts of the text that state: "Tiger sharks are deadly hunters" (p. 12), and "Tiger sharks are at the top of many food chains. No one knows for certain, but they may live up to 40 years" (p. 13). While acknowledging the student's logical use of prior knowledge, the importance of justifying one's inferences with specific information from the text and of verifying facts through multiple sources of information should be emphasized.

**Help students use multiple sources of information.** Teachers will likely need to help students use additional sources to clarify meaning. After discussing the probability that even a baby tiger shark would be able to defend itself, the teacher might suggest reading more about tiger sharks in books such as Deborah Nuzzolo's (2008) *Tiger Shark*, to gather additional information to answer the question, "Do newborn tiger sharks need to be cared for?"

## 3. Visualize information.

Visualization, the forming of mental images reflective of as many senses as possible during reading, enhances the reader's recall of significant details, leading to increased comprehension and memory of the text. Skilled readers spontaneously and purposefully create mental images as they read. Based on the reader's prior knowledge and sensory experiences, the images are used to provide the reader with rich details that give depth and dimension to the reading. As readers engage more deeply, the text becomes more comprehensible, allowing for more accurate inferences and for distinct and unique interpretations of the text. Good readers often adapt their initial images as a result of both further reading in the text and discussion with others about the text. Their revised images represent new information and interpretations of the text.

### TEACHING TIPS

**Point out how authors use words to help readers create "mind pictures."** In *Apples for Everyone,* author Jill Esbaum's (2009a) rich use of words arouses all of the readers' senses. Ask children to listen for words that help them picture exactly what Esbaum wanted them to notice when she wrote the following three sentences: "Drawn by the sweet smell, bees buzz from blossom to blossom" (p. 2). "Slowly the baby apples grow bigger, turning all shades of red" (p. 3). "Your teeth sink in—crunch!—and the tart-sweet juice dribbles down your chin" (p. 7).

**Make your thinking and mental images visual to students.** To support all children's ability to employ the strategy of visualization, teachers can begin by modeling—thinking aloud about their own processes of evoking images during reading. For example, in *Heavier and Lighter*, April Barth (2009) asks readers to imagine how it would feel to lift a sheep and then a lamb. When you come to this part in the book, pause to think aloud for children about how you think it would feel to lift a sheep:

- Your arms would feel tight, and your back and legs might hurt because you are straining to pick up something heavy.
- Your hands and arms might feel itchy from the wool of the sheep's coat, and you might possibly be scratched by the sheep's hooves as he struggled in your grasp.
- Depending on how the sheep smells, you might be holding your breath, and the wool from the sheep's coat may be tickling your nose.
- You would probably be making an "ugh" sound as you strained to lift the sheep.
- The sheep would possibly be making a bleating sound.

After thinking aloud and adding greater sensory details, discuss how thinking about images prompted by the text and one's prior knowledge helps us better understand and remember what we read.

**Help children use their five senses to form more complete images.** Gradually, invite students to use their five senses to share their own images. To continue with the example from Barth's (2009) *Heavier and Lighter*, after thinking aloud for children how you visualize yourself lifting a sheep, ask them to use their senses to imagine how it would feel to lift a lamb. Prompt students to talk about what would they would see, hear, feel, smell, and perhaps even taste. Always be true to the text, however, and don't trot students through the five senses with every visualization.

## 4. Ask and answer questions.

Good readers are able to use questions to focus their attention on important components of the text. They ask and answer questions as they seek to construct and clarify meaning, make and justify predictions, and seek evidence in the text to prove their predictions. Teachers can help beginning readers learn to ask good questions by modeling the construction of good questions and by following a predictable sequence of questioning.

### TEACHING TIPS

**Teach children to ask themselves "before reading" questions.** When reading expository text, good readers begin by asking themselves questions such as the following: "What do I already know about this topic?" "What do I think the author is going to tell me about this topic?" "Why am I reading this text?" and "What do I want to find out about this topic?" As they read, they actively seek information to answer these questions, and they are aware of new questions that occur to them during reading. By engaging in self-questioning as we read aloud from an expository piece of text, we can model a predictable line of questioning as well as how to construct answers. For example, let's say we are going to read aloud the section "Ocean" from *National Geographic Little Kids First Big Book of Animals* (Hughes, 2010). We might tell children we are going to think aloud, so they can hear the types of questions that we ask ourselves when we read. Then we share the first question, "What do I already know about oceans?" and a response. Next, we might pose the question: "What will the author tell me about oceans?" We could turn quickly through the pages in this section and read just the headings that appear in big, bold type: bottlenose dolphin, green sea turtle, short-head seahorse, sea otter, giant Pacific octopus, humpback whale, blue-striped grunt—and then decide to read first about the humpback whale. Again, we could ask, "What do I already know?" and then model a response: "I know that whales are mammals, that they are really big and live in the ocean, and that there are other kinds of whales, such as the beluga whale and great white whale. I wonder how the humpback whale is different from other whales." Point out to the students that we just asked ourselves a question about something we want to find out. Ask students to share something they want to know about this ocean animal.

**Teach children to ask themselves "during reading" questions.** Good readers pause periodically in their reading to ask themselves questions about what they are reading. This helps them stay focused on the text and gives them a personal reason to keep reading. Continuing with the example from above, point out that the heading on the first page reads, "Humpbacks do not have teeth" (Hughes, 2010, p. 45). Pause to model a question: "How does the humpback whale chew its food?" Continue reading to find out that the humpback whale has baleen instead of teeth, and then pause to ask, "What is baleen?"

**Model how to locate correct answers to one's questions.** Beginning readers may not yet be able to determine whether a question can be answered by the text, whether they will need to infer the answer from the text, or if the answer is left to the reader's interpretation. Through thinking aloud, teachers can model how skilled readers locate correct answers. After modeling how to ask questions about something you want to find out (e.g., how the humpback whale chews its food), read on to infer that the whale doesn't chew its food. The text reads,

> The humpback whale opens its mouth wide to eat. Its mouth fills with water as well as small fish and other creatures that live in the water. . . . The baleen lets the water out, but keeps the fish and other sea creatures inside. It acts as a strainer. When no water is left, the whale swallows. That's dinner! (pp. 46–47)

The children may want to know more than this text tells about baleen. There is a photograph showing baleen, and its purpose is discussed; however, the author doesn't provide other information to help one understand what baleen feels like. Examples such as these provide opportunities to discuss that sometimes readers have questions that are not answered in the text.

**Ask higher level thought questions to prompt close reading of text.** Questioning also plays a key role in readers' motivation and engagement with text; just the right question posed at just the right time can serve to propel readers further into closer examination of the text. For example, rather than beginning with lower level, literal questions to prompt higher level thinking, teachers can begin by asking questions that require students to make an inference. The teacher might ask, "How are humpback whales and beluga whales alike and different?" If children cannot respond, text-based questions, such as, "What did we learn about beluga whales?" and "What did this author tell us about humpback whales?" can then be asked to prompt their recall of key ideas and details. The teacher would help the children return to the text to find the information, and then think aloud to model how that information enables answering of the first question about how humpback whales and beluga whales are alike and different.

## 5. Compare and contrast text and pictures.

Strategies that engage students in comparative thinking have been shown to have a strong positive impact on student achievement (Marzano, 2007; Marzano, Pickering, & Pollock, 2001). Asking students to discuss likenesses and differences strengthens their recall of key ideas and details, and increases their capacity for metacognitive thinking. Teachers can help beginning readers learn to think comparatively by asking them to compare and contrast familiar objects, such as a pencil and a crayon. Moving to literature, students can be led to discuss similarities and differences between characters in a familiar story, such as the classic tale "The City Mouse and the County Mouse," or between two versions of the same story.

When reading informational text, students can be led to make comparisons between two or more concepts presented or between two or more books on the same topic. For example, they may listen to or read one or more nonfiction books about cats and then compare and contrast domestic and wild cats as they seek to determine which might make the better pet.

## TEACHING TIPS

**Ask a central question to focus the students' listening and/or reading.** The central question, "Which types of cats make the best pets?" would serve to focus the students' listening and/or reading of informational texts about cats. Students would first read/listen to gather text-based details and evidence, and then would make an inference leading to the answer for the central question.

**Use books that invite comparison.** Some books for beginning readers lend themselves to development of comparison thinking. For example, *National Geographic Kids Cats vs. Dogs* (Carney, 2011), and *Transportation Past and Present* (Frank, 2009), a part of the Then and Now series by Benchmark Education, provide an appropriate scaffold for beginning readers who are just learning to detect likenesses and differences in illustrations and in text.

**Provide opportunities for comparing and contrasting information from multiple texts.** As students gain skill in comparing and contrasting information located within the same text, branch out to other texts to provide opportunities for discussion of information provided by two books on the same topic. Students learning about modes of transportation could compare the information found in Zimmerman's (2012) *The Stourbridge Lion: America's First Locomotive*, with that found in *Train* (Shields, 2011b).

## 6. Determine key ideas and details.

As proficient readers, we make both purposeful and spontaneous decisions about what is important in a particular text. We consider the words the author uses, key sentences, and key ideas, concepts, and themes. What we judge to be most important is also affected by our schema for the text content; those ideas most closely connected to our prior knowledge are often the ones we deem to be most important. Similarly, our beliefs, opinions, and experiences related to the text will influence our opinions, and often our memory of key ideas and details. After reading *Cats vs. Dogs* (Carney, 2011), children with a pet dog will likely remember more information to support the belief that dogs make the better pets. Those with cats will find the facts about their chosen pet to be most memorable, most important.

## TEACHING TIPS

**Help students look for key words and sentences.** The words *survive, protect, predator,* and *prey* are repeated frequently in *Amazing Animals* (Wasp, 2006), and provide a strong clue to the theme of this book. Although key words often appear in bold type, other words may also be important to note, so be sure students understand that we need to be on the lookout for all words that provide clues to an author's message. Good readers also look for key sentences—ones that carry the weight of meaning for a paragraph, passage, or section. In informational texts for young children, these may be presented in bold type and/or at the beginning or ending of a passage. At the end of page 1 in *Amazing Animals* is the key sentence, "Animals survive in amazing ways!" On the last page we find, "We saw lots of amazing animals! How does each one survive?" (p. 14). These sentences confirm the key idea or theme that animals possess ways to protect themselves from harm.

**Point out text features used to alert the reader to important information.** Clues such as use of bold type, italics, or a different font or ink color signal beginning readers to pay attention, much like a traffic light signals motorists. Illustrations and graphics, such as diagrams, word bubbles, and charts, also help direct our attention to essential information and ideas. Discussing with students why authors use these techniques and how they can and should be used by readers is one way to support students' identification of key ideas and details.

**Help students identify examples and nonexamples of key ideas and details.** Sometimes, helping children to think of elements of the text that are not the more important ideas (nonexamples) is a way to build understanding of what might be considered the key, or most important, ideas. For example, in *Cats vs. Dogs*, the author includes additional information in textboxes located on several of the pages. In one appears the heading "Pet Words" with definitions and examples of the words *canine, predator,* and *domesticated.* Another textbox is labeled "Weird but True" and contains a statement about wolves howling to communicate with pack members. During the reading of this book, the teacher could draw children's attention to the textboxes and discuss whether the information provided supported either animal as the best pet. Through discussion, the teacher would guide children to discover that good readers are able to distinguish between more and less important information provided by the author.

## 7. Interpret information from graphs, charts, and diagrams.

While skills involved in interpreting information from graphs, charts, diagrams, and special illustrative features may seem a bit of a reach for beginning readers, even students at this level need to learn how titles, headings, pictures, and captions help us gain meaning from a text. Through exposure to informational text, beginning readers develop more complex print concepts (e.g., author's use of italics, bold type. or enlarged font), concepts about genres, and concepts about text structures that help them construct meaning from different types of text (Duke, 2004).

Widespread awareness of the expectations found within the Common Core State Standards has prompted the publication of many new nonfiction texts for children. While not all contain graphs, charts, and diagrams, these features are finding their way into more texts for use in the lower elementary grades. Also found in an increasing number of informational texts for beginning readers is the use of graphics, such as maps, cut-aways, cross-sections, enlargements, overlays, and word bubbles, the use of which needs to be modeled for beginning readers.

### TEACHING TIPS

**Help students locate and use information found in graphs, charts, and diagrams.**
Direct students' attention to graphs, charts, diagrams, and other such features appearing within text. Pose questions that require students to examine the graphic to form a response, and discuss why the author/illustrator decided to use a graph, (chart, diagram, et cetera) to convey that particular information. Help students look for information that is provided only through these tools, as opposed to information found in both the text and the graphic.

**Point out features illustrators use to help readers comprehend text.** In Figure 4.3 we see a photograph from Jill Esbaum's *Apples for Everyone* (2009a). Note the enlarged section of the photograph used to focus the reader's attention on a specific part discussed in the text: "As time passes petals flutter to the grass, and fuzzy bumps appear" (p. 3). Books such as this one provide opportunities to share with students the role illustrations can play in conveying the author's message. For example, we might read the first line of text at the top of the page and then point to the photograph in the circle, saying: "Oh, I see that Jill Esbaum has a close-up photo here of just the part of the plant where the fuzzy bumps appear. This is helpful because we can't see the fuzzy bumps in the picture that shows apples on the branches. We have learned that authors sometimes provide clues to help us better understand what we are reading. Illustrators can do that, too."

**FIGURE 4.3** Enlarged Section of Photograph

*Source:* Esbaum (2009a)

## 8. Use references and resources.

While different from other reading comprehension strategies, learning to use references and resources to answer questions, verify facts, and gain information is critical for successful reading of informational text. Reading multiple texts on the same topic allows teachers to model how good readers and writers use various sources to gather and verify information across sources. At the same time, students are provided opportunities to build a depth of knowledge about a particular topic.

### TEACHING TIPS

**Provide students with access to multiple texts on the same topic.** To assist you in locating multiple titles for a number of themes and topics typically included in the K–2 curriculum, we have included a list of books organized by topic (see Appendix D), and an annotated bibliography of those books (see Appendix E).

**Show students how references and resources can be used to answer questions.** Take advantage of everyday questions that arise from students to model use of references and resources. Make a habit of saying, "Let's look that up," and then DO look it up. When it is not feasible to locate an answer immediately, write the question on a "Things We Want To Know" chart, so you will have a tangible reminder to refer to at a later, more convenient time.

**Integrate instruction in use of references and resources into interdisciplinary units of study.** The CCSS encourages an interdisciplinary approach through which students apply their reading, speaking, listening, and writing skills to gain disciplinary knowledge. There's no better time to teach use of grade-appropriate references and resources than during a unit of study on a topic that holds strong interest and appeal for your students.

## 9. Summarize and synthesize.

Although similar in that they both require presentation of key ideas and details in one's own words, summarizing and synthesizing are distinctly different. Good readers periodically pause in their reading to summarize—to reflect about what they have read, to restate key content in their own words. Summarizing aids in comprehension and recall and is an essential strategy for reading both narrative and expository text. Synthesizing encompasses summarization of information and ideas from multiple sources, including making connections to one's prior knowledge (Harvey & Goudvis, 2007). Techniques for teaching summarization and synthesis entail many of the same strategies and are dependent upon the reader's ability to determine key ideas and details. For this reason, these are typically the most challenging strategies for students, and they are introduced after students demonstrate the ability to locate key ideas and details.

### TEACHING TIPS

**Chunk text into shorter, more manageable sections for reading and discussion.** Many informational texts are already divided into chapters or sections. Sometimes, as in the case with *National Geographic Little Kids First Big Book of Animals* (Hughes, 2010), sections are further divided by subtopic. For example, the section discussed above, "Ocean," included two to four pages of information about each of six ocean animals. Whether or not the text you wish to use is divided into manageable parts, we strongly encourage you to identify an appropriate number of pages for your students to read and discuss at a time.

**Model, model, model.** Summarizing and synthesizing are difficult skills for many students and will require much teacher modeling and many opportunities for scaffolded practice. After you have introduced the text to the students, and have either modeled or asked for prereading questions, read just the first part of the text to the students. Stop to explain to the students that good readers pause periodically in their reading to paraphrase, or repeat, the key information in their own words. For example, after reading the section on humpback whales, the teacher might say: "Good readers know they cannot always remember everything they read, so they pay attention to key ideas and details and stop after reading each part of a text to think about what they learned. One way they remember the key ideas and details is to say or write them in their own words. An important thing to remember about the humpback whale is that it doesn't have teeth, it has baleen. The humpback whale catches a lot of water and small fish in its mouth. The baleen lets the water out but keeps the fish in, and the whale swallows them whole."

**Use semantic maps and other graphic organizers to integrate reading, writing, and summarizing.** Semantic maps and other graphic organizers can be used during teacher modeling and whole group discussions, with students gradually assuming greater responsibility for recalling key ideas and details, and for restating that information in their own words. (See Chapter 7 for an example of one graphic organizer.) Shared writing can then be used to record students' summary statements and the connections they make to prior knowledge and experiences.

## 10. Monitor comprehension and use fix-up tips.

The ultimate goal of reading is to understand what is read; to do so, readers must be able to monitor their own reading and know what to do when the process breaks down. Skilled readers monitor their comprehension during reading. They know when the text they are reading or listening to makes sense, when it does not, what does not make sense, and whether the unclear portions are critical to overall understanding of the piece. They are able to pinpoint difficulties they have in comprehending at the word, sentence, and whole text level, and are flexible in their use of methods to solve different types of comprehension problems. The methods used to solve problems, sometimes referred to as "roadblocks," encountered during reading include, but are not limited to, the following:

- Pause and think about what makes sense and what doesn't.
- Reread a part of the text.
- Read ahead in the text.
- Look for clues in the text and illustrations.
- Think about what you already know about the topic.
- Recall the sequence of the information presented.
- Discuss the text with another reader.

When we engage in comprehension monitoring instruction with beginning readers, we are seeking to help students notice what they *do* understand, recognize what they *do not* understand, and use fix-up strategies to resolve difficulties in comprehension (National Reading Panel, 2000). Developing as a reader requires development of one's own set of fix-up strategies; as teachers we can model these for children through think-alouds and explicitly show students how these strategies work with text.

### TEACHING TIPS

**Teach one fix-up tip at a time.** It is best to teach these one at a time, and allow children ample opportunities to practice utilizing each one before adding another. For example, in the text discussed earlier about the humpback whale, there are several places where K–2 children may not immediately grasp the author's meaning. Rather than think aloud about all of these during the same lesson, choose just one to model, saving other tips to discuss at a later time, in another text.

To model a tip, call students' attention to the portion of the text where comprehension could break down, and think aloud for students how to apply the selected fix-up tip. A teacher might say, "On page 45 the author states that the baleen hangs from the whale's upper jaw. Although there's a picture on this page with an arrow pointing to the baleen, I don't understand exactly what baleen is and how it helps the humpback whale eat. There's nothing else on this page to help me, so I'm going to do what good readers sometimes have to do when they hit a roadblock to understanding—I'm going to read ahead." The teacher could pause when she gets to the part that tells how baleen acts as a strainer to keep the food in and the water out of the whale's mouth and discuss with the students how this information provides a "fix" to help the reader better understand what the author wanted to share about baleen.

Teacher modeling should be followed with opportunities for students to apply the tip, with guidance. For example, next the teacher could read the section on blue-striped grunts, where another opportunity exists for readers to read ahead to better understand the text. The teacher could ask the students to give her a "thumbs down" if they hear something in the text they do not quite understand. She can then ask them to recall the new fix-up tip, to listen as she continues reading, and to give her a "thumbs up" when they hear the information that helps them understand.

**Post fix-up tips in the classroom for children's use.** Some teachers find it helpful to actually post a list of fix-up tips in the classroom so that students can look at the charts to remind themselves what to do when they hit a roadblock. A sample chart is shown in Figure 4.4. You'll notice that this chart contains tips for both K–1 students and for students in Grades 1–2. You may want to begin the year with first graders using just the tips listed under K–1. As first graders mature in their sophistication, you may want to add more tips so that at the end of the year, the chart includes all of the tips listed under 1–2.

| Fix-Up Tips for K-1 | Fix-Up Tips for 1-2 |
|---|---|
| Re-read | Re-read |
| Look at the pictures and illustrations | Sequence events or steps |
| Think about what makes sense | Recall details |
| Read ahead | Summarize |
| Ask someone | Look at the pictures and illustrations |
| | Think about what makes sense |
| | Read ahead |
| | Ask someone |

FIGURE 4.4 Have Students Contribute Ideas to Fix-Up Tips Charts

## In Summary

Reading comprehension is an active, constructive process, greatly affected by one's background knowledge. Research has shown that teachers who model and explain effective comprehension strategies help students become strategic readers (Almasi, 2003; Pressley, 2002). Highly effective teachers intentionally model the metacognitive strategies involved in comprehension, and carefully scaffold students' use of these through interactive read-aloud experiences.

In this chapter, we shared tips for teaching students to apply ten evidence-based strategies appropriate for use with informational text. In Chapters 5–8, we introduce a lesson template and examples to assist you in further translating into practice the information from this and previous chapters. Specifically, we address goals for preparing students to read, guiding students' reading, explicitly teaching from the text, and facilitating connections.

We want to leave you with two final thoughts before we introduce the lesson template in Chapter 5. First, while differences exist with respect to the consistency and classification of comprehension skills and strategies recommended by various researchers, as Caldwell and Leslie (2013) state, "In the end, however, it doesn't matter which strategies you choose as long as they help your students engage in deep processing of text" (p. 239). And second, ultimately, each student's personal toolbox for reading comprehension is filled over the course of many years of instruction, as teachers across grade levels engage in intentional, strategic teaching of evidence-based tools for comprehending different types of text. With these thoughts in mind, turn to the next chapter to learn how you can design effective lessons that feature use of informational text.

# 5

# Demystifying What Makes Lessons Effective

## The Lesson Plan Template

Lesson planning can be daunting given the pressure to design our curricula around the Common Core State Standards, high-quality texts, and the unique needs of primary children who are learning to read. That's why we have developed a template that we use for any kind of informational text lessons, whether an interactive read-aloud or a small group lesson. We've found it makes planning and teaching more efficient and intentional. In this chapter, we'll look at the components of the template, and then, in subsequent chapters, we provide sample lessons for kindergarten, first grade, and second grade, so you can see the template in action in classrooms.

## The Overarching Goal of Informational Text Lessons: Rigorous Text Experiences for All Students

An important distinction regarding the pedagogical foundation of this book was stated in Chapter 2 and must be reiterated here, as it is embedded in the design of the lesson plan template. In the primary grades the lesson design reflects the frequent use of a common, grade-level informational text with *all* students. This is done in order to ensure that all students have exposure to grade-level concepts and materials and to common academic language and content.

The lesson in which the teacher utilizes the informational text may be part of the literacy block or part of the content studies (science, social studies, health) block, or it may be worked in during a read-aloud time of the day.

Beginning readers are unique in that they are utilizing texts of differing levels of complexity for different purposes. As teachers of beginning readers, we have to understand when and how these different text types come into play. Let's think about how this applies within the literacy block. During the literacy block, students' *core instruction* refers to the sequential, systematic teaching of the foundational skills of reading, with the application of those skills in appropriate text, text that children can read themselves. For example, K–1 students receive instruction in phonics and apply their phonics skills to read decodable texts that match their decoding skills. The decodable controls give way to grade-level text as their decoding skills become solid. But *in addition to that core instruction,* we want to build meaningful informational text experiences utilizing high-quality text for which students may not have the skills to read independently; this is where interactive read-alouds come in. See Figures 5.1 and 5.2 for a summary of the types of text experiences primary children need to have.

The lesson plan template is designed to be used in the read-aloud, shared reading, or guided reading formats, and can be used at any time of the day.

Beginning readers are not just small versions of readers. They are at a unique stage of development in that they are forming the neural pathways to unlock the alphabetic code in order to make sense of print. We want to ensure that they are receiving exemplary instruction in how to read, utilizing a strong core program and research-based instructional practices in the essential skills of reading. But that is not the entirety of their reading instruction or reading experience. While receiving that core instruction, students will also receive instruction utilizing informational text of appropriate grade-level complexity, and you will see in the pages to follow how the lesson will be adjusted for each group of readers as necessary to provide both access to the meaning of that text (Lesson Steps 1 and 2) and opportunities to apply the reading skills and strategies appropriate to the readers' needs and development (Lesson Step 3). In utilizing one text for all students, it is acknowledged there is great worth for all children (not just the advanced readers) to make extensions and connections (Lesson Step 4). This is an important distinction from the common and widespread exclusive use of leveled text; if leveled text is used for all reading experiences in the classroom, students may not all get equal opportunities for informational text experiences of appropriate complexity and content.

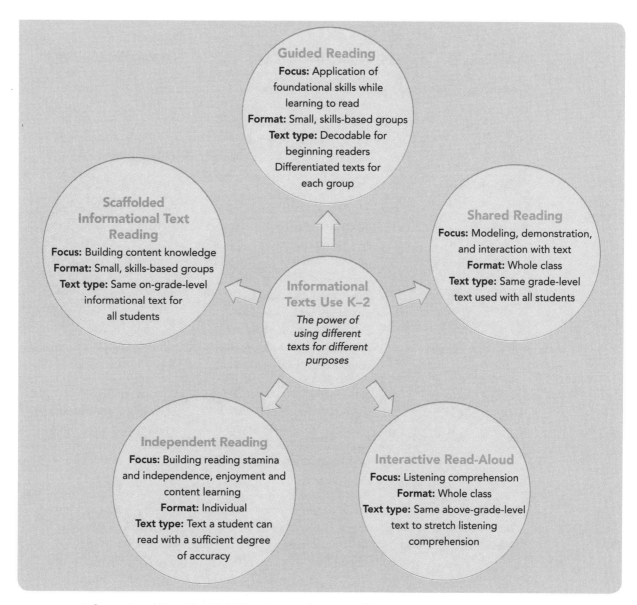

**FIGURE 5.1** Informational Text Use K–2: The Power of Using Different Texts for Different Purposes

## Lesson Planning

Informational text is typically rich with ideas and opportunities for learning about the world. Because of this, it is sometimes easy for a lesson to take on a life of its own and go off in multiple directions. While being responsive to students' needs and open to their contributions and questions is important, primary teachers well know how easily students can get distracted! Thorough preparation prior to a lesson will assist a teacher not only in keeping a focus but also in anticipating and planning for student responses.

Becoming completely familiar with the text is the first step for teachers in lesson planning. A thorough reading of the text will allow the teacher to answer the critical first question regarding the *purpose* for the lesson: "What are the big ideas (essential information) I want my students to know after reading this text?" Knowing the answer to that question will facilitate planning and guide a teacher to provide a more focused lesson.

| Lesson Format | What This Means | Type of Informational Text |
|---|---|---|
| **Interactive Read-Aloud** (typically whole class) | The teacher chooses books/texts to read aloud to children (preferably several times a day) that are written at a higher level than that at which children are able to read on their own. The read-aloud experience is interactive, with the teacher modeling, questioning, and interacting with students. The goal is to model vocabulary, fluency, and strategies that children will eventually internalize and gradually be able to use as their burgeoning skills allow them to read more complex text independently. | Texts written above the children's current reading level, texts of sufficient depth to relay important concepts, develop strong vocabulary, and stretch children's listening comprehension level. |
| **Shared Reading** (typically whole class) | Similar to reading aloud, a shared reading experience allows the beginning reader to have a more intimate glimpse of the text as it is shared in an interactive lesson. | Same as read-aloud text, but typically shared reading text is enlarged in a big-book format or a digital format. |
| **Guided Reading (With Focus on Foundational Skills and Word Work)** (core instruction is typically whole class initially, with differentiated instruction as indicated by assessments; text reading is done in small, skills-based groups) | This is core instruction of sequential, systematic skills that all beginning readers need to be able to learn to read. | Text that has phonetic and readability controls so that students are practicing the application of their emerging skills; decodable text needs to be progressively and cumulatively decodable, matching the sequence of phonetic elements as children are learning them. |
| **Small Group Scaffolded Informational Text Reading** (small, skills-based group) | Students work in small, skills-based groups designed to provide a more focused reading experience; the teacher guides students through text with an emphasis on meaning while also providing the appropriate instruction to teach children *how to read* the text. | Text that is at grade level or above for all students; it is imperative that below-level students receive accelerated instruction of sufficient duration and intensity to bring them to grade level. |

**FIGURE 5.2** Classroom Use of Informational Text

## The Four Lesson Steps

The basic lesson plan template involves four steps:

1. Prepare to read.
2. Guide reading.
3. Explicitly teach from the text.
4. Facilitate connections.

Figure 5.3 offers a brief explanation of these four steps.

| Lesson Step | Purpose |
|---|---|
| Prepare to read. | • Get the students ready for the reading. |
| Guide reading. | • Make the text accessible, and guide students to meaning. |
| Explicitly teach from the text. | • Return to the text after the initial reading to teach or model skills and strategies that good readers use. The goal is to help students develop metacognitive awareness of the process of making meaning from print. |
| Facilitate connections. | • Make interdisciplinary connections. |

**FIGURE 5.3** Purpose of Lesson Steps

## A Detailed Look at the Lesson Template

For each step of the lesson, teachers need to make instructional decisions based on the purpose of the lesson, the opportunities presented in the text, and their students' readiness for the content. Let's take a closer look at each step and the questions teachers might ask themselves in preparing for the reading.

### LESSON STEP 1: PREPARE TO READ.

**GOAL: Access or establish vocabulary and schema.**
**ASK:** What background knowledge about this topic do my students possess? Which concepts and vocabulary need to be elicited from the students or developed through instruction before the reading?

**GOAL: Build text knowledge.**
**ASK:** Which text features (if any) will need to be taught before the reading?

**GOAL: Set a purpose for reading.**
**ASK:** What is our overall purpose for the reading (essential information I want my students to know), and how can I state this for the students?

**GOAL: Preview text.**
**ASK:** How can I build excitement for reading by engaging students in previewing the text (using the cover, illustrations, or other features)?

> **TIP**
>
> **Remember:** Read the text first. Think about what you want your students to learn (the essential information) from reading this text.

## LESSON STEP 2: GUIDE READING.

Lesson Step 2 is the initial reading of the text. It will take on different forms depending on the group of students you are working with; sometimes the reading will be teacher modeled; sometimes students will read independently. As you prepare for this step, keep in mind that the comprehension strategies taught will depend on the opportunities presented in the text itself. We also want to consider the high-impact reading strategies supported by research that were introduced in Chapter 4 (see Figure 5.4).

A note about vocabulary: As you begin to use the lesson plan template, keep in mind that whether you are preteaching vocabulary or explaining vocabulary within the text as you read, it is helpful to plan in advance your child-friendly definitions and sentences. In the sample lesson plans, examples of these will be provided.

- Use prior knowledge.
- Make inferences (predict, determine cause and effect, draw and support conclusions).
- Visualize information.
- Ask and answer questions.
- Compare and contrast text and pictures.
- Determine key ideas and details.
- Interpret information from graphs, charts, and diagrams.
- Use references and resources.
- Summarize and synthesize.
- Monitor comprehension and use fix-up tips.

FIGURE 5.4 High-Impact Reading Strategies

**TIP**

Text features include the following:

- Table of contents
- Headings
- Index
- Glossary
- Captions
- Photos
- Drawings
- Bullets
- Sidebars
- Textboxes
- Bold type

**GOAL: Make text accessible for students.**

**ASK:** What vocabulary or concepts should be taught during the reading so that my students can understand the text? What text features and illustrations need to be utilized in order to make the text accessible?

**GOAL: Teach or model appropriate reading strategies.**

**ASK:** Given the big, important ideas of this text I want my students to understand, what strategies can I teach or model that are appropriate for this text?

**GOAL: Demonstrate understanding.**

**ASK:** How can I check students' understanding? What reteaching will I need to do if they do not demonstrate understanding?

## LESSON STEP 3: EXPLICITLY TEACH FROM THE TEXT.

In Lesson Step 3, immediately after you and students have read the entire text, you spend a few minutes going back into the text to teach a specific reading skill or strategy. This is where the lesson dovetails with the work that might be going on in the core instruction of the foundational skills. The great thing here, though, is that everyone in the class is using the same grade-level text to absorb the lesson. This step is unique in that you will typically choose one option rather than trying to meet all the goals below. Also, remember that this step takes place after the initial reading of the text, so essentially you are returning to the text to provide a context for these instructional opportunities. This is part of the scaffolding process; just as you are being deliberate in your teacher modeling, this step allows you to gradually lead students to apply the same skills or strategies in their own reading.

**TIP**

See Chapter 4 for a detailed discussion of high-impact reading strategies.

This step is unique to the use of informational text with young children who are learning to read. As discussed in Chapter 2, you are striving to ensure that all students have access to grade-level texts, while considering specific instructional techniques that integrate the foundational skills of reading within that text. So the possible goals within this step include the following:

- Teach decoding.
- Build fluency.
- Teach a skill or strategy.
- Teach comprehension monitoring and the use of fix-up strategies.

As you will see from the questions below, the option you choose is based on the needs of the readers.

**POSSIBLE GOAL: Teach decoding within a meaningful context.**
**ASK:** Are my students able to decode this text? If not, what phonetic elements and decoding strategies do I need to teach and/or review? How can I utilize words or passages from this text to help students practice decoding?

**POSSIBLE GOAL: Build fluency.**
**ASK:** Are my students fluent readers? How can I use this text to model characteristics of fluent reading? Can I follow up the reading with shared and unison reading for practicing fluency? Are there other ways for students to utilize this text for fluency building (assisted reading with CD, partner reading, choral reading)?

**POSSIBLE GOAL: Teach comprehension strategies.**
**ASK:** Which comprehension skills and strategies are appropriate to this text? How can I explicitly teach those skills or strategies? What follow-up activities can I provide that will enable my students to apply the skill or strategy in their own reading?

**POSSIBLE GOAL: Teach children how to monitor their own comprehension and use fix-up tips when they don't understand.**
**ASK:** How can I use this text to teach students to apply fix-up tips during their independent reading? (See the discussion of fix-up tips in Chapter 4.)

**TIP**

Fix-up tips include the following:

- Reread.
- Look at pictures and illustrations.
- Think about what makes sense.
- Read ahead.
- Sequence events or steps.
- Recall details.
- Summarize.

### ◢ LESSON STEP 4: FACILITATE CONNECTIONS.

In Lesson Step 4, you want to exploit the richness of the informational text to demonstrate and then have children participate in connecting the information, topics, or big idea themes to a wider context. For example, after reading a selection about the water cycle, you might demonstrate how water evaporates by leaving drops of water on a window ledge or under a bulb. Like Lesson Step 3, these are options to choose from if and when it is appropriate based on the text opportunities, student need, and time.

**GOAL: Expand the reading experience by connecting the text to other interdisciplinary areas.**

**Ask:** Does this text experience authentically lend itself to making connections in writing, technology, additional text reading, content areas, or the fine arts? How can I formulate a meaningful follow-up activity to help students make these connections?

## Summary of the Lesson Plan Action Steps

Before the lesson, read the text thoroughly, and ask yourself, What are the big ideas (essential information) I want my students to understand through this text? Then follow the four lesson steps and the related action steps as shown in Figure 5.5. Figure 5.6 is a template that includes the four Lesson Steps, the action steps within each Lesson Step, and a space for you to write your own ideas for each step. (A reproducible copy of this template is included in Appendix C for your own use in lesson planning.)

| Steps in the Lesson | Goals/Purposes | Action Steps—Teacher Determines: |
|---|---|---|
| Prepare to read. | • Access or establish vocabulary and schema.<br>• Build text knowledge.<br>• Set a purpose for reading.<br>• Preview text. | • What is my students' background knowledge in content? Which concepts and vocabulary need to be elicited or developed before the reading?<br>• Which text features will be taught before the reading?<br>• What is our overall purpose for the reading, and how can I state this for the students?<br>• How can I preview the text to build excitement for the reading (using the cover, illustrations, or other features)? |
| Guide reading. | • Make text accessible for students.<br>• Teach or model appropriate reading strategies.<br>• Demonstrate understanding. | • What vocabulary or concepts should be taught during the reading so that my students can understand the text?<br>• What text features and illustrations need to be taught or pointed out in order to make the text accessible?<br>• What are the big, important ideas of this text I want my students to understand?<br>• What strategies are appropriate for this text that I can teach/model? |

| Steps in the Lesson | Goals/Purposes | Action Steps—Teacher Determines: |
|---|---|---|
| | | • What questions can I ask students to check their understanding?<br>• What reteaching will I need to do if they do not demonstrate understanding? |
| Explicitly teach from the text. | • Teach decoding within a meaningful context.<br>• Build fluency.<br>• Teach comprehension strategies.<br>• Teach children how to monitor their own comprehension and use fix-up tips when they don't understand. | • Are my students able to decode this text? If not, what phonetic elements and decoding strategies do they need to work on? How can I utilize words or passages from this text to practice decoding?<br>• Are my students fluent readers? How can I model fluency in this text? Can I follow up the reading with shared and unison reading for practicing fluency? Are there other ways for students to utilize this text for fluency building (assisted reading with CD, partner reading, choral reading)?<br>• Which comprehension skills and strategies are needed to comprehend this text? How can I teach one of those skills or strategies explicitly? What practice opportunities can I follow up with to allow my students to apply that skill or strategy?<br>• What fix-up tips can I teach based on the reading of the text that will allow students to learn self-help skills in their independent reading? |
| Facilitate connections. | • Expand the reading experience by connecting the text to other interdisciplinary areas. | • Does this text experience authentically lend itself to any of these connections?<br><br>  o Engaging in shared, guided, and independent writing<br>  o Using technology to discover and share information<br>  o Reading additional texts, comparing and contrasting information in each<br>  o Pairing fiction and nonfiction<br>  o Exploring related knowledge and concepts in science, social studies, math, et cetera.<br>  o Linking to art, music, movement, and/or drama<br><br>• How can I formulate a meaningful follow-up activity to make these connections? |

**FIGURE 5.5** Lesson Steps and Related Action Steps

*Note:* The steps in the lesson and action steps in this chart are included in the lesson plan template in Figure 5.6, which is also reproduced in Appendix C.

**Name of Text:**

**Big Ideas for This Lesson (essential information):**

| Step in the Lesson | Action Steps |
| --- | --- |
| Prepare to read. | • What is my students' background knowledge in content? Which concepts and vocabulary need to be elicited or developed before the reading?<br>• Which text features will be taught before the reading?<br>• What is our overall purpose for the reading, and how can I state this for the students?<br>• How can I preview the text to build excitement for the reading (using the cover, illustrations, or other features)? |

**Ideas for This Text:**

| Step in the Lesson | Action Steps |
| --- | --- |
| Guide reading. | • What vocabulary or concepts should be taught during the reading so that my students can understand the text?<br>• What text features and illustrations need to be taught or pointed out in order to make the text accessible?<br>• What are the big, important ideas of this text I want my students to understand?<br>• What strategies are appropriate for this text that I can teach/model?<br>• What questions can I ask students to check their understanding?<br>• What reteaching will I need to do if they do not demonstrate understanding? |

**Ideas for This Text:**

| Step in the Lesson | Action Steps |
|---|---|
| **Explicitly teach from the text.** <br> (Choose one focus area for each group of students.) | • Are my students able to decode this text? If not, what phonetic elements and decoding strategies do they need to work on? How can I utilize words or passages from this text to practice decoding? <br> • Are my students fluent readers? How can I model fluency in this text? Can I follow up the reading with shared and unison reading for practicing fluency? Are there other ways for students to utilize this text for fluency building (assisted reading with CD, partner reading, choral reading)? <br> • Which comprehension skills and strategies are needed to comprehend this text? How can I teach one of those skills or strategies explicitly? What practice opportunities can I follow up with to allow my students to apply that skill or strategy? <br> • What fix-up tips can I teach based on the reading of the text that will allow students to learn self-help skills in their independent reading? |
| **Ideas for This Text:** | |

| Step in the Lesson | Action Steps |
|---|---|
| **Facilitate connections.** <br> (Choose one focus area for each group of students.) | • Does this text experience authentically lend itself to making connections in writing, technology, additional text reading, content areas, or the fine arts? How can I formulate a meaningful follow-up activity to make these connections? |
| **Ideas for This Text:** | |

 **FIGURE 5.6** Lesson Plan Template

Available for download at **www.corwin.com/theeverythingguide.**

Copyright © 2014 by Corwin. All rights reserved. Reprinted from *The Everything Guide to Informational Texts, K–2: Best Texts, Best Practices* by Kathy Barclay and Laura Stewart with Deborah M. Lee. Thousand Oaks, CA: Corwin, www.corwin.com. Reproduction authorized only for the local school site or nonprofit organization that has purchased this book.

*Note:* This template for lesson planning is also included in Appendix C.

## How the Template Addresses
## CCSS for Informational Text

Figure 5.7 shows how the Reading Standards for Informational Text are met within the steps of the lesson plan template. Notice that the standards are fully met, yet the instructional protocol within the template provides significantly more depth and supportive scaffolding than is specified in the standards.

## How the Template Helps
## You Model Text-Based Responses

As students move from kindergarten to Grade 2 and their reading abilities become fluent, teachers increasingly remove the scaffolds to allow students to do more and more reading on their own, independently. Teacher-supported instruction becomes more focused on showing students how to deeply comprehend texts, and ideally, fewer and fewer students need support with decoding, fluency, and other foundational skills. That's the ideal, and it's reflected in the Common Core's goal that students "show a steadily growing ability to discern more from and make fuller use of text" (NGA/CCSSO, 2010b, p. 8) as they grow in sophistication as readers.

| Steps in the Lesson | Kindergarten Standards | Grade 1 Standards | Grade 2 Standards |
| --- | --- | --- | --- |
| Prepare to read. | Identify the front cover, back cover, and title page of a book. (5)<br><br>Name the author and illustrator of a text and define the role of each in presenting the ideas or information in a text. (6) | Know and use various text features to locate facts or information in a text. (5) | |
| Guide reading.<br><br>Goal 1: Make text accessible. | With prompting and support, ask and answer questions about unknown words in a text. (4) | Ask and answer questions to help determine or clarify the meaning of words and phrases in a text. (4) | Determine the meaning of words and phrases in a text relevant to a Grade 2 topic or subject area. (4) |
| Guide reading.<br><br>Goal 2: Build understanding. | With prompting and support, describe the relationship between illustrations and the text in which they appear. (7)<br><br>With prompting and support, identify the reasons an author gives to support points in a text. (8) | Distinguish between information provided by pictures or other illustrations and information provided by the words in a text. (6)<br><br>Use the illustrations and details in a text to describe its key ideas. (7) | Know and use various text features to locate key facts or information in a text efficiently. (5) |

| Steps in the Lesson | Kindergarten Standards | Grade 1 Standards | Grade 2 Standards |
|---|---|---|---|
| Guide reading.<br><br>Goal 3: Demonstrate understanding. | With prompting and support, ask and answer questions about key details in a text. (1)<br><br>With prompting and support, identify the main topic and retell key details of a text. (2) | Ask and answer questions about key details in a text. (1)<br><br>Identify the main topic and retell key details of a text. (2) | Ask and answer such questions as who, what, when, where, why and how to demonstrate understanding of key details in a text. (1)<br><br>Identify the main topic of a multiparagraph text as well as the focus of specific paragraphs within the text. (2) |
| | With prompting and support, describe the connection between two individuals, events, ideas, or pieces of information in a text. (3) | Describe the connection between two individuals, events, ideas, or pieces of information in a text. (3)<br><br>Identify the reasons an author gives to support points in a text. (8) | Describe the connection between a series of historical events, scientific ideas or concepts, or steps in technical procedures in a text. (3)<br><br>Identify the main purpose of a text, including what the author wants to answer, explain, or describe. (6)<br><br>Explain how specific images contribute to and clarify a text. (7)<br><br>Describe how reasons support specific points the author makes in a text. (8) |
| Facilitate connections. | With prompting and support, identify basic similarities in and differences between two texts on the same topic. (9) | Identify basic similarities and differences between two texts on the same topic. (9) | Compare and contrast the most important points presented by two texts on the same topic. (9) |

FIGURE 5.7 CCSS in the Lesson Plan Template

But as any primary grade teacher knows, despite the ideal, each year we have a broad range of reading abilities in any one class, and we still support students plenty. One of the best ways to get students of a wide range of levels all on the same page is to give them lots of opportunities to refer back to the text to provide text-based responses to our inquiries.

**TIP**

Follow-up questions:

- What makes you say that?
- Show me where you found that in the text.
- Read the section to us that confirms where you found that answer.

According to the standards, students must make "an increasing number of connections among ideas and between texts, considering a wider range of textual evidence . . . becoming more sensitive to inconsistencies, ambiguities, and poor reasoning in texts" (NGA/CCSSO, 2010b, p. 8).

When using the lesson plan template, remember that one of the goals of Lesson Step 2, guide reading, is for students to demonstrate understanding. There are a number of questions or prompts teachers can use throughout the reading to check for students' understanding. For example, saying to students, "Tell me what this text is about" will give you a sense of their understanding of the main idea of the text. Asking students, "What does the author want us to know about this topic?" yields insight into their understanding or the purpose of the text. To assess students' understanding of the key details, *who, what, when, where,* and *why* questions are helpful. Most important, when you ask those comprehension questions, it is important to follow up with such prompts as, "What makes you say that?" "Show me where you found that in the text," or "Read the section to us that confirms where you found that answer." With these follow-up prompts, we are guiding students back to the text to help them use textual evidence in their responses.

Figure 5.8 lists key tasks we want students to be able to complete for a text. As we pause throughout the reading to check for students' understanding, these are important

- Identify main topic.
- Recall details.
- Answer *who, what, when, where, why,* and *how* questions.
- Describe connections between characters, events, or pieces of information.
- Ask and answer questions about vocabulary.
- Identify text features and the roles of the author and illustrator.
- Compare and contrast this text with another on the same topic.
- Identify the purpose of the text.

**FIGURE 5.8** Text-Based Responses to Demonstrate Understanding

**TIP**

**Remember:** In addition to having informational text experiences, K–2 children are daily receiving systematic, explicit instruction in the foundational skills of reading, and are practicing the application of those skills to appropriate text.

to keep in mind. Specific examples will be provided in the following chapters throughout the sample lesson plans.

## How the Template Addresses Foundational Skills

As discussed in Chapter 1, the Foundational Skills of the Common Core State Standards are "directed toward fostering students' understanding and working knowledge of concepts of print, the alphabetic principle, and other basic conventions of the English writing system" (NGA/CCSSO, 2010b, p. 15) but are not "an end in and of themselves."

Although the primary goal of using informational text is to teach essential information, informational text also provides a meaningful platform for the reinforcement and application of the Foundational Skills. As teachers work with informational text, they can discern the level of instructional support needed to meet the needs of students in the areas of

- Print concepts (K–1)
- Phonological awareness (K–1)
- Phonics and word recognition (K–2)
- Fluency (K–2)

Based on the needs of the learners, these specific skills may be taught and applied within the steps of the lesson plan template, as shown in Figure 5.9.

| Skill | Initial Teaching | Application/Assessment |
|---|---|---|
| Print concepts | Prepare to read. | Prepare to read. |
| Phonics | Initial teaching of phonetic elements and decoding is done systematically and explicitly before the elements are encountered in text. | Phonics and word recognition skills are applied in Lesson Step 2 (guide reading) and reinforced in Lesson Step 3 (explicitly teach from the text). |
| Word recognition (irregularly spelled words) | Prepare to read. | Guide reading. |
| Fluency | Explicitly teach from the text. | Explicitly teach from the text. |

FIGURE 5.9 Foundational Skills in the Lesson Plan Template

*Note:* Phonological awareness goals include the awareness of spoken words, syllables, and sounds. These are all auditory and oral skills and should be taught outside of the reading of informational text. However, within an informational text read-aloud experience, a teacher can isolate words and attend to their phonologic attributes as a way to apply the taught phonological awareness skills within a listening comprehension lesson.

## How the Template Addresses Interdisciplinary Learning

The Common Core State Standards fully support an integrated model of literacy, motivated by "extensive research, establishing the need for college and career ready students to be proficient in reading complex informational text independently in a variety of content areas." The lesson plan template attends to this goal in Lesson Step 4, make connections, specifically in the use of text as a springboard for the following:

- Engaging in shared, guided, and independent writing
- Using technology to discover and share information
- Reading additional texts, comparing and contrasting information in each
- Pairing fiction and nonfiction
- Exploring related knowledge and concepts in science, social studies, math, et cetera
- Linking to art, music, movement, and/or drama

## In Summary

The lesson plan template is designed to streamline planning for meeting the Common Core State Standards through informational text lessons. It is also designed to go beyond the standards and provide an outline for a deep and thorough lesson designed to teach children how to make meaning from text. If this all seems like a lot of new information, don't worry! In the next chapters we will examine sample lessons using the template for a read-aloud lesson, a guided reading lesson using leveled text, and a guided reading lesson using magazine articles. Important: Although these sample lessons are arranged by grade level, we encourage you to read all of these chapters, as you can generalize the ideas to your specific grade. For example, the read-aloud lesson sample is from a kindergarten class, but the basic outline for a read-aloud lesson applies whether you are teaching kindergarten, first grade, or second grade. The same goes for the two guided reading lessons. Also, there is a lot of practical information about differentiation and classroom management woven throughout. So don't miss a single chapter for many tried and true ideas that you can begin to use immediately. Onward and upward!

# 6

# Informational Text Read-Aloud Lessons in Kindergarten

One of the most iconic images of a kindergarten classroom is children gathered on a rug for a read-aloud. From *Chicka, Chicka, Boom, Boom* to *Strega Nona* and *Rosie's Walk*, charming narratives read aloud, and then discussed, retold, and maybe even dramatized, can lead young children down the path to independent reading and writing. As discussed in previous chapters, a strong research base supports the practice, too. The key is to make sure the instructional read-aloud is an interactive experience for children.

As children are developing their foundational skills and learning how to read text themselves, teachers engage them in rich interactive read-aloud experiences, which help the young learners build oral language, vocabulary, conceptual knowledge, and knowledge about the world, and develop reading behaviors and a love of reading. The case we've made in this book, of course, is that children's experiences are enriched if teachers read aloud high-quality informational books, too, so that an informative, imaginative book like *What Do You Do With a Tail Like This?*, a Caldecott Honor Book by Jenkins and Page (2003), brings content knowledge and concepts about animals and their senses into the mix. In this chapter we look more closely at how informational text read-alouds present unique opportunities to maximize this treasured time within every classroom day.

## The Common Core Standards for Informational Text Read-Alouds

Using informational text for read-alouds is fully supported by the Common Core State Standards. According to the Common Core State Standards, Appendix A,

> Children in the early grades—particularly kindergarten through grade 3—benefit from participating in rich, structured conversations with an adult in response to written texts that are read loud. (NGA/CCSSO, 2010a, p. 27)

The standards indicate why read-alouds are so critical:

> By reading a story or nonfiction selection aloud, teachers allow children to experience written language without the burden of decoding, granting them access to content that they may not be able to read and understand by themselves. Children are then free to focus their mental energy on the words and ideas presented in the text, and they will eventually be better prepared to tackle rich content on their own. (NGA/CCSSO, 2010a, p. 27)

An extensive number of read-aloud exemplars appropriate for K–2 are included in Appendix E of this book.

These read-aloud experiences don't replace the explicit, systematic instruction in the foundational skills of reading. Rather, they complement the foundational skills work:

> Time should be devoted to reading fiction and content-rich selections aloud to young children, just as it is to providing those same children with the skills they will need to decode and encode. (NGA/CCSSO, 2010a, p. 27)

## Benefits of Informational Text Read-Alouds in Kindergarten

According to the Common Core State Standards,

- "Preparation for reading complex informational texts should begin at the very earliest elementary school grades.... Having students listen to informational read-alouds in the early grades helps lay the necessary foundation for students' reading and understanding of increasingly complex texts on their own in subsequent grades" (NGA/CCSSO, 2010b, p. 33).

- In the grade-level standards, kindergartners "actively engage in group reading activities with purpose and understanding" (NGA/CCSSO, 2010b, p. 11).

Each day it is important to provide several read-aloud text experiences for kindergarten students. In addition to supporting the development of language comprehension skills and meeting the demands of the Common Core State Standards for informational text, read-aloud time also has these benefits:

- Models fluent reading; reading with appropriate pace, accuracy, and prosody or expression (CCSS Foundational Skills)
- Develops awareness of print concepts and conventions of print (CCSS Foundational Skills)
- Provides a context for teaching phonics and word recognition skills (CCSS Foundational Skills)
- Develops a love of and excitement for reading

## Using the Lesson Plan Template for the Read-Aloud

**TIP**

**Remember:** Before beginning the lesson steps, always read the book to yourself first!

In a read-aloud experience, especially for kindergartners, it is important not to overplan. A read-aloud selection is usually rich in language and concepts, so it is important not to try to do too much with the book; interrupting the reading repeatedly can take young listeners so far away from the through-line of the text that it may be counterproductive. So in applying the lesson plan template to the read-aloud, it is wise to keep it simple. Also, the first rule of thumb is to remember to read the book yourself ahead of the lesson, so you can make an instructional plan and be prepared to read with fluency and expression.

In the sections below, suggestions will be provided to assist in the lesson planning. First, we'll provide some general suggestions for a kindergarten read-aloud with informational text. Next, we'll provide a sample read-aloud lesson using the template. The lesson is designed to provide some ideas that may be generalized to other read-aloud lessons. Where an action addresses a specific standard for kindergarten reading, the number of the standard is given in parentheses after the action (e.g., CCSS 6).

**TIP**

Some expected behaviors to model and reinforce:

- Eyes on book
- Body facing the book
- Hands to self
- Ears and lips ready to LISTEN first
- Raise hand to volunteer

### Step 1: Prepare to Read

For the beginning of the year in kindergarten, it is important to remember that children may have had little exposure to books and reading aloud, so they need explicit instructions about expected behavior for listening to a book read aloud and responding to what they hear. Those expectations must be modeled and reinforced daily to establish an appropriate routine.

During a read-aloud with kindergartners, preparing the students for informational text typically involves the actions below.

- Point out the title, author, and illustrator, making connections to other books/texts by the same author if appropriate (CCSS 6).
- If you are using a book, show students the cover and back, and even preview some of the inside illustrations to generate enthusiasm for the reading (CCSS 5).
- Discuss that this is nonfiction text, or text that is "real life" and "true information." Contrast that with fiction stories you have read.
- Teach any vocabulary you think is critical to listening to the text with understanding.
- Set the purpose for reading by telling the students what the text will be about and what they will learn.

## Step 2: Guide Reading

You will want to read with expression and appropriate pacing. If it is appropriate (in other words, it does not interfere with the fluency and enjoyment of the reading), you can run your finger under the words to help children follow text. Allow time for students to hear the text and examine the illustrations. Allow time for students to share with each other and with you.

During the reading, you will want to pause occasionally to discuss the text and illustrations, focusing on the strategies below.

- Help students understand new vocabulary.
- Point out text features and illustrations that will help students understand the text (CCSS 7).
- Ask questions to check for understanding, focusing on the main ideas and key details. Be sure to give students ample "think time" for answering questions (CCSS 1–3, 8):
  o What was this book all about?
  o What important information did you learn from this book?
  o How are these (ideas, pieces of information, events) alike or different?

And remember, to reinforce text-based responses, we want to follow up the questions with prompts to get children back into the text, for example, "Let's look at the words we read to find out where it tells us. . . . "

- Give opportunities for children to ask questions. Prompt them to give reasons for their responses, but keep the discussions short.
- If children have trouble answering questions, reread text, show illustrations, and provide a think-aloud model for how you might find answers to the question.

## Step 3: Explicitly Teach From the Text

Depending on the purpose of the reading, you may go back into the text for any of these purposes:

- Examine a particular word for decoding and word recognition skills (Foundational Skills).
- Revisit an important concept word from the book. Have students tell you about the word to check for meaning (CCSS 4).

- Return to a passage to model fluency (Foundational Skills).
- Provide a think-aloud to revisit a comprehension strategy demonstrated in the reading or to model a fix-up tip.

## Step 4: Facilitate Connections

Depending on the opportunities presented in the text, the goals of the lesson, and the time, you may follow up the read-aloud with a short discussion of content learned, a writing activity, reading additional related text for comparison (CCSS 9), or linking the reading to art, music, or movement.

**TIP**

Fix-up tips include the following:
- Reread
- Look at pictures and illustrations
- Think about what makes sense
- Read ahead
- Sequence events or steps
- Recall details
- Summarize

## Miss Webb's Kindergarten Class: A Sample Informational Text Read-Aloud Lesson

### Setting the Stage

Miss Webb's kindergarten class is made up of 25 children, 17 boys and 8 girls. She teaches in a working class neighborhood with an ever-increasing population of students in poverty. She values the read-aloud time as an opportunity to build classroom community and develop children's listening comprehension, vocabulary, and conceptual understanding. With the CCSS's acknowledgment of both digital and print sources, she is utilizing a digital read-aloud text called *Play Ball!* (The excerpted text and lesson plan are taken from the Super Smart series published by the Rowland Reading Foundation. This series of digital texts is designed to meet the kindergarten standards for informational text literacy.) This interactive digital text includes multimedia features (audio, video, interactive capabilities) whose use can be modeled by the teacher and that can also activated by children. In the lesson plan you will see sample pages of the text, not the entire 19-page text.

From the beginning of the year, Miss Webb has patiently, consistently, and explicitly stated, modeled, and allowed her children to practice the expected routines for the read-aloud time. Her read-alouds generally take place at the reading rug, where she has a comfortable chair to sit in for her text-based read-alouds, and a screen where she projects digital read-alouds. At the beginning of the year, she taught children to quietly move to the reading rug for read-aloud time and take their places on the floor. She began the year with hula hoops on the floor to help children define their own personal seating areas; by midyear students no longer needed the hula hoops to determine their space. Miss Webb taught the children to "take five"; she instructed them on five behaviors she expected during read-aloud time:

- Eyes on book
- Body facing the book (having children orient their entire bodies toward the instructional source enhances engagement)
- Hands to self (in the beginning of the year, the hula hoops helped to define this)
- Ears and lips ready to LISTEN ("lips ready to listen" means no talking during the initial reading)
- Raise hand to volunteer

She introduced each of these behaviors by providing an example (modeling what the behavior looks like) and a nonexample (what it looks like when the behavior is not present). She drew a simple hand on a poster, with small words and pictures on each finger (for example, a pair of eyes and the word "eyes" on the thumb, a small stick figure and the word "body" on the index finger) to remind students of the behaviors. She used her hand to remind students to "take five." The nonverbal reminder is a powerful signal that cuts down on interruptions—eventually all students need to see is her hand to remember the expected behaviors.

To prepare for the lesson, Miss Webb has **read the text thoroughly** and identified the **essential information** she wants the children to know after reading the text. She also thought about her students' background knowledge and what schema and vocabulary she might need to elicit or build to give them access to the text. Utilizing the lesson plan template, she developed her action steps for the lesson. Finally, she considered the Common Core State Standards and how she would work toward meeting the standards within this read-aloud experience. You will see the steps of the lesson plan template, the guiding questions she asked herself in developing her action steps; Lesson Step 1 in Figure 6.1, Lesson Step 2 in Figure 6.4, Lesson Step 3 in Figure 6.11, and Lesson Step 4 in Figure 6.12. You can also read the script of her lesson plan.

## Before the Lesson

Big ideas (essential information) I want the students to know:

- People play many sports and games that use balls. These balls come in many different sizes, weights, colors, and coverings.
- Each sport or game uses a specific kind of ball in a specific way. For some sports, you might hit a ball with a bat, racquet, or mallet. For other sports, you might kick, bounce, shoot, or pass the ball.

| Step in the Lesson | Action Steps |
| --- | --- |
| Prepare to read. | • What is my students' background knowledge in content? Which concepts and vocabulary need to be elicited or developed before the reading?<br>• Which text features will be taught before the reading?<br>• What is our overall purpose for the reading and how can I state this for the students?<br>• How can I preview the text to build excitement for the reading (using the cover, illustrations, or other features)? |

FIGURE 6.1 Lesson Step 1: Prepare to Read

# MY LESSON PLAN

Today's Super Smart will tell about some sports and games that people play using balls. You'll learn about how different sports or games use different balls in different ways. I am thinking many of you already know some of these! Let's start by looking at some of these balls used in games and sports.

**Unit Opener:** (See Figure 6.2.) What does the picture show? Let's name as many of the balls as we can. Each kind of ball is used to play a specific sport or game, and there are different ways to play with these balls.

DETERMINE KEY IDEAS AND DETAILS

**Title Page; Set Purpose and Preview:** (See Figure 6.3.) [Point to the title and read it, tracking underneath.] Boys and girls, this is the title. Listen while I read it; then read it again with me. As I read aloud, you can listen to add to what you already know about games that use balls and maybe learn about a game that is new. These kids look really excited to be playing, and I know you all will enjoy our text today about playing ball!

**FIGURE 6.2** Super Smart Unit 6 Opener

*Source:* Rowland Reading Foundation (2012)

**FIGURE 6.3** *Play Ball!* Title Page

*Source:* Rowland Reading Foundation (2012)

| Step in the Lesson | Action Steps |
| --- | --- |
| Guide reading. | • What vocabulary or concepts should be taught during the reading so that my students can understand the text?<br>• What text features and illustrations need to be taught or pointed out in order to make the text accessible?<br>• What are the big, important ideas of this text I want my students to understand?<br>• What strategies can I teach or model that are appropriate for this text?<br>• What questions can I ask students to check their understanding?<br>• What reteaching will I need to do if they do not demonstrate understanding? |

**FIGURE 6.4** Lesson Step 2: Guide Reading

This is nonfiction, or true information. Sometime we call this "real life" reading that will provide information as we read. How do we know? What clues to you have already that this is nonfiction?

**Read Page 2:** (See Figure 6.5.) Let's think about how all these balls are different from one another. When I look at this page, I see these things: They are different sizes and colors. They would also feel different when picked up. I'm wondering how these would feel if I picked them up. Can any of you think of words to describe them? [Elicit or use these words: *heavy, light, hard, soft, bumpy,* or *smooth.*]

FIGURE 6.5  *Play Ball!* Page 2

*Source:* Rowland Reading Foundation (2012)

**Read Page 3:** (See Figure 6.6.) Before I play this, I want you to visualize what you think is going to happen in this video. [Play animation to show girl hitting the ball. Then read.] What kind of ball is this page all about? Here is what I saw happen: The ball was **pitched** toward the **hitter**, she **swung** her **bat**, the bat hit the ball, and the ball flew into the **baseball field**.

Sometimes an author makes important words on a page look different from the other words. On this page, the word *hit* is bigger and darker than the other words. That makes sense. Hit is an important word, because it tells what you can do with a baseball. Let's look for other important words like this as I keep reading.

FIGURE 6.6  *Play Ball!* Page 3 (Includes Animation of a Girl Hitting a Baseball With a Bat)

*Source:* Rowland Reading Foundation (2012)

**Read Page 4:** (See Figure 6.7.) Why is the word *kick* bigger and darker than the other words? What happens when a soccer player kicks the ball into the net? How do you know? Let's look back and find it out from the text.

ASK AND ANSWER QUESTIONS

DETERMINE KEY IDEAS AND DETAILS

FIGURE 6.7 *Play Ball!* Page 4

*Source:* Rowland Reading Foundation (2012)

ASK AND ANSWER QUESTIONS

DETERMINE KEY IDEAS AND DETAILS

**Read Page 5:** (See Figure 6.8.) What do you notice about the word *bounce?* When you bounce a ball, what does the ball do?

FIGURE 6.8 *Play Ball!* Page 5

*Source:* Rowland Reading Foundation (2012)

**Read Page 10:** (See Figure 6.9.) How is a bocce ball like a bowling ball (from a previous page)? How is it different? What does it say in the text about bocce balls and bowling balls? Let's look at one of the words in our text. The word is *target*. Can you say it with me? Say target. Let's do the syllables: tar-get. Target. Do it with me. [Students can hold out a fist for each of the syllables *tar* and *get*, and then say it all together by bringing their fists together: target.] A target is something you aim for or try to get close to in a game. In this game, the people are trying to toss some balls close to the target ball, and the ball that is closest wins. The target is the location where you aim for in a game. When I shoot an arrow with a bow, I try to hit the target. When someone does something right, we sometimes say "that was right on target," meaning it was correct. Can you think of examples of targets? [Take suggestions.]

COMPARE AND CONTRAST TEXT AND PICTURES

DETERMINE KEY IDEAS AND DETAILS

FIGURE 6.9  *Play Ball!* Page 10

*Source:* Rowland Reading Foundation (2012)

**Read Page 12:** (See Figure 6.10.) Before I read this, what questions do you have about this? What information do you want to know? [Take student responses; then read.] When you *tap* a **croquet ball**, what are you doing? Where does it tell us this in the text?

ASK AND ANSWER QUESTIONS

There is a word here that is confusing to me. It is the word *mallet*. [Read the sentence with the word *mallet*.] When I read something and I don't know what it means, I need to stop and use my fix-up ideas to try to figure it out. So I start by rereading. "In croquet you use a mallet to tap your ball through the wickets, metal hoops that are stuck in the grass." So I use a mallet to tap a ball. I know that "tap" means to hit. So the mallet must be what the child is holding and swinging at the ball. So I read it again to see if that makes sense. It does! Are there any words on these pages that are confusing to you? [When children identify *wickets*, take them through the fix-up ideas again.]

**MONITOR COMPREHENSION AND USE FIX-UP TIPS**

FIGURE 6.10  *Play Ball!* Page 12

*Source:* Rowland Reading Foundation (2012)

**Wrapping Up the Reading:** Ask

- What is *Play Ball!* all about?
- What is something new you learned about playing with balls?
- What else would you like to know about one of the balls or games *Play Ball!* told about?
- Do children and adults enjoy playing with balls? How do you know?
- Which ball from this text would you most like to play with? Why?

SUMMARIZE AND
SYNTHESIZE

DETERMINE KEY
IDEAS AND DETAILS

ASK AND ANSWER
QUESTIONS

MAKE INFERENCES

So far, you have read about Miss Webb's class, some of the groundwork she has laid to prepare for the read-aloud, and the selected scripts from her Lesson Steps 1 and 2 from the lesson plan template. Before we go on to Lesson Steps 3 and 4, pause and jot down your thoughts about these concepts:

What steps have you taken or will you take to provide a classroom environment conducive to the read-aloud?

Why is reading the text ahead of time so critical?

Look back at how Miss Webb sometimes thinks aloud and then guides children to utilize her strategy. How do you balance teacher-talk (think-alouds) with student response? How do you guide students to apply what you are modeling?

## Moving to Lesson Steps 3 and 4

Let's go on to see where Miss Webb goes with this lesson after the reading. Remember that Lesson Steps 3 and 4 are summarized in Figures 6.11 and 6.12. Here is how she thinks about these next two lesson steps:

For Lesson Step 3 (explicitly teach from the text; see Figure 6.11), I need to consider that at this level, my students are receiving their decoding and fluency instruction during my core reading time. During that time, I am providing explicit instruction in the foundational skills of reading, and I am utilizing decodable text so that my kindergartners are getting appropriate, cumulative practice in applying their emerging reading skills as they are learning them. I am using this informational text read-aloud to build listening comprehension. So it makes sense that I would return to the essential understandings I wanted my students to come away with, and do an activity to help bring that home for them. So for my action step, I am going to focus on an activity that will allow them to return to the strategy compare/contrast to think about what they have learned. I'm going to model this for them by creating a compare/contrast chart.

For Lesson Step 4 (see Figure 6.12), I usually think of several extensions for my students. This informational text provided many verbs, so I am going to begin to lay the groundwork for that particular part of speech, but in an age-appropriate way, through movement and discovery.

Because the reading of this text was rather lengthy for my kindergartners, I decided to do these lesson steps on another day.

I will create a chart with the students to develop their ability to compare and contrast. I'll start the chart by modeling how a baseball looks and feels and how it is used. Together, we will develop the rest of the chart (see Figure 6.13) using the balls from the text.

As an independent activity I will have the students go back to their seats, draw a picture of a ball (from the text or not), and write underneath how it looks and feels. I will also have them write about what they can do with that ball. Some of my children will

| Step in the Lesson | Action Steps |
|---|---|
| Explicitly teach from the text. <br><br> (Choose one focus area for each group of students.) | • Are my students able to decode this text? If not, what phonetic elements and decoding strategies do they need to work on? How can I utilize words or passages from this text to practice decoding? <br><br> • Are my students fluent readers? How can I model fluency in this text? Can I follow up the reading with shared and unison reading for practicing fluency? Are there other ways for students to utilize this text for fluency-building (assisted reading with CD, partner reading, choral reading)? <br><br> • Which comprehension skills and strategies are needed to comprehend this text? How can I teach one of those skills or strategies explicitly? What practice opportunities can I follow up with to allow my students to apply that skill or strategy? <br><br> • What fix-up tips can I teach based on the reading of the text that will allow students to learn self-help skills in their independent reading? |

FIGURE 6.11  Lesson Step 3: Explicitly Teach From the Text

| Step in the Lesson | Action Steps |
| --- | --- |
| Facilitate connections.<br>(Choose one focus area for each group of students.) | • Does this text experience authentically lend itself to making connections in writing, technology, additional text reading, content areas, or the fine arts? How can I formulate a meaningful follow-up activity to make these connections? |

FIGURE 6.12 Lesson Step 4: Facilitate Connections

| Ball | Looks | Feels | What can I do with it? |
| --- | --- | --- | --- |
| Baseball | Small, white | Smooth | Throw, hit, catch |
| Soccer ball | | | |
| Basketball | | | |

FIGURE 6.13 Compare/Contrast Chart for Balls

write independently, utilizing their phonetic spelling. Other children will draw the picture, and I will do some guided writing to model key words as captions on their drawings.

I am going to focus on vocabulary by returning to the text to pick out all the key action words that were bold-faced in the text: *bounce, swat, shoot, swing, tap, flick.* For movement activity, I'll have the children act out the motions. I will then name some other verbs, and have children act them out, to extend the idea of "action words."

## How Does This Lesson Fit Within a Broader Framework of Kindergarten Reading?

We've examined a singular kindergarten read-aloud lesson plan utilizing a lesson template. It is important to remember that this is one aspect of the reading instruction going on in Miss Webb's kindergarten. Figure 6.14 summarizes the different goals of the different texts utilized in her reading block.

| Component and Text | Goal | Schedule and Grouping |
|---|---|---|
| Instruction in foundational skills with application in phonetically controlled text | Providing comprehensive, integrated, cumulative instruction on the predictable progression of skills necessary to learn to read | Children are receiving this core instruction daily, and in kindergarten this instruction dominates the core reading block. Although the core instruction should take *all* children through the sequence of grade-level skills, differentiated instruction in the skills and utilizing appropriate text takes place in small, differentiated groups. |
| Read-aloud using narrative text | Developing vocabulary, conceptual understanding, listening comprehension, and understanding of narrative story structure. Narrative text is also designed to nurture a love of literature and story. | Read-aloud time is provided each day, preferably several times a day. Both narrative and informational read-alouds are important, striving for an equal balance of both over time (not necessarily every day). Read-alouds can be focused on simply enjoying the story or can follow a more detailed lesson structure.<br><br>Read-aloud time is typically whole group, although lessons utilizing aspects of the text may take place in small, differentiated groups. |
| Read-aloud using informational text | Developing vocabulary, conceptual knowledge, content-specific knowledge, listening comprehension, and understanding of expository text structure. Informational text is also designed to spark curiosity about the world. | Read-aloud time is provided each day, preferably several times a day. Both narrative and informational read-alouds are important, striving for an equal balance of both over time (not necessarily every day). Read-alouds can be focused on simply enjoying the story or can follow a more detailed lesson structure.<br><br>Read-aloud time is typically whole group, although lessons utilizing aspects of the text (for example, Lesson Step 3 in the lesson plan template) may take place in small, differentiated groups. |

FIGURE 6.14 Goals for Use of Texts in Miss Webb's Reading Block

## Kindergarten Informational Text Standards Included

As previously illustrated, as Miss Webb prepares her lessons, she considers the Common Core State Standards and how she will work toward meeting the standards within her read-aloud experiences. She finds it helpful to always return to the end-of-year standards and check off how she is progressing as she formulates her lessons.

An example of how this lesson included kindergarten Informational Text Standards is included in Figure 6.15. A copy of this checklist is included in Appendix B of this volume.

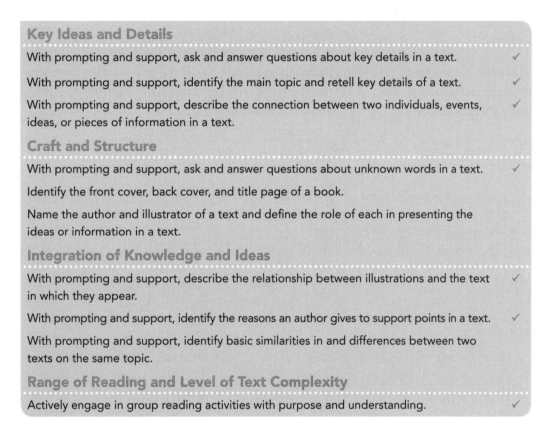

**Key Ideas and Details**

With prompting and support, ask and answer questions about key details in a text. ✓

With prompting and support, identify the main topic and retell key details of a text. ✓

With prompting and support, describe the connection between two individuals, events, ideas, or pieces of information in a text. ✓

**Craft and Structure**

With prompting and support, ask and answer questions about unknown words in a text. ✓

Identify the front cover, back cover, and title page of a book.

Name the author and illustrator of a text and define the role of each in presenting the ideas or information in a text.

**Integration of Knowledge and Ideas**

With prompting and support, describe the relationship between illustrations and the text in which they appear. ✓

With prompting and support, identify the reasons an author gives to support points in a text. ✓

With prompting and support, identify basic similarities in and differences between two texts on the same topic.

**Range of Reading and Level of Text Complexity**

Actively engage in group reading activities with purpose and understanding. ✓

**FIGURE 6.15** Kindergarten Standards for Informational Text Chart

In addition to the Informational Text Standards checked off on the chart in Figure 6.15, these standards from other areas were included in this lesson plan:

## SPEAKING AND LISTENING STANDARDS (NGA/CCSSO, 2010B, P. 23)

- Participate in collaborative conversations with diverse partners about kindergarten topics and texts with peers and adults in small and larger groups.
- Confirm understanding of a text read aloud or information presented orally or through other media by asking or answering questions about key details and requesting clarification if something is not understood.

## LANGUAGE STANDARDS (NGA/CCSSO, 2010B, P. 27)

- With guidance and support from adults, explore word relationships and nuances in word meanings.

## In Summary

Read-aloud experiences in kindergarten have many benefits and have always been beloved by teachers and children. While simply reading aloud to children in a supportive and nurturing environment is valuable, particularly in the area of language development, with careful planning the read-aloud experience can also meet important key goals within the Common Core State Standards. As we look to meet the demands of reading complex text in an information-rich global world, maximizing these well-planned and carefully delivered early experiences will help launch our children forward as confident and competent readers of informational text.

Where does informational text read-aloud time fit within your classroom day or week?

How can you use the ideas presented in this sample lesson in your classroom?

# 7

# Informational Text Lessons in First Grade

I n the previous chapter, we presented an informational text lesson using a read-aloud format. The general guidelines of the kindergarten example, presented on pages 69–75, and the lesson structure itself also apply to first-grade read-aloud lessons, so adapt the structure to your needs.

In this chapter, we look at how to use the lesson template to plan and teach in a guided reading format for beginning readers. The guided reading lesson will differ from a read-aloud lesson in significant ways. First and most obvious, the lesson will be done in a small group setting. Because of that, teachers need to deeply understand the makeup of the group; they will group students together based on their current abilities and needs as readers; these are considered "skills-based groups." For example, you might group students who need support with decoding, or fluency, or comprehension. Second, guided reading lessons are customized to meet those needs. As you plan any guided reading lesson, you choose the instructional focus that will help all the members of the group. Doing so requires the careful integration of the foundational skills with the goals for informational text reading.

## What's Different About First Grade?

In first grade, we want to develop children's independence as readers, their identity as readers who can read and enjoy books on their own. From the child who is still cementing a concept of words to the child who is already reading, our orientation is to have all children reading on or above grade level by the end of the year. The Common Core State Standards for Grade 1 reflect this push for independent reading of grade-level texts. Whereas almost all the standards in kindergarten begin with the phrase "with prompting and support," in Grade 1 only one standard includes this phrase: "With prompting and support, read informational texts appropriately complex for grade 1" (NGA/CCSSO, 2010b, p. 3, CCSS for Informational Text, Grade 1 Standard 10).

The way we interpret Standard 10 is that *all* first graders need to be utilizing grade-level informational text; the teacher then differentiates the amount of support (instruction) needed to help each reader access the text. Standards 1–9 define specific tasks students need to be able to do with that text; for example, according to the Informational Text Standards within the Key Ideas and Details (NGA/CCSSO, 2010b, p. 13) category, first graders should be able to

- ask and answer questions about key details in a text.
- identify the main topic and retell key details of a text.
- describe the connection between two individuals, events, ideas, or pieces of information in a text.

Again, notice the CCSS language and the distinction these expectations draw between kindergarten and first grade: While in kindergarten the focus was "engaging in group activities," the focus in first grade really shifts to students being sufficiently able to read texts independently.

As discussed in Chapter 6, complex text in kindergarten is provided in the form of read-alouds. In first grade, the challenge is not only to provide complex text through read-alouds, but also to choose text that is "appropriately complex for grade 1." This emphasis on grade-appropriate text is one of the most critical shifts teachers are asked to make with the adoption of the Common Core.

## Mrs. Stocker's First Graders: A Sample Informational Text Guided Reading Lesson

### *Setting the Stage*

Mrs. Stocker's class is made up of 22 eager first graders, the vast majority of whom are English language learners. She teaches in an urban setting with a transient population.

The range of preparedness for first grade is wide; she has students who are reading, others "on their way," and still others without a solid foundation of sounds and letters. She has many students who do not have a strong oral language foundation in either English or their native language, so she is always operating with deliberate intention to build language and vocabulary. She welcomes the increased use of informational text in her classroom as a vehicle for developing content knowledge and vocabulary and as a highly motivating context for teaching children to read.

With the adoption of the Common Core in her state, Mrs. Stocker has increased the use of informational text in her classroom. During her regularly scheduled read-aloud time, she utilizes informational text about 40% of the time. She sees this as a tremendous advantage, because she chooses read-alouds that fit her science and social studies themes, saving her instructional time as she meets multiple goals for both reading and content studies. While she is developing children's listening comprehension and content knowledge through read-alouds, she is also providing the core instruction in the foundational skills in whole group, with practice in decodable text in small groups. In small group **guided reading**, she strives for a 50/50 balance of narrative and informational text.

While complex informational text (above grade level, appropriate for listening comprehension) is used during read-aloud time, both phonetically decodable text and grade-level informational text are utilized in small groups. Phonetically decodable text is used in small groups until students have a firm grasp of decoding. Informational text is used in small groups as well, with one common text used for all students. Mrs. Stocker adheres to the "grouping without tracking" approach to informational text as explained in the beginning of this book. She utilizes a common, grade-level text with all of her students so that they all have exposure to grade-appropriate content; however, she groups them according to where they are in their development as readers, providing a bridge from *learning to read* to *reading to learn*. The big ideas or essential information are the same for all her first graders, but she uses the text in different ways with different small groups to make that information accessible for all students.

To help you set a context for the lesson examples in this chapter, you may wish to reread pages 24–26 in Chapter 2, which discuss how to differentiate instruction while using a common text with below-level, on-level, and above-level readers. Figure 7.1 is a quick summary of this differentiated instruction model.

When we refer to *below level, on level,* and *above level* we do so to provide you with a general outline of how instruction may be differentiated by skill need. We do not suggest any particular system of readability measures; how you assess to make these determinations we leave to you. Generally speaking, we encourage teachers to utilize formal and informal assessments, benchmarks, and observation of children's reading, writing, listening, and speaking. This daily knowing and observing of your readers is crucial. So much can learned from listening to our students read aloud to us, too. Taken together, we use all these forms of assessment to inform our decisions about exactly where a child is along the spectrum of reading development.

**TIP**

Be sure to use multiple texts in your classroom for multiple purposes, for example, read-aloud texts that can be above grade level for developing listening comprehension, instructional text (such as phonetically decodable text for beginning readers), and grade-level literature and informational text for guided reading.

| Readers | Characteristics in First Grade | Tips and Considerations for Informational Text |
|---|---|---|
| Below grade level | Focus: decoding and word recognition skills, language development | • Spend additional time building concepts and vocabulary before reading; frontload through discussion, additional reading, and use of media.<br>• Consider reading the selection to students first, so they have a model of fluent reading and can learn concepts through listening comprehension.<br>• Chunk the text into manageable units based on the essential information in the text. (Often, informational text is already divided by text features such as headings or chapters.)<br>• After focusing on the essential information, utilize the text as a forum for teaching the decoding and word recognition skills students are working on in their core reading instructional time.<br>• Remember to balance the time in small group utilizing grade-level informational text with using other texts more accessible to their independent reading, such as phonetically decodable text, as they are building their skills as readers. |
| On grade level | Focus: consolidation of foundational skills. As decoding and word recognition skills become solid, the emphasis shifts to building fluency. | • Continually assess students by listening to them read aloud; ensure they are using appropriate word recognition strategies and not guessing.<br>• Even if they are decoding accurately, pay particular attention to vocabulary, as they will likely still need you to teach and support their conceptual development.<br>• Encourage students to monitor for meaning, and use fix-up strategies when their understanding falters.<br>• Provide ample opportunities for rereading and guided oral reading. |
| Above grade level | Focus: development of independent reading capabilities | • Think of ways to elicit vocabulary and prior knowledge from students rather than teaching it explicitly.<br>• Move to silent reading, but still continue to check in by listening to them read orally, to ensure they are indeed "really reading."<br>• Look for opportunities to scaffold students' higher level comprehension skills, modeling inferring, identifying main idea/theme, connecting information to other texts, and so on.<br>• Continue to focus on the essential understandings of the core text, but provide additional, more challenging text to supplement it. |

FIGURE 7.1 Summary of Differentiating Instruction in Reading

## Phased-In Classroom Management to Prepare for Differentiated Instruction

As you read in Chapter 6, establishing routines early in the year, explicitly teaching children these expected routines, and continually expecting and reinforcing the routines is a critical part of the success of the reading instruction time. Mrs. Stocker has general "productive behaviors" that are taught with great detail and explicitness right from the start of the year. Here are her "three R's of the classroom":

- Respect everyone's right to learn.
- Respect Mrs. Stocker's right to teach.
- Respect each other's property and this classroom.

Because first graders don't necessarily know what any of this means, it is futile to just post rules and expect compliance. These behaviors are modeled, and students participate in defining "what our classroom looks like" when all of the members are adhering to these behaviors. The amount of explicit detail the students can generate in defining these behaviors is directly related to their understanding of what is expected.

In order to effectively work with students in small groups, Mrs. Stocker has to ensure that students can operate within these expectations so that she is not interrupted while with a group of students. It is essential at the beginning of the year that time is taken to carefully build these expectations and practice them in whole group during core instruction time; this is Phase 1 of establish the classroom management. Once children can follow the guidelines during whole group instruction and articulate the behaviors, they practice them in small groups, with Mrs. Stocker monitoring. During this Phase 2 of classroom management, Mrs. Stocker gives small groups of children specific tasks, but she herself does not meet with a group; instead she circulates and ensures that children can enact the expected behaviors in a small group setting. In Phase 3 of classroom management, children are given independent tasks as seatwork or in small groups (centers), while Mrs. Stocker begins to meet with small groups for teacher-led instruction. At first these are short segments, gradually lengthening until children can carry out tasks independently or in centers for a long enough period of time for Mrs. Stocker to meet with her small groups, typically 45–60 minutes total time (15–20 minutes per group). It is helpful at the end of the small group time to have a short class meeting to discuss how things went and set goals for additional improvements that might be necessary in the future to make sure everyone can be productive.

So what kinds of tasks does she teach children to do so that they are productively engaged during the times they are not with her? While a detailed explanation of all of the options goes beyond the scope of the book, here are some suggestions:

- Complete any skill work that has been previously assigned
- Partner reading of previously read text
- Listen to recordings of text, either as a follow-up or a frontloading (important for ELLs or children who come less prepared in the area of language and vocabulary)
- Practice handwriting or editing exercises
- Practice spelling words with a partner

- Journal writing or reading response
- Online or computer-based skill games,
- Center activities such as alphabet games, word work, or other previously taught manipulative activities that can now be done independently

One key concept to remember about these independent activities is that once children know the routine, you can infuse these activities with different content, so the concepts and content grow with the students' maturing understandings, but the routines are just that—known and routine—so that students can focus on productive learning, undistracted by "What do I do?"

It is also important to keep in mind that students need some explicit guidance and practice on anything you eventually decide will be an independent task. For example, during Phase 1 you are modeling these tasks and doing these tasks together. During Phase 2 children are completing these tasks in small groups while you circulate and monitor. By Phase 3, students will be prepared to carry out these tasks independently.

Although phasing in classroom management appears time consuming, it indeed saves countless hours of instructional time that is sometimes spent redirecting children or attending to repeated interruptions that characterize a classroom where children do not know, understand, or adhere to the expected behaviors.

Once the classroom is set for small guided-reading groups, and Mrs. Stocker has utilized her formal assessments as well as informal observations and oral reading, she can start to pull groups for guided reading.

**TIP**

Phasing in your classroom management, setting up consistent expectations, and providing lots of guided practice will help ensure your system will work.

The sample lesson in this chapter is from the *National Geographic Kids* series of nonfiction texts. This book is a Level 1 book. There are no specific guidelines for the leveling, but the publisher describes the level this way: "Level 1 books are just right for kids who are beginning to read on their own." (To determine if this book is suitable for her students and to meet the demands of the CCSS, a teacher would need to factor in the qualitative factors and the reader and task considerations discussed briefly in Chapter 2.) What follows is not the entire lesson but excerpts from certain pages of the book.

Although the bulk of the lesson is taking place in small, differentiated, guided reading groups, one advantage in utilizing core text is that some of the lesson steps can be done in whole group. For example, in this lesson, Mrs. Stocker is going to start a K-W-L (know, wonder, learn) chart. Because all students will be reading this selection, this step could be done in the whole class setting. After all students have read the text, the chart can be revisited to wrap up the reading.

To prepare for the lesson, Mrs. Stocker has **read the text thoroughly** and identified the **essential information** she wants the children to know after reading the text. She has also thought about her students' background knowledge and what schema and vocabulary she might need to elicit or build to give them access to the text. Utilizing the lesson plan template (see Appendix C), she developed her action steps for the lesson.

Finally, she considered the Common Core State Standards and how she would work toward meeting the standards within this guided reading experience. You will see the steps of the lesson plan template, the guiding questions she asked herself in developing her action steps (Lesson Step 1 in Figure 7.2, Lesson Step 2 in Figure 7.6, Lesson Step 3 in Figure 7.12, and Lesson Step 4 in Figure 7.13), and the script of her lesson plan below.

This is her on-level group lesson; modifications for her other groups will adhere to guidelines in Figure 7.1.

## Before the Lesson

Big ideas (essential information) I want the students to know:

- Spiders live in many habitats and can look very different from one another.
- Spiders all share some features: eight legs, two body parts, the ability to spin silk, meat eating, egg laying.
- Spiders can be helpful.

| Step in the Lesson | Action Steps |
|---|---|
| Prepare to read. | • What is my students' background knowledge in content? Which concepts and vocabulary need to be elicited or developed before the reading?<br>• Which text features will be taught before the reading?<br>• What is our overall purpose for the reading, and how can I state this for the students?<br>• How can I preview the text to build excitement for the reading (using the cover, illustrations, or other features)? |

FIGURE 7.2 Lesson Step 1: Prepare to Read

# MY LESSON PLAN

USE PRIOR
KNOWLEDGE

**Before Reading (in Whole Group):** (See Figure 7.3). [Chart with the class what they currently know about spiders. Add a second column, charting the questions they have about spiders that they hope will be answered in the reading.]

| What do we KNOW? | What do we WONDER? | What did we LEARN? |
|---|---|---|
| Spiders are scary. | Why do we have spiders? | |
| Spiders are black. | How many eggs do they lay? | |
| Spiders lay eggs. | Do spiders have teeth? | |
| Spiders bite. | How do they make webs? | |
| Spiders eat bugs. | | |
| Spiders make webs. | | |

FIGURE 7.3  Know-Wonder-Learn Chart 1

FIGURE 7.4  *Spiders* Cover

*Source:* Marsh (2011)

[After doing the K-W columns of the chart in whole group, assign students to work independently in order to pull small groups for guided reading.]

**Cover, Set Purpose, Preview (in Small Group):** Boys and girls, welcome to the reading group. I want you to sit in your chairs with both feet on the ground and face me. I want your book flat in front of you and closed. Please put your hand on the cover of your book so I know you are ready to begin. Eyes on me for now.

Today we will be learning a lot about an animal that sometimes people are very afraid of, but we'll learn what makes spiders special and important. Look at the cover (see Figure 7.4). This is nonfiction, or true information. Sometime we call this "real life" reading that will provide information as we read. How do we know? What clues to you have already that this is nonfiction?

Let's read the title together. [Read title.]

Let's look at the picture on the cover. Are there any notes we put on our chart that the cover picture confirms?

**Table of Contents**

It's a Spider! . . . . . . . . . . . . . . . . 4
Spiders, Spiders Everywhere! . . . . . 6
A Spider's Body . . . . . . . . . . . . . 8
Spider Food . . . . . . . . . . . . . . . 10
Senses . . . . . . . . . . . . . . . . . . 14
Web Builders . . . . . . . . . . . . . . 16
Spinning Silk . . . . . . . . . . . . . . 18
Super Spiders! . . . . . . . . . . . . . 20
Baby Spiders. . . . . . . . . . . . . . 24
Helpful Spiders. . . . . . . . . . . . . 28
What in the World?. . . . . . . . . . 30
Glossary. . . . . . . . . . . . . . . . . 32

**FIGURE 7.5** *Spiders* Table of Contents

*Source:* Marsh (2011)

Now I want you to use your pointing finger to find the author. Who remembers what *author* means? That's right; the author is the person who wrote this book. I'll read it to you. The author is Laura Marsh. There is one other item on the cover. It is the name of the publisher. The publisher is National Geographic.

**Preview Table of Contents:** (See Figure 7.5.) Boys and girls, remember that this is called a *table of contents*. This lists all the contents, or the information, included in this book. [Read through the table of contents, either having students take turns or reading it to them while they follow along.] What are you most excited to read about? Turn to your neighbor and share. Where will we read if we want to learn about what spiders eat? Where will we read if we want to learn about spider babies?

**Guided Reading:** (See Figure 7.6). [Continue with Lesson Step 2, Guide Reading.]

USE PRIOR KNOWLEDGE

MAKE INFERENCES

COMPARE AND CONTRAST TEXT AND PICTURES

DETERMINE KEY IDEAS AND DETAILS

USE PRIOR KNOWLEDGE

USE REFERENCES AND RESOURCES

ASK AND ANSWER QUESTIONS

DETERMINE KEY IDEAS AND DETAILS

| Step in the Lesson | Action Steps |
|---|---|
| Guide reading. | • What vocabulary or concepts should be taught during the reading so that my students can understand the text? <br> • What text features and illustrations need to be taught or pointed out in order to make the text accessible? <br> • What are the big, important ideas of this text I want my students to understand? <br> • What strategies can I teach or model that are appropriate for this text? <br> • What questions can I ask students to check their understanding? <br> • What reteaching will I need to do if they do not demonstrate understanding? |

**FIGURE 7.6** Lesson Step 2: Guide Reading

**Students Take Turns Reading Page 4:** (See Figure 7.7.) Now look at the picture. What does that look like? Why doesn't it look like a spider? How do you think the photographer took that picture?

COMPARE AND CONTRAST TEXT AND PICTURES

MAKE INFERENCES

Sometimes photographers can use cameras that can take pictures very close up. These special cameras have telephoto lenses—say that with me—that allow photographers taking a picture to magnify, or make larger, whatever it is they are taking a picture of.

**Students Take Turns Reading Page 5:** Can spiders hurt people? How do you know? Read where you learned that in the text. It is important to know that *most* does not mean *all*. In our class today, if I say, "Most of the students are wearing jeans," it means almost all of you but not everyone. So, thumbs up if this is true: All spiders are harmless. [Reteach as necessary.]

DETERMINE KEY IDEAS AND DETAILS

ASK AND ANSWER QUESTIONS

I'm going to read the first question for you. [Read aloud.] Sometimes when we come across a word we don't know, we can look at the picture. Sometimes we can figure out the

**FIGURE 7.7** *Spiders,* Pages 4 and 5

*Source:* Marsh (2011)

DETERMINE KEY
IDEAS AND DETAILS

ASK AND ANSWER
QUESTIONS

word by reading the sentence or more sentences. In this case, if I don't know what *fang* means, I can look at the Web Word that the author included on the page. [Read or have a student read the definition.] Show me the fang on the photo of the spider.

So I learned that spiders have fangs, and most are harmless. What other facts did we learn about spiders? That's right. They have eight legs and are hairy, which means they have a lot of hair on their bodies. Point to the text that told me those facts, and let's read

DETERMINE KEY
IDEAS AND DETAILS

together. Let's examine, or look closely at the picture to see that they are hairy.

The last thing to notice. Did you see the "Q and A"? [Have students read or read to them.]

**Pages 8 and 9:** (See Figure 7.8.) I'm going to read these pages, and then pause and let you visualize each of the spiders I am describing. *Visualize* means to close your eyes and picture in your mind what I am describing. [Read aloud this page, and pause after each

VISUALIZE
INFORMATION

DETERMINE KEY
IDEAS AND DETAILS

sentence.] Before you open your eyes, hold up the number of fingers to show me how many body parts they have. Hold up your fingers to show me how many legs spiders have.

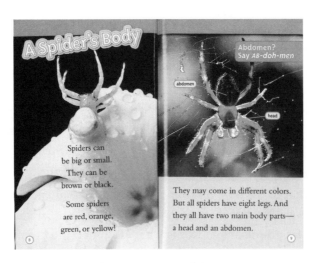

**FIGURE 7.8** *Spiders,* Pages 8 and 9

*Source:* Marsh (2011)

Now I want you to take turns reading these sentences on page 8 to me. [Have students read.]

How are spiders the same? How are they different? How do you know from the text?

DETERMINE KEY IDEAS AND DETAILS

SUMMARIZE AND SYNTHESIZE

Now I want you to take turns reading the sentences on page 9 to me. What are the spiders' main body parts? Show me on the picture.

DETERMINE KEY IDEAS AND DETAILS

SUMMARIZE AND SYNTHESIZE

There was one tricky word I think we need to talk about today. It is the last word on page 9. You read *abdomen,* and maybe you remember that is how I pronounced it. But if you had read this by yourself it might have been tricky for some of you. Let me use my white board to show you how we can chunk this word to make it easier to read. [Show and slash ab/do/men.] Now I think I can read the first chunk: *ab.* And the last one is easy: *men.* The second one is a little harder. *Do* usually spells /doo/, but here it is pronounced "doh." If I look up at the top of the page I see a pronunciation guide. Let's read the word parts together. [Read.] If I come across a word that tricks me up, I remember to chunk it and look for help if the author has provided it for me.

Also, the author gives us some tools to use to figure out what that tricky word means. What do you see on the page that helps us know the meaning? That's right, we see labels. Let's read the labels together. [Read.]

MONITOR COMPREHENSION AND USE FIX-UP TIPS

Is this picture a good picture of a spider for this page? Why or why not? [Take ideas.] I think it is a good picture for this page, because it shows the eight legs and the two body parts.

COMPARE AND CONTRAST TEXT AND PICTURES

INTERPRET INFORMATION FROM GRAPHS, CHARTS, AND DIAGRAMS

Because we are part way through the reading and have already learned a lot, let's go back to our chart to see if we have confirmed any of the things we wrote down that we know about spiders, and if we have answered any of our questions. [Answers will vary based on the chart. Just do this orally, as you want to use this same chart with other small groups as well.]

SUMMARIZE AND SYNTHESIZE

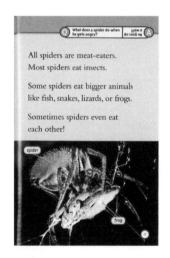

**FIGURE 7.9** *Spiders,* Page 11

*Source:* Marsh (2011)

**Page 11:** (See Figure 7.9.) Before you read this page, I want you to cover up the words and just look at the picture. Read the labels to yourself, and raise your hand if you can describe what is happening in that picture. [Take responses.] So is it a fact to say that spiders eat frogs? Do ALL spiders eat frogs? Let's read to find out. [Students take turns reading.] Thumbs up if it is a fact that all spiders each frogs. Let's read again where it says that SOME spiders eat frogs. [Read.] Is there one thing that ALL spiders eat? [Have students read the first sentence again.] That's right. All spiders eat meat. What else do spiders eat? [Take responses.]

COMPARE AND CONTRAST TEXT AND PICTURES

DETERMINE KEY IDEAS AND DETAILS.

When I read this page, I had a bit of trouble with the first two sentences. When I read "All spiders are meat eaters," I visualized, or pictured in my mind, a spider actually eating meat, like we do. And I knew that couldn't be right. Then I read, "Most spiders eat insects." So then I had to draw the conclusion that insects are considered "meat" for the spider to eat. If a spider eats a frog, he is eating meat. Maybe not the kind of meat we eat, but a frog is meat, not a plant. And or course that makes sense, because frogs certainly are not plants! So I had to reread the sentences and then pause and think about how they fit together. That was my fix-up strategy. When you read this page, did you find any words or sentences tricky? [Take responses and model a fix-up tip as necessary.]

**Have Students Take Turns Reading Page 25:** (See Figure 7.10.) Okay, when you were reading, what were all the ways the author and photographs taught you the meaning of the phrase *egg sac?* That's right. We have three pictures and we have the blue Web Word box.

I'm going to read this page again for you, and as I read where the spider keeps her egg sac, I want you to point to the right picture.

**DETERMINE KEY
IDEAS AND DETAILS.**

**ASK AND ANSWER
QUESTIONS**

**COMPARE AND
CONTRAST TEXT
AND PICTURES**

**Glossary:** (See Figure 7.11.) Look at the top of this page, and let's sound out the word. Read *glossary.* A glossary in a text lists words that are interesting and maybe unfamiliar to us, and it gives the meanings of the words. [Have students partner up, and have each child read one definition to another child.] Okay, now, were any of these words tricky for you? [Answers will vary; use strategies to help students with words and meanings as appropriate.] Now I'm going to ask you some questions, and I want you to point to the correct box. Sometimes I will ask you to read or answer a question. Make sure your book is flat on your table in front of you and your pointing finger is ready. Where will I look to find the meaning of *prey?* Read the definition of *venom.* Find the picture of the spider eggs. Where are spider eggs held?

**SUMMARIZE AND
SYNTHESIZE**

Now I'll have you each create a sentence using these terms. [Answers will vary; assist students as necessary.]

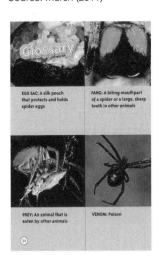

**FIGURE 7.10** *Spiders,*
Page 25

*Source:* Marsh (2011)

**FIGURE 7.11** *Spiders*
Glossary

*Source:* Marsh (2011)

# PAUSE & REFLECT

At this point, you have read about Mrs. Stocker's classroom management, some of the preparation she has done for determining her groups, and the selected scripts from her Lesson Steps 1 and 2 from the lesson plan template. Before we go on to Lesson Steps 3 and 4, pause and jot down your thoughts about these concepts:

What steps have you taken or will you take to provide a classroom environment conducive to small group instruction?

_____

_____

_____

_____

How do you phase in your management system?

_____

_____

_____

_____

Why is reading the text ahead of time so critical?

_____

_____

_____

What parts of the lesson are whole group? Which are small group?

Mrs. Stocker has many ELLs in her classroom. Look back at the lesson and notice the ways she pays particular attention to building vocabulary and concepts, explicitly teaching word meanings and leaving nothing to chance. How do you utilize some of these strategies for your ELLs?

## Moving to Lesson Steps 3 and 4

What does Mrs. Stocker think about the first two lesson steps? Where does Mrs. Stocker go with this lesson after the reading? Here is her thinking, reflecting on where she has been and where she is going:

# MY LESSON PLAN

For Lesson Steps 1 and 2, my focus was making sure all my students, regardless of their reading abilities, had access to the essential information. So doing the K-W-L in whole group made sense, and I'll return to that at the end, after all my students have read the text, in order to bring closure to the lesson.

As I guided students through the text (Lesson Step 2) it made sense to keep essentially the same questions and prompts for all groups, because again my focus was on comprehending the big ideas.

When I reflect on how my lesson plan script really reflects what I do with each group, it is pretty accurate. With my below-level readers I will tweak the lesson to do more of the reading to them before I ask them to read themselves. My above-level readers do more independent reading. But for the most part the prompts and questions are applicable for all groups, because my content goals are the same for all students.

For Lesson Step 3 (explicitly teach from the text; see Figure 7.12), I need now to really think about the different types of readers in my class. This is where the differentiation really comes in. I've scripted out how I differentiate the instruction in each group for this lesson step.

In this sample lesson, I would do all of Lesson Step 4 (facilitate connections; see Figure 7.13) in whole group. I would return to our K-W-L chart, and we would do this together, because we have all taken away the same content. This informational text provided many verbs, so I am going to begin to lay the groundwork for that particular part of speech, but in an age-appropriate way, through movement and discovery. For other extension activities, I have chosen two of my favorites, art and writing.

**For Students Who Are Still Working on Decoding:** Now that we have read the text and learned some facts about spiders, let's use this book to practice our reading skills. Please return

| Step in the Lesson | Action Steps |
|---|---|
| Explicitly teach from the text. (Choose one focus area for each group of students.) | • Are my students able to decode this text? If not, what phonetic elements and decoding strategies do they need to work on? How can I utilize words or passages from this text to practice decoding? <br> • Are my students fluent readers? How can I model fluency in this text? Can I follow up the reading with shared and unison reading for practicing fluency? Are there other ways for students to utilize this text for fluency-building (assisted reading with CD, partner reading, choral reading)? <br> • Which comprehension skills and strategies are needed to comprehend this text? How can I teach one of those skills or strategies explicitly? What practice opportunities can I follow up with to allow my students to apply that skill or strategy? <br> • What fix-up tips can I teach based on the reading of the text that will allow students to learn self-help skills in their independent reading? |

**FIGURE 7.12** Lesson Step 3: Explicitly Teach From the Text

to page 25. [On the white board, write the words *she, keep, safe.*] Let's look at these words and read them together. What do you notice about all the vowel sounds? They are long. How do we know these are long vowels when we read?

How do we know to say the long *e* in *she?* This is called an *open vowel pattern;* the vowel is at the end of the word and not "fenced in on both sides" by consonants. When you have an open vowel at the end of a word or syllable, it is usually the long sound. [List on the white board and read: *he, me, hi, no.*] There are some words that don't follow that pattern, but try the long sound when the vowel is open, and if it doesn't sound right you can adjust. Let me give you an example. [Write "I went to school" on the white board. Read it aloud.] Let's look at the word *to.* If this is an open vowel, I would read this: "I went toe school." Does this sound right? Sometimes you have to try it out and adjust.

How do we know to say the long *e* in *keep? ee* is a vowel pair. When we have two vowels together, one is telling the other its name, so we remember to use the long sound (or the name sound) of the vowel. [Write and read these words: *sleep, deep, feet,* any others you wish to practice.]

How do we know to say the long *a* in *safe?* I know you all know the "silent *e*" rule—if we have an *e* at the end of the word, the *e* is signaling the first vowel to say its long sound or its name. Let's practice with some words we know. [Write and read: *take, tame, lone, lane,* any others you wish to practice.]

[Return to page 25 for reading; have each student practice reading for fluency.]

**For Students Who Can Decode But Are Working on Building Fluency:** Let's turn back to page 5. [Read aloud the selection as if it had no punctuation. Then read aloud with expression.] What did you notice? That's right, the first time I read this I didn't pay any attention to the punctuation. And it was hard to understand the meaning of the sentences! It is important to remember that punctuation gives us signals on how to read, and how we read helps us understand what we are reading. [Have students practice reading page 5 with expression and attending to the punctuation chorally (all together), then with partners. Make the recorded reading available in the listening center.]

**For Students Who Are Reading Well, Use This Text for Building Ability to Monitor Comprehension and Use Fix-Up Tips:** In this text the author provided us with several ways to make sure we understood our reading. One was the vocabulary boxes. Let's go back and look at those. How is this helpful to me? If I'm reading and don't understand, I can read this explanation of what the word means and then put it into my sentence. For example, on page 5, if I read that first sentence and don't know what *fang* means, I can look at the Web Word box. I read that a fang is a "biting mouthpart." So I can go back to the first sentence and put "biting mouthpart" in place of the word *fang.* That helps me make sense of the sentence. The author and illustrator were also very helpful in providing good pictures with labels. I learned in reading page 9 that spiders "all have two main body parts—a head and an abdomen." But I don't know where they are. Notice the labels tell me where they are on a spider's body. There are often these features in a nonfiction text that I can use when I am reading and don't understand what I'm reading. Let's practice using the Web Word on page 25. [Have students practice thinking out loud using this strategy.]

**Wrapping Up the Reading:** [In whole group, after each small group has read the text, return to the opening chart. Reread the first column.] Were any of our "knows" disproven or proven? [Go through and strike out any the class cannot prove (see Figure 7.14).]

| Step in the Lesson | Action Steps |
|---|---|
| Facilitate connections. (Choose one focus area for each group of students) | • Does this text experience authentically lend itself to making connections in writing, technology, additional text reading, content areas, or the fine arts? How can I formulate a meaningful follow-up activity to make these connections? |

FIGURE 7.13  Lesson Step 4: Facilitate Connections

| What do we KNOW? | What do we WONDER? | What did we LEARN? |
|---|---|---|
| ~~Spiders are scary.~~ | Why do we have spiders? | Spiders have eight legs, fangs, and hair. |
| ~~Spiders are black.~~ | How many eggs do they lay? | Spiders live everywhere. |
| Spiders lay eggs. | Do spiders have teeth? | Most spiders can't hurt people. |
| ~~Spiders bite.~~ Some spiders bite. | How do they make webs? | Spiders have two body parts. |
| ~~Spiders eat bugs.~~ Most spiders eat insects. | ~~Do spiders make good pets?~~ | Spiders can be all different colors. |
| Spiders make webs. | | Spiders can eat meat like animals and each other. |
| | | Spiders help us by eating pests. |

FIGURE 7.14  Know-Wonder-Learn Chart 2

[Reread the "wonder" column.] Which of our questions were answered? [Strike out any for which an answer was not found.]

Now boys and girls, let's write in our final column, which is an *L* for "What we learned." [Chart the children's responses to "What did we learn?" Be sure to add any that you know were in the book. Have the children return to the text to show where they found the facts.]

## Connections

- **Art:** To illustrate the physical characteristics of spiders (two body parts and eight legs), create spider models from Styrofoam balls and pipe cleaners.
- **Writing:** Read *The Important Book* by Margaret Wise Brown. Following the pattern of each page of the original text, create *The Important Book About Spiders*.

Learn more about spiders: www.kids.nationalgeographic.com

## First Grade Informational Text Standards Included

As Mrs. Stocker prepares her guided reading lessons, she considers the Common Core State Standards and how she will work toward meeting the standards within her guided reading experiences. She finds it helpful to always return to the end-of-year standards and check off how she is progressing as she formulates her lessons. An example of how this lesson included first-grade Informational Text Standards is included in Figure 7.15. A copy of this checklist is included in Appendix B of this volume.

| | |
|---|---|
| **Key Ideas and Details** | |
| Ask and answer questions about key details in a text. | ✓ |
| Identify the main topic and retell key details of a text. | ✓ |
| Describe the connection between two individuals, events, ideas, or pieces of information in a text. | |
| **Craft and Structure** | |
| Ask and answer questions to help determine or clarify the meaning of words and phrases in a text. | ✓ |
| Know and use various text features to locate key facts or information in a text. | ✓ |
| Distinguish between information provided by pictures or other illustrations and information provided by the words in a text. | ✓ |
| **Integration of Knowledge and Ideas** | |
| Use the illustrations and details in a text to describe its key ideas. | ✓ |
| Identify the reasons an author gives to support points in a text. | ✓ |
| Identify basic similarities in and differences between two texts on the same topic. | |
| **Range of Reading and Level of Text Complexity** | |
| With prompting and support, read informational texts appropriately complex for grade 1. | ✓ |

**FIGURE 7.15** First Grade Standards for Informational Text

*Source:* NGA/CCSSO (2010b). Copyright © 2010 National Governors Association Center for Best Practices and Council of Chief State School Officers. All rights reserved.

## Other Standards Addressed

In addition to the Informational Text Standards checked off on the chart in Figure 7.15, these standards from other areas were included in this lesson plan:

## FOUNDATIONAL SKILLS STANDARDS (NGA/CCSSO, 2010B, P. 15)

- Demonstrate understanding of the organization and basic features of print.

## SPEAKING AND LISTENING STANDARDS (NGA/CCSSO, 2010B, P. 23)

- Participate in collaborative conversations with diverse partners about Grade 1 topics and texts with peers and adults in small and larger groups.

## LANGUAGE STANDARDS (NGA/CCSSO, 2010B, P. 27)

- Determine or clarify the meaning of unknown and multiple-meaning words and phrases based on Grade 1 reading and content, choosing flexibly from an array of strategies.

## In Summary

This chapter tackled two challenging tasks we have as primary teachers. The first is setting up and maintaining a classroom management system that will allow us to meet productively in small, teacher-led groups while the rest of the students are also productively engaged. This is not an easy thing to do, but remember that young children can learn and adhere to systems of expected behavior if those behaviors have been explicitly taught and modeled, sufficiently practiced, and consistently reinforced. Children want to be a part of an orderly and systematic classroom, where they can know what to expect and they feel safe. A positive and productive climate is crucial for real teaching and learning to take place.

> **TIP**
>
> Keeping a chart of the CCSS for your grade, and checking off standards as you address them throughout the year, is a great way to stay grounded in the standards as you develop lesson plans.

The second challenge we face is embracing and employing a system of differentiated instruction that puts instruction at the forefront: modifying and changing our instructional approach based on the needs of the reader, not based on levels of books. If our goals are to have all children at grade level and to give all children equal access to important and motivating nonfiction content, we need to consider how we can use grade-level informational text for all students. This requires us to understand how children progress and develop as readers, and how critical our instruction is to that process. The lesson template provides an effective roadmap for working within this paradigm.

In conclusion, a first grade guided reading lesson utilizing informational text requires careful planning. A teacher must consider the needs of the different levels of readers in the lesson design, paying particular attention to modifying the lesson to adapt to their unique stages of development. She must also set up a classroom environment conducive to providing those lessons in small group. Overall, the goal is to provide a reading experience in which all students are stretched to meet the demands of reading grade-level, complex text, so that they can all benefit from the important content that informational text presents.

How do you utilize your understanding of different readers' needs to determine your groupings? How do you adjust your use of text and your guided reading for your different groups?

How can you use the ideas presented in this sample lesson in your classroom?

# 8

# Informational Text Lessons in Second Grade

With the strong foundation of decoding and fluency built into K–1 instruction, the world of reading really opens up for second graders! Reading instruction in second grade looks as unique as second graders themselves. While we want to expose them to a wide variety of genres and meet the quantitative guidelines for complex text as outlined in the Common Core, we need to ensure that their foundational skills are firmly in place. Informational text provides a sturdy platform upon which to build both students' reading experience and their content area knowledge.

The information presented in previous chapters really kicks in as you implement the second-grade model. Concepts to borrow from previous chapters include these:

- Text complexity becomes increasingly important in Grade 2. For a thorough look at text complexity, see Chapter 2.
- Read-aloud lessons continue to be important in second grade. Using high-quality children's nonfiction literature that meets the criteria as outlined in Chapter 6 along with the basic template from Chapter 5 will support you as you maximize your read-aloud time with informational text.
- Differentiating instruction as outlined in Chapters 2 and 7 will provide you with the basic outline for differentiating your small groups in Grade 2.
- The phasing in of classroom management and the independent activities briefly discussed in Chapter 7 will assist you in setting up your classrooms for small group instruction.

## The Common Core Standards for Informational Text in Second Grade

In Chapter 5, we examined how the standards are met in the basic outline of the lesson plan template. The standards put much more emphasis on second graders' independent reading of informational text that meets certain criteria for complexity:

By the end of the year, [students will] read and comprehend informational texts including history/social studies, science and technical texts, in the grades 2–3 complexity band proficiently, with scaffolding needed at the high end of the range. (NGA/CCSSO, 2010b, p. 13)

What exactly is meant by the "text complexity band"? As discussed in previous chapters, *text complexity* describes how difficult a text is to read and comprehend, and the Common Core State Standards use a three-part model to determine text complexity, including qualitative factors, quantitative measures, and reader and task considerations. While the three components are considered throughout the standards (see NGA/CCSSO, 2010a, pp. 2–10), quantitative requirements formally begin in second grade. A variety of readability measures can be used to identify books that are within the text complexity band, and these are specified in the Common Core State Standards document (NGA/CCSSO, 2012b) for Grades 2–12.

In keeping with the demands for independent reading, the standards for informational text require students to "ask and answer," "identify," "describe," "know and use," and "compare and contrast" as *independent* readers. This of course requires that they be reading texts with accuracy, fluency, and comprehension *on their own*.

## What About Students Who Are Not Reading With Grade-Level Proficiency?

According to the standards, "students who struggle greatly to read texts within (or even below) their text complexity grade band must be given the support needed to enable them to read at a grade-appropriate level of complexity" (NGA/CCSSO, 2010a, p. 9). This is when the foundational skills come into play in second grade.

The Foundational Skills in second grade assume the mastery of phonological awareness and print concepts and expect that students will

- "know and apply grade-level phonics and word analysis skills in decoding words" and
- "read with sufficient accuracy and fluency to support comprehension." (NGA/CCSSO, 2012b, p. 16)

By second grade, continued instruction in the Foundational Skills is differentiated and focused only on students who are struggling with grade-level text. This requires that we do everything we can to get them to grade level in kindergarten and first grade, through a strong foundation of explicitly taught and carefully applied skills so that decoding and word recognition is automatic and brain energy is freed up for comprehension. When students are not yet fluent in grade-level text in second grade, we need to apply the appropriate explicit teaching of the foundational skills to establish the strong neural pathway for automatic decoding, and provide them with appropriate text to solidify these essential word recognition skills. At the same time, students need to be exposed to high-quality, grade-level informational text. This will meet two goals: (1) In addition to providing guided reading utilizing differentiated instruction to meet their needs as readers, we are providing scaffolded instruction to allow them to have access to grade-level text, and (2) all students are provided with grade-appropriate content of sufficient complexity and sophistication.

The lesson sample on the next page is designed to provide that access to high-quality, grade-level text. Just as in the first grade lesson sample, we recommend you use such text with all students, but differentiate the approach you use based on the group with which you are working. If you are using this text with readers who are not yet proficient with decoding, you will still focus on the big ideas within the text; however, you may be reading excerpts of the text to the students, and utilizing parts of the lesson and excerpts from the text as opportunities for them to continue to develop their foundational skills. If you are using this text with readers who are decoding but not yet fluent, you will again still focus on the big ideas within the text; however, you may be using the text to develop their fluency, particularly in Lesson Step 3. If you are using this text with grade-level or above readers, your focus may be on the deeper comprehension and evidence-based/text-based questions, again, with the purpose of focusing on the big ideas. (See Chapters 2 and 7 for additional information on utilizing grade-level informational text in differentiated groups.)

Regardless of how you differentiate your approach, you will want all students to have access to and mastery of the big ideas available to them in high-quality informational text. It is imperative that all students are given the opportunities to learn from text of sufficient grade-level complexity, and it is through our *differentiated instruction* we can make that possible.

This model lesson is designed to show how this differentiated approach within common text can be achieved. However, as was true in the first grade model lesson, remember that *below-level readers, in addition to needing a grade-level informational text experience, will also need to continue explicit, systematic practice in the necessary foundational skills and in applying those emerging skills to appropriate text.* In other words, while using grade-level, core text with all students, we are also providing differentiated text reading outside of this lesson, in guided and independent practice.

## Mr. Morris's Second Graders: A Model Informational Text Guided Reading Lesson

Mr. Morris is a relatively new teacher with a class of overall high-achieving students who come to school well prepared and from affluent backgrounds. The parents are involved in their children's education and expect that their children will be sufficiently challenged to assure academic progress. The unspoken premise of the parent culture is, "My child is smart and college bound, so you better be at the top of your game as a teacher."

Mr. Morris is a product of a teacher preparation program that emphasized evidence-based instructional practices, so he has identified one of the major challenges inherent in his population of students: There are some students who appeared to be readers in kindergarten and first grade but have started to slip through the cracks in Grade 2. Their foundation in reading was built on using picture cues and patterned text; they were encouraged to "think about what makes sense," "look at the pictures," and "skip and read on" without regard to phonetic decoding. Now that text has become less patterned and has fewer picture supports, they are starting to stumble, having no strong neural networks in place for understanding the underlying structure of the English alphabetic code and the language foundations of reading. Mr. Morris works diligently to fill in the missing pieces so all of his students can fearlessly decode and utilize word recognition strategies with automaticity so that they use all their cognitive energy for comprehending text. (See Chapter 7, page 104 for an outline of differentiating instruction for different levels of readers; more detail is provided in Chapter 2.)

As a new teacher, Mr. Morris struggled somewhat with classroom management, not realizing the importance of setting goals and boundaries from the first day of school. Now in his third year of teaching, Mr. Morris continues to work on setting classroom guidelines, phasing in the management system over time, being diligent in reinforcing the class rules, and enforcing productive independent work time so that he can effectively work in small guided reading groups. (See Chapter 7 for a more detailed discussion of setting up classroom management and independent activities.)

He uses the gradual release of responsibility model ("I do, we do, you do"), ever aware that a recurring flow of teacher demonstrations, we-do-it-together group learning, and independent—"you do it"—study and learning cultivates independence while providing enough instruction.

The lesson that follows utilizes informational text within the band of complexity for second grade recommended by the standards. This particular lesson shows how short selections within a magazine also provide excellent opportunities for examining multiple texts on the same topic. As stated in the Common Core

**TIP**

Be sure to use multiple texts in your classroom for multiple purposes; for example, read-aloud texts that are at or above grade level for developing listening comprehension, instructional text (such as phonetically decodable text for beginning readers), and grade-level literature and informational text for guided reading.

Standards, "Within a grade level, there should be an adequate number of titles on a single topic that would allow children to study that topic for a sustained period." (NGA/CCSSO, 2010b, p. 33)

This text (and excerpted lesson plan ideas) are taken from a second-grade nonfiction magazine called *Splish Splash,* part of a series of theme-based magazines called SUPER (published by Rowland Reading Foundation), written specifically for second grade. The ideas for the text are designed to provide more ideas than would be used in any given lesson; because this lesson is designed as a small group guided reading, these are possibilities that may be pursued depending on the students in the group.

A special note about vocabulary: Because the vocabulary is not taught explicitly in the text, note that for vocabulary teaching ideas, the key word is provided, followed by a student-friendly definition and sentence. These key words may be *elicited* from the students, rather than taught explicitly, again, depending on your students.

To prepare for the lesson, Mr. Morris has **read the text thoroughly** and identified the **essential information** he wants the children to know after reading the text. He has also thought about his students' background knowledge and what schema and vocabulary he might need to *elicit or build* to give them access to the text. Utilizing the lesson plan template, he developed his action steps for the lesson. Finally, he considered the Common Core State Standards and how he would work toward meeting the standards within this guided reading experience. You will see the steps of the lesson plan template and the guiding questions he asked himself in developing the action steps (Lesson Step 1 in Figure 8.1, Lesson Step 2 in Figure 8.2, Lesson Step 3 in Figure 8.6, Lesson Step 4 in Figure 8.7), and the script of his lesson plan below. Remember, this lesson is done in small skills-based guided reading groups, differentiated by students' current skill level. Because of that, remember that although the lesson plan may indicate that children will read the text for themselves, he may need to read the text to some children.

## "Water, Water, Everywhere" and "The Never-Ending Story": Before the Lesson

Big ideas (essential information) I want the students to know:

- Even though the earth is made mostly of water, only a tiny amount of that water is suitable for drinking, and it must be shared by everyone on the planet.
- There is a natural water cycle that allows us to use and reuse all the water we have available to us.
- There is a human-made water cycle that directs water to and from our homes.

**TIP**

Some productive independent activities for students to complete while you are meeting in groups include the following:

- Complete any skill work that has been previously assigned
- Partner reading of previously read text
- Listen to recordings of text, either as a follow-up or a frontloading (important for ELLs or children who come less prepared in the area of language and vocabulary)
- Practice handwriting or editing exercises
- Practice spelling words with a partner
- Journal writing or reading response
- Online or computer-based skill games,
- Center activities such as alphabet games, word work, or other previously taught manipulative activities that can now be done independently

**TIP**

Refer to Figure 7.1 in Chapter 7 for a summary of key modifications to make with different readers.

| Step in the Lesson | Action Steps |
| --- | --- |
| Prepare to read. | • What is my students' background knowledge in content? Which concepts and vocabulary need to be elicited or developed before the reading?<br>• Which text features will be taught before the reading?<br>• What is our overall purpose for the reading, and how can I state this for the students?<br>• How can I preview the text to build excitement for the reading (using the cover, illustrations, or other features)? |

**FIGURE 8.1** Lesson Step 1: Prepare to Read

# MY LESSON PLAN

**Before Reading:** Let's talk about water! I want to find out what you know now about water, so I'm going to ask you a couple of questions so I know what else we need to learn through our reading today. Is water is important? In what ways? Where do we get water for our daily use?

<small>USE PRIOR KNOWLEDGE</small>

**Set Purpose and Preview:** In your lifetime, you'll probably drink enough water to fill a swimming pool! We are going to read two articles today; one is called *Water, Water Everywhere* and the other is called *The Never-Ending Story*. From these two articles, you will learn how we get all of that water, where it comes from, and where it goes.

Remember that these are magazine articles. Let's review the features of a magazine and examine the features in the articles we will be reading. Look at pages 6–7, and you'll see the title of the article, the text that provides the information, and a small sidebar at the bottom with an interesting fact. Look at pages 8–9, and you'll see the title again, the text that provides the information, and a very detailed diagram that will help us understand what the text is explaining. See that the diagram has labels and arrows and short text. When you finish this article you will understand something called the *water cycle*. Let's look at pages 10–11, and you'll see another diagram. Take a moment and look at some of the labels and arrows. What do you think this diagram will help explain? [Take responses, leading children to the understanding that this diagram is designed to show how we get water in our homes and where water goes when it leaves our homes.]

<small>DETERMINE KEY IDEAS AND DETAILS

MAKE INFERENCES

COMPARE AND CONTRAST TEXT AND PICTURES

INTERPRET INFORMATION FROM GRAPHS, CHARTS, AND DIAGRAMS</small>

| Step in the Lesson | Action Steps |
|---|---|
| Guide reading. | • What vocabulary or concepts should be taught during the reading so that my students can understand the text?<br>• What text features and illustrations need to be taught or pointed out in order to make the text accessible?<br>• What are the big, important ideas of this text I want my students to understand?<br>• What strategies can I teach or model that are appropriate for this text?<br>• What questions can I ask students to check their understanding?<br>• What reteaching will I need to do if they do not demonstrate understanding? |

FIGURE 8.2 Lesson Step 2: Guide Reading

**Students Read Opening Text on Page 6:** What nickname does the Earth have? Where did you read that? Why do you think it is called the "water planet?" [Take responses.] That's right, when we look at the picture taken from outer space, you can see how much blue there is. All the blue areas are water.

<small>MAKE INFERENCES

ASK AND ANSWER QUESTIONS

DETERMINE KEY IDEAS AND DETAILS</small>

**Students Take Turns Reading Text on Pages 6 and 7:** (See Figure 8.3.) When we read this, it confirms our understanding that our planet is mostly water. It was interesting to me when I heard you read that the white areas are clouds and ice, which are also made of water, and that we also have a lot of water underground, which can't be seen. So there is a lot of water on Earth! Now I want you to read like a detective. By yourself, read again the first paragraph on page 7, and find out why we cannot use most of the water on Earth. [Allow students time to read, and then take responses, leading them to understand that most of the water is salt water, which cannot be used for drinking or for watering plants that we need to eat.]

**FIGURE 8.3** *Water, Water Everywhere, Pages 6 and 7*

*Source:* Rowland Reading Foundation (2009b)

**DETERMINE KEY IDEAS AND DETAILS** → I would like someone to go back into the text and read a sentence for me that tells us why we don't have a lot of water that we can drink. [Have a student find and read, "Most of it is ocean water, which is too salty to drink."]

What does *salt-free* mean? How do you know? [Guide students to find the sentence where the text reads "salt-free, or fresh."]

So another name for salt-free water is *fresh* water. Let me read the last paragraph to you. [Read the last paragraph.]

**DETERMINE KEY IDEAS AND DETAILS** → So I can conclude that fresh water means water that is not salty, and it is the water we need for drinking.

**USE PRIOR KNOWLEDGE** → Have you ever tasted salt water? What was it like? Were you surprised by the taste? If not, think about what it would taste like. Would it be easy to drink? Why or why not?

There is one last part of this page I want you to read. It is the red text, which I earlier called a sidebar. This means that it is not really part of the main text in this article, but it adds important information. Go ahead and read that to yourself. [Allow time for students to read.]

There is one word I want to make sure we all understand. It is the last word on the page. Can someone read that to me? It is a long word, so I'm guessing you read it by dividing the word into two parts: *drink* and *able*. But when you actually read it, it is not pronounced like those two separate words. When we read it, we change the long a in able to a schwa sound, a little like a short u sound. Let's pronounce it together.

*Drinkable* means something that is good and healthy to drink; let me use it in a sentence for you: He spat out the water from the swimming pool because it wasn't drinkable. [Ask students to generate sentences using the word *drinkable*.] Were there any other words that were tricky for you on this page? [If there were, help students read the word and generate meaning.]

ASK AND ANSWER QUESTIONS

DETERMINE KEY IDEAS AND DETAILS

MONITOR COMPREHENSION AND USE FIX-UP TIPS

**Page 8:** Before we read the next article, I want to tell you about what we will be learning. We will read to find out about the Earth's natural water cycle and the human-made cycle that brings water from rivers and lakes to our homes and back again. So the first word I need you to know is *cycle*. You might know *cycle* from *bicycle* or *tricycle*. The word *cycle* in those words means "circular." *Bi* means two, and *tri* means three. So a bicycle has two circular wheels, and a tricycle has three circular wheels. Something that is circular has no beginning and no end. In this article, we'll be reading about the water cycle, but it doesn't have anything to do with wheels! The word *cycle* in this case also means "no beginning and no end." A cycle is a process that repeats itself in the same order; the seasons of the year—spring, summer, winter, fall—make a complete cycle. So the *water cycle* refers to the series of events where water gets used over and over again.

Another word I need you to know is *vapor*. So as you read the first page, be looking for that word and thinking of how you can explain vapor to me.

**Have Students Read Page 8:** Look at the diagram (see Figure 8.4). Let's begin at the lake where the star tells us to start. What kind of lake is this? [Have students read "freshwater lake."] Look at the wiggly arrows pointing up. Follow them up with your fingers. What does the caption tell us these arrows mean? [Have a student read the caption.] How does the diagram show us the water vapor is moving? [Guide students to respond that the wiggly arrows are designed to show movement.] Continue with your fingers to the clouds and fog. [Have a student read the caption.] So, now the water vapor is rising into the air. Can anyone tell me what *vapor* is? [Take responses. If students aren't able to explain *vapor*, provide them with a definition: *Vapor* means tiny drops of water in the air that can take the form of steam, fog, or clouds.] Here is a sentence with the word *vapor*: Even when I can't see vapor in the air, I can feel its moisture on hot, muggy days.

DETERMINE KEY IDEAS AND DETAILS

MAKE INFERENCES

ASK AND ANSWER QUESTIONS

INTERPRET INFORMATION FROM GRAPHS, CHARTS, AND DIAGRAMS

What do you think the next page is going to explain? [Take student responses, guiding them to the conclusion that the next page will tell them how the cycle goes back to the beginning.]

**Page 9:** Now I want you to read the first paragraph on page 9. I want you to read carefully to be able to answer the question, "What happens when vapor cools?" [Have students read.] Now I want you to explain to a partner what happens when vapor cools. [Monitor responses to make sure the students understand that when vapor cools, it forms drops of water.] Now I want you to find out what makes the water drops into rain. What makes them into snow or hail? [Students respond.] Read me the text that confirms your answers.

## The Never-Ending Story

The water that we drink has been on Earth since our planet was formed. New water never gets made. The same water just keeps moving around and getting recycled.

How does that happen? The sun warms water in oceans and lakes. Some of the water gets so hot that it turns to vapor. Most of the time, we can't see the vapor. The vapor rises into the air.

When vapor cools, it forms little drops of water. Those tiny drops are what make steam, fog, and clouds. When the drops of water get large and heavy, they become rain. If the water drops freeze in the cold air, they turn to snow or hail. Drops of fallen rain and melted snow trickle deep into the ground or flow into rivers, lakes, and oceans.

Water in the ocean is salty. When salt water turns to vapor, the salt gets left behind in the ocean. That's why rain is never salty!

All of the water in the world has been going through this cycle for a long, long time. In fact, the water you drink today is the same water dinosaurs used to drink!

**FIGURE 8.4** *The Never-Ending Story*, Pages 8 and 9

*Source:* Rowland Reading Foundation (2009a)

DETERMINE KEY IDEAS AND DETAILS

MAKE INFERENCES

ASK AND ANSWER QUESTIONS

INTERPRET INFORMATION FROM GRAPHS, CHARTS, AND DIAGRAMS

[Students should read "When drops of water get large and heavy, they become rain. If the water drops freeze in the cold air, they turn to snow or hail."]

Go ahead and read the rest of page 9 and be able to tell your neighbor why rain is not salty. [Students read and respond. Monitor responses to be sure students understand that when salt water turns to vapor, the salt gets left behind in the ocean.] Is there anything surprising or interesting you learned from this text today? I know I was surprised to learn that the water we drink is the same water the dinosaurs drank! [Take responses.]

DETERMINE KEY IDEAS AND DETAILS

MAKE INFERENCES

Let's look at the entire diagram on pages 8–9. Find the labels under the clouds that show rain and snow. Next to the clouds on page 9, it says drops of rain and melted snow run into the rivers, lakes, or ground. I can see the "freshwater river" label right below this, so the rain and snow must go into this river. Then where does that river water flow? [Guide students to see that it goes back to the freshwater lake.] So that shows us what

INTERPRET INFORMATION FROM GRAPHS, CHARTS, AND DIAGRAMS

we just read in the text. The cycle starts in a freshwater lake, moves into the clouds, and comes back down into the freshwater river that flows into the freshwater lake. Use your finger to start at the lake, move up into the clouds, back down to the river, and then over to the lake. Do you see how your finger is making a circle? That circle is the water cycle.

INTERPRET INFORMATION FROM GRAPHS, CHARTS, AND DIAGRAMS

Look at the part of the diagram on page 9 labeled "saltwater ocean." Using your finger, trace for me the water cycle from the ocean. [Monitor students to make sure they create a counterclockwise circle going from the ocean to "freshwater vapor" to "drops of rain and melted snow run into rivers and lakes or the ground" back to the freshwater river and the ocean.]

**Page 10:** (See Figure 8.5.) So you have learned about the water cycle on the earth, how water keeps moving around and around, from the earth to the sky and back again. Now we will read about another kind of water cycle, the one that explains how water gets into some of our homes and where it goes when it leaves those homes. Let's start by looking at the question on page 9. [Have a student read the question, "How does water get to your faucet?"] Boys and girls, what did you notice about the print? Yes, it is blue. Look at the key right below the text. Notice the blue pipe. What does the blue pipe show? [Guide students to respond that the blue pipe will show how clean water travels.] So if we follow the blue pipe, I think it means we will answer the question in blue: "How does water get to your faucet?" Put your finger on the diagram and find where it says "start here." Follow the blue pipe. Does it show us how the water gets from the lake to the house? [Guide students to respond that it does.] Now I want you to follow your finger again, but this time stop when you have a word or words to read. [Guide students to start by reading "lake," and then follow the blue pipe and read "pumping station," "water treatment plant," "underground pipes," and "storage tower" as they follow the pipe to the home.] Where does our water come from first? How does it get out of the lake? [Guide students to respond that the water begins in the lake and that there are pumps in the pumping station that pump the water out of the lake.] Where does it go next? What happens in a water treatment plant? [Guide students to understand that the water is pumped through the water treatment plant, where it is cleansed.] Now here is where it gets a little tricky. All the clean water is stored in the storage tower. Then notice that there are three homes where the blue pipes are going. What does that mean? [Guide students to understand that all the homes receive the clean water from the storage tower.]

INTERPRET INFORMATION FROM GRAPHS, CHARTS, AND DIAGRAMS

ASK AND ANSWER QUESTIONS

Look at the blue pipes in the house. What rooms do the pipes go to? [Guide students to respond basement (furnace, washer), kitchen (sink), bathrooms (sink, toilet, tub).]

INTERPRET INFORMATION FROM GRAPHS, CHARTS, AND DIAGRAMS

DETERMINE KEY IDEAS AND DETAILS

MAKE INFERENCES

[Note: Some houses get water directly from underground wells, but this diagram was designed to show how water gets to houses when they don't have their own water supply.]

Now I want you to read the text on page 10 to see if everything we discovered in the diagram is correct. [Students read.] Did you notice any new information or anything that was different from what we read? [Take responses.] What other questions do you have about clean water in your homes? [Take responses.]

ASK AND ANSWER QUESTIONS

MAKE INFERENCES

COMPARE AND CONTRAST TEXT AND PICTURES

DETERMINE KEY IDEAS AND DETAILS

**Page 11:** The last page we are going to read today will answer what question? [Guide students to read, "Where does the water go once you have used it?"] What color pipes will we be following for this segment? How do you know? [Guide students to find the key and to discover that the yellow pipe will show dirty water.]

MAKE INFERENCES

INTERPRET INFORMATION FROM GRAPHS, CHARTS, AND DIAGRAMS

Before you read, there is a word you need to know: *sewer.* Say it with me. A sewer is an underground drain that carries away waste water. Here is how I might use it in a sentence: The ball rolled into the storm sewer so we couldn't play ball anymore. [Ask students to generate sentences using *sewer.*]

USE PRIOR KNOWLEDGE

DETERMINE KEY IDEAS AND DETAILS

I would like you to read the paragraph for yourself. [Allow students time to read.] So let's see what we learned. Start by putting your finger at the bathtub. Picture that water from the bath going down through the yellow pipe. Follow your finger down and over, and name the places where the water goes. [Monitor students to make sure they read "sewer" and "sewage treatment plant."] After the sewage treatment plant, why does the pipe turn blue again? [Guide students to understand that the sewage treatment plant turns the water clean, so the clean water goes back to the river.] Where does it go from there? [Guide students to understand that the river flows back to the lake.] How is this a cycle? [Guide students to understand that this process repeats over and over again.]

MAKE INFERENCES

ASK AND ANSWER QUESTIONS

COMPARE AND CONTRAST TEXT AND PICTURES

DETERMINE KEY IDEAS AND DETAILS

INTERPRET INFORMATION FROM GRAPHS, CHARTS, AND DIAGRAMS

SUMMARIZE AND SYNTHESIZE

**FIGURE 8.5** *The Never-Ending Story,* Pages 10 and 11

*Source:* Rowland Reading Foundation (2009a).

There is one last thing I want to point out to you in your reading. I want to read one sentence for you: "The dirty water flows to a sewage treatment plant." The text doesn't tell us what sewage is, but I can figure it out. Here is how. First of all, the author did tell me how to pronounce it, with the "say it: Soo-ij" clue. I just finished reading that dirty water goes to a sewer, and the words *sewer* and *sewage* start the same. So the word *sewage* must have something to do with dirty water. Then I read on to learn that the "dirty water flows to a sewage treatment plant." So the treatment plant treats sewage, which must be the same as the dirty water. Does that make sense? So as I am reading, if I come to a word I don't know, it is important to stop and use the text clues to help me figure it out. Remember, we call these fix-up tips: rereading, looking at pictures or illustrations, thinking about what makes sense, recalling details. [Refer to the fix-up tips chart in the room to remind children of these strategies.]

MONITOR COMPREHENSION AND USE FIX-UP TIP

Did you use any fix up tips today? [Take responses.]

DETERMINE KEY IDEAS AND DETAILS

SUMMARIZE AND SYNTHESIZ

**Wrapping Up the Reading:** What was our purpose for reading? Did we accomplish that purpose? Let's chart what we learned today. [Guide students to recall that we read to find out how much water we have on earth and how we need to share it. We also read to find out where all that water comes from and where it goes. We read to learn about the water cycle. Chart if feasible.]

DETERMINE KEY IDEAS AND DETAILS

SUMMARIZE AND SYNTHESIZ

Why do you think this article is called "The Never-Ending Story"? [Take students' responses, guiding them to understand that the cycle never ends.]

DETERMINE KEY IDEAS AND DETAILS

SUMMARIZE AND SYNTHESIZ

MAKE INFERENCES

Was it important to read "Water, Water Everywhere" before "The Never-Ending Story"? [Take student responses, guiding them to think about the first article's main idea, that water is relatively scarce. The second article explained how, if water is scarce, we can continue to receive and use water.]

> **TIP**
>
> Fix-up tips include the following:
>
> - Reread
> - Look at pictures and illustrations
> - Think about what makes sense
> - Read ahead
> - Sequence events or steps
> - Recall details
> - Summarize

At this point, you have read Mr. Morris's selected scripts from Lesson Steps 1 and 2 from the lesson plan template. Before we go on to Lesson Steps 3 and 4, pause and jot down your thoughts about these concepts:

Mr. Morris develops vocabulary for the reading by identifying words he believes children need to know and don't. He has the children pronounce each of these words, and he provides a student-friendly definition and example sentences. Often, he will ask students to also generate example sentences. How can you use this routine within your reading groups?

Informational text often has charts, graphs, diagrams, and other visual supports. Sometimes children may want to skip the reading and just gather information from the visuals. How do you sustain the balance between the visuals and the text, helping children primarily utilize text, but support the text with the visuals?

How would you have changed any parts of this lesson to meet the specific needs of your students?

## Moving to Lesson Steps 3 and 4

Many of us assume, when we conduct a guided reading, that we are "over teaching" the text—that perhaps if we interrupt the reading too much, we don't allow the students time to read deeply and discover meaning for themselves. Mr. Morris feels the same way but offers this advice:

When I plan lessons around informational text, I try to always keep in mind the big ideas or essential information I want my children to take away. So it helps me to keep my guidance and questioning focused. I also like to use the action step questions as I plan my lessons, because they provide options within each lesson step to support my thinking. Finally, I usually write the lesson with several ideas and options, knowing that I will be responsive to the students as we move through the lesson. For example, I think ahead and write child-friendly definitions for the vocabulary words, and I even generate some context sentences so I'm not caught short. But sometimes kids in one group may already know the word's meaning, so I don't need to use that part of my lesson plan for that group.

Good advice! Use the lesson plan template as a framework for guiding children through text; use the action step questions to guide your thinking about *how* to guide them to understandings. These planning tools will help you internalize solid lesson structures; this kind of preparation ultimately frees you up to be more responsive to the children within your group.

Moving on to Lesson Steps 3 and 4 (Figures 8.6 and 8.7), you'll notice that Mr. Morris plans for the different readers in his groups, in a similar format to the first grade model lesson in Chapter 7. Remember that the power of Lesson Step 3 is to bridge reading from the core skills-based instruction to application in grade-level informational text. Lesson Step 3 always comes after the comprehension-focused Lesson Steps 1 and 2.

| Step in the Lesson | Action Steps |
| --- | --- |
| Explicitly teach from the text.<br><br>(Choose one focus area for each group of students) | • Are my students able to decode this text? If not, what phonetic elements and decoding strategies do they need to work on? How can I utilize words or passages from this text to practice decoding?<br>• Are my students fluent readers? How can I model fluency in this text? Can I follow up the reading with shared and unison reading for practicing fluency? Are there other ways for students to utilize this text for fluency building (assisted reading with CD, partner reading, choral reading)?<br>• Which comprehension skills and strategies are needed to comprehend this text? How can I teach one of those skills or strategies explicitly? What practice opportunities can I follow up with to allow my students to apply that skill or strategy?<br>• What fix-up tips can I teach based on the reading of the text that will allow students to learn self-help skills in their independent reading? |

**FIGURE 8.6** Lesson Step 3: Explicitly Teach From the Text

| Step in the Lesson | Action Steps |
| --- | --- |
| Facilitate connections.<br><br>(Choose one focus area for each group of students.) | • Does this text experience authentically lend itself to making connections in writing, technology, additional text reading, content areas, or the fine arts? How can I formulate a meaningful follow-up activity to make these connections? |

**FIGURE 8.7** Lesson Step 4: Facilitate Connections

# MY LESSON PLAN

**For Students Who Are Still Working on Decoding:** Let's return to page 7. [On the white board, write *mostly, many, salty, only, tiny.*] Let's read these words together. [Read through list.] What do you notice? [Guide students to notice that these are all words where the ending *y* represents the /e/ sound.]

[Add to the list: *very, penny, puppy, messy, silly, cry, sky, fly.*] Let's read these words together. [Read through list.] What do you notice? [Guide students to notice that sometimes the ending *y* represents the long /e/ sound, and sometimes it represents the long /i/.] What are the differences between these words? [Do a word sort, where you list all the /e/ words in one column and the /i/ words in another. Determine when *y* represents /e/ (two-syllable words) and when it represents /i/ (single syllable words). Brainstorm other words that fit those categories.]

[Practice reading word list. Return to page 7 and have students read sentences (or words) containing –*y* endings. Add to the columns.]

**For Students Who Can Decode But Are Working on Building Fluency:** Boys and girls, I want to return to page 6 and read aloud of the first paragraph. [Model a reading with incorrect phrasing, ignoring punctuation, pausing repeatedly. Then model fluent reading.] What did you notice about my two readings? [Guide students to discuss how the second model used natural phrasing, which made it easier to understand.]

[Divide the pages into three paragraphs. Conduct a choral reading with all three. Have children partner up and do a partner reading with one of the paragraphs. Make the recorded reading available in the listening center.]

**For Students Who Are Reading Well, Use This Text for Building Ability to Monitor Comprehension and Use Fix-Up Tips.** When we are reading and something doesn't make sense, we can use pictures or diagrams or charts to help us understand. Look back at pages 10–11. Cover up the pictures and just read the text. Are there parts that are confusing? [Take responses from students. If they don't identify any confusing parts, share that without the diagram, we are left to visualize, and if we don't know what a water treatment plant is or haven't been shown one, or if we don't know what a water tower is or haven't been shown one, this entire water cycle is very difficult to visualize.] What does the diagram allow us to do as we read the text? [Guide students to understand that the diagram confirms the text.] On the other hand, let's look just at the diagram and see if we would be missing any information if we didn't have the text. [Guide students to understand that the diagram alone doesn't provide all the details; for example, the text helps them pronounce two key words. The text clarifies that once the clean water goes back to the river, it then goes from there to lakes or oceans, which isn't really clear from the diagram alone.] It is important to use the pictures as we read to assist us in getting meaning from the text. But it is important to remember that we can't get accurate and detailed information from the diagram alone. Look at our poster of fix-up tips, and point to the one I am modeling for you now. [Guide students to point to "look at pictures and illustrations." Make sure they understand that pictures are designed to confirm meaning, not to replace text.]

## Possible Ideas for This Text

- **Science:** Demonstrate how water evaporates by leaving drops of water on a window ledge or under a light bulb.
- **Fine arts:** Act out the water cycle.
- **Additional reading:** Read an excerpt from "The Rime of the Ancient Mariner" by Samuel Taylor Coleridge, and ask students what this line means: "Water, water everywhere, nor any drop to drink."

Learn more about the water cycle: www.epa.gov

## Second Grade Informational Text Standards Included

**TIP**

Keeping a chart of the CCSS for your grade, and checking off standards as you address them throughout the year, is a great way to stay grounded in the standards as you develop lesson plans.

As Mr. Morris prepares his lessons, he considers the Common Core State Standards and how he will work toward meeting the standards within his guided reading experiences. He finds it helpful to always return to the end-of-year standards and check off how he is progressing as he formulates his lessons. An example of how this lesson included second-grade Informational Text Standards is included in Figure 8.8. A copy of this checklist is included in Appendix B of this volume.

## Other Standards Addressed

In addition to the Informational Text Standards checked off on the chart in Figure 7.15, these standards from other areas were included in this lesson plan:

### SPEAKING AND LISTENING STANDARDS (NGA/CCSSO, 2010B, P. 23)

- Participate in collaborative conversations with diverse partners about Grade 2 topics and texts with peers and adults in small and larger groups.
- Recount or describe key ideas or details from a text read aloud or information presented orally or through other media.

### LANGUAGE STANDARDS (NGA/CCSSO, 2010B, P. 27)

- Determine or clarify the meaning of unknown and multiple-meaning words and phrases based on Grade 2 reading and content, choosing flexibly from an array of strategies.
- Demonstrate understanding of word relationships and nuances in word meanings.

## In Summary

By the time students reach second grade, "complex text" is more fully defined within quantitative guidelines of the Common Core. The complexity of the texts they are reading requires that they have grade-level proficiency. While we are continuing to build and

### Key Ideas and Details

Ask and answer such questions as who, what, where, when, why, and how to demonstrate understanding of key details in a text. ✓

Identify the main topic of a multiparagraph text as well as the focus of specific paragraphs within the text. ✓

Describe the connection between a series of historical events, scientific ideas or concepts, or steps in technical procedures in a text. ✓

### Craft and Structure

Determine the meaning of words and phrases in a text relevant to a grade 2 topic or subject area. ✓

Know and use various text features to locate key facts or information in a text efficiently. ✓

Identify the main purpose of a text, including what the author wants to answer, explain, or describe. ✓

### Integration of Knowledge and Ideas

Explain how specific images contribute to and clarify a text. ✓

Describe how reasons support specific points the author makes in a text. ✓

Compare and contrast the most important points presented by two texts on the same topic. ✓

### Range of Reading and Level of Text Complexity

By the end of year, read and comprehend informational texts, including history/ social studies, science, and technical texts, in the grades 2–3 text complexity band proficiently, with scaffolding as needed at the high end of the range. ✓

**FIGURE 8.8** Second Grade Standards for Informational Text

*Source:* NGA/CCSSO (2010b, p. 13). Copyright © 2010 National Governors Association Center for Best Practices and Council of Chief State School Officers. All rights reserved.

support the development of the foundational skills for those second graders who are not yet fluent, we are ensuring all students have access to high-quality informational text written at grade level. This requires a nuanced understanding of how to approach a text with readers who may not have the skills to independently read that text. The lesson plan template allows us as teachers to keep an eye on the big ideas (essential information) we want our children to know while adapting the lesson to meet the unique needs of each reader.

According to the CCSS, "Students who struggle greatly to read texts within (or even below) their text complexity grade band must be given the support needed to enable them to read at a grade-appropriate level of complexity" (NGA/CCSSO, 2010a, p. 9). What have you learned from the lesson samples about how you can support all students in utilizing grade-appropriate text? Specifically, how will you support using grade-level text with students who are not yet reading at grade level?

What other texts will you be utilizing in your instruction besides grade-level informational text?

Have you had students like the ones identified by Mr. Morris, students who appeared to be on track but are starting to fall apart as text becomes more complex? How will you go back and fill in the gaps that are apparent, especially in the area of phonetic decoding?

# 9

# Embedding Informational Texts in Units of Study

Ok, you now have specific criteria you can use to select high-quality informational literature, and you are ready to use the lesson plan template in your classroom. But there's more! In this final chapter we'll explore how informational text experiences fit within the broader context of interdisciplinary units of study and within the balance of literary experiences in your classroom. Finally, we'll close with a few thoughts about meeting the Common Core State Standards for Informational Literature.

## An Interdisciplinary Focus

Current research within the fields of science and social studies supports interdisciplinary approaches for developing young students' vocabulary, conceptual, and content knowledge (Goldschmidt, 2010; Halvorsen et al., 2012; Vitale & Romance, 2011). Not surprisingly, within and across the CCSS English Language Arts Standards, we see a strong and growing across-the-curriculum emphasis on student ability not only to read and comprehend informational text but also to use knowledge gained from those texts to support opinions and arguments as well as informative/explanatory speaking and writing. The support we see within the CCSS for interdisciplinary instruction is tied to a systematic progression of carefully crafted units of study. As stated in the *Common Core State Standards for English Language Arts & Literacy in History/Social Studies, Science, and Technical Subjects,*

> Building knowledge systematically in English language arts is like giving children various pieces of a puzzle in each grade that, over time, will form one big picture. At a curricular or instruction level, texts—with and across grade levels—need to be selected around topics or themes that systemically develop the knowledge base of students. (NGA/CCSSO, 2010b, p. 33)

Although the Common Core State Standards for the elementary grades include only Standards for English language arts and mathematics, movement toward identification of common standards in other disciplines has followed. For example, the newly released Next Generation Science Standards for K–12 (see http://nextgenscience.org), based on the *Framework for K–12 Science Education* developed by the National Research Council (2012), provide guidance for both instructional content and practice. In 2010, the same year the Common Core State Standards were issued, the National Council on Social Studies published a revised version of their national curriculum standards for social studies, *National Curriculum Standards for Social Studies: A Framework for Teaching, Learning, and Assessment. These include standards for the early grades, middle grades, and high school, and they state clearly what students in the elementary, middle, and high school grades should know and be able to do with respect to 10 broad themes of social studies.*

The Common Core State Standards, along with those from the content areas, provide us with the big pictures that all students should develop by the end of their K–12 school experience. To ensure that our students are forming these big pictures, we must carefully and systematically provide the specific curricular pieces appropriate for each grade level. With these ideas in mind, how do we design interdisciplinary instruction that enables us to *systematically* develop students' content knowledge *and* literacy skills?

## Planning Units of Study: Who Does What?

Planning of interdisciplinary units for today's classrooms must be a collaborative endeavor based upon shared standards. Consider again the puzzle metaphor: The goal is for students to acquire more and more puzzle pieces in each grade level, so that by the time they graduate from high school, they possess "big pictures"—that is, key content and conceptual knowledge related to each discipline. Without a systematic progression of content and conceptual knowledge, teachers at each grade level run the risk of providing students with pieces of, at best, loosely related puzzles. Students could receive a few puzzle pieces related to bears, oceans, and fruits and vegetables in kindergarten. In Grade 1 they might receive a few puzzle pieces related to dinosaurs, penguins, the five senses, and community helpers. Similarly, Grade 2 teachers may provide them with a few pieces related to planets, seasons, weather, and plants. If this scenario continues, by the time the students graduate from high school, they will have thousands of puzzle pieces, but few complete puzzles. In contrast, curricula based on a systematic progression of concepts and content knowledge will enable students to fit the pieces together in a way that permits deep understanding.

## Identifying Goals and Objectives

Adherence to shared standards for social studies and science, across grade levels, enables teachers to better determine "who does what" with respect to the teaching of specific content knowledge and skills. To illustrate this, let's examine the systematic progression of understandings related to the human body found in this example from the Common Core State Standards document (see Figure 9.1).

From the example shown in Figure 9.1, it is very easy to see which pieces of the puzzle would be included in the curriculum at each grade level from K through 3. Once this has been determined, teachers at each level can begin to plan instruction that incorporates application of the CCSS for English Language Arts—reading, writing, speaking and listening—into the discipline-specific area of study. The chart in Figure 9.2 provides a suggested sequence of steps to help you get started.

## Balancing Teacher- and Child-Initiated Learning Experiences

An important consideration when planning an interdisciplinary unit of study is a balance of teacher-directed and child-initiated learning opportunities. Teacher-directed learning experiences that promote use and understanding of informational text would include the types of lessons demonstrated in Chapters 6 through 8:

- Engaging students in a discussion about their prior knowledge about the topic
- Conducting a shared reading of an informational big book related to the unit topic
- Reading aloud to students from multiple nonfiction texts related to the topic, pausing periodically to think aloud about text features, new vocabulary and/or concepts presented
- Guiding students' reading in grade-appropriate text with information about the topic
- Modeling and guiding students' writing of informational and opinion pieces

Child-initiated experiences might include activities such as the following:

- Self-selected reading on related subtopics
- Peer discussions and sharing of ideas and opinions about an aspect of the unit that holds special interest or relevance for the student
- Inquiry projects prompted by whole group discussion, reading, or topic-related resources and materials brought into the classroom during the unit

### The Five Senses and Associated Body Parts

- *My Five Senses* by Aliki
- *Hearing* by Maria Rius
- *Sight* by Maria Rius
- *Smell* by Maria Rius
- *Taste* by Maria Rius
- *Touch* by Maria Rius

### Taking Care of Your Body

- *My Amazing Body: A First Look at Health and Fitness* by Pat Thomas
- *Get Up and Go!* by Nancy Carlson
- *Go Wash Up* by Doering Tourville
- *Sleep* by Paul Showers
- *Fuel the Body* by Doering Tourville

## The Human Body: Grade 1

### Introduction to Systems of the Human Body and Body Parts

- *Under Your Skin: Your Amazing Body* by Mick Manning
- *Me and My Amazing Body* by Joan Sweeny
- *The Human Body* by Gallimard Jeunesse
- *The Busy Body Book* by Lizzy Rockwell
- *First Encyclopedia of the Human Body* by Fiona Chandler

### Taking Care of Your Body: Germs, Diseases, and Preventing Illness

- *Germs Make Me Sick* by Marilyn Berger
- *Tiny Life on Your Body* by Christine Taylor-Butler
- *Germ Stories* by Arthur Kornberg
- *All About Scabs* by Genichiro Yagu

## The Human Body: Grades 2 to 3

### Digestive and Excretory Systems

- *What Happens to a Hamburger* by Paul Showers
- *The Digestive System* by Rebecca Johnston
- The Digestive System by Kristin Petrie

### Taking Care of Your Body: Healthy Eating and Nutrition

- *Good Enough to Eat* by Lizzy Rockwell
- *Showdown at the Food Pyramid* by Rex Barron

### Muscular, Skeletal, and Nervous Systems

- *The Mighty Muscular and Skeletal Systems* (Crabtree Pub.)
- *Muscles* by Seymour Simon

- *Bones* by Seymour Simon
- *The Astonishing Nervous System* (Crabtree Pub.)
- *The Nervous System* by Joelle Riley

**FIGURE 9.1** Sample Progression of Units Related to the Human Body

*Source:* NGA/CCSSO (2010b, p. 33). Copyright © 2010 National Governors Association Center for Best Practices and Council of Chief State School Officers. All rights reserved.

## Selecting High-Quality Informational Literature for Units of Study

In Chapter 3 we discussed criteria for selecting stellar nonfiction, and then in subsequent chapters we demonstrated techniques for planning and implementing lessons designed to move K–2 students toward mastery of the CCSS for Informational Text. Now let's talk about selecting nonfiction texts to support interdisciplinary units of study. A range of texts on your selected topic will be needed to support both teacher- and child-initiated learning experiences. These need to include both texts designed to be read aloud by the teacher and texts that might be used in a guided reading situation. Still other texts might be selected for students to use independently as they gain new information about the topic through reading and/or examination of illustrations.

To help you get started, we've compiled a list of books for a number of themes commonly included within the K–2 classroom curriculum. In Appendix D you will find a selection of more recently published books with a few classic titles included for the following topics: animals, birds, civics/citizenship, culture, dinosaurs, ecology, family, five senses, friendship, garden, habitats, healthy living, holidays/special celebrations, human body, insects, jobs, life cycle of animals, natural disasters, ocean animals, pets, plants, presidents and their families, ranch/farm life, reptiles, safety, seasons, space, sports and recreation, transportation, and weather. You'll also find books for curriculum-based topics, such as the alphabet, biographies, geography, history, maps, math, measurement, money, patterns/symmetry, physical science/chemistry/simple machines, science, and space. Appendix E contains an annotated bibliography for the books listed in Appendix D, with notations indicating (1) the number of pages; (2) whether the book contains a table of contents, glossary, and/or index; (3) use of photos and/or illustrations; (4) use of captions; (5) if the book is part of a leveled book series; and (6) availability of the book in big book format.

## Providing a Balance of Texts

As you reflect on the big picture of your classroom library and meeting the Common Core State Standards, overall, it is important to remember that children need a balance of literature to promote wide reading across multiple genres. Although the emphasis of this text is nonfiction text, literature for children in the early grades encompasses an expansive range—from nursery rhymes and concepts books to picture books, beginning

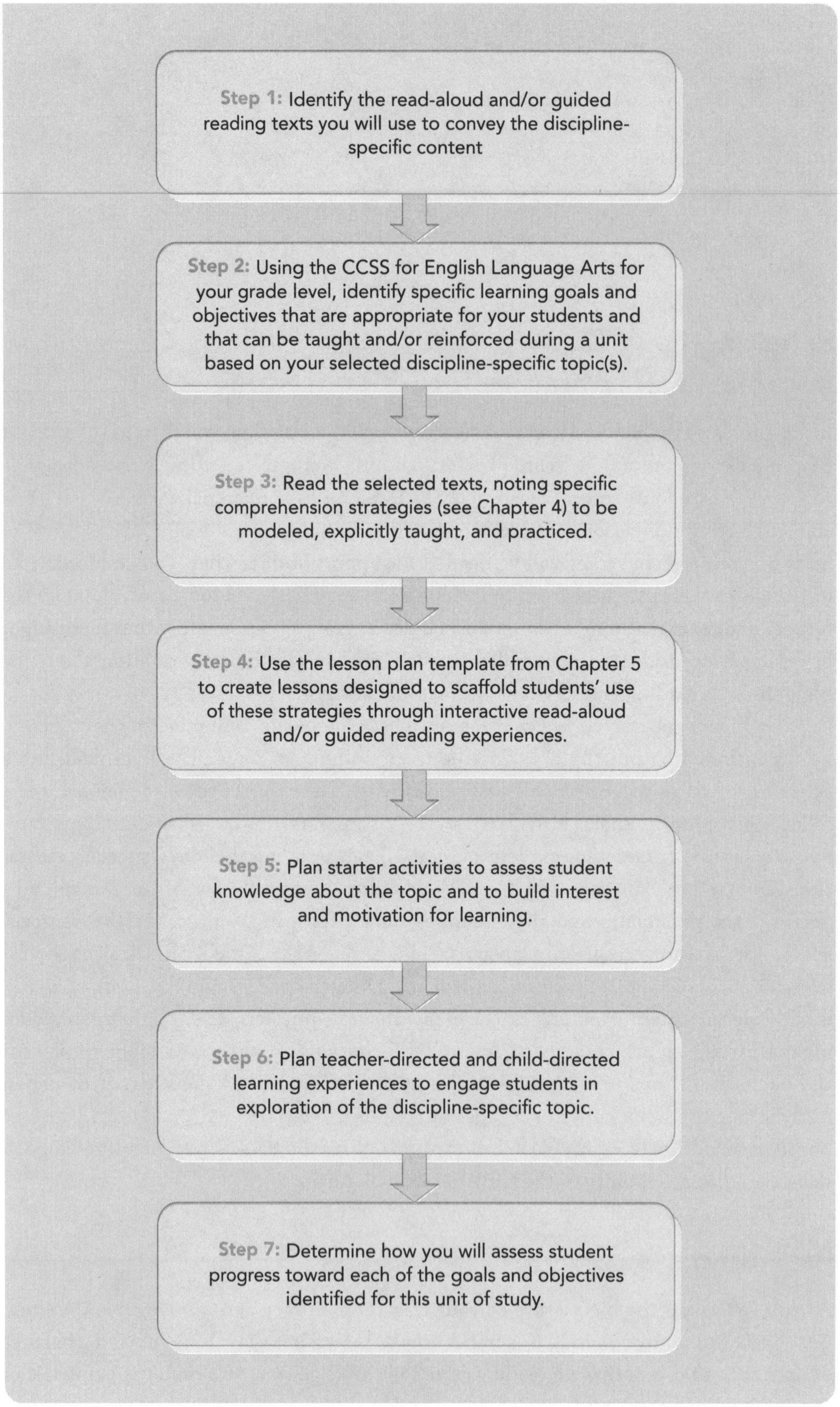

**Step 1:** Identify the read-aloud and/or guided reading texts you will use to convey the discipline-specific content

**Step 2:** Using the CCSS for English Language Arts for your grade level, identify specific learning goals and objectives that are appropriate for your students and that can be taught and/or reinforced during a unit based on your selected discipline-specific topic(s).

**Step 3:** Read the selected texts, noting specific comprehension strategies (see Chapter 4) to be modeled, explicitly taught, and practiced.

**Step 4:** Use the lesson plan template from Chapter 5 to create lessons designed to scaffold students' use of these strategies through interactive read-aloud and/or guided reading experiences.

**Step 5:** Plan starter activities to assess student knowledge about the topic and to build interest and motivation for learning.

**Step 6:** Plan teacher-directed and child-directed learning experiences to engage students in exploration of the discipline-specific topic.

**Step 7:** Determine how you will assess student progress toward each of the goals and objectives identified for this unit of study.

**FIGURE 9.2** Planning for Interdisciplinary Learning

chapter books, and informational books. An important part of becoming an effective lifelong reader is learning to love books, something more likely to happen when students have access to a wide selection of books and to teachers with expertise about varying types of literature. To this end, let's look at how books are categorized and classified. Our overall goal is to equip you with the knowledge and skills needed to provide your K–2 students with a strong balance of both fiction and nonfiction literature.

## *What's in Your Classroom Library?*

There are a number of different ways to categorize and classify texts. On a very basic level, texts can be grouped into prose or poetry, narrative or expository, fiction or nonfiction. These categories can be further divided. For example, fiction may be fantasy or realistic; realistic may be contemporary realistic or historical. Similarly, traditional literature—that is, stories, songs, and rhymes with unknown authorship passed down orally from generation to generation—can be divided into myths, fables, ballads, legends, tall tales, fairy tales, and rhymes (Anderson, 2013). These categories are not finite, as varying experts in the field of children's literature may use slightly different categories or labels; however, books for young children are typically classified by format and/or genre.

This leads us to an important question for this book: What's the difference between nonfiction and informational text? Although a brief explanation was given in Chapter 1, let's flesh this out a little more here. "Ninety-five percent of school and public libraries organize nonfiction text by the Dewey Decimal System" (Johnson, 2012, p. 281). This system includes 10 main classes: (1) computers, information, and general reference; (2) philosophy and psychology; (3) religion; (4) social sciences; (5) language; (6) science; (7) technology; (8) arts and recreation; (9) literature; and (10) history and geography. While all types of nonfiction text are important, not all are informational text. Although many people tend to use these terms—*nonfiction* and *informational text*—interchangeably, a distinction exists between the two. Nell Duke and Susan Bennett-Armistead are two leading researchers in the use of informational text for young children. In their book, *Reading and Writing Informational Text in the Primary Grades: Research-Based Practices* (2003), they discuss the distinction between nonfiction and informational text. Biography and nonfiction narrative, or "true stories," are nonfiction but not informational text, because their primary purpose is to tell of an event or series of events that have occurred.

Categorizing books by genre—by similar style, form, or content—provides us with a framework for talking about and selecting books representative of a range of text types. The chart shown in Figure 9.3 contains a brief description of each genre and major subgenre with examples of each.

One important feature not evident within the genre classification chart is the author's use of either expository or narrative prose. Expository writing is used in informational text, whereas narrative is used in both fiction and biography. Significant differences exist between most narrative and expository text, not the least of which is the primary purpose for which we read—to understand and enjoy a story, or to learn more about a topic of interest.

| Poetry | | Prose | | | |
| --- | --- | --- | --- | --- | --- |
| Nursery Rhymes | Poems | Fiction | Realism | Contemporary Realistic Fiction | Historical Fiction |
| Brief stories that have been passed down orally from generation to generation and are the beginning of poetry for children. | A kind of imaginative writing and artistic writing including ballads, narrative (story) poetry, and lyric poetry. | Stories created from the author's imagination, even though they may be based on real happenings. | Imaginative writing that reflects life as it is lived today or could have been lived in the past; stories are possible though not necessarily probable. | Possible, though not necessarily probable, stories with a contemporary setting. | Realistic stories set in the past involving fictional characters, historic figures in fictional situations, or a combination. |

**Nursery Rhymes**

Examples

*Pocketful of Posies, A Treasury of Nursery Rhymes* by Salley Mavor

*Favorite Nursery Rhymes from Mother Goose* by Scott Gustafson

**Contemporary Realistic Fiction**

Characteristics

- Plots include events that could actually happen.
- Settings are real or realistic places and modern times.
- Stories are often told from child's point of view.
- Author uses contemporary language that fits the characters and setting

Examples

*Alexander and the Terrible, Horrible, No Good, Very Bad Day* by Judith Viorst

*Amazing Grace* by Mary Hoffman

*Knuffle Bunny: A Cautionary Tale* by Mo Willems

**Historical Fiction**

Characteristics

- Setting is in the past.
- Author's style of writing may include words drawn from time and place of story.

| Poetry | Prose |
|---|---|
| **Examples**<br><br>*Cousins of Clouds, Elephant Poems* by Tracie Zimmer<br><br>*Red Sings from Treetops, a Year in Colors* by Joyce Sidman | • Characters, places, and plot events can be imaginary, or real persons and/or places may be used in combination with a fictional plot.<br>• Theme pertains not only to historical period but also to society.<br><br>**Examples**<br><br>*Aunt Harriet's Underground Railroad in the Sky* by Faith Ringold<br><br>*Dandelions* by Eve Bunting<br><br>**Modern Fantasy**<br><br>Stories that are created around another world or in the real world with fantasy occurrences (or a combination of the two); events, settings, or characters are outside the realm of possibility.<br><br>**Characteristics**<br><br>• Characters may include humans, personified objects or animals, or fantastic creatures.<br>• Setting may be in a realistic world or a completely imaginary world, or characters may travel between real and imaginary settings. |

*(Continued)*

| Poetry | Prose |
|---|---|

- Themes are universal (e.g., good versus evil, friendship, life-changing discoveries or insights).
- Reader is encouraged to suspend disbelief—to believe that seemingly unbelievable events could occur.

**Examples**

*Franklin* books by Paulette Bourgeois

*Arthur* books by Marc Brown

*The Little Engine That Could* by Watty Piper

*Duck and Goose* by Tad Hills

**Traditional Literature**

Stories written or "retold" from original versions that were passed orally from one generation to another with no recorded authorship.

**Characteristics**

- Characters have expected traits and behaviors (e.g., fairy godmother, prince, princess).
- Settings are often generalized ones with no specific place and only a feeling that story takes place "in the past."
- Plots are relatively brief and follow a logical, predictable sequence.

**Folktales**

Tales passed down by word of mouth.

**Examples**

*The Three Little Pigs*

*The Three Billy Goats Gruff*

*The Little Red Hen*

**Fairy Tales**

Tales dealing with magic and the supernatural.

**Examples**

*Jack and the Beanstalk*

*Cinderella*

*Sleeping Beauty*

**Myths and Legends**

Myths are invented to explain how some aspect of the world or its cultures came

(Continued)

| Poetry | Prose |
|---|---|

**Prose**

- Themes deal with basic values (good versus evil).
- Magic is often a key element in solving problems.

to be, whereas legends may have a foundation in historical truth.

Examples

*Johnny Appleseed*

*Hercules*

Tall Tales

Tales in which exaggeration is used to achieve humor in relaying stories about characters performing impossible acts.

Examples

*Paul Bunyan*

*John Henry*

Fables

Tales used to convey a moral.

Examples

*The Town Mouse and the Country Mouse*

*The Tortoise and the Hare*

*Aesop's Fables*

Trickster Tales

Tales in which the characters play tricks on one another.

Examples

*Anansi the Spider*

*Iktomi and Coyote*

(Continued)

(Continued)

| Poetry | Prose | | |
|---|---|---|---|
| | Nonfiction | | |
| | Informational Books | Concept Books | Nonfiction Picture Books |
| | Texts written for the purpose of sharing factual or conceptual information to answer questions and satisfy the natural curiosity of the reader. | Books designed to help children explore basic concepts, such as shapes, colors, numerals, and letters. | A picture book format is used to convey factual information and ideas. |
| | Characteristics | Examples | Examples |
| | • Logical organization | *Eric Carle's ABC* by Eric Carle | *Who Has This Tail?* by Laura Hulbert |
| | • Clear, understandable words and phrases | *Shape by Shape* by Suse MacDonald | *A Den Is a Bed for a Bear* by Becky Baines |
| | • Wide range of topics | | *Alphabet of Ocean Animals* by Laura Gates Galvin |
| | • Realistic illustrations or photographs | | How-To Books |
| | | | Pictures and words are used to present a step-by-step process for completing a task. |
| | | | Examples |
| | | | *How to Make Bubbles* by Erika Shores |
| | | | *How to Make a Bouncing Egg* by Jennifer Marks |

| Poetry | Prose |
| --- | --- |
| | **Experiment and Activity Books**<br><br>Illustrated directions for completing hands-on experiments and activities.<br><br>**Examples**<br><br>*Nature in a Nutshell for Kids* by Jean Potter<br><br>*Art Lab for Kids: 52 Creative Adventures in Drawing, Painting, Printmaking, Paper, and Mixed Media* by Susan Schwake<br><br>**Authentic Biographies**<br><br>A factual and objective view of a person's life.<br><br>**Examples**<br><br>*My Name Is Celia/Me Llamo Celia, The Life of Celia Cruz* by Monica Brown<br><br>*The Watcher: Jane Goodall's Life with the Chimps* by Jeanette Winter<br><br>**Fictionalized Biographies**<br><br>A primarily factual view of a person's life in which authors may have changed the sequence of events or fictionalized the context of an event in an attempt to achieve a greater sense of story.<br><br>**Examples**<br><br>*If a Bus Could Talk: The Story of Rosa Parks* by Faith Ringold<br><br>*Maria's Comet* by Deborah Hopkinson |
| | **Biography**<br><br>A biography is a history of a person's life.<br><br>**Characteristics**<br><br>• Facts are gathered through research about the person and time period.<br>• Information is presented in a way that is suitable and appealing for the reader. |

**FIGURE 9.3** Genre Classifications and Examples

## Characteristics of Narrative and Expository Text

The structure of narrative text provides the reader with highly predictable elements—characters, setting, plot, and theme, all organized within a logical sequence of events. The reader expects to encounter a plot that will move the story forward, and knows to read the story from beginning to end. When reading fiction, the reader understands that the story did not actually happen. When reading biography, the reader understands that the events and facts presented did actually happen, even though the text is written as a story, and past tense is used.

Authors of expository text write in present tense and use completely different text structures that follow a logical order in the presentation of factual information (e.g., cause and effect, description, classification/example, problem/solution, and compare/contrast). While both narrative and expository texts may contain a table of contents, indexes and glossaries are typically included only within expository text. Other characteristics of expository text not found in narrative text are headings, subheadings, charts, tables, and other such means of graphically portraying the information for the reader. Unlike authors of narrative text, authors of expository text do not use dialogue, nor do they avoid use of technical vocabulary or discussion of abstract concepts.

Readers of expository text expect that what they read will be well organized, authentic, and accurate. They know the text does not have to be read from cover to cover, the information conveyed by the author can be read in any order, and that they are free to read just those portions of the text that are of interest. They also realize the need for a slower rate of reading than that used with narrative text. Understanding when and how to use visual text features (e.g., headings, subheadings, captions, charts, graphs, tables, indexes, and glossaries), effective readers are able to successfully gain information from expository text.

## Categorizing by Format

Books for younger readers are often categorized by format. *Format* refers to the way the book is made—how it looks, as opposed to what it says. Typically the purview of the publisher, format is heavily influenced by the illustrations, the text, and the audience. A book's format includes its overall size and shape, the weight of its pages, the font size, the spacing and placement of illustrations and text, its binding, and a whole host of other factors that impact a book's durability, appeal, and suitability for a particular audience and purpose. Consider, for example, the importance of sturdy pages in an interactive lift-the-flap or pop-up book, or the interest that an enlarged or big book version of an illustrated storybook generates among children in kindergarten or Grade 1 as they engage in shared reading of a familiar text. There are a number of popular formats used in books for young children. Picture books, wordless books, beginning or easy-to-read books, beginning chapter books, toy and board books, and books with unusual formats are among the most common.

### PICTURE BOOKS

While some sources include all picture books as a separate genre, more typically, when a book is described as a picture book, the description pertains to its format. The text in picture books can be prose or poetry, narrative or expository, fiction or nonfiction. It is important to note that not every book with pictures is considered a picture book, and not every picture book is suitable for young children. A picture book is a book in which pictures are used to convey the message with only a small amount of text. A good rule of thumb is if the book contains more pictures than words, it is classified under the umbrella heading of *picture book*. Picture books are generally 32 to 64 pages in length (in multiples of 16 because of the way the books are printed). The majority of picture books are 32 pages long, and often they do not have page numbers. Some picture books are intended primarily as read-aloud books; their illustrations and sometimes their text is large enough to be clearly visible to children in a group situation. Others, especially those picture books with smaller, more detailed illustrations, are best suited for individual readers, as are the easy-to-read books, another common book format for young readers.

Since the term *picture book* refers primarily to the format of the book, individuals of many ages can enjoy listening to and reading picture books. However, because picture books vary in complexity, the appropriateness of a specific picture book for any given learner will depend greatly upon the interest and prior knowledge of the individual. Careful evaluation of picture books in terms of both format and content is the key to their selection and use with young learners.

## WORDLESS BOOKS

Carefully sequenced illustrations are used to convey the story in wordless picture books, such as *Frog Goes to Dinner* (Mayer, 2003) and the Caldecott Award–winning *The Lion and the Mouse* (Pinkney, 2009). Wordless books are uniquely appropriate for use as instructional classroom tools. For example, children in kindergarten through Grade 2 will benefit from careful analysis and discussion of the characters and action. Teachers can also seize the opportunity to expand children's use of descriptors for characters and setting, and discuss use of temporal words (e.g., *first, then, next, finally*) to signal a sequence of events. Younger children can be engaged in creating a group-dictated version of the story, whereas older children can write their own written stories to accompany the illustrations.

## BEGINNING OR EASY-TO-READ BOOKS

Books to be read by children in the beginning stage of reading development are referred to as beginning or easy-to-read books. These books contain pictures, fewer words, and simple sentences and dialogue that serve to both engage and support young readers. Dr. Seuss's *The Cat in the Hat* is a classic book for beginning readers. The My First I Can Read and the I Can Read books for beginning readers, both by HarperCollins, include both fiction and nonfiction titles and are perfect for emergent readers and for readers who are just beginning to sound out words.

## CHAPTER AND SERIES BOOKS

Once children master the basics of reading, they are ready for easy or beginning chapter books. Beginning chapter books include several short chapters containing independent episodes. While a few illustrations are included, the text carries the story. The move from easy-to-read books into chapter books with fewer illustrations and more text can be quite challenging for many children. The familiar writing style and characters found in series books, such as those featuring Cam Jansen, Nate the Great, Judy Moody, and Junie

B. Jones, provide needed scaffolding for beginning readers. Similarly, nonfiction series books such as Scholastic's Welcome Books and National Geographic Readers contain a consistent format and element of predictability that enables young readers to tackle more complex informational topics. A suitable choice for independent reading, both fiction and nonfiction series books help children build skill and confidence as readers.

## *Reading Wide and Deep*

Key to the development of students' ability to read and respond to text at the level of proficiency mandated by the Common Core State Standards is our providing them with ample opportunities for both deep and wide reading in and across genres. As discussed in previous chapters, in the early grades we prepare students for the close reading of complex text required in the later grades. We do this through both read-aloud and scaffolded guided reading experiences. Since the challenge for many K–2 teachers is the identification and use of a sufficient number of high-quality informational texts, this has been the focus of our book. At the same time, we heartily acknowledge the importance of wide reading across genres. As many researchers have discovered (Kuhn, 2005; Kuhn et al., 2006), wide reading in different types of text (narrative, expository, and poetic), and across a range of genres (e.g., fantasy, fairy tales, myths, science fiction, historical fiction, biographies, autobiographies, information) builds good readers.

## Concluding Thoughts

Understanding all there is to know about the Common Core State Standards requires time and effort, and to translate the standards to everyday classroom instruction requires synthesizing a great deal of information. It is our hope that this book has offered clarity on the Standards and has provided you with practical, easy-to-use ideas to translate the Standards to classroom practice. To summarize the big ideas from this book,

- The Common Core State Standards provide us with a blueprint for teaching literacy, with the ultimate goal of leading us to college and career readiness for all students.
- The Common Core State Standards draw particular attention to the use of informational text in all grades, in preparation for real world reading.
- There is a great deal of research supporting the use of informational text in the primary grades.
- In choosing informational text for use in primary classrooms, it is important to consider visual appeal, accuracy, and engaging writing style.
- When utilizing informational text, we need to consider the distinct features of informational text in designing effective lessons. Primary readers present a unique challenge in that they are acquiring the foundational skills of reading as they access informational text. These foundational skills will need to be considered in designing differentiated lessons.

So, where to begin? If you have just finished this book and are wondering what first steps to take, we offer you this advice:

- It is helpful to keep in mind what is being taught in the grades both before and after the grade level at which you teach, so become more familiar with the CCSS for informational text for your grade, but also look at the "staircase of complexity" that moves from grade to grade.
- Both teachers and students need to be discriminating users of informational text, so use the criteria in this book and the checklists provided to select high-quality informational text.
- An appropriate lesson template makes lesson planning easier, so use the samples provided in this book to develop a lesson plan template that works for you, and use it consistently for designing read-aloud and guided reading lessons.

Our last piece of advice may well be the most important:

- Primary students are eager to learn about the world around them, so enjoy using informational text with your K–2 students!

# Checklist for Evaluating Informational Literature

## Evaluating Format and Visual Appeal

| Is the format visually appealing? | Yes | No |
| --- | --- | --- |
| Is there an attractive cover? | ☐ | ☐ |
| Are the font, letter size, and type large, simple, and easy to read? | ☐ | ☐ |
| Are there high-quality, appealing photographs and/or illustrations in which appropriate media have been used? | ☐ | ☐ |
| Do illustrations contribute to the visual appeal of the book? | ☐ | ☐ |
| Are the illustrations clear and large but not overly crowded? | ☐ | ☐ |
| Do the illustrations appropriately explain and enhance the content? | ☐ | ☐ |
| Do illustrations depict accurate size relationships? | ☐ | ☐ |
| Are labels and captions simple yet sufficient? | ☐ | ☐ |
| Is there a wide variety of illustrative materials (maps, charts, and graphs) that serve to clarify and extend the text? | ☐ | ☐ |
| Does the text layout (headings, sidebars, and/or other visual features, such as special fonts or letter size) serve to highlight key information for readers? | ☐ | ☐ |
| Is there an appropriate amount of text and illustrations on each page? | ☐ | ☐ |
| Is there a table of contents, index, and/or glossary? | ☐ | ☐ |

## Evaluating Accuracy and Authenticity

| Is the book accurate? | Yes | No |
| --- | --- | --- |
| Is information about the authors' qualifications or process for research of the topic included? | ☐ | ☐ |
| Does the book have a recent copyright date and/or is the information based on up-to-date research? | ☐ | ☐ |
| Do illustrations accurately depict the text? | ☐ | ☐ |
| Can facts presented in the text be verified with other authoritative sources? | ☐ | ☐ |
| Are animals depicted accurately without being given human characteristics? | ☐ | ☐ |
| Do authors refrain from making value-laden statements and/or statements of opinion, rather than fact? | ☐ | ☐ |
| Are statements of opinion clearly stated as such? | ☐ | ☐ |
| If the book is a blend of fact and fiction, is it clear which parts are fact and which are fiction? | ☐ | ☐ |

## Evaluating Writing Style and Appropriateness

| Is the writing style engaging? | Yes | No |
|---|:---:|:---:|
| Does the author draw the reader in with an engaging lead? | ☐ | ☐ |
| Are ideas logically ordered? | ☐ | ☐ |
| Is the background knowledge of the reader considered? | ☐ | ☐ |
| Are new ideas presented in a way that helps children make connections to what they already know? | ☐ | ☐ |
| Is the language appropriate for the children? | ☐ | ☐ |
| Does the author explain difficult concepts clearly and simply? | ☐ | ☐ |
| Are there any interactive elements that involve the reader? | ☐ | ☐ |
| Are new terms explained, highlighted, or defined? | ☐ | ☐ |
| Do the sound and meaning devices employed by the author enhance the rhythm and flow of the language and the child's understanding of the content? | ☐ | ☐ |
| Is the author's choice of text structure appropriate for presenting the content? | ☐ | ☐ |

## Evaluating Potential Content and Curricular Connections

| Does the text lend itself to both content and curricular connections? | Yes | No |
|---|:---:|:---:|
| Is the text is aligned to standards and curricular components? | ☐ | ☐ |
| Can the text be used across the curriculum in conjunction with other content areas? | ☐ | ☐ |
| Does the text relate to topics and themes that serve to build children's knowledge base? | ☐ | ☐ |

Available for download at **www.corwin.com/theeverythingguide**

# Common Core State Standards (CCSS) Checklists

## Kindergarten CCSS Checklist

### Kindergarten Standards for Informational Text

| Key Ideas and Details | |
|---|---|
| With prompting and support, ask and answer questions about key details in a text. | ☐ |
| With prompting and support, identify the main topic and retell key details of a text. | ☐ |
| With prompting and support, describe the connection between two individuals, events, ideas, or pieces of information in a text. | ☐ |
| **Craft and Structure** | |
| With prompting and support, ask and answer questions about unknown words in a text. | ☐ |
| Identify the front cover, back cover, and title page of a book. | ☐ |
| Name the author and illustrator of a text and define the role of each in presenting the ideas or information in a text. | ☐ |
| **Integration of Knowledge and Ideas** | |
| With prompting and support, describe the relationship between illustrations and the text in which they appear. | ☐ |
| With prompting and support, identify the reasons an author gives to support points in a text. | ☐ |
| With prompting and support, identify basic similarities in and differences between two texts on the same topic. | ☐ |
| **Range of Reading and Level of Text Complexity** | |
| Actively engage in group reading activities with purpose and understanding. | ☐ |

### Kindergarten Standards for Foundational Skills

| Print Concepts | |
|---|---|
| Demonstrate understanding of the organization and basic features of print. | ☐ |
| **Phonological Awareness** | |
| Demonstrate understanding of spoken words, syllables, and sounds. | ☐ |
| **Phonics and Word Recognition** | |
| Know and apply grade-level phonics and word analysis skills in decoding words. | ☐ |
| **Fluency** | |
| Read emergent-reader texts with purpose and understanding. | ☐ |

# Kindergarten Standards for Speaking and Listening

### Comprehension and Collaboration

Participate in collaborative conversations with diverse partners about kindergarten topics and texts with peers and adults in small and larger groups. ☐

Confirm understanding of a text read aloud or information presented orally or through other media by asking or answering questions about key details and requesting clarification if something is not understood. ☐

Ask and answer questions in order to seek help, get information, or clarify something that is not understood. ☐

### Presentation of Knowledge and Ideas

Describe familiar people, places, things, and events and, with prompting and support, provide additional detail. ☐

Add drawings or other visual displays to descriptions as desired to provide additional detail. ☐

Speak audibly and express thoughts, feelings, and ideas clearly. ☐

# Kindergarten Standards for Language

### Conventions of Standard English

Demonstrate command of the conventions of standard English grammar and usage when writing and speaking. ☐

Demonstrate command of the conventions of standard English capitalization, punctuation, and spelling when writing. ☐

### Vocabulary Acquisition and Use

Determine or clarify the meaning of unknown and multiple-meaning words and phrases based on kindergarten reading and content. ☐

With guidance and support from adults, explore word relationships and nuances in word meanings. ☐

Use words and phrases acquired through conversation, reading and being read to, and responding to texts. ☐

# Kindergarten Standards for Writing

### Text Types and Purposes

Use a combination of drawing, dictating, and writing to compose opinion pieces in which they tell a reader the topic or the name of the book they are writing about and state an opinion or preference about the topic or book. ☐

Use a combination of drawing, dictating, and writing to compose informative/explanatory texts in which they name what they are writing about and supply some information about the topic. ☐

Use a combination of drawing, dictating, and writing to narrate a single event or several loosely linked events, tell about the events in the order in which they occurred, and provide a reaction to what happened. ☐

### Production and Distribution of Writing

With guidance and support from adults, respond to questions and suggestions from peers and add details to strengthen writing as needed. ☐

With guidance and support from adults, explore a variety of digital tools to produce and publish writing, including in collaboration with peers. ☐

| **Research to Build and Present Knowledge** | |
| --- | :---: |
| Participate in shared research and writing projects. | ☐ |
| With guidance and support from adults, recall information from experiences or gather information from provided sources to answer a question. | ☐ |

# First Grade CCSS Checklist

## First Grade Standards for Informational Text

| **Key Ideas and Details** | |
| --- | :---: |
| Ask and answer questions about key details in a text. | ☐ |
| Identify the main topic and retell key details of a text. | ☐ |
| Describe the connection between two individuals, events, ideas, or pieces of information in a text. | ☐ |
| **Craft and Structure** | |
| Ask and answer questions to help determine or clarify the meaning of words and phrases in a text. | ☐ |
| Know and use various text features to locate key facts or information in a text. | ☐ |
| Distinguish between information provided by pictures or other illustrations and information provided by the words in a text. | ☐ |
| **Integration of Knowledge and Ideas** | |
| Use the illustrations and details in a text to describe its key ideas. | ☐ |
| Identify the reasons an author gives to support points in a text. | ☐ |
| Identify basic similarities in and differences between two texts on the same topic. | ☐ |
| **Range of Reading and Level of Text Complexity** | |
| With prompting and support, read informational texts appropriately complex for grade 1. | ☐ |

## First Grade Standards for Foundational Skills

| **Print Concepts** | |
| --- | :---: |
| Demonstrate understanding of the organization and basic features of print. | ☐ |
| **Phonological Awareness** | |
| Demonstrate understanding of spoken words, syllables, and sounds. | ☐ |
| **Phonics and Word Recognition** | |
| Know and apply grade-level phonics and word analysis skills in decoding words. | ☐ |
| **Fluency** | |
| Read with sufficient accuracy and fluency to support comprehension. | ☐ |

# First Grade Standards for Speaking and Listening

| Comprehension and Collaboration | |
| --- | --- |
| Participate in collaborative conversations with diverse partners about grade 1 topics and texts with peers and adults in small and larger groups. | ☐ |
| Ask and answer questions about key details in a text read aloud or information presented orally or through other media. | ☐ |
| Ask and answer questions about what a speaker says in order to gather additional information or clarify something that is not understood. | ☐ |
| **Presentation of Knowledge and Ideas** | |
| Describe people, places, things, and events with relevant details, expressing ideas and feelings clearly. | ☐ |
| Add drawings or other visual displays to descriptions when appropriate to clarify ideas, thoughts, and feelings. | ☐ |
| Produce complete sentences when appropriate to task and situation. | ☐ |

# First Grade Standards for Language

| Conventions of Standard English | |
| --- | --- |
| Demonstrate command of the conventions of standard English grammar and usage when writing or speaking. | ☐ |
| Demonstrate command of the conventions of standard English capitalization, punctuation, and spelling when writing. | ☐ |
| **Vocabulary Acquisition and Use** | |
| Determine or clarify the meaning of unknown and multiple-meaning words and phrases based on grade 1 reading and content, choosing flexibly from an array of strategies. | ☐ |
| With guidance and support from adults, demonstrate understanding of word relationships and nuances in word meanings. | ☐ |
| Use words and phrases acquired through conversations, reading and being read to, and responding to texts, including using frequently occurring conjunctions to signal simple relationships. | ☐ |

# First Grade Standards for Writing

| Text Types and Purposes | |
| --- | --- |
| Write opinion pieces in which they introduce the topic or name the book they are writing about, state an opinion, supply a reason for the opinion, and provide some sense of closure. | ☐ |
| Write informative/explanatory texts in which they name a topic, supply some facts about the topic, and provide some sense of closure. | ☐ |
| Write narratives in which they recount two or more appropriately sequenced events, include some details regarding what happened, use temporal words to signal event order, and provide some sense of closure. | ☐ |
| **Production and Distribution of Writing** | |
| With guidance and support from adults, focus on a topic, respond to questions and suggestions from peers, and add details to strengthen writing as needed. | ☐ |
| With guidance and support from adults, use a variety of digital tools to produce and publish writing, including in collaboration with peers. | ☐ |

| Research to Build and Present Knowledge | |
|---|---|
| Participate in shared research and writing projects (e.g., explore a number of "how-to" books on a given topic and use them to write a sequence of instructions). | ☐ |
| With guidance and support from adults, recall information from experiences or gather information from provided sources to answer a question. | ☐ |

## Second Grade CCSS Checklist

## Second Grade Standards for Informational Text

| Key Ideas and Details | |
|---|---|
| Ask and answer such questions as who, what, where, when, why, and how to demonstrate understanding of key details in a text. | ☐ |
| Identify the main topic of a multiparagraph text as well as the focus of specific paragraphs within the text. | ☐ |
| Describe the connection between a series of historical events, scientific ideas or concepts, or steps in technical procedures in a text. | ☐ |
| **Craft and Structure** | |
| Determine the meaning of words and phrases in a text relevant to a grade 2 topic or subject area. | ☐ |
| Know and use various text features to locate key facts or information in a text efficiently. | ☐ |
| Identify the main purpose of a text, including what the author wants to answer, explain, or describe. | ☐ |
| **Integration of Knowledge and Ideas** | |
| Explain how specific images contribute to and clarify a text. | ☐ |
| Describe how reasons support specific points the author makes in a text. | ☐ |
| Compare and contrast the most important points presented by two texts on the same topic. | ☐ |
| **Range of Reading and Level of Text Complexity** | |
| By the end of year, read and comprehend informational texts, including history/social studies, science, and technical texts, in the grades 2–3 text complexity band proficiently, with scaffolding as needed at the high end of the range. | ☐ |

## Second Grade Standards for Foundational Skills

| Phonics and Word Recognition | |
|---|---|
| Know and apply grade-level phonics and word analysis skills in decoding words. | ☐ |
| **Fluency** | |
| Read with sufficient accuracy and fluency to support comprehension. | ☐ |

# Second Grade Standards for Speaking and Listening

| **Comprehension and Collaboration** | |
|---|---|
| Participate in collaborative conversations with diverse partners about grade 2 topics and texts with peers and adults in small and larger groups. | ☐ |
| Recount or describe key ideas or details from a text read aloud or information presented orally or through other media. | ☐ |
| Ask and answer questions about what a speaker says in order to clarify comprehension, gather additional information, or deepen understanding of a topic or issue. | ☐ |
| **Presentation of Knowledge and Ideas** | |
| Tell a story or recount an experience with appropriate facts and relevant, descriptive details, speaking audibly in coherent sentences. | ☐ |
| Create audio recordings of stories or poems; add drawings or other visual displays to stories or recounts of experiences when appropriate to clarify ideas, thoughts, and feelings. | ☐ |
| Produce complete sentences when appropriate to task and situation in order to provide requested detail or clarification. | ☐ |

# Second Grade Standards for Language

| **Conventions of Standard English** | |
|---|---|
| Demonstrate command of the conventions of standard English grammar and usage when writing or speaking. | ☐ |
| Demonstrate command of the conventions of standard English capitalization, punctuation, and spelling when writing. | ☐ |
| **Knowledge of Language** | |
| Use knowledge of language and its conventions when writing, speaking, reading, or listening. | ☐ |
| **Vocabulary Acquisition and Use** | |
| Determine or clarify the meaning of unknown and multiple-meaning words and phrases based on grade 2 reading and content, choosing flexibly from an array of strategies. | ☐ |
| Demonstrate understanding of word relationships and nuances in word meanings. | ☐ |
| Use words and phrases acquired through conversations, reading and being read to, and responding to texts, including using adjectives and adverbs to describe. | ☐ |

# Second Grade Standards for Writing

| **Text Types and Purposes** | |
|---|---|
| Write opinion pieces in which they introduce the topic or book they are writing about, state an opinion, supply reasons that support the opinion, use linking words to connect opinion and reasons, and provide a concluding statement or section. | ☐ |
| Write informative/explanatory texts in which they introduce a topic, use facts and definitions to develop points, and provide a concluding statement or section. | ☐ |

### Text Types and Purposes

Write narratives in which they recount a well elaborated event or short sequence of events, include details to describe actions, thoughts, and feelings, use temporal words to signal event order, and provide a sense of closure. ☐

### Production and Distribution of Writing

With guidance and support from adults and peers, focus on a topic and strengthen writing as needed by revising and editing. ☐

With guidance and support from adults, use a variety of digital tools to produce and publish writing, including in collaboration with peers. ☐

### Research to Build and Present Knowledge

Participate in shared research and writing projects ☐

Recall information from experiences or gather information from provided sources to answer a question. ☐

 Available for download at **www.corwin.com/theeverythingguide**

# Lesson Plan Template

**Name of Text:**

**Big Ideas for This Lesson (essential information):**

| Step in the Lesson | Action Steps |
| --- | --- |
| **Prepare to read.** | • What is my students' background knowledge in content? Which concepts and vocabulary need to be elicited or developed before the reading?<br>• Which text features will be taught before the reading?<br>• What is our overall purpose for the reading, and how can I state this for the students?<br>• How can I preview the text to build excitement for the reading (using the cover, illustrations, or other features)? |

**Ideas for This Text:**

| Step in the Lesson | Action Steps |
| --- | --- |
| **Guide reading.** | • What vocabulary or concepts should be taught during the reading so that my students can understand the text?<br>• What text features and illustrations need to be taught or pointed out in order to make the text accessible?<br>• What are the big, important ideas of this text I want my students to understand?<br>• What strategies are appropriate for this text that I can teach/model?<br>• What questions can I ask students to check their understanding?<br>• What reteaching will I need to do if they do not demonstrate understanding? |

**Ideas for This Text:**

| Step in the Lesson | Action Steps |
|---|---|
| **Explicitly teach from the text.**<br><br>(Choose one focus area for each group of students.) | • Are my students able to decode this text? If not, what phonetic elements and decoding strategies do they need to work on? How can I utilize words or passages from this text to practice decoding?<br>• Are my students fluent readers? How can I model fluency in this text? Can I follow up the reading with shared and unison reading for practicing fluency? Are there other ways for students to utilize this text for fluency building (assisted reading with CD, partner reading, choral reading)?<br>• Which comprehension skills and strategies are needed to comprehend this text? How can I teach one of those skills or strategies explicitly? What practice opportunities can I follow up with to allow my students to apply that skill or strategy?<br>• What fix-up tips can I teach based on the reading of the text that will allow students to learn self-help skills in their independent reading? |

**Ideas for This Text:**

| Step in the Lesson | Action Steps |
|---|---|
| **Facilitate connections.**<br><br>(Choose one focus area for each group of students.) | • Does this text experience authentically lend itself to making connections in writing, technology, additional text reading, content areas, or the fine arts? How can I formulate a meaningful follow-up activity to make these connections? |

**Ideas for This Text:**

# Topical List of Informational Literature

ABCs   174
Animals—General   174
Animals—Wild: Exotic   177
Animals—Wild: Native   179
Biographies   179
Birds   180
Civics/Citizenship   181
Culture   181
Dinosaurs   182
Ecology   182
Family   183
Five Senses   183
Friendship   183
Garden   184
Geography   184
Habitats   184
Healthy Living   186
History   187
Holidays/Special Celebrations   188
Human Body   188
Insects   188
Jobs   189
Life Cycles of Animals   190

Maps   190
Math   190
Measurement   192
Money   192
Natural Disasters   192
Ocean Animals   193
Patterns/Symmetry   194
Pets   194
Physical Science (Physics,
    Chemistry, Simple Machines)   194
Plants   195
Presidents and Their Families   196
Ranch/Farm Life   197
Reptiles   197
Safety   198
Science   198
Seasons   198
Shapes   199
Space   199
Sports/Recreation   200
Transportation   200
Weather   201

| Title | Author | pp | TC | P | ILL | C | G | I | L | BB | Series |
|---|---|---|---|---|---|---|---|---|---|---|---|
| | | | | | **ABCs** | | | | | | |
| *Alphabet of Ocean Animals* | Laura Gates Galvin | 40 | | | X | | X | | | | |
| *D Is for Dinosaur* | Todd Chapman & Lita Judge | 48 | | | X | | | | | | |
| *S Is for S'Mores* | Helen Frost James | 38 | | | X | | | | | | |
| *W Is for Windy City* | Steven Layne & Deborah Dover | 40 | | | X | X | | | | | |
| *A Zeal of Zebras: An Alphabet Collection of Nouns* | Woop Studios | 64 | | | X | | | | | | |
| | | | | | **Animals—General** | | | | | | |
| *All Kinds of Animals* | Megan Wasp | 14 | X | X | | X | X | X | X | X | Big Book Science |
| *Amazing Animal Journeys* | Laura Marsh | 48 | X | X | | X | X | X | | | National Geographic Kids |
| *Amazing Animal Senses* | Caroline Hutchinson | 16 | X | X | | | | | | | Rising Readers Leveled Books: Science |
| *Amazing Animals* | Megan Wasp | 14 | X | X | | X | X | X | X | X | Big Book Science |
| *Animal Baths* | Bob Barner | 32 | | | X | | | | | | |
| *Animal Eyes* | Beth Fielding | 36 | | X | | X | | X | X | | Explorations |
| *Animal Fathers* | Jill Eggleton | 16 | | X | | | X | X | | | |
| *Animals and the Seasons* | Margaret McNamara | 16 | X | X | | X | X | X | X | X | Science Content Connections |
| *Animals in Fall* | Martha Rustad | 24 | X | X | | | X | X | | | Pebble Plus: All About Fall |
| *Animals Nobody Loves* | Seymour Simon | 48 | X | X | | | | | | | |
| *Animals That Store Food* | Kerrie Shanahan | 24 | X | X | | X | X | | X | | Flying Start to Literacy |
| *Baby Animals at Night* | Kingfisher Editors | 14 | | X | | X | | | | | Kingfisher: Baby Animals |
| *Baby Animal Pop!* | Sarah Wassner Flynn | 20 | | X | | X | | | | | National Geographic Little Kids |
| *Changing Colors* | Jill Eggleton | 16 | | X | | X | | X | X | | Abrams Learning Trends |

*Legend:* pp = Number of pages; TC = Table of contents; P = Photos; ILL = Illustrated; C = Captioned; G = Glossary; I = Index; L = Leveled book; BB = Available in big book format

| Title | Author | pp | TC | P | ILL | C | G | I | L | BB | Series |
|---|---|---|---|---|---|---|---|---|---|---|---|
| | | | | | **Animals—General (Continued)** | | | | | | |
| *Count* | National Geographic Kids | 24 | | X | | | | | | | National Geographic Little Kids: Look and Learn |
| *Deadliest Animals* | Melissa Stewart | 48 | X | X | | X | X | X | | | National Geographic Kids |
| *Decomposers* | Megan Lappi | 24 | X | X | | X | X | X | X | | AV2: Food Chain |
| *Different or the Same?* | Jill Eggleton | 16 | | X | | | | X | X | | |
| *Even an Octopus Needs a Home* | Irene Kelly | 32 | | | X | | | | | | |
| *First Big Book of Animals* | Catherine Hughes | 128 | X | X | | X | X | X | | | National Geographic Little Kids |
| *Friends: True Stories of Extraordinary Animal Friendships* | Catherine Thimmesh | 32 | | X | | X | | | | | |
| *Great Migrations: Whales, Wildebeests, Butterflies, Elephants, and Other Amazing Animals on the Move* | Elizabeth Carney | 44 | X | X | | | | X | | | |
| *How Do Baby Animals Grow?* | Caroline Hutchinson | 16 | | X | | | | | X | | Rising Readers Leveled Books: Science |
| *How Many Ways Can You Catch a Fly?* | Steve Jenkins & Robin Page | 32 | | | X | | | | | | |
| *I Wonder Why Kangaroos Have Pouches* | Jenny Wood | 32 | X | | X | X | | X | | | I Wonder Why |
| *Inside-Out Skeletons* | Lynda Nunweek | 20 | X | X | | | | X | X | | |
| *Kate and Pippin: An Unlikely Love Story* | Martin Springett | 32 | | X | | | | | | | |
| *Living Color* | Steve Jenkins | 32 | | | X | X | | | | | |
| *Living Things Are Everywhere!* | Jayne Smith | 14 | X | X | | | X | X | X | X | Big Book Science |
| *Look! No Tail!* | Jill Eggleton | 14 | | X | | | | X | X | | |
| *Loud and Quiet: An Animal Opposites Book* | Lisa Bullard | 32 | | X | | | X | X | | | |
| *Mammals* | David Burne | 48 | X | X | | X | X | X | | | |

*Legend:* pp = Number of pages; TC = Table of contents; P = Photos; ILL = Illustrated; C = Captioned; G = Glossary; I = Index; L = Leveled book; BB = Available in big book format

| Title | Author | pp | TC | P | ILL | C | G | I | L | BB | Series |
|---|---|---|---|---|---|---|---|---|---|---|---|
| | | | | | | Animals—General (Continued) | | | | | |
| *Match!* | National Geographic Kids | 24 | | X | | X | | | | | National Geographic Little Kids: Science |
| *Move!* | Steve Jenkins & Robin Page | 32 | | | X | | | | | | |
| *The Nature of Things* | Jill Eggleton | 20 | X | X | | | | | X | | |
| *No Bones* | Jill Eggleton | 14 | X | | | | | X | X | | |
| *North: The Amazing Story of Arctic Migration* | Nick Dowson | 55 | | X | | | X | | | | |
| *A Place to Live* | Jill Eggleton | 16 | | X | | X | | X | X | | Abrams Learning Trends |
| *Sisters and Brothers: Sibling Relationships in the Animal World* | Steve Jenkins & Robin Page | 32 | | | X | | | | | | |
| *Sleeping Animals* | Jill Eggleton | 16 | | X | | | | X | X | | |
| *Stay Away!* | Jenny Feely | 16 | X | X | | | | X | X | | Explorations |
| *Teach Me How* | Kerrie Shanahan | 16 | | X | | | | | X | | Flying Start to Literacy |
| *Time for a Bath* | Steve Jenkins & Robin Page | 24 | | X | | | | | | | Time to |
| *Time to Eat* | Steve Jenkins & Robin Page | 24 | | X | X | | | | | | Time to |
| *Using Color* | Hannah Reed | 16 | X | X | | | | X | X | | Explorations |
| *What Am I?* | Hannah Reed | 16 | | X | | | | | X | | Flying Start to Literacy |
| *What Animal Am I?* | Caroline Hutchinson | 16 | | X | | | | | X | | Rising Readers Leveled Books: Science |
| *What Do Animals Need?* | Margaret McNamara | 16 | X | X | | X | X | X | X | X | Science Content Connections |
| *What Do You Do With a Tail Like This?* | Steve Jenkins & Robin Page | 32 | | | X | | | | | | |
| *What Is Long?* | Jill Eggleton | 16 | | X | | X | | X | X | | Abrams Learning Trends |
| *What's That?* | Jill Eggleton | 20 | X | X | | | | | X | | |
| *Where Can They Live?* | Jill Eggleton | 16 | | X | | X | | | X | | Abrams Learning Trends |

*Legend:* pp = Number of pages; TC = Table of contents; P = Photos; ILL = Illustrated; C = Captioned; G = Glossary; I = Index; L = Leveled book; BB = Available in big book format

| Title | Author | pp | TC | P | ILL | C | G | I | L | BB | Series |
|-------|--------|-----|-----|-----|-----|-----|-----|-----|-----|-----|--------|
| **Animals—General (Continued)** | | | | | | | | | | | |
| *Whiskers* | Jill Eggleton | 16 | | X | | X | | | X | X | Abrams Learning Trends |
| *Who Has These Feet?* | Laura Hulbert | 40 | | | X | | | | | | |
| *Who Has This Tail?* | Laura Hulbert | 40 | | | X | | | | | | |
| *A Zeal of Zebras: An Alphabet Collection of Nouns* | Woop Studios | 64 | | | X | | | | | | |
| **Animals—Wild: Exotic** | | | | | | | | | | | |
| *Almost Gone: The World's Rarest Animals* | Steve Jenkins | 32 | | | X | | | | | | |
| *Animal Fathers* | Jill Eggleton | 16 | | X | | | | | X | X | |
| *Ape* | Martin Jenkins | 48 | | | X | X | | X | | | |
| *Baby Animals in the Snow* | Kingfisher Editors | 14 | | X | | X | | | | | Kingfisher: Baby Animals |
| *Baby Animals in the Wild* | Kingfisher Editors | 14 | | X | | X | | | | | Kingfisher: Baby Animals |
| *Baby Bonobos Alone* | Jill Eggleton | 16 | | X | | X | | | X | X | Abrams Learning Trends |
| *Big Gorilla* | Jill Eggleton | 14 | | X | | | | | X | X | |
| *Can We Save the Tiger?* | Martin Jenkins | 56 | | | X | X | | | | | |
| *Cheetahs* | Laura Marsh | 32 | X | X | | X | X | | | | National Geographic Kids |
| *Crocodile Mother* | Jill Eggleton | 14 | | X | | | | | X | X | |
| *Count* | National Geographic | 24 | | X | | | | | | | National Geographic Little Kids: Look and Learn |
| *Counting at the Zoo* | Kathleen Fischer | 14 | | X | | | | | X | X | Big Book Math |
| *Cousins of Clouds: Elephant Poems* | Tracie Vaughn Zimmer | 31 | | | X | X | | | | | |
| *Down by the Waterhole* | Jill Eggleton | 16 | | X | | | | | X | X | |
| *Elephants* | Laura Marsh | 48 | X | X | | X | X | X | | | National Geographic Kids: Great Migrations |
| *Elephants of Africa* | Gail Gibbons | 32 | | | X | X | | | | | |

*Legend:* pp = Number of pages; TC = Table of contents; P = Photos; ILL = Illustrated; C = Captioned; G = Glossary; I = Index; L = Leveled book; BB = Available in big book format

| Title | Author | pp | TC | P | ILL | C | G | I | L | BB | Series |
|---|---|---|---|---|---|---|---|---|---|---|---|
| | | | | | | Animals—Wild: Exotic (Continued) | | | | | |
| *Food for Zebras* | Jill Eggleton | 14 | | X | | | | X | X | | |
| *Giant Pandas* | Kari Schuetz | 24 | X | X | | | X | X | X | | Blast Off Readers: Animal Safari |
| *The Griffin Vulture* | Jill Eggleton | 20 | X | X | | X | | X | X | | |
| *Harpy Eagle Chick* | Jill Eggleton | 16 | | X | | X | | X | X | | |
| *How Do Baby Animals Grow?* | Caroline Hutchinson | 16 | | X | | | | | | | Rising Readers Leveled Books: Science |
| *How Many Baby Pandas?* | Sandra Markle | 24 | | X | | X | X | X | | | |
| *Knut: A Pet or Not?* | Jill Eggleton | 16 | | X | | | | X | X | | |
| *Little Kids' African Animal Book* | Beverly & Derek Joubert | 48 | | X | | X | X | | | | |
| *Looking Closely in the Rain Forest* | Frank Serafini | 40 | | X | | | | | | | |
| *Lucky Water Buffalo Calf* | Jill Eggleton | 16 | X | X | | X | | X | X | | |
| *Mother to Tigers* | George Ella Lyon | 32 | | | X | | | | | | |
| *Moving Elephants* | Jill Eggleton | 16 | | X | | X | | X | X | | Abrams Learning Trends |
| *Pandas* | Willow Clark | 24 | X | X | | X | X | X | | | Animals of Asia |
| *Penguins* | Penelope Arlon | 80 | X | X | | X | X | X | | | Scholastic: Discover More |
| *Polar Bears* | Mark Newman | 32 | | X | | X | | | | | |
| *Rainforest: Discover Earth's Ecosystems* | Sean Callery | 32 | X | X | | X | X | X | | | |
| *Teach Me How* | Kerrie Shanahan | 16 | | | X | | | | X | | Flying Start to Literacy |
| *Tigers* | Laura Marsh | 32 | X | X | | X | X | | | | National Geographic Kids |
| *What Did One Elephant Say to the Other?* | Becky Baines | 29 | | X | | | | | | | |
| *What Would You Eat in the Rain Forest?* | Caroline Hutchinson | 16 | | X | | | | | X | | Rising Readers Leveled Books: Science |
| *Wildlife Detective* | Jill Eggleton | 20 | | X | | | | | X | | |
| *The World's Greatest Lion: A True Story of Survival* | Ralph Helfer | 40 | | | X | | | | | | |

Legend: pp = Number of pages; TC = Table of contents; P = Photos; ILL = Illustrated; C = Captioned; G = Glossary; I = Index; L = Leveled book; BB = Available in big book format

| Title | Author | pp | TC | P | ILL | C | G | I | L | BB | Series |
|---|---|---|---|---|---|---|---|---|---|---|---|
| **Animals—Wild: Native** | | | | | | | | | | | |
| *Animals in the Fall* | Martha Rustad | 24 | X | X | | | X | X | | | Pebble Plus: All About Fall |
| *Animals That Store Food* | Kerrie Shanahan | 24 | X | X | | X | X | | X | | Flying Start to Literacy |
| *At Home With the Gopher Tortoise* | Madeline Dunphy | 32 | | | X | | | | | | |
| *Brown Bear* | Jill Eggleton | 14 | | X | | | X | X | | | |
| *Day and Night in the Desert* | Jill Eggleton | 14 | | X | | | X | X | | | |
| *A Den Is a Bed for a Bear* | Becky Baines | 30 | | X | | X | | | | | |
| *Hungry Fox* | Jill Eggleton | 16 | | X | | X | | X | X | | Abrams Learning Trends |
| *Little Cub* | Caitlin Fraser | 16 | | | X | | | | X | | Flying Start to Literacy |
| *Lucky Seal* | Jill Eggleton | 14 | | X | | | X | X | | | |
| *Ponies* | Laura Marsh | 32 | X | X | | X | X | | | | National Geographic Kids |
| *Sea Otters in the Kelp Forest* | Hannah Reed | 16 | | | X | X | | | X | | Flying Start to Literacy |
| *Seabird of the Forest: The Mystery of the Marbled Murrelet* | Joan Dunning | 32 | | | X | X | | | | | |
| *Vulture View* | April Pulley Sayre | 32 | | | X | | | | | | |
| *What Lives at the Pond?* | Caroline Hutchinson | 16 | | X | | | | | X | | Rising Readers Leveled Books: Science |
| *Where Are the Bats?* | Jill Eggleton | 14 | | X | | | X | X | | | |
| **Biographies** | | | | | | | | | | | |
| *Amazing Scientists* | Donna Merritt | 14 | X | X | | X | X | X | X | X | Big Book Science |
| *Balloons Over Broadway: The True Story of the Puppeteer of Macy's Parade* | Melissa Sweet | 40 | | | X | X | | X | | | |
| *Betsy Ross* | Alexandra Wallner | 32 | | | X | | | | | | |

*Legend:* pp = Number of pages; TC = Table of contents; P = Photos; ILL = Illustrated; C = Captioned; G = Glossary; I = Index; L = Leveled book; BB = Available in big book format

| Title | Author | pp | TC | P | ILL | C | G | I | L | BB | Series |
|---|---|---|---|---|---|---|---|---|---|---|---|
| **Biographies (Continued)** | | | | | | | | | | | |
| *Betsy Ross* | Becky White | 32 | | | X | | | | | | |
| *Eleanor, Quiet No More* | Doreen Rappaport | 48 | | | X | | | | | | |
| *George: George Washington, Our Founding Father* | Frank Keating | 32 | | | X | | | | | | |
| *Moses: When Harriet Tubman Led Her People to Freedom* | Carole Boston Weatherford | 48 | | X | X | | X | X | | | |
| *A President from Hawai'i* | Terry & Joanna Carolan | 24 | | | | | | | | | |
| *Stand Tall, Abe Lincoln* | Judith St. George | 48 | | | X | | | | | | |
| *Thank You, Sarah: The Woman Who Saved Thanksgiving* | Laurie Halse Anderson | 49 | | | X | | | | | | |
| *Theodore* | Frank Keating | 32 | | | X | | | | | | |
| *Will Rogers: An American Legend* | Frank Keating | 32 | | | X | | | | | | |
| *Yellowstone Moran* | Lita Judge | 32 | | | X | X | | | | | |
| **Birds** | | | | | | | | | | | |
| *Bird Talk: What Birds Are Saying and Why* | Lita Judge | 48 | | | X | | | | | | |
| *Even an Ostrich Needs a Nest* | Irene Kelly | 20 | | | X | | | | | | |
| *The Griffin Vulture* | Jill Eggleton | 20 | X | X | | X | | X | X | | |
| *Harpy Eagle Chick* | Jill Eggleton | 16 | | X | | X | | X | X | | |
| *The Hoatzin Bird* | Lynda Nunweek | 20 | X | X | | X | | X | X | | |
| *It's a Hummingbird's Life* | Irene Kelly | 32 | | | X | X | | | | | |
| *Penguins* | Penelope Arlon | 80 | X | X | | X | X | X | | | Scholastic: Discover More |
| *Seabird in the Forest: The Mystery of the Marbled Murrelet* | Joan Dunning | 32 | | | X | X | | | | | |

*Legend:* pp = Number of pages; TC = Table of contents; P = Photos; ILL = Illustrated; C = Captioned; G = Glossary; I = Index; L = Leveled book; BB = Available in big book format

| Title | Author | pp | TC | P | ILL | C | G | I | L | BB | Series |
|---|---|---|---|---|---|---|---|---|---|---|---|
| | | | | | **Civics/Citizenship** | | | | | | |
| *Being a Good Citizen* | John Serrano | 16 | X | X | | X | | | X | | Rising Readers Leveled Books: Social Studies |
| *Discover Local and State Government* | Barbara Brannon | 24 | X | X | | X | X | X | | | English Explorers Social Studies |
| *Getting Along* | Cathy Torrisi | 14 | X | X | | | X | X | | X | Big Book Social Studies |
| *How Do Laws Get Passed?* | Leslie Harper | 24 | X | X | | X | X | X | | | Civics Q&A |
| *Local and State Government* | Etta Johnson | 24 | X | X | | X | X | X | | | English Explorers Social Studies: Government & Citizenship |
| *My Community* | Cathy Torrisi | 14 | X | X | | | X | X | | X | Abrams Learning Trends |
| *Our Country* | Cathy Torrisi | 14 | X | X | X | | X | X | | X | Big Book Social Studies |
| *Take a Stand* | Cathy Torrisi | 14 | X | X | | | X | X | | X | Big Book Health & Safety |
| *We Need Rules* | Cathy Torrisi | 14 | X | X | | | X | X | X | X | Abrams Learning Trends |
| *What Are Some Rules at Home?* | Margaret McNamara | 16 | X | X | | X | X | X | X | X | Social Studies Content Connections |
| *What Are Some Rules at School?* | Margaret McNamara | 16 | X | X | | X | X | X | X | X | Social Studies Content Connections |
| *Why Do We Have Rules?* | Margaret McNamara | 16 | X | X | | X | X | X | X | X | Social Studies Content Connections |
| | | | | | **Culture** | | | | | | |
| *Birthdays Around the World* | Mary Lankford | 32 | X | | X | | X | | | | |
| *The Call of the Sea* | Jill Eggleton | 20 | X | X | | | X | | | | |
| *Hello, World!* | Cathy Torrisi | 14 | X | X | | | X | X | X | X | Abrams Learning Trends |
| *Kimonos* | Annelore Parot | 36 | | | X | | | | | | |
| *Living in a Cave* | Jill Eggleton | 16 | | X | | | X | X | | | |
| *A Real Tree House* | Jill Eggleton | 16 | | X | | X | X | X | | | |
| *Shades of People* | Shelley Rotner & Sheila Kelly | 32 | | X | | | | | | | |

*Legend:* pp = Number of pages; TC = Table of contents; P = Photos; ILL = Illustrated; C = Captioned; G = Glossary; I = Index; L = Leveled book; BB = Available in big book format

| Title | Author | pp | TC | P | ILL | C | G | I | L | BB | Series |
|---|---|---|---|---|---|---|---|---|---|---|---|
| **Dinosaurs** | | | | | | | | | | | |
| *Born to be Giants: How Baby Dinosaurs Grew to Rule the World* | Lita Judge | 48 | | | X | | | | | | |
| *D Is for Dinosaur* | Todd Chapman & Lita Judge | 48 | | | X | | | | | | |
| *Dinosaur Science* | Megan Wasp | 14 | X | X | X | X | X | X | X | X | Big Book Science |
| *Dinosaurs* | Judy Allen | 18 | | | X | | X | | | | |
| *Dinosaurs* | Gail Gibbons | 32 | | | X | X | | | | | |
| *Dinosaurs* | Kathy Weidner Zoehfeld | 32 | X | | X | X | X | | | | National Geographic Kids |
| *First Big Book of Dinosaurs* | Catherine Hughes | 127 | X | | X | | X | X | | | |
| **Ecology** | | | | | | | | | | | |
| *Almost Gone: The World's Rarest Animals* | Steve Jenkins | 34 | | | X | | | | | | |
| *At Home With the Gopher Turtle: The Story of a Keystone Species* | Madeline Dunphy | 32 | | | X | | | | | | |
| *Can We Save the Tigers?* | Martin Jenkins | 56 | | | X | X | | | | | |
| *Decomposers* | Megan Lappi | 24 | X | X | | X | X | X | X | | AV2: Food Chain |
| *Garbage Helps our Garden Grow* | Linda Glazer | 32 | | X | | | | | | | |
| *Garbage in the River* | Jill Eggleton | 16 | | X | | X | | X | X | | |
| *How Many Baby Pandas?* | Sandra Markle | 24 | | X | | X | X | X | | | |
| *Human Footprint: Everything You Will Eat, Use, Wear, Buy, and Throw Out in Your Lifetime* | Ellen Kirk | 32 | X | X | | | | | | | National Geographic Kids |
| *The Junk Raft Journey* | Lynda Nunweek | 16 | | X | | X | | X | X | | |
| *Leopard and Silkie: One Boy's Quest to Save the Seal Pups* | Brenda Peterson | 32 | | X | | | | | | | |
| *The Mangrove Trees: Planting Trees to Feed Families* | Susan Roth & Cindy Trumbore | 40 | | | X | X | X | | | | |
| *Meadowlands: A Wetlands Survival Story* | Thomas Yezerski | 40 | | | X | X | | | | | |
| *Samso: The Green Dream* | Lynda Nunweek | 20 | X | X | | X | | X | X | | |

Legend: pp = Number of pages; TC = Table of contents; P = Photos; ILL = Illustrated; C = Captioned; G = Glossary; I = Index; L = Leveled book; BB = Available in big book format

| Title | Author | pp | TC | P | ILL | C | G | I | L | BB | Series |
|---|---|---|---|---|---|---|---|---|---|---|---|
| | | | | | | **Ecology (Continued)** | | | | | |
| *Saving Our Planet* | Megan Wasp | 14 | X | X | | X | X | X | X | X | Big Book Science |
| *Wildlife Detective* | Jill Eggleton | 20 | | X | | | | | X | | |
| | | | | | | **Family** | | | | | |
| *At Lunchtime* | James Talia | 20 | | X | | | | | X | | Explorations |
| *Don't Forget, God Bless Our Troops* | Jill Biden | 40 | | | X | | | | | | |
| *Families Are Special* | Cathy Torrisi | 14 | X | X | | | X | X | X | X | Abrams Learning Trends |
| *I'm Adopted* | Shelley Rotner & Sheila Kelly | 32 | | X | | | | | | | |
| *Many Ways: How Families Practice Their Beliefs and Religions* | Shelley Rotner & Sheila Kelly | 32 | | X | | | | | | | |
| | | | | | | **Five Senses** | | | | | |
| *Hearing* | Sharon Gordon | 32 | | X | | | X | X | | | Rookie Read About Health |
| *I Learn With My Senses* | Christopher Raymond | 14 | X | X | | | X | X | X | X | Big Book Science |
| *Seeing* | Sharon Gordon | 32 | | X | | | X | X | | | Rookie Read About Health |
| *Senses in the City* | Shelley Rotner | 32 | | X | | | | | | | |
| *Senses on the Farm* | Shelley Rotner | 32 | | X | | | | | | | |
| *What Do You See?* | Caroline Hutchinson | 16 | | X | | | | | X | | Rising Readers Leveled Books: Science |
| | | | | | | **Friendship** | | | | | |
| *Friends: True Stories of Extraordinary Animal Friendships* | Catherine Thimmesh | 32 | | X | | X | | | | | |
| *Getting Along* | Cathy Torrisi | 14 | X | X | | | X | X | | X | Big Book Social Studies |
| *The Guardian Team: On the Job With Rena and Roo* | Cat Urbigkit | 32 | | X | | | | | | | |
| *Kate and Pippin: An Unlikely Love Story* | Martin Springett | 32 | | X | | | | | | | |
| *One Step, Two Step* | Marilyn Wooley | 12 | | X | | | | | X | | Explorations |

*Legend:* pp = Number of pages; TC = Table of contents; P = Photos; ILL = Illustrated; C = Captioned; G = Glossary; I = Index; L = Leveled book; BB = Available in big book format

| Title | Author | pp | TC | P | ILL | C | G | I | L | BB | Series |
|---|---|---|---|---|---|---|---|---|---|---|---|
| **Garden** | | | | | | | | | | | |
| *From Seed to Pumpkin* | Jan Kottke | 23 | | X | | | X | X | X | | Welcome Books |
| *From Seed to Pumpkin* | Wendy Pfeffer | 33 | | | X | | | | X | | Let's-Read-And-Find-Out: Science |
| *Garbage Helps our Garden Grow* | Linda Glazer | 32 | | X | | | | | | | |
| *Night in the Garden* | Jill Eggleton | 16 | | X | | X | | X | | | Abrams Learning Trends |
| *Tools for the Garden* | Mari Schuh | 24 | X | X | | | X | X | | | Pebble Books: Gardens |
| **Geography** | | | | | | | | | | | |
| *Comparing Two Cities* | Anna Lee | 16 | | X | | X | X | | X | | Early Explorers |
| *Different Villages* | Jill Eggleton | 20 | X | X | | | | X | | | |
| *Life in a Rural Community* | Margaret McNamara | 16 | X | X | | X | X | X | X | X | Social Studies Content Connections |
| *Life in a Suburban Community* | Margaret McNamara | 16 | X | X | | X | X | X | X | X | Social Studies Content Connections |
| *Life in an Urban Community* | Margaret McNamara | 16 | X | X | | X | X | X | X | X | Social Studies Content Connections |
| *My Community* | Cathy Torrisi | 14 | X | X | | X | X | X | X | | Abrams Learning Trends |
| *Our Earth* | John Thomas Matthews | 14 | X | X | | X | X | X | X | | Big Book Science |
| *Where Are We?* | Cathy Torrisi | 14 | X | X | | X | X | X | X | | Abrams Learning Trends |
| **Habitats** | | | | | | | | | | | |
| *Animals in Their Habitats* | Debra Castor | 16 | X | X | | X | X | X | X | X | Science Content Connections |
| *Baby Animals in the Forest* | Kingfisher Editors | 14 | | X | | X | | | | | Kingfisher: Baby Animals |
| *Baby Animals in the Sea* | Kingfisher Editors | 14 | | X | | X | | | | | Kingfisher: Baby Animals |
| *Baby Animals in the Snow* | Kingfisher Editors | 14 | | X | | X | | | | | |
| *Baby Animals in the Wild* | Kingfisher Editors | 14 | | X | | X | | | | | |

*Legend:* pp = Number of pages; TC = Table of contents; P = Photos; ILL = Illustrated; C = Captioned; G = Glossary; I = Index; L = Leveled book; BB = Available in big book format

| Title | Author | pp | TC | P | ILL | C | G | I | L | BB | Series |
|-------|--------|-----|-----|-----|-----|-----|-----|-----|-----|-----|--------|
| | | | | Habitats (Continued) | | | | | | | |
| *Coral Reefs* | Gail Gibbons | 32 | | | X | X | | | | | |
| *Day and Night in the Desert* | Jill Eggleton | 14 | | X | | | | X | X | | |
| *Down at the Waterhole* | Jill Eggleton | 16 | | X | | | | X | X | | |
| *Down, Down, Down: A Journey to the Bottom of the Sea* | Steve Jenkins | 40 | | | X | | | | | | |
| *Going Under* | Jill Eggleton | 16 | | X | | X | | X | X | | Abrams Learning Trends |
| *Going Up* | Jill Eggleton | 16 | | X | | X | | X | X | | Abrams Learning Trends |
| *Habitats Around the World* | Debra Castor | 16 | X | X | | X | X | X | X | X | Science Content Connections |
| *In a Nutshell* | Jill Eggleton | 16 | | X | | X | | X | | | Abrams Learning Trends |
| *Life Cycles: Ocean* | Sean Callery | 32 | X | X | | X | X | X | | | Kingfisher: Life Cycles |
| *Looking Closely in the Rain Forest* | Frank Serafini | 40 | | X | | | | | | | |
| *Night in the Garden* | Jill Eggleton | 16 | | X | | X | | X | X | | Abrams Learning Trends |
| *Ocean: Discover Earth's Ecosystems* | Sean Callery | 32 | X | X | | X | X | X | | | Kingfisher: Discover Earth's Ecosystems |
| *Oceans and Seas* | Nicola Davies | 56 | X | X | | X | | X | | | Science Kids |
| *Plants in Their Habitats* | Debra Castor | 16 | X | X | | X | X | X | X | X | Science Content Connections |
| *Rainforest: Discover Earth's Ecosystems* | Sean Callery | 32 | X | X | | X | X | X | | | Kingfisher: Discover Earth's Ecosystems |
| *Step Gently Out* | Helen Frost & Rick Lieder | 32 | | X | | | | | | | |
| *The Tall Tree* | Jill Eggleton | 16 | | X | | X | | X | | | Abrams Learning Trends |
| *Under the Ice* | Jill Eggleton | 16 | | X | | X | | X | X | | Abrams Learning Trends |

*Legend:* pp = Number of pages; TC = Table of contents; P = Photos; ILL = Illustrated; C = Captioned; G = Glossary; I = Index; L = Leveled book; BB = Available in big book format

| Title | Author | pp | TC | P | ILL | C | G | I | L | BB | Series |
|---|---|---|---|---|---|---|---|---|---|---|---|
| | | | | | | **Habitats (Continued)** | | | | | |
| *What Can We See in Nature?* | Caroline Hutchison | 16 | | X | | | | | X | | Rising Readers Leveled Books: Science |
| *What Lives at the Pond?* | Caroline Hutchinson | 16 | | X | | | | | | | Rising Readers Leveled Books: Science |
| *What Would You Eat in the Rainforest?* | Caroline Hutchinson | 16 | | X | | | | | X | | Rising Readers Leveled Books: Science |
| *Where Can They Live?* | Jill Eggleton | 16 | | X | | X | | X | | | Abrams Learning Trends |
| *Where Do Plants Live?* | Caroline Hutchinson | 16 | | X | | | | | X | | Rising Readers Leveled Books: Science |
| | | | | | | **Healthy Living** | | | | | |
| *Eat All Your Colors* | Cathy Torrisi | 14 | X | X | | | X | X | X | X | Big Book Health & Safety |
| *Get Up and Go!* | Cathy Torrisi | 14 | X | X | | | X | X | X | X | Big Book Health & Safety |
| *Healthy Days* | Cathy Torrisi | 14 | X | X | | | X | X | X | X | Big Book Health & Safety |
| *How Do You Stay Well* | Caroline Hutchinson | 16 | | X | | | | | X | | Rising Readers Leveled Books: Science |
| *I Am Clean, I Am Healthy* | Nicole Desalle | 14 | X | X | | X | | X | X | X | Big Book Health & Safety |
| *I Have Chicken Pox* | Gillian Gosman | 24 | X | X | | X | X | X | | | Get Well Soon |
| *I Keep Myself Healthy* | Brenda Dominello | 14 | X | X | | X | X | X | X | X | Big Book Science |
| *I Know First Aid* | Cathy Torrisi | 14 | X | X | | | X | X | X | X | Big Book Health & Safety |
| *Let's Eat* | Donna Merritt | 14 | X | X | | | X | X | X | X | Big Book Science |
| *Staying Clean* | Robin Nelson | 32 | | X | | | X | X | | | Pull Ahead Books: Health |
| *Vegetables on My Plate* | Mari Schuh | 24 | X | X | | | X | X | | | Pebble Plus: What's on My Plate? |
| *What Should I Put on My Plate?* | Cathy Torrisi | 14 | X | X | | X | X | X | X | X | Big Book Science |

*Legend:* pp = Number of pages; TC = Table of contents; P = Photos; ILL = Illustrated; C = Captioned; G = Glossary; I = Index; L = Leveled book; BB = Available in big book format

| Title | Author | pp | TC | P | ILL | C | G | I | L | BB | Series |
|---|---|---|---|---|---|---|---|---|---|---|---|
| | | | | | History | | | | | | |
| *Balloons Over Broadway: The True Story of the Puppeteer of Macy's Parade* | Melissa Sweet | 40 | | | X | X | | X | | | |
| *The Beatitudes: From Slavery to Civil Rights* | Carole Boston Weatherford | 36 | | | X | | | | | | |
| *Betsy Ross* | Alexandra Wallner | 32 | | | X | | | | | | |
| *Betsy Ross* | Becky White | 32 | | | X | | | | | | |
| *The Cemetery Keepers of Gettysburg* | Linda Oatman High | 32 | | | X | | | | | | |
| *Children Past and Present* | Matthew Frank | 16 | X | X | | X | X | X | X | X | Social Studies Content Connections |
| *Clothes Then and Now* | Vickey Herold | 20 | X | X | X | X | X | X | X | | Early Explorers: Social Studies: Then and Now |
| *Inventions Changed Our Lives* | Colleen Barile | 14 | X | X | | X | X | X | X | X | Big Book Science |
| *Long Ago and Now* | Cathy Torrisi | 14 | X | X | | | X | X | X | X | Abrams Learning Trends |
| *Moses: When Harriet Tubman Led Her People to Freedom* | Carole Boston Weatherford | 48 | | | X | | | | | | |
| *Needs Past and Present* | Matthew Frank | 16 | X | X | X | | X | X | X | X | Social Studies Content Connections |
| *One Thousand Tracings: Healing the Wounds of World War II* | Lita Judge | 40 | | | X | | | | | | |
| *Over the Bridge* | Jeannie Kennedy | 20 | X | X | | X | | X | X | | |
| *Schools Then and Now* | Cynthia Swain | 16 | | X | X | | X | | X | | Social Studies Then and Now |
| *Thank You, Sarah: The Woman Who Saved Thanksgiving* | Laurie Halse Anderson | 49 | | | X | | | | | | |
| *Titanic* | Melissa Stewart | 48 | X | X | | X | X | X | | | National Geographic Kids |
| *Transportation Past and Present* | Matthew Frank | 16 | X | X | | X | X | X | X | X | Social Studies Content Connections |

*Legend:* pp = Number of pages; TC = Table of contents; P = Photos; ILL = Illustrated; C = Captioned; G = Glossary; I = Index; L = Leveled book; BB = Available in big book format

| Title | Author | pp | TC | P | ILL | C | G | I | L | BB | Series |
|---|---|---|---|---|---|---|---|---|---|---|---|
| **Holidays/Special Celebrations** | | | | | | | | | | | |
| *Balloons Over Broadway: The True Story of the Puppeteer of Macy's Parade* | Melissa Sweet | 40 | | | X | X | | X | | | |
| *Birthdays Around the World* | Mary Lankford | 32 | X | | X | | | X | | | |
| *Earth Day* | Clara Cella | 24 | X | X | | | X | X | | | Pebble Plus: Let's Celebrate! |
| *Groundhog Day!* | Gail Gibbons | 32 | | | X | X | | | | | |
| *Presidents' Day* | Robin Nelson | 23 | | X | | | X | X | | | First Step Nonfiction |
| *Thank You, Sarah: The Woman Who Saved Thanksgiving* | Laurie Halse Anderson | 49 | | | X | | | | | | |
| **Human Body** | | | | | | | | | | | |
| *Bones* | Steve Jenkins | 44 | | | X | X | | | | | |
| *The Bones You Own* | Becky Baines | 28 | | X | X | | | | | | |
| *I Can Move* | Caroline Hutchinson | 16 | | X | | | | | X | | Rising Readers Leveled Books: Science |
| *Me* | Emily Wood | 16 | | X | | | X | | X | | Flying Start to Literacy |
| *My Wonderful Body* | Donna Merritt | 14 | X | X | | X | X | X | X | X | Big Book Science |
| *Your Body Has Parts* | Caroline Hutchinson | 16 | | X | | | | | X | | Rising Readers Leveled Books: Science |
| *Your Skin Holds You In* | Becky Baines | 29 | | X | X | | | | | | National Geographic Kids |
| **Insects** | | | | | | | | | | | |
| *Ants! They Are Hard Workers* | Brenda Iasevoli | 32 | X | X | | X | X | | | | Time for Kids: Science Scoops |
| *The Beetle Book* | Steve Jenkins | 40 | | | X | | X | | | | |
| *Bug Hunters* | Jill Eggleton | 16 | | X | | X | X | X | | | |
| *Bully Bugs* | Lynda Nunweek | 16 | | X | | X | X | X | | | |
| *Butterflies* | Laura Marsh | 48 | X | X | | X | X | X | | | National Geographic Kids: Great Migrations |

*Legend:* pp = Number of pages; TC = Table of contents; P = Photos; ILL = Illustrated; C = Captioned; G = Glossary; I = Index; L = Leveled book; BB = Available in big book format

| Title | Author | pp | TC | P | ILL | C | G | I | L | BB | Series |
|---|---|---|---|---|---|---|---|---|---|---|---|
| **Insects (Continued)** ||||||||||||
| *A Butterfly Is Patient* | Dianna Hutts Aston & Sylvia Long | 40 | | | X | X | | | | | |
| *The Buzz on Bees* | Shelley Rotner & Anne Woodhull | 32 | | X | | X | | | | | |
| *Caterpillar to Butterfly* | Laura Marsh | 32 | X | X | | X | X | | | | National Geographic Kids |
| *Caterpillars* | Marilyn Singer | 40 | | X | | X | X | X | | | |
| *It's a Butterfly's Life* | Irene Kelly | 32 | | | X | X | | | | | |
| *Ladybug* | Gail Gibbons | 32 | | | X | X | | | | | |
| *The Life Cycle of a Butterfly* | Margaret McNamara | 16 | X | X | | X | X | X | X | X | Science Content Connections |
| *The Life of a Butterfly* | Ann Murphy | 14 | X | X | | | X | X | X | X | Big Book Science |
| *Monarch and Milkweed* | Helen Frost & Leonid Gore | 40 | | | X | | | | | | |
| *Monarch Butterfly* | Gail Gibbons | 32 | | | X | X | | | | | |
| *Spiders* | Laura Marsh | 32 | X | X | | X | X | | | | |
| **Jobs** ||||||||||||
| *Before It Gets to the Store* | Cathy Torrisi | 14 | X | X | | | X | X | X | X | Abrams Learning Trends |
| *Bug Hunters* | Jill Eggleton | 16 | | X | | X | | X | X | | |
| *Circus Performers* | Jeannie Kennedy | 20 | X | X | | | | X | X | | |
| *Demolition* | Sally Sutton | 32 | | | X | | | | | | |
| *Helicopters Help* | Jill Eggleton | 16 | | X | | | | X | X | | |
| *How Did That Get in My Lunch Box?* | Chris Butterworth | 32 | | | X | X | | X | | | |
| *Hunting for Treasure* | Lynda Nunweek | 20 | X | X | | X | | X | X | | |
| *My Community* | Cathy Torrisi | 14 | X | X | | | X | X | X | X | Abrams Learning Trends |
| *A Photographer's Diary* | Jill Eggleton | 20 | | X | | | | | X | | |
| *Smoke Jumpers Help* | Jill Eggleton | 16 | | X | | X | | | X | | Abrams Learning Trends |
| *The Snake Wrangler* | Lynda Nunweek | 16 | | X | | X | | X | X | | |
| *The Story of Silk: From Worm Spit to Woven Scarves* | Richard Sobol | 37 | | X | | X | X | | | | |

*Legend:* pp = Number of pages; TC = Table of contents; P = Photos; ILL = Illustrated; C = Captioned; G = Glossary; I = Index; L = Leveled book; BB = Available in big book format

| Title | Author | pp | TC | P | ILL | C | G | I | L | BB | Series |
|---|---|---|---|---|---|---|---|---|---|---|---|
| **Jobs (Continued)** | | | | | | | | | | | |
| *Whose Shoes?* | Stephen Swinburne | 32 | | X | | | | | | | |
| *Wildlife Detective* | Jill Eggleton | 20 | | X | | | | | X | | |
| **Life Cycles of Animals** | | | | | | | | | | | |
| *Caterpillar to Butterfly* | Laura Marsh | 32 | X | X | | X | X | | | | National Geographic Kids |
| *It's a Butterfly's Life* | Irene Kelly | 32 | | | X | X | | | | | |
| *It's a Hummingbird's Life* | Irene Kelly | | | | | | | | | | |
| *The Life Cycle of a Butterfly* | Margaret McNamara | 16 | X | X | | X | X | X | X | X | Science Content Connections |
| *The Life Cycle of a Frog* | Margaret McNamara | 16 | X | X | | X | X | X | X | X | Science Content Connections |
| *The Life of a Butterfly* | Ann Murphy | 14 | X | X | | X | X | X | X | | Big Book Science |
| *Monarch and Milkweed* | Helen Frost & Leonid Gore | 40 | | | X | | | | | | |
| *Monarch Butterfly* | Gail Gibbons | 32 | | | X | X | | | | | |
| *What Is In That Egg?* | Becky Baines | 29 | | X | | | | | | | |
| **Maps** | | | | | | | | | | | |
| *Bird's-Eye View of a Neighborhood* | Matthew Frank | 16 | X | X | X | X | X | X | X | X | Social Studies Content Connections |
| *Map Keys* | Rebecca Aberg | 32 | | X | X | X | X | | | | Rookie Read About Geography |
| *Map Skills* | Matthew Frank | 16 | X | X | X | X | X | | X | X | Social Studies Content Connections |
| *Maps of My School* | Matthew Frank | 16 | X | X | X | X | X | X | X | X | Social Studies Content Connections |
| *We Need Directions* | Sarah De Capua | 32 | | X | | X | X | | | | Rookie Read About Geography |
| *Where Are We?* | Cathy Torrisi | 14 | X | X | | X | X | X | X | | Abrams Learning Trends |
| **Math** | | | | | | | | | | | |
| *Adding Two-Digit Numbers* | April Barth | 16 | X | X | | X | X | X | X | X | Math Content Connections |
| *Addition and Subtraction* | April Barth | 16 | X | X | | X | X | X | X | X | Math Content Connections |
| *Addition Strategies* | April Barth | 16 | X | X | | X | X | X | X | X | Math Content Connections |

*Legend:* pp = Number of pages; TC = Table of contents; P = Photos; ILL = Illustrated; C = Captioned; G = Glossary; I = Index; L = Leveled book; BB = Available in big book format

| Title | Author | pp | TC | P | ILL | C | G | I | L | BB | Series |
|---|---|---|---|---|---|---|---|---|---|---|---|
| | | | | | | Math (Continued) | | | | | |
| *Are They Equal?* | Brianna Cain | 14 | | X | | X | | | X | X | Big Book Math |
| *Centimeter and Meter* | April Barth | | X | X | | X | X | X | X | X | Math Content Connections |
| *Compare and Order Numbers to 1,000* | April Barth | | X | X | | X | X | X | X | X | Math Content Connections |
| *Compare Numbers to 100* | April Barth | | X | X | | X | X | X | X | X | Math Content Connections |
| *Counting to 10 and Beyond* | Elizabeth Huff Bennett | 14 | | X | | X | | | X | X | Big Book Math |
| *Estimating Sums and Differences* | April Barth | | X | X | | X | X | X | X | X | Math Content Connections |
| *How Else Can We Show It?* | Miguel Ortega Rodriguez | 14 | | X | | | | | X | X | Big Book Math |
| *How Many Are Left?* | Kay Jackson | 14 | | X | | | | | X | X | Big Book Math |
| *How Many in All?* | April Barth | 16 | X | X | | X | X | X | X | X | Math Content Connections |
| *How Many Parts?* | Linh Nguyen | 14 | | X | | X | | | X | X | Big Book Math |
| *Is It Likely to Happen?* | Donna Merritt | 14 | | X | | X | | | X | X | Big Book Math |
| *It All Adds Up* | Claire Johnson | 14 | | X | | | | | X | X | Big Book Math |
| *Let's Figure It Out!* | Donna Merritt | 14 | | X | | X | | | X | X | Big Book Math |
| *Match-Up Fun* | Cathy Torrisi | 14 | | X | | | | | X | X | Big Book Math |
| *Numbers to 100: Before, After, and Between* | April Barth | 16 | X | X | X | X | X | X | X | X | Math Content Connections |
| *One More, One Less* | April Barth | 16 | X | X | | X | X | X | X | X | Math Content Connections |
| *Same, More, Less?* | April Barth | 16 | X | X | | X | X | X | X | X | Math Content Connections |
| *Subtracting Two-Digit Numbers* | April Barth | 16 | X | X | | X | X | X | X | X | Math Content Connections |
| *Subtraction Strategies* | April Barth | 16 | X | X | | X | X | X | X | X | Math Content Connections |
| *Understanding Place Value* | April Barth | 16 | X | | X | X | X | X | X | X | Math Content Connections |
| *Understanding Tens and Ones* | April Barth | 16 | X | X | | X | X | X | X | X | Math Content Connections |
| *We Can Graph It!* | Ann Murphy | 14 | | X | | | | | X | X | Big Book Math |

Legend: pp = Number of pages; TC = Table of contents; P = Photos; ILL = Illustrated; C = Captioned; G = Glossary; I = Index; L = Leveled book; BB = Available in big book format

| Title | Author | pp | TC | P | ILL | C | G | I | L | BB | Series |
|-------|--------|-----|----|----|-----|---|---|---|---|----|--------|
| *Actual Size* | Steve Jenkins | 28 | | | X | | | | | | |
| *Centimeter and Meter* | April Barth | 16 | X | X | | X | X | X | X | X | Math Content Connections |
| *Finding Length* | April Barth | 16 | X | X | | X | X | X | X | X | Math Content Connections |
| *Heavier and Lighter* | April Barth | 16 | X | X | | X | X | X | X | X | Math Content Connections |
| *How Do We Measure?* | Ann Murphy | 14 | | X | | | | | X | X | Big Book Math |
| *How Do We Tell Time?* | Kathleen Fischer | 14 | | X | | | | | X | X | Big Book Math |
| *Inch, Foot, Yard* | April Barth | 16 | X | X | | X | X | X | X | X | Math Content Connections |
| *Just a Second* | Steven Jenkins | 40 | | | X | | | | | | |
| *Let's Measure With Tools* | Christine Casteel | 14 | | X | | X | | | X | X | Big Book Math |
| *What Is Longer? What Is Shorter?* | April Barth | 16 | X | X | | X | X | X | X | X | Math Content Connections |
| *What Time Is It?* | Marie Mulcahy | 14 | | X | | X | | | X | X | Big Book Math |

<table>
<thead>
<tr><th colspan="12" align="center">Money</th></tr>
</thead>
</table>

| Title | Author | pp | TC | P | ILL | C | G | I | L | BB | Series |
|-------|--------|-----|----|----|-----|---|---|---|---|----|--------|
| *Dimes* | Kara Kenna & Judy Ostarch | 24 | | X | | | | | | | All About Coins |
| *Lots and Lots of Coins* | Margarette Reid | 32 | | X | | X | | | | | |
| *Money Matters* | BreAnn Rumsch | 32 | X | X | | X | X | X | | | Economy in Action |
| *Nickels* | Kara Kenna & Judy Ostarch | 24 | | X | | | | | | | All About Coins |
| *Pennies* | Kara Kenna & Judy Ostarch | 24 | | X | | | | | | | All About Coins |
| *Quarters* | Kara Kenna & Judy Ostarch | 24 | | X | | | | | | | All About Coins |

<table>
<thead>
<tr><th colspan="12" align="center">Natural Disasters</th></tr>
</thead>
</table>

| Title | Author | pp | TC | P | ILL | C | G | I | L | BB | Series |
|-------|--------|-----|----|----|-----|---|---|---|---|----|--------|
| *A Big Earthquake* | Jill Eggleton | 16 | | X | | X | | X | | | Abrams Learning Trends |
| *The Hand of Nature* | Jill Eggleton | 20 | X | X | | | | | X | | |
| *Hurricanes* | Gail Gibbons | 32 | | | X | X | | | | | |
| *Tornado!* | Amanda Jenkins | 16 | | | | X | | X | | | Reader's Theater: Science |
| *Tornadoes!* | Gail Gibbons | | | | X | X | | | | | |
| *Volcanoes!* | Anne Schreiber | 32 | X | X | | X | X | | | | National Geographic Kids |

*Legend:* pp = Number of pages; TC = Table of contents; P = Photos; ILL = Illustrated; C = Captioned; G = Glossary; I = Index; L = Leveled book; BB = Available in big book format

| Title | Author | pp | TC | P | ILL | C | G | I | L | BB | Series |
|---|---|---|---|---|---|---|---|---|---|---|---|
| | | | | **Ocean Animals** | | | | | | | |
| *Alphabet of Ocean Animals* | Laura Gates Galvin | 40 | | | X | | | | | | |
| *Baby Animals in the Sea* | Kingfisher Editors | 14 | | X | | X | | | | | Kingfisher: Baby Animals |
| *A Battle in the Deep Sea* | Lynda Nunweek | 16 | | X | | X | | X | X | | |
| *A Battle to Breathe* | Lynda Nunweek | 16 | | X | | | | X | X | | |
| *Coral Reefs* | Gail Gibbons | 32 | | | X | X | | | | | |
| *Do Whales Have Belly Buttons?* | Melvin & Gilda Berger | 47 | X | | X | | | X | | | |
| *Dolphins to the Rescue* | Jill Eggleton | 16 | | X | | X | | X | X | | Abrams Learning Trends |
| *Down, Down, Down: A Journey to the Bottom of the Sea* | Steve Jenkins | 40 | | | X | | | | | | |
| *In the Sea* | David Elliott | 32 | | | X | | | | | | |
| *Leopard and Silkie: One Boy's Quest to Save the Seal Pups* | Brenda Peterson | 32 | | X | | | | | | | |
| *Life in a Coral Reef* | Wendy Pfeffer | 34 | | | X | | | | | | Let's-Read-And-Find-Out: Science |
| *Monsters of the Deep* | Nicola Davies | 32 | | X | | X | | | | | |
| *Ocean: Discover Earth's Ecosystems* | Sean Callery | 32 | X | X | | X | X | X | | | |
| *Oceans and Seas* | Nicola Davies | 56 | X | X | | X | | X | | | Science Kids |
| *Oceans: Dolphins, Sharks, Penguins, and More* | Johanna Rizzo | 64 | X | X | | X | X | X | | | |
| *Octopus Mother* | Jill Eggleton | 16 | | X | | X | | X | X | | Abrams Learning Trends |
| *Robot Crab* | Jill Eggleton | 14 | | X | | | | X | X | | |
| *Sea Turtles* | Laura Marsh | | | | | | | | | | |
| *Splash: A Book About Whales and Dolphins* | Melvin & Gilda Berger | 40 | | X | | | | | X | | Hello Reader: Science |
| *Tiger Shark* | Deborah Nuzzolo | 32 | | X | | X | X | X | | | |
| *The Turtle's Journey* | Jill Eggleton | 14 | | X | | | | X | X | | |
| *Weird Sea Creatures* | Laura Marsh | 32 | X | X | | X | X | | | | National Geographic Kids |
| *Whales and Dolphins: Open Your Eyes to a World of Discovery* | Caroline Bingham | 47 | X | X | | X | X | X | | | |

*Legend:* pp = Number of pages; TC = Table of contents; P = Photos; ILL = Illustrated; C = Captioned; G = Glossary; I = Index; L = Leveled book; BB = Available in big book format

| Title | Author | pp | TC | P | ILL | C | G | I | L | BB | Series |
|---|---|---|---|---|---|---|---|---|---|---|---|
| **Patterns/Symmetry** | | | | | | | | | | | |
| *Bees, Snails, & Peacock Tails: Patterns and Shapes . . . Naturally* | Betsy Franco & Steve Jenkins | 40 | | | X | | | | | | |
| *Let's Make Patterns* | Marsha Grant | 14 | | X | | | | | X | X | Big Book Math |
| *Right Down the Middle* | Cathy Torrisi | 14 | | X | X | | | | X | X | Big Book Math |
| *Seeing Symmetry* | Loreen Leedy | 32 | | X | | X | | | | | |
| *What Is Next?* | Gloria Chen | 16 | | X | | | | | X | | Rising Readers Leveled Books: Math |
| **Pets** | | | | | | | | | | | |
| *Brave Dogs, Gentle Dogs* | Cat Urbigkit | 32 | | X | | | | | | | |
| *Cats vs. Dogs* | Elizabeth Carney | 48 | X | X | | | X | X | | | |
| *Dogs* | Emily Wood | 16 | | X | | | | | X | | Flying Start to Literacy |
| *Dogs and Cats* | Steve Jenkins | 40 | | | X | X | | | | | |
| *Everything Dogs* | Becky Baines | 64 | X | X | | | X | X | X | | National Geographic Kids |
| *A Handy Horse* | Jill Eggleton | 16 | | X | | X | | | X | X | Abrams Learning Trends |
| *Meet the Dogs of Bedlam Farm* | Jon Katz | 32 | | X | | X | | | | | |
| *Over, Under, In, and Out* | Marie Mulcahy | 14 | | X | | X | | | X | X | Big Book Math |
| *Pets* | Kingfisher Editors | 14 | | X | | X | | | | | Kingfisher: Baby Animals |
| *Puppies, Puppies Everywhere!* | Cat Urbigkit | 22 | | X | | | | | | | |
| *Saving Audie: A Pit Bull Puppy Gets a Second Chance* | Dorothy Hinshaw Patent | 48 | | X | | X | | | | | |
| *Super Dog* | Jill Eggleton | 16 | | X | | X | | | X | X | Abrams Learning Trends |
| **Physical Science (Physics, Chemistry, Simple Machines)** | | | | | | | | | | | |
| *Discover Forensic Chemistry* | Libby Romero | 24 | X | X | | | X | X | X | | English Explorers Chemistry |
| *Discover Kitchen Chemistry* | Libby Romero | 24 | X | X | | | X | X | X | | English Explorers Chemistry |

*Legend:* pp = Number of pages; TC = Table of contents; P = Photos; ILL = Illustrated; C = Captioned; G = Glossary; I = Index; L = Leveled book; BB = Available in big book format

| Title | Author | pp | TC | P | ILL | C | G | I | L | BB | Series |
|-------|--------|----|----|---|-----|---|---|---|---|----|--------|
| **Physical Science (Physics, Chemistry, Simple Machines) (Continued)** | | | | | | | | | | | |
| *Discover Medical Chemistry* | Libby Romero | 24 | X | X | | X | X | X | | | English Explorers Chemistry |
| *Earth Rocks!* | Brenda Dominello | 14 | X | X | | X | X | X | X | X | Big Book Science |
| *Energy All Around* | Mark Ramirez | 14 | X | X | | X | X | X | X | X | Big Book Science |
| *Feel the Force* | Tom Adams | 20 | | | X | X | | X | | | |
| *Force and Motion* | Mark Ramirez | 14 | X | X | | X | X | X | X | X | Big Book Science |
| *Forensic Chemistry* | Libby Romero | 32 | X | X | | X | X | X | | | English Explorers Chemistry |
| *Kitchen Chemistry* | Libby Romero | 32 | X | X | | X | X | X | | | English Explorers Chemistry |
| *Medical Chemistry* | Libby Romero | 32 | X | X | | X | X | X | | | English Explorers Chemistry |
| *Playground Science* | Donna Merritt | 14 | X | X | | | X | X | X | X | Big Book Science |
| *Robots* | Rod Rees | 24 | X | X | | X | | | X | | Explorations |
| *Rocks and Minerals* | Steve Tomecek | 32 | | X | X | X | X | X | X | X | Big Book Science |
| *Watch What Happens!* | Marsha Grant | 14 | X | X | | | X | X | X | X | Big Book Science |
| *Water* | Gallimard Jeunesse & Pierre-Marie Valat | 34 | | | X | X | | | | | My First Discoveries |
| *The Water Cycle* | Donna Merritt | 14 | X | X | | X | X | X | X | X | Big Book Science |
| **Plants** | | | | | | | | | | | |
| *Amazing Plants* | Rosario Ortiz Santiago | 14 | X | X | | | X | X | X | X | Big Book Science |
| *Apples for Everyone* | Jill Esbaum | 16 | | X | | | | | | | |
| *Corn* | Elaine Landau | 50 | X | X | | X | | | | | A True Book |
| *Different Plants* | Jill Eggleton | 16 | | X | | | | X | X | | |
| *From Seed to Pumpkin* | Jan Kottke | 23 | | X | | | X | X | X | | Welcome Books |
| *From Seed to Pumpkin* | Wendy Pfeffer | 33 | | | X | | | | X | | Let's-Read-And-Find-Out: Science |
| *It Started With a Plant* | Jill Eggleton | 16 | | X | | | | X | X | | Abram Learning Trends |
| *Living Things Are Everywhere!* | Jayne Smith | 14 | X | X | | | X | X | X | X | Big Book Science |

*Legend:* pp = Number of pages; TC = Table of contents; P = Photos; ILL = Illustrated; C = Captioned; G = Glossary; I = Index; L = Leveled book; BB = Available in big book format

| Title | Author | pp | TC | P | ILL | C | G | I | L | BB | Series |
|---|---|---|---|---|---|---|---|---|---|---|---|
| **Plants (Continued)** | | | | | | | | | | | |
| *Looking Closely in the Rain Forest* | Frank Serafini | 40 | | X | | | | | | | |
| *The Mangrove Trees: Planting Trees to Feed Families* | Susan Roth & Cindy Trumbore | 40 | | | X | X | X | | | | |
| *Moving Seeds* | Jill Eggleton | 14 | | X | | | | X | X | | |
| *The Mystery Seeds* | Christopher Raymond | | | | | | | | | | |
| *An Oak Tree Has a Life Cycle* | Debra Castor | 16 | X | X | | X | X | X | X | X | Science Content Connections |
| *Parts of a Plant* | Debra Castor | 16 | X | X | | X | X | X | X | X | Science Content Connections |
| *Plants and the Seasons* | Margaret McNamara | 16 | X | X | | X | X | X | X | X | Science Content Connections |
| *Plants in Their Habitat* | Debra Castor | 16 | X | X | | X | X | X | X | X | Science Content Connections |
| *Seed, Sprout, Pumpkin, Pie* | Jill Esbaum | 16 | | X | | | | | | | |
| *The Tall Tree* | Jill Eggleton | 16 | | X | | X | | X | X | | Abrams Learning Trends |
| *Tell Me, Tree: All About Trees for Kids* | Gail Gibbons | 32 | | | X | X | | | | | |
| *Up Pops a Mushroom* | Jill Eggleton | 16 | X | X | | X | | X | X | | |
| *The Vegetables We Eat* | Gail Gibbons | 32 | | | X | X | | | | | |
| *What Do Plants Need?* | Debra Castor | 16 | X | X | | X | X | X | X | X | Science Content Connections |
| *Where Do Plants Live?* | Caroline Hutchinson | 16 | | X | | | | | X | | Rising Readers Leveled Books: Science |
| **Presidents and Their Families** | | | | | | | | | | | |
| *Camping With the President* | Ginger Wadsworth | 32 | | | X | | | | | | |
| *Eleanor, Quiet No More* | Doreen Rappaport | 48 | | | X | | | | | | |
| *First Dog Fala* | Elizabeth Van Steenwyk | 32 | | | X | | | | | | |
| *George: George Washington, Our Founding Father* | Frank Keating | 32 | | | X | | | | | | |

*Legend:* pp = Number of pages; TC = Table of contents; P = Photos; ILL = Illustrated; C = Captioned; G = Glossary; I = Index; L = Leveled book; BB = Available in big book format

| Title | Author | pp | TC | P | ILL | C | G | I | L | BB | Series |
|---|---|---|---|---|---|---|---|---|---|---|---|
| **Presidents and Their Families (Continued)** | | | | | | | | | | | |
| A President from Hawai'i | Terry & Joanna Carolan | 24 | | X | X | X | X | | | | |
| Stand Tall, Abe Lincoln | Judith St. George | 48 | | | X | | | | | | |
| Theodore | Frank Keating | 32 | | | X | | | | | | |
| **Ranch/Farm Life** | | | | | | | | | | | |
| Brave Dogs, Gentle Dogs | Cat Urbigkit | 32 | | X | | | | | | | |
| Cattle Kids: A Year on the Western Ranch | Cat Urbigkit | 32 | | X | | | | | | | |
| The Dingo Fence | Jill Eggleton | 20 | X | X | | X | | X | X | | |
| The Guardian Team: On the Job With Rena and Roo | Cat Urbigkit | 32 | | X | | | | | | | |
| Meet the Dogs of Bedlam Farm | Jon Katz | 32 | | X | | X | | | | | |
| Senses on the Farm | Shelley Rotner | 32 | | X | | | | | | | |
| The Shepherd's Trail | Cat Urbigkit | 32 | | X | | | | | | | |
| World of Farming: Food From Farms | Nancy Dickman | 24 | X | X | | | X | X | | | World of Farming |
| World of Farming: Jobs on the Farm | Nancy Dickman | 24 | X | X | | | X | X | | | World of Farming |
| World of Farming: Seasons on a Farm | Nancy Dickman | 24 | X | X | | | X | X | | | World of Farming |
| A Young Shepherd | Cat Urbigkit | 32 | | X | | | | | | | |
| **Reptiles** | | | | | | | | | | | |
| Lizards | Laura Marsh | 32 | X | X | | X | X | | | | National Geographic Kids |
| A Photographer's Diary | Jill Eggleton | 20 | | X | | | | | X | | |
| Reptiles | Belinda Weber | 56 | X | X | | X | X | X | | | Kingfisher Young Knowledge |
| The Snake Wrangler | Lynda Nunweek | 16 | | X | | X | | X | X | | |
| Snakes | Gail Gibbons | 32 | | | X | X | | | | | |
| Snakes! | Melissa Stewart | 32 | X | X | | X | X | | | | National Geographic Kids |

*Legend:* pp = Number of pages; TC = Table of contents; P = Photos; ILL = Illustrated; C = Captioned; G = Glossary; I = Index; L = Leveled book; BB = Available in big book format

| Title | Author | pp | TC | P | ILL | C | G | I | L | BB | Series |
|-------|--------|-----|-----|-----|------|-----|-----|-----|-----|------|--------|
| **Safety** | | | | | | | | | | | |
| *I Keep Myself Safe* | Cathy Torrisi | 14 | X | X | | | X | X | X | X | Big Book Science |
| *I Know First Aid* | Cathy Torrisi | 14 | X | X | | | X | X | X | X | Big Book Health & Safety |
| *Safe at Home* | Nicole Desalle | 14 | X | X | | | X | X | | X | Big Book Health & Safety |
| *Safe at Play* | Nicole Desalle | 14 | X | X | | | X | X | | X | Big Book Health & Safety |
| *Safe at School* | Nicole Desalle | 14 | X | X | | | X | X | | X | Big Book Health & Safety |
| *Tell Someone You Trust* | Cathy Torrisi | 14 | X | X | | | X | X | X | X | Big Book Health & Safety |
| **Science** | | | | | | | | | | | |
| *Amazing Scientists* | Donna Merritt | 14 | X | X | | X | X | X | X | X | Big Book Science |
| *First Big Book of Why* | Amy Shields | 128 | X | X | | X | X | X | | | National Geographic Little Kids |
| *How Scientists Observe* | Marie Mulcahy | 14 | X | X | | X | X | X | X | X | Big Book Science |
| *Science Detectives* | Christopher Raymond | 14 | X | X | | X | X | X | X | X | Big Book Science |
| *Science Is Everywhere!* | Nancy Yu | 14 | X | X | X | X | X | X | X | X | Big Book Science |
| *Tell Me All About It* | Christopher Raymond | 14 | X | X | | | X | X | X | X | Big Book Science |
| **Seasons** | | | | | | | | | | | |
| *Animals and the Seasons* | Margaret McNamara | 16 | X | X | | X | X | X | X | X | Science Content Connections |
| *Animals in the Fall* | Martha Rustad | 24 | X | X | | | X | X | | | Pebble Plus: All About Fall |
| *A Den Is a Bed for a Bear* | Becky Baines | 30 | | X | X | | | | | | |
| *Every Season* | Shelley Rotner & Anne Love Woodhull | 32 | | X | | | | | | | |
| *Everything Spring* | Jill Esbaum | 16 | | X | | | | | | | |
| *Plants and the Seasons* | Margaret McNamara | 16 | X | X | | X | X | X | X | X | Science Content Connections |
| *Weather and the Seasons* | Margaret McNamara | 16 | X | X | | X | X | X | X | X | Science Content Connections |

*Legend:* pp = Number of pages; TC = Table of contents; P = Photos; ILL = Illustrated; C = Captioned; G = Glossary; I = Index; L = Leveled book; BB = Available in big book format

| Title | Author | pp | TC | P | ILL | C | G | I | L | BB | Series |
|---|---|---|---|---|---|---|---|---|---|---|---|
| **Seasons (Continued)** | | | | | | | | | | | |
| *What Season Is It?* | Caroline Hutchinson | 16 | | X | | | | | X | | Rising Readers Leveled Books: Science |
| *Winter Wonderland* | Jill Esbaum | 16 | | X | | | | | | | |
| *World of Farming: Seasons on a Farm* | Nancy Dickman | 24 | X | X | | | X | X | | | World of Farming |
| **Shapes** | | | | | | | | | | | |
| *Building With Solid Shapes* | April Barth | 16 | X | X | | X | X | X | X | X | Math Content Connections |
| *Designing With Plane Shapes* | April Barth | 16 | X | X | | X | X | X | X | X | Math Content Connections |
| *Look for Shapes* | Alison Schmerler | 14 | | X | | | | | X | X | Big Book Math |
| *Plane Shapes* | April Barth | 16 | X | X | X | X | X | X | X | X | Math Content Connections |
| *Solid Shapes* | April Barth | 16 | X | X | | X | X | X | X | X | Math Content Connections |
| *Solid Shapes* | Alison Schmerler | 14 | | X | | | | | X | X | Big Book Math |
| *Where Are the Solid Shapes?* | April Barth | 16 | X | X | | X | X | X | X | X | Math Content Connections |
| **Space** | | | | | | | | | | | |
| *Every Planet Has a Place* | Becky Baines | 32 | | | X | | | | | | National Geographic Kids |
| *Galaxies* | Gail Gibbons | 32 | | | X | X | | | | | |
| *I Wonder Why Stars Twinkle* | Carol Stott | 32 | X | | X | X | | X | | | I Wonder Why |
| *Living in Space* | Jill Eggleton | 14 | | X | | | X | X | | | |
| *A Mammoth Eclipse* | Joseph Nunweek | 20 | X | X | | | X | X | | | |
| *Our Solar System* | Megan Wasp | 14 | X | X | | X | X | X | X | X | Big Book Science |
| *Planets* | Penelope Arlon | 79 | X | X | | X | X | X | | | Scholastic: Discover More |
| *Robot Lander on Mars* | Jill Eggleton | 16 | | X | | | X | X | | | |
| *The Stars Above* | Jill Eggleton | 16 | | X | | X | X | X | | | |
| *A Suit for Spacewalking* | Jill Eggleton | 20 | X | X | | X | X | X | | | |

*Legend:* pp = Number of pages; TC = Table of contents; P = Photos; ILL = Illustrated; C = Captioned; G = Glossary; I = Index; L = Leveled book; BB = Available in big book format

| Title | Author | pp | TC | P | ILL | C | G | I | L | BB | Series |
|---|---|---|---|---|---|---|---|---|---|---|---|
| **Space (Continued)** | | | | | | | | | | | |
| *Sun and Shadows, Sky and Space* | Maria Sanchez | 14 | X | X | | X | X | X | X | X | Big Book Science |
| *A Trip to Space Camp* | Jeannie Kennedy | 20 | X | X | | | | | X | X | |
| **Sports/Recreation** | | | | | | | | | | | |
| *Climbing a Rock Wall* | Janine Scott | 20 | X | X | | X | | X | X | | |
| *My Baseball Book* | Gail Gibbons | 22 | | | X | X | X | | | | |
| *My Basketball Book* | Gail Gibbons | 22 | | | X | X | X | | | | |
| *My Soccer Book* | Gail Gibbons | 22 | | | X | X | X | | | | |
| *On the Ball* | Jeannie Kennedy | 14 | | X | | | | X | X | | |
| *Same, More, Less?* | April Barth | 16 | X | X | | X | X | X | X | X | Math Content Connections |
| *The Unforgettable Season: The Story of Joe DiMaggio, Ted Williams, and the Record-Setting Summer of '41* | Phil Bildner | 32 | | | X | | | | | | |
| **Transportation** | | | | | | | | | | | |
| *Bulldozers* | Amanda Askew | 24 | X | X | | X | X | X | | | Mighty Machines |
| *Cars* | Ian Graham | 24 | X | X | | X | X | X | | | Mighty Machines |
| *Diggers* | Amanda Askew | 24 | X | X | | X | X | X | | | Mighty Machines |
| *Dump Trucks and Other Big Machines* | Ian Graham | 24 | X | X | | X | X | X | | | Mighty Machines |
| *Fire Trucks and Rescue Vehicles* | Jean Coppendale | 24 | X | X | | X | X | X | | | Mighty Machines |
| *Helicopters Help* | Jill Eggleton | 16 | | X | | | | X | X | | |
| *Monster Trucks* | Ian Graham | 24 | X | X | | X | X | X | | | Mighty Machines |
| *Race to the Finish* | Janine Scott | 20 | X | X | | X | | X | X | | |
| *Racing* | Jill Eggleton | 16 | | X | | | | X | X | | |
| *The Stourbridge Lion: America's First Locomotive* | Karl Zimmerman | 32 | | | X | | | | | | |
| *Tractors and Farm Vehicles* | Jean Coppendale | 24 | X | X | | X | X | X | | | Mighty Machines |

*Legend:* pp = Number of pages; TC = Table of contents; P = Photos; ILL = Illustrated; C = Captioned; G = Glossary; I = Index; L = Leveled book; BB = Available in big book format

| Title | Author | pp | TC | P | ILL | C | G | I | L | BB | Series |
|-------|--------|-----|-----|---|-----|---|---|---|---|-----|--------|
| **Transportation (Continued)** | | | | | | | | | | | |
| *Train* | Amy Shields | 32 | X | X | | | X | | | | |
| *Transportation Past and Present* | Matthew Frank | 16 | X | X | | X | X | X | X | X | Social Studies Content Connections |
| *Trucks* | Jean Coppendale | 24 | X | X | | X | X | X | | | Mighty Machines |
| *Wheels* | Jill Eggleton | 14 | | X | | | X | X | | | |
| **Weather** | | | | | | | | | | | |
| *How the Weather Works* | Christiane Dorion | 20 | | | X | X | | | | | |
| *Hurricanes* | Gail Gibbons | 32 | | | X | X | | | | | |
| *It's Snowing* | Gail Gibbons | 32 | | | X | X | | | | | |
| *Tornado!* | Amanda Jenkins | 16 | | | | | X | | X | | Reader's Theater: Science |
| *Tornadoes!* | Gail Gibbons | | | | X | X | | | | | |
| *Weather and the Seasons* | Margaret McNamara | 16 | X | X | | X | X | X | X | X | Science Content Connections |
| *What Is Weather?* | Cathleen Bartholomew | 14 | X | X | | | X | X | X | X | Big Book Science |

 Available for download at **www.corwin.com/theeverythingguide**

# Annotated Bibliography of Children's Books

The following is an annotated list of informational books that can be used in grades K–2. Some books would best be read aloud by the teacher; some could be part of guided reading; some could be read independently by children. This is not an exhaustive list. Because there have been so many high-quality informational books published recently, we have concentrated on those new titles, with a few classic nonfiction books added in as well. If you find a book in a series that you like or an author you like, we encourage you to look for other books in that series or by that author.

**Aberg, Rebecca. *Map Keys*. Scholastic, 2003.**
This book provides an explanation of what map keys are and how they can be used. (32 pp, P, G, I)

**Adams, Tom. *Feel the Force!* Templar Books, 2011.**
This creative, fun, and colorful book is both interactive and informative. Flaps can be lifted to discover the science and mechanics of physics while learning about pitch and intonation. Tabs can be pulled to fly a blimp or to give an electrical shock to Frankenstein. (20 pp, ILL, C, I)

**Allen, Judy. *Dinosaurs*. Kingfisher, 2008.**
Simple information about dinosaurs (food, size, babies, et cetera.) is presented in a lift-the-flap format, where questions are on one side and the answers are on the part revealed when the flap is lifted. (18 pp, ILL, I)

**Anderson, Laurie Halse. *Thank You, Sarah: The Woman Who Saved Thanksgiving*. Simon and Schuster Books for Young Readers, 2002.**
The true story of Sarah Hale, composer of "Mary Had a Little Lamb." During the Civil War, Sarah became concerned that people were ignoring Thanksgiving, so she wrote a letter asking President Lincoln to make Thanksgiving a national holiday. (40 pp, ILL)

**Arlon, Penelope. *Penguins*. Scholastic, 2012.**

Using colorful photographs, this book tells of the different types of penguins, where they live, what their diets are, and how they build nests. (80 pp, TC, P, C, G, I, Series: Scholastic: Discover More)

**Arlon, Penelope. *Planets*. Scholastic, 2012.**

Dense with information, this book presents details about the planets and our exploration of the solar system. Each page gives facts accompanying photographs and could be a stand-alone study in itself. (79 pp, TC, P, C, G, I, Series: Scholastic: Discover More)

**Askew, Amanda. *Bulldozers*. QEB Publishing, 2010.**

Large photographs show the different parts of a bulldozer. Many examples of how bulldozers are used to build roads, on the farm, in mining, in the army, et cetera, are given. (24 pp, TC, P, C, G, I, Series: Mighty Machines)

**Askew, Amanda. *Diggers*. QEB Publishing, 2010.**

This book includes photographs of the various parts of excavators as well as photographs of the many uses for these machines, such as for digging, mining, and demolition. (24 pp, TC, P, C, G, I, Series: Mighty Machines)

**Aston, Dianna Hutts, & Long, Sylvia. *A Butterfly is Patient*. Chronicle Books, 2011.**

With detailed paintings of many different butterflies, this book tells the life cycle of butterflies from eggs to the beautiful creatures that fly away. (40 pp, ILL, C)

**Baines, Becky. *The Bones You Own: A Book About the Human Body*. National Geographic Society, 2009.**

With simple, clear, and engaging pictures, Baines explains what bones are and how they work, and gives the names of many of them. (28 pp, P, C)

**Baines, Becky. *A Den Is a Bed for a Bear: A Book About Hibernation*. National Geographic Society, 2008.**

Baines shares through simple text and photographs how bears hibernate over the winter. (30 pp, P, C)

**Baines, Becky. *Every Planet Has a Place: A Book About Our Solar System*. National Geographic, 2008.**

Bright pages engage readers as they learn about our solar system, from the sun to the Kuiper Belt. (32 pp, ILL, Series: National Geographic Kids)

**Baines, Becky. *Everything Dogs*. National Geographic, 2012.**

Filled with adorable photographs and interesting facts, this book shares information about man's best friend. (64 pp, TC, P, C, G, I, Series: National Geographic Kids)

---

*Legend:* pp = Number of pages; TC = Table of contents; P = Photos; ILL = Illustrated; C = Captioned; G = Glossary; I = Index; L = Leveled book; BB = Available in big book format

**Baines, Becky.** *What Did One Elephant Say to the Other? A Book About Communication.* **National Geographic Society, 2008.**
This book explains how elephants communicate by using their whole bodies for talking. (29 pp, P)

**Baines, Becky.** *What Is In That Egg? A Book About Life Cycles.* **National Geographic Society, 2009.**
Baines presents an egg on the first page and asks, "What's in that egg?" She considers a turtle, a fish, a frog, a butterfly, and a swan. In fascinating colored photographs following the development in the egg, the reader learns it is a chick. (29 pp, P)

**Baines, Becky.** *Your Skin Holds You In.* **National Geographic Society, 2008.**
Colorful photographs of young children are used to illustrate what skin does and why it is important. (29 pp, P, C, Series: National Geographic Kids)

**Barile, Colleen.** *Inventions Change Our Lives.* **Abrams Learning Trends, 2007.**
Barile presents examples of how telephones, cars, and lights have changed the lives of people over the years. The book includes photographs of the earliest telephones, cars, and lights as well as those of the present day. (14 pp, TC, P, C, G, I, L, BB, Series: Big Book Science)

**Barner, Bob.** *Animal Baths.* **Chronicle Books, 2011.**
Adorable collage illustrations and simple text show how a variety of animals keep clean. (32 pp, ILL)

**Barth, April.** *Adding Two-Digit Numbers.* **Benchmark Education Company, 2009.**
Using mental math, models, and place value, readers learn to add two-digit numbers. (16 pp, TC, P, C, G, I, L, BB, Series: Math Content Connections)

**Barth, April.** *Addition and Subtraction.* **Benchmark Education Company, 2009.**
Using the concepts of parts and whole, Barth illustrates how addition and subtraction are related and how these relationships can be used to develop fact families. (16 pp, TC, P, C, G, I, L, BB, Series: Math Content Connections)

**Barth, April.** *Addition Strategies.* **Benchmark Education Company, 2009.**
Barth provides examples of how to add using counting on, making doubles, and making 10. (16 pp, TC, P, C, G, I, L, BB, Series: Math Content Connections)

**Barth, April.** *Building With Solid Shapes.* **Benchmark Education Company, 2009.**
Providing examples of real buildings from around the world, Barth illustrates how architects, particularly I. M. Pei, use solid shapes in their designs. (16 pp, TC, P, C, G, I, L, BB, Series: Math Content Connections)

**Barth, April.** *Centimeter and Meter.* **Benchmark Education Company, 2009.**
Barth provides a simple explanation of the metric system's centimeter and meter. Challenges are provided to readers for using these units in measuring common distances. (16 pp, TC, P, C, G, I, L, BB, Series: Math Content Connections)

---

*Legend:* pp = Number of pages; TC = Table of contents; P = Photos; ILL = Illustrated; C = Captioned; G = Glossary; I = Index; L = Leveled book; BB = Available in big book format

**Barth, April. *Compare and Order Numbers to 1,000*. Benchmark Education Company, 2009.**

This book illustrates how comparison terms such as *equal to, greater than*, and *less than* can be represented by symbols (=, >, and <). (16 pp, TC, P, C, G, I, L, BB, Series: Math Content Connections)

**Barth, April. *Compare Numbers to 100*. Benchmark Education Company, 2009.**

Ways to determine comparisons of *equal to, greater than*, and *less than* are presented using models, a hundred chart, and a number line. (16 pp, TC, P, C, G, I, L, BB, Series: Math Content Connections)

**Barth, April. *Designing With Plane Shapes*. Benchmark Education Company, 2009.**

Barth presents the plane shapes of rectangle, square, and triangle and illustrates how they can be combined in a variety of ways to make new shapes or pictures. (16 pp, TC, P, C, G, I, L, BB, Series: Math Content Connections)

**Barth, April. *Estimating Sums and Differences*. Benchmark Education Company, 2009.**

After providing examples of when estimation might be used, Barth shares with readers how to estimate using mental math and using tens for both sums and differences. (16 pp, TC, P, C, G, I, L, BB, Series: Math Content Connections)

**Barth, April. *Finding Length*. Benchmark Education Company, 2009.**

This book provides examples of how both nonstandard and standard units of measure can be used to measure length and why one system might be preferable to the other. Units of measure discussed include centimeters, inches, cubes, and paper clips. (16 pp, TC, P, C, G, I, L, BB, Series: Math Content Connections)

**Barth, April. *Heavier and Lighter*. Benchmark Education Company, 2009.**

Barth first gives definitions of heavy and light. Then she compares adult and baby animals to illustrate the concepts of heavier and lighter. The concept of weighing the same is also touched on briefly. (16 pp, TC, P, C, G, I, L, BB, Series: Math Content Connections)

**Barth, April. *How Many in All?* Benchmark Education Company, 2009.**

Using a circus theme, this book presents addition story problems for the reader to complete. (16 pp, TC, P, C, G, I, L, BB, Series: Math Content Connections)

**Barth, April. *Inch, Foot, Yard*. Benchmark Education Company, 2009.**

The customary units of inch, foot, and yard and their relationship to each other are presented in this book. Examples of when it is best to use each unit are also provided. (16 pp, TC, P, C, G, I, L, BB, Series: Math Content Connections)

---

*Legend:* pp = Number of pages; TC = Table of contents; P = Photos; ILL = Illustrated; C = Captioned; G = Glossary; I = Index; L = Leveled book; BB = Available in big book format

**Barth, April. *Numbers to 100: Before, After, and Between*. Benchmark Education Company, 2009.**

Using engaging photographs and illustrations, Barth presents how to count forward and backward using a number line. (16 pp, TC, P, ILL, C, G, I, L, BB, Series: Math Content Connections)

**Barth, April. *One More, One Less*. Benchmark Education Company, 2009.**

With the help of adorable pets, Barth shows how to match items to determine if one set has more or less than another. Use of a number line is also included. (16 pp, TC, P, C, G, I, L, BB, Series: Math Content Connections)

**Barth, April. *Plane Shapes*. Benchmark Education Company, 2009.**

Barth explains the characteristics of circles, rectangles, squares, and triangles and provides examples of where to find these shapes in the world around us. (16 pp, TC, P and ILL, C, G, I, L, BB, Series: Math Content Connections)

**Barth, April. *Same, More, or Less?* Benchmark Education Company, 2009.**

Various types of sports equipment are used to illustrate how to match sets up one-to-one to determine which sets have the same, more, or less. (16 pp, TC, P, C, G, I, L, BB, Series: Math Content Connections)

**Barth, April. *Solid Shapes*. Benchmark Education Company, 2009.**

Three-dimensional shapes such as cones, cubes, cylinders, and spheres are described, and examples of them in the world around are given. (16 pp, TC, P, C, G, I, L, BB, Series: Math Content Connections)

**Barth, April. *Subtracting Two-Digit Numbers*. Benchmark Education Company, 2009.**

To find the difference between two quantities, or subtract, Barth provides examples of using mental math, models, place value, and regrouping. (16 pp, TC, P, C, G, I, L, BB, Series: Math Content Connections)

**Barth, April. *Subtraction Strategies*. Benchmark Education Company, 2009.**

Using photographs of enticing food, Barth demonstrates how to subtract using counting back, addition, and doubles. (16 pp, TC, P, C, G, I, L, BB, Series: Math Content Connections)

**Barth, April. *Understanding Place Value*. Benchmark Education Company, 2009.**

A friendly frog shows the reader how to illustrate, read, and write up to three-digit numbers using the concept of place value. (16 pp, TC, ILL, C, G, I, L, BB, Series: Math Content Connections)

**Barth, April. *Understanding Tens and Ones*. Benchmark Education Company, 2009.**

Barth uses photographs of adorable kittens and puppies among others to illustrate how to group items by tens to determine quantity. (16 pp, TC, P, C, G, I, L, BB, Series: Math Content Connections)

---

*Legend:* pp = Number of pages; TC = Table of contents; P = Photos; ILL = Illustrated; C = Captioned; G = Glossary; I = Index; L = Leveled book; BB = Available in big book format

**Barth, April.** *What is Longer? What is Shorter?* **Benchmark Education Company, 2009.**

Examples from the animal world offer readers the opportunity to compare organisms of differing lengths. (16 pp, TC, P, C, G, I, L, BB, Series: Math Content Connections)

**Barth, April.** *Where Are the Solid Shapes?* **Benchmark Education Company, 2009.**

A backyard, the beach, the city, and the farm are locales that readers are offered in which to find solid shapes. Once the shapes are found, readers are to use positional words to describe each shape's location. (16 pp, TC, P, C, G, I, L, BB, Series: Math Content Connections)

**Bartholomew, Cathleen.** *What Is Weather?* **Abrams Learning Trends, 2012.**

In answering the question, "What is weather?" Bartholomew address how weather affects how we dress and what we do. She also provides examples of a day during each of the four seasons. (14 pp, TC, P, G, I, L, BB, Series: Big Book Science)

**Bennett, Elizabeth Huff.** *Counting to 10 and Beyond!* **Abrams Learning Trends, 2005.**

Using photographs of plants and animals that might be found on a farm, Bennett illustrates how to group by ten to count items. (14 pp, P, C, L, BB, Series: Big Book Math)

**Berger, Melvin & Gilda.** *Do Whales Have Belly Buttons? Questions and Answers About Whales and Dolphins.* **Scholastic, 1999.**

Stunning photographs help this book answer a variety of sea life questions, such as, "How did the fin get its name?" and "Can dolphins save humans?" (47 pp, TC, ILL, I)

**Berger, Melvin & Gilda.** *Splash: A Book About Whales and Dolphins.* **Scholastic, 2001.**

Many details and facts about whales and dolphins accompany photographs of these creatures of the sea. (40 pp, P, L, Series: Hello Reader: Science)

**Biden, Jill.** *Don't Forget, God Bless Our Troops.* **Simon and Schuster Books for Young People, 2012.**

Second Lady Jill Biden tells a story of a family waiting for the return of their father deployed to war. (40 pp, ILL)

**Bildner, Phil.** *The Unforgettable Season: The Story of Joe DiMaggio, Ted Williams, and the Record-Setting Summer of '41.* **Putnam Juvenile, 2011.**

The baseball season of 1941 has held many records and provided many legends for the sport. Bildner shares this season with readers, introducing them to the personalities that have made the sport so special. (32 pp, ILL)

---

*Legend:* pp = Number of pages; TC = Table of contents; P = Photos; ILL = Illustrated; C = Captioned; G = Glossary; I = Index; L = Leveled book; BB = Available in big book format

**Bingham, Caroline.** *Whales and Dolphins: Open Your Eyes to a World of Discovery.* **DK Publishing, 2002.**
This book explores whales and dolphins, these fascinating mammals of the ocean. (47 pp, TC, P, C, G, I)

**Brannon, Barbara.** *Discover Local and State Government.* **Benchmark Learning, 2005.**
Brannon provides simple descriptions of positions in local and state governments and what each position's responsibilities are. (24 pp, TC, P, C, G, I, Series: English Explorers Social Studies: Government and Citizenship)

**Bullard, Lisa.** *Loud and Quiet: An Animal Opposites Book.* **Capstone Press, 2006.**
This exciting book explores loud and quiet animals with colorful photographs that will engage young readers. (32 pp, P, G, I)

**Burnie, David.** *Mammals.* **Kingfisher, 2011.**
From the north tip of the Earth to the south, the world is populated by many fascinating mammals. This book introduces some of them through colorful pictures and accompanying text. (48 pp, TC, P, C, I, G)

**Butterworth, Chris.** *How Did That Get In My Lunch Box? The Story of Food.* **Candlewick Press, 2011.**
Butterworth follows the path of many common foods from field to store in this book that answers the question, "Where did my lunch come from?" (32 pp, ILL, C, I)

**Cain, Brianna.** *Are They Equal?* **Abrams Learning Trends, 2005.**
Using photographs of children of many different ethnicities, Cain provides problems for the reader to solve in determining whether two quantities are equal. (14 pp, P, C, L, BB, Series: Big Book Math)

**Callery, Sean.** *Life Cycles: Ocean.* **Kingfisher, 2011.**
Following a brief introduction to food chains, the book explores three food chains from oceans in different parts of the world: the Indian Ocean, the Pacific Ocean, and the Atlantic Ocean. (32 pp, TC, P, C, G, I, S)

**Callery, Sean.** *Ocean: Discover Earth's Ecosystems.* **Kingfisher, 2011.**
The book lists different life forms in the oceans and describes the ocean food chains. Additional "did you know" facts are presented in boxes. (32 pp, TC, P, C, G, I, S)

**Callery, Sean.** *Rainforest: Discover Earth's Ecosystems.* **Kingfisher, 2011.**
This colorful book introduces us to rain forest animals. Each page is filled with interesting information about amphibians, snakes, and mammals that are found in the rain forest. (32 pp, TC, P, C, G, I, S)

---

*Legend:* pp = Number of pages; TC = Table of contents; P = Photos; ILL = Illustrated; C = Captioned; G = Glossary; I = Index; L = Leveled book; BB = Available in big book format

**Carney, Elizabeth.** *Cats vs. Dogs.* **National Geographic, 2011.**
Carney compares cats and dogs across a number of characteristics from hearing to sleep habits and declares for each which is the winner. As to which makes the best pet, it is a tie. (48 pp, TC, P, G, I)

**Carney, Elizabeth.** *Great Migrations: Whales, Wildebeests, Butterflies, Elephants, and Other Amazing Animals on the Move.* **National Geographic, 2010.**
Many animals migrate. Beautiful, colorful, often close-up pictures and text tell the story of some of these creatures. (44 pp, TC, P, I)

**Carolan, Terry & Joanna.** *A President From Hawai'i.* **Candlewick Press, 2012.**
Photographs of President Barack Obama are part of collage illustrations that introduce the reader to the first American president born in Hawai'i. Many Hawaiian words are introduced, and quotes by President Obama are used to illustrate the values the president learned while growing up in this state. (24 pp, P, ILL, C, G)

**Casteel, Christine.** *Let's Measure With Tools.* **Abrams Learning Trends, 2006.**
The book demonstrates how tools of measurement, such as scales, rulers, and thermometers, can be used to measure weight, length, and temperature. In the conclusion, readers are asked to determine which measurement tool would be best to use in measuring some common items. (14 pp, P, C, L, BB, Series: Big Book Math)

**Castor, Debra.** *Animals in Their Habitats.* **Benchmark Education Company, 2009.**
Close-up photographs show some of the animals that live in ponds, in forests, in deserts, and in the Arctic. Examples are given of how the animals have adapted to their respective habitats. (16 pp, TC, P, C, G, I, L, BB, Series: Science Content Connections)

**Castor, Debra.** *Habitats Around the World.* **Benchmark Education Company, 2009.**
In beautiful photographs, Castor presents four habitats, and their plants and animals, from across the globe—a savanna, the Arctic, a tropical rain forest, and a coral reef. (16 pp, TC, P, C, G, I, L, BB, Series: Science Content Connections)

**Castor, Debra.** *An Oak Tree Has a Life Cycle.* **Benchmark Education Company, 2009.**
Using clear, close-up photographs, Castor illustrates the life cycle of an oak tree from an acorn to a tree that can live for hundreds of years. (16 pp, TC, P, C, G, I, L, BB, Series: Science Content Connections)

**Castor, Debra.** *The Parts of a Plant.* **Benchmark Education Company, 2009.**
Castor uses photographs of plants, from mangrove trees to cacti to sunflowers, to illustrate the different parts of a variety of flora. (16 pp, TC, P, C, G, I, L, BB, Series: Science Content Connections)

---

*Legend:* pp = Number of pages; TC = Table of contents; P = Photos; ILL = Illustrated; C = Captioned; G = Glossary; I = Index; L = Leveled book; BB = Available in big book format

**Castor, Debra.** *Plants in Their Habitats.* **Benchmark Education Company, 2009.**
This book has many colorful photographs of plants that live near ponds, in a tropical rain forest, in a desert, and in the Arctic. Examples of how these plants are suited to survive in their habitat are also included. (16 pp, TC, P, C, G, I, L, BB, Series: Science Content Connections)

**Castor, Debra.** *What Do Plants Need?* **Benchmark Education Company, 2009.**
Accompanied by beautiful photographs, Castor's text explains why plants need water, air, light, and space to grow. (16 pp, TC, P, C, G, I, L, BB, Series: Science Content Connections)

**Cella, Clara.** *Earth Day.* **Capstone Press, 2013.**
Using old black-and-white photographs and more colorful modern ones, Cella tells the history of Earth Day, why it is important, and how it can be celebrated. (24 pp, TC, P, G, I, Series: Pebbles Plus: Let's Celebrate!)

**Chapman, Todd, & Judge, Lita.** *D is for Dinosaur: A Prehistoric Alphabet.* **Sleeping Bear Press, 2007.**
In simple rhyme, each letter of the alphabet is presented as an aspect of dinosaurs. Additional information is given in sidebars. (48 pp, ILL)

**Chen, Gloria.** *What Is Next?* **Newmark Learning, 2010.**
In this book, patterns are presented using animals and other items. Readers are asked to determine what comes next in the pattern. (16 pp, P, L, Series: Rising Readers Leveled Books: Math)

**Clark, Willow.** *Pandas.* **PowerKids Press, 2013.**
Adorable photographs introduce the reader to the giant panda and the red panda, who make their homes in Asia. (24 pp, TC, P, C, G, I, Series: The Animals of Asia)

**Coppendale, Jean.** *Fire Trucks and Rescue Vehicles.* **QEB Publishing, 2007.**
Photographs present fire trucks, fire boats, ambulances, police cars, and motorcycle patrols. Text tells how each vehicle is used to keep people safe. (24 pp, TC, P, C, G, I, Series: Mighty Machines)

**Coppendale, Jean.** *Tractors and Farm Vehicles.* **QEB Publishing, 2007.**
This book has photographs and information about a variety of farm vehicles, from tractors to combines to plows. (24 pp, TC, P, C, G, I, Series: Mighty Machines)

**Coppendale, Jean.** *Trucks.* **QEB Publishing, 2007.**
Many examples of trucks from small to monster are portrayed in the large photographs. Explanations are also given of what each type of truck does. (24 pp, TC, P, C, G, I, Series: Mighty Machines)

**Davies, Nicola.** *Monsters of the Deep.* **National Geographic Society, 2011.**
Fascinating, sometimes terrifying, photographs and text tell of the large creatures that live in the sea. The book also contains action cards and directions on how to access additional information on the Internet. (32 pp, P, C)

---

*Legend:* pp = Number of pages; TC = Table of contents; P = Photos; ILL = Illustrated; C = Captioned; G = Glossary; I = Index; L = Leveled book; BB = Available in big book format

**Davies, Nicola. *Oceans and Seas*. Kingfisher, 2011.**

Beautiful, intriguing photographs introduce the reader to life in and near the oceans and seas. Projects for children and information for parents and teachers are also included. (56 pp, TC, P, C, I, Series: Science Kids)

**De Capua, Sarah. *We Need Directions*. Scholastic, 2002.**

Simple text accompanies photographs of children illustrating the need for the directions north, south, east, and west in finding almost any place. (32 pp, P, G, I)

**Desalle, Nicole. *I Am Clean, I Am Healthy*. Abrams Learning Trends, 2011.**

Simple text and photographs of young children doing the activities necessary to be clean and healthy provide the reader with models for doing the same. (14 pp, TC, P, G, I, L, BB only, Series: Big Book Health & Safety)

**Desalle, Nicole. *Safe at Home*. Abrams Learning Trends, 2011.**

Each page has ideas for staying safe at home and then asks, "What can you do to stay safe?" so that readers are encouraged to generate their own ideas. (14 pp, TC, P, G, I, BB only, Series: Big Book Health & Safety)

**Desalle, Nicole. *Safe at Play*. Abrams Learning Trends, 2011.**

In addition to giving advice for staying safe on a bicycle, playing in the sun, and playing at the park, this book challenges the reader to think of additional things to do to stay safe at play. (14 pp, TC, P, G, I, BB only, Series: Big Book Health & Safety)

**Desalle, Nicole. *Safe at School*. Abrams Learning Trends, 2011.**

Basic safety rules at school are presented, and readers are also asked to generate their own ideas. (14 pp, TC, P, G, I, BB only, Series: Big Book Health & Safety)

**Dickman, Nancy. *World of Farming: Food From Farms*. Capstone Global Library, 2011.**

Simple text and photographs depict all the different foods that come from farms. (24 pp, TC, P, G, I, Series: World of Farming)

**Dickman, Nancy. *World of Farming: Jobs on the Farm*. Capstone Global Library, 2011.**

There are a variety of jobs on a farm, and this book portrays many of them in photographs with accompanying simple text. (24 pp, TC, P, G, I, Series: World of Farming)

**Dickman, Nancy. *World of Farming: Seasons on a Farm*. Capstone Global Library, 2011.**

This book explains the seasonal changes that occur on a farm using photographs and simple text. (24 pp, TC, P, G, I, Series: World of Farming)

**Dominello, Brenda. *Earth Rocks!* Abrams Learning Trends, 2007.**

Clear and colorful photograph illustrate the differences between minerals and rock as well as how they change in the rock cycle. (14 pp, TC, P, C, G, I, L, BB, Series: Big Book Science)

---

*Legend:* pp = Number of pages; TC = Table of contents; P = Photos; ILL = Illustrated; C = Captioned; G = Glossary; I = Index; L = Leveled book; BB = Available in big book format

**Dominello, Brenda. *I Keep Myself Healthy*. Abrams Learning Trends, 2007.**
Photographs of children of many ethnicities depict how to stay healthy and why it is important. (14 pp, TC, P, C, G, I, L, BB, Series: Big Book Science)

**Dorion, Christiane. *How the Weather Works: A Hands-On Guide to Our Changing Climate*. Templar Books, 2011.**
With pop-ups, pull-tabs, and colorful illustrations, this book explains how our climate is changing. (20 pp, ILL, C)

**Dowson, Nick. *North: The Amazing Story of Arctic Migration*. Candlewick Press, 2011.**
Simple text and beautiful illustrations tell the story of the many animals that migrate north to the Arctic each spring. (55 pp, ILL, G)

**Dunning, Joan. *Seabird in the Forest: The Mystery of the Marbled Murrelet*. Boyds Mills Press, 2011.**
This book tells how the mystery of the marbled murrelet was solved. This bird lives by the ocean, but no one had ever seen its nest. In recent years it has been discovered that the murrelet makes its nest 20 miles inland in the California forest. Beautiful drawings illustrate the bird's life. (32 pp, ILL, C)

**Dunphy, Madeleine. *At Home With the Gopher Tortoise: The Story of a Keystone Species*. Web of Life Children's Books, 2010.**
Dunphy shows readers how this one species, the gopher tortoise, has many other species dependent on it for survival, making it a keystone species. (32 pp, ILL)

**Eggleton, Jill. *Animal Fathers*. Abrams Learning Trends, 2008.**
Eggleton presents father penguins, red back poison frogs, and seahorses and their important jobs taking care of their babies. Suggestions to guide the adult in using the book with children are included. (16 pp, P, I, L)

**Eggleton, Jill. *Baby Bonobos Alone*. Global Education Systems, 2008.**
This book shares the story of a woman who cared for two orphaned bonobos until they could be released back into the wild. Suggestions to guide the adult in using the book with children are included. (16 pp, P, C, I, L, Series: Abrams Learning Trends)

**Eggleton, Jill. *A Big Earthquake*. Global Education Systems, 2008.**
This book tells of a big earthquake in China and its devastating aftermath. Suggestions to guide the adult in using the book with children are included. (16 pp, P, C, I, Series: Abrams Learning Trends)

**Eggleton, Jill. *Big Gorilla*. Abrams Learning Trends, 2009.**
The big gorilla, leader of a group of gorillas in the forest, has an important job. He stands up and shows his teeth to scare away a leopard. Then he is able to take a much-needed nap. Suggestions to guide the adult in using the book with children are included. (14 pp, P, I, L)

---

*Legend:* pp = Number of pages; TC = Table of contents; P = Photos; ILL = Illustrated; C = Captioned; G = Glossary; I = Index; L = Leveled book; BB = Available in big book format

**Eggleton, Jill.** *Brown Bear*. **Abrams Learning Trends, 2009.**

Eggleton presents a brown bear during each season and the important work she needs to do to survive. Suggestions to guide the adult in using the book with children are included. (14 pp, P, I, L)

**Eggleton, Jill.** *Bug Hunters*. **Abrams Learning Trends, 2009.**

This book follows entomologists as they look for bugs all over the world. They hope to find the bugs' secrets so that this information can help people. Suggestions to guide the adult in using the book with children are included. (16 pp, P, C, I L)

**Eggleton, Jill.** *The Call of the Sea*. **Abrams Learning Trends, 2009.**

Eggleton introduces the Moken people who live by the sea, where they fish and gather most of the food they need. Knowing the signs of the sea, they are also able to find safety from a tsunami. Suggestions to guide the adult in using the book with children are included. (20 pp, TC, P, L)

**Eggleton, Jill.** *Changing Colors*. **Global Education Systems, 2008.**

Photographs and simple text follow a snowshoe hare from summer when its fur is brown through winter when its fur is white, explaining why this is important for its survival. Suggestions to guide the adult in using the book with children are included. (16 pp, P, C, I, L, Series: Abrams Learning Trends)

**Eggleton, Jill.** *A Crocodile Mother*. **Abrams Learning Trends, 2009.**

This book tells of a mother crocodile that lays her eggs in the sand and guards them until it is time for them to hatch. As the time nears, she digs up the nest and helps the hatchling emerge. Suggestions to guide the adult in using the book with children are included. (14 pp, P, I, L)

**Eggleton, Jill.** *Day and Night in the Desert*. **Abrams Learning Trends, 2009.**

Beautiful photographs of the desert landscape are paired with photographs of wildlife that make the desert their home. Hiding underground or under rocks during the hot day, these animals come out to cross the sand during the cooler night. Suggestions to guide the adult in using the book with children are included. (14 pp, P, I, L)

**Eggleton, Jill.** *Different or the Same?* **Abrams Learning Trends, 2009.**

Eggleton presents an albino gorilla, peacock, lion, and alligator and asks if these animals are the same as or different from their colored brethren. Suggestions to guide the adult in using the book with children are included. (16 pp, P, I, L)

**Eggleton, Jill.** *Different Plants*. **Abrams Learning Trends, 2009.**

Some plants catch flies to eat them; some plants have very large flowers that smell yucky; some plants have seed pods that pop. All these unusual plants and more are presented in colorful photographs. Suggestions to guide the adult in using the book with children are included. (16 pp, P, I, L)

---

*Legend:* pp = Number of pages; TC = Table of contents; P = Photos; ILL = Illustrated; C = Captioned; G = Glossary; I = Index; L = Leveled book; BB = Available in big book format

**Eggleton, Jill.** *Different Villages.* **Abrams Learning Trends, 2009.**
After defining what a village is, Eggleton explores those by the sea, in the mountains, and in the rain forest. Suggestions to guide the adult in using the book with children are included. (20 pp, TC, P, L)

**Eggleton, Jill.** *The Dingo Fence.* **Abrams Learning Trends, 2009.**
This book tells of the Dingo Fence, which stretches across Australia and is the longest fence in the world. Its job is to keep dingoes, a doglike animal, from killing ranchers' sheep. Suggestions to guide the adult in using the book with children are included. (20 pp, TC, P, C, I, L)

**Eggleton, Jill.** *Dolphins to the Rescue.* **Global Education Systems, 2008.**
Eggleton shares the story of a surfer who was attacked by a shark but rescued by a group of dolphins. Suggestions to guide the adult in using the book with children are included. (16 pp, P, C, I, L, Series: Abrams Learning Trends)

**Eggleton, Jill.** *Down at the Waterhole.* **Abrams Learning Trends, 2008.**
This African waterhole attracts many different animals from early in the morning till late at night. An analog clock accompanies each photograph of animals as they go about their day. Suggestions to guide the adult in using the book with children are included. (16 pp, P, I, L)

**Eggleton, Jill.** *Food for Zebras.* **Abrams Learning Trends, 2009.**
The zebras in this book have no food. It is hot, and the grass is brown. In searching for food, they meet a lion and a crocodile that are also looking for food. The zebras are able to quickly escape to the other side of the river, where there is green grass to eat. Suggestions to guide the adult in using the book with children are included. (14 pp, P, I, L)

**Eggleton, Jill.** *Garbage in the River.* **Abrams Learning Trends, 2009.**
After briefly explaining the water cycle, Eggleton proceeds to explain why clean water in rivers is important and how garbage in the river endangers the living things that depend on the water. Suggestions to guide the adult in using the book with children are included. (16 pp, P, C, I, L)

**Eggleton, Jill.** *Going Under.* **Global Education Systems, 2008.**
As the submarine goes down deep in the sea, the divers see many strange and fascinating creatures. Suggestions to guide the adult in using the book with children are included. (16 pp, P, C, I, L, Series: Abrams Learning Trends)

**Eggleton, Jill.** *Going Up.* **Global Education Systems, 2008.**
Photographs with accompanying descriptions show what lives at each level of a very tall mountain. Suggestions to guide the adult in using the book with children are included. (16 pp, P, C, I, L, Series: Abrams Learning Trends)

---

*Legend:* pp = Number of pages; TC = Table of contents; P = Photos; ILL = Illustrated; C = Captioned; G = Glossary; I = Index; L = Leveled book; BB = Available in big book format

**Eggleton, Jill. *The Griffin Vulture*. Abrams Learning Trends, 2009.**

Griffin vultures are large birds with short, heavy beaks. They eat dead animals. They have an important job—to clean. Eggleton shares how these birds use updrafts to fly, how they spot food, how they use nests, and how they feed their young. Suggestions to guide the adult in using the book with children are included. (20 pp, TC, P, C, I, L)

**Eggleton, Jill. *The Hand of Nature*. Abrams Learning Trends, 2009.**

With accompanying photographs, Eggleton describes what happens in natural disasters such as avalanches, volcanoes, hurricanes, and droughts. Suggestions to guide the adult in using the book with children are included. (20 pp, TC, P, L)

**Eggleton, Jill. *A Handy Horse*. Global Education Systems, 2008.**

Eggleton tells the story of Cuddles, a small horse who is smart and has very good eyesight. Her job is to help her owner, Dan, who is blind. Suggestions to guide the adult in using the book with children are included. (16 pp, P, C, I, L, Series: Abrams Learning Trends)

**Eggleton, Jill. *Harpy Eagle Chick*. Abrams Learning Trends, 2009.**

This book tells of Alex and Ruth, who ventured into the rain forest to find a chick of the harpy eagle, a very large bird with very large claws. Once they find the chick, they put a GPS on its back so they can study where it goes. Suggestions to guide the adult in using the book with children are included. (16 pp, P, C, I, L)

**Eggleton, Jill. *Helicopters Help*. Abrams Learning Trends, 2008.**

Helicopters are used to rescue people who are hurt on large mountains, injured on boats at sea, or stranded because of a flood. Photographs depict the rescues. Suggestions to guide the adult in using the book with children are included. (16 pp, P, I, L)

**Eggleton, Jill. *Hungry Fox*. Global Education Systems, 2008.**

Following its tracks, the reader finds a fox's den and discovers what it does at night when it is hungry. Suggestions to guide the adult in using the book with children are included. (16 pp, P, C, I, L, Series: Abrams Learning Trends)

**Eggleton Jill. *In a Nutshell*. Global Education Systems, 2008.**

An acorn can be more than just food for a squirrel. Eggleton shows how weevils, moths, and ants can use a nut as a place to lay their eggs. Suggestions to guide the adult in using the book with children are included. (16 pp, P, C, I, Series: Abrams Learning Trends)

**Eggleton, Jill. *It Started With a Plant*. Global Education Systems, 2008.**

This book portrays a simple food chain that begins with a plant and moves on to a caterpillar and then a bird. The next link in the chain, a cat, is not so lucky today. Suggestions to guide the adult in using the book with children are included. (16 pp, P, C, I, L, Series: Abrams Learning Trends)

---

*Legend:* pp = Number of pages; TC = Table of contents; P = Photos; ILL = Illustrated; C = Captioned; G = Glossary; I = Index; L = Leveled book; BB = Available in big book format

**Eggleton, Jill. *Knut, a Pet or Not?* Abrams Learning Trends, 2009.**

Eggleton tells of Knut, a polar bear cub who was born in a zoo. Unlike cubs in the wild, Knut's mother did not take care of him. A man named Thomas had to be a mother to Knut, but Knut was not his pet. Knut is too big to play with Thomas now. Suggestions to guide the adult in using the book with children are included. (16 pp, P, I, L)

**Eggleton, Jill. *Living in a Cave.* Abrams Learning Trends, 2009.**

A young Chinese girl introduces the reader to the large cave she lives in high in the mountains. The cave is so large that many people live there. She even goes to school and plays inside the cave! While the cave is much different than a house, it is where she likes to live. Suggestions to guide the adult in using the book with children are included. (16 pp, P, I, L)

**Eggleton, Jill. *Living in Space.* Abrams Learning Trends, 2009.**

Eggleton compares living in space to living on Earth. Side-by-side differences in housing, moving around, eating food, venturing outside, and sleeping are noted. Even the view out of windows is compared. Suggestions to guide the adult in using the book with children are included. (14 pp, P, I, L)

**Eggleton, Jill. *Look! No Tail!* Abrams Learning Trends, 2009.**

In this book Eggleton depicts how lizards, crabs, and octopi can lose a limb and then regenerate another. Suggestions to guide the adult in using the book with children are included. (14 pp, P, I, L)

**Eggleton, Jill. *Lucky Seal.* Abrams Learning Trends, 2009.**

When a seal pokes his head out a hole in the ice, a polar bear spots him. The polar bear, intent on capturing his dinner, chases the seal across the ice. When the seal finds a hole in the ice, he jumps in and escapes the bear. Suggestions to guide the adult in using the book with children are included. (14 pp, P, I, L)

**Eggleton, Jill. *Lucky Water Buffalo Calf.* Abrams Learning Trends, 2009.**

An African water buffalo calf could not run fast enough to get away from the lions who wanted to eat it. When both the buffalo and lion fell into the river, a crocodile decides he also wants to eat the calf. The lion wins the contest, but as he is dragging the calf out of the water, the calf's herd charges the lion and saves the calf. Suggestions to guide the adult in using the book with children are included. (16 pp, TC, P, C, I, L)

**Eggleton, Jill. *Moving Elephants.* Global Education Systems, 2008.**

To protect elephants in Kenya, sometimes it is necessary to move them. This book follows the elephants' journey to their safe new home. Suggestions to guide the adult in using the book with children are included. (16 pp, P, C, I, L, Series: Abrams Learning Trends)

**Eggleton, Jill. *Moving Seeds.* Abrams Learning Trends, 2009.**

Eggleton explains that though seeds have no wings to fly or feet to walk, they do have many ways to get from their original plant to a new place to grow. The wind, birds, and

---

*Legend:* pp = Number of pages; TC = Table of contents; P = Photos; ILL = Illustrated; C = Captioned; G = Glossary; I = Index; L = Leveled book; BB = Available in big book format

water, among other things, help seeds get from here to there. Suggestions to guide the adult in using the book with children are included. (14 pp, P, I, L)

**Eggleton, Jill.** *The Nature of Things.* **Abrams Learning Trends, 2009.**
Eggleton presents numerous animals with strange features that help them survive. Included, among others, are the coconut crab, tapir, and bulldog ant. Suggestions to guide the adult in using the book with children are included. (20 pp, TC, P, L)

**Eggleton, Jill.** *Night in the Garden.* **Global Education Systems, 2008.**
Spotlighting the animals in the dark night, Eggleton shows what animals are doing at that time. Suggestions to guide the adult in using the book with children are included. (16 pp, P, C, I, L, Series: Abrams Learning Trends)

**Eggleton, Jill.** *No Bones.* **Abrams Learning Trends, 2009.**
While many animals have bones, some do not. This book introduces the reader to those that do not, such as butterflies, worms, slugs, snails, and jellyfish. Suggestions to guide the adult in using the book with children are included. (14 pp, P, I, L)

**Eggleton, Jill.** *Octopus Mother.* **Global Education Systems, 2008.**
Photographs and text describe how an octopus mother survives in the deep to care for the eggs she laid. Suggestions to guide the adult in using the book with children are included. (16 pp, P, C, I, L, Series: Abrams Learning Trends)

**Eggleton, Jill.** *A Photographer's Diary.* **Abrams Learning Trends, 2009.**
In diary format, Eggleton presents the adventures of a photographer who goes to Komodo Island to photograph komodo dragons, the heaviest lizards. On the fourth day he gets to see the dragon lizard up close. Suggestions to guide the adult in using the book with children are included. (20 pp, P, L)

**Eggleton, Jill.** *A Place to Live.* **Global Education Systems, 2008.**
Beautiful photographs and very simple text show bears, foxes, and tigers and the different habitats in which they can live. Suggestions to guide the adult in using the book with children are included. (16 pp, P, C, I, L, Series: Abrams Learning Trends)

**Eggleton, Jill.** *Racing.* **Abrams Learning Trends, 2009.**
In the photographs, the reader will see race cars, boats, trucks, hot air balloons, bicycles, planes, and people in wheelchairs race. On the final page the reader can determine which car came in first, second, and third. (16 pp, P, I, L)

**Eggleton, Jill.** *A Real Tree House.* **Abrams Learning Trends, 2009.**
Some children have tree houses to play in, but some people who live in the rain forest live in real tree houses. Up high these people can keep cool and be safe from floods. Suggestions to guide the adult in using the book with children are included. (16 pp, P, C, I, L)

---

*Legend:* pp = Number of pages; TC = Table of contents; P = Photos; ILL = Illustrated; C = Captioned; G = Glossary; I = Index; L = Leveled book; BB = Available in big book format

**Eggleton, Jill.** *Robot Crab*. **Abrams Learning Trends, 2009.**
Modeled after crabs that walk sideways on their eight legs, a robot was built that could go in the water. However, unlike the crab, the robot does not grow. Also unlike a crab, the robot can flip itself upright when flipped over by a wave. Suggestions to guide the adult in using the book with children are included. (14 pp, P, I, L)

**Eggleton, Jill.** *Robot Lander on Mars*. **Abrams Learning Trends, 2009.**
Robot landers are on Mars investigating. They bring information back to scientists who want to learn if people can go to Mars. Suggestions to guide the adult in using the book with children are included. (16 pp, P, I, L)

**Eggleton, Jill.** *Sleeping Animals*. **Abrams Learning Trends, 2009.**
By looking at the photographs, readers will determine which wild animals are asleep. Animals included are a leopard, bear, hippo, owl, bat, and snake. Suggestions to guide the adult in using the book with children are included. (16 pp, P, I, L)

**Eggleton, Jill.** *Smoke Jumpers Help*. **Global Education Systems, 2008.**
Smoke jumpers have a dirty, dangerous job. This book shows what they need to do to put out a mountain fire. Suggestions to guide the adult in using the book with children are included. (16 pp, P, C, I, Series: Abrams Learning Trends)

**Eggleton, Jill.** *The Stars Above*. **Abrams Learning Trends, 2009.**
Astronomers study the stars out in space. They know some things about stars but are always learning new information. Brief descriptions of black holes and supernovas are included in this book. Suggestions to guide the adult in using the book with children are provided. (16 pp, P, C, I L)

**Eggleton, Jill.** *A Suit for Spacewalking*. **Abrams Learning Trends, 2009.**
In space astronauts need protection from the sun's rays. They also need to breathe good air. That is why they wear special suits. Eggleton describes the different parts of the suit and their functions. Suggestions to guide the adult in using the book with children are included. (20 pp, TC, P, C, I, L)

**Eggleton, Jill.** *Super Dog*. **Global Education Systems, 2008.**
There are many ways that Endal, a service dog, can help Allen, his owner who uses a wheelchair. Suggestions to guide the adult in using the book with children are included. (16 pp, P, C, I, L, Series: Abrams Learning Trends)

**Eggleton, Jill.** *The Tall Tree*. **Global Education Systems, 2008.**
Through photographs and simple text Eggleton introduces readers to all the animals that call a very tall tree home. Suggestions to guide the adult in using the book with children are included. (16 pp, P, C, I, L, Series: Abrams Learning Trends)

*Legend:* pp = Number of pages; TC = Table of contents; P = Photos; ILL = Illustrated; C = Captioned; G = Glossary; I = Index; L = Leveled book; BB = Available in big book format

**Eggleton, Jill.** *The Turtle's Journey.* **Abrams Learning Trends, 2009.**

Eggleton follows the turtle's journey over sand to lay eggs and then go back to the sea. When the hatchlings emerge from the eggs, they have a dangerous journey from their nest to the safety of the water. Suggestions to guide the adult in using the book with children are included. (14 pp, P, I, L)

**Eggleton, Jill.** *Under the Ice.* **Global Education Systems, 2008.**

Eggleton leads the reader under the ice into the cold water below. With brief descriptions and photographs, she shares what can be found in that murky world. Suggestions to guide the adult in using the book with children are included. (16 pp, P, C, I, L, Series: Abrams Learning Trends)

**Eggleton, Jill.** *Up Pops a Mushroom.* **Abrams Learning Trends, 2009.**

Mushrooms are fungi. There are many different kinds. Some are poisonous, some are slimy and smell, some glow in the dark, and others are red with white spots. Suggestions to guide the adult in using the book with children are included. (16 pp, TC, P, C, I, L)

**Eggleton, Jill.** *What Is Long?* **Global Education Systems, 2008.**

From long claws, legs, and horns to long necks and noses, Eggleton presents animals with long body parts. For each long body part, there is also an illustration of an animal that does not have that part at all. Suggestions to guide the adult in using the book with children are included. (16 pp, P, C, I, L, Series: Abrams Learning Trends)

**Eggleton, Jill.** *What Next?* **Abrams Learning Trends, 2009.**

Three sequences from egg to adult animal are portrayed in this book. These include a chicken, a frog, and a crocodile. Suggestions to guide the adult in using the book with children are included. (14 pp, P, I, L)

**Eggleton, Jill.** *What's That?* **Abrams Learning Trends, 2009.**

Eggleton presents some animals that appear strange. These include the star-nosed mole, the aye-aye, the jerboa, the thorny devil, and more. Suggestions to guide the adult in using the book with children are included. (20 pp, TC, P, L)

**Eggleton, Jill.** *Wheels.* **Abrams Learning Trends, 2009.**

Sets of pages within this book each present a wheel and three choices of vehicles to which the wheel could belong. The second page in each set shows the correct vehicle with the wheel. Scooter, bus, and bicycle wheels are presented. Suggestions to guide the adult in using the book with children are included. (14 pp, P, I, L)

**Eggleton, Jill.** *Where Are the Bats?* **Abrams Learning Trends, 2009.**

In the book's photographs, bats are sleeping in the caves during the day, but at night they wake up and venture out of their caves. Eggleton shows a bat hunting a moth and a fly. Suggestions to guide the adult in using the book with children are included. (14 pp, P, I, L)

---

*Legend:* pp = Number of pages; TC = Table of contents; P = Photos; ILL = Illustrated; C = Captioned; G = Glossary; I = Index; L = Leveled book; BB = Available in big book format

**Eggleton, Jill. *Where Can They Live?* Global Education Systems, 2008.**
In this book, questions are asked and answered about whether a bird, a snake, and a frog can live on land or in the water. Close-up photographs of the surface of each animal give the reader additional information. Suggestions to guide the adult in using the book with children are included. (16 pp, P, C, I, L, Series: Abrams Learning Trends)

**Eggleton, Jill. *Whiskers*. Global Education Systems, 2008.**
With simple text and close-up photographs, Eggleton presents the whiskers on a lion, a wolf, and a seal. The biggest set of whiskers, however, is that of the marmoset monkey. Suggestions to guide the adult in using the book with children are included. (16 pp, P, C, I, L, Series: Abrams Learning Trends)

**Eggleton, Jill. *Wildlife Detective*. Abrams Learning Trends, 2009.**
In this book written as a diary, Eggleton presents the work of a wildlife detective who is trying to locate smugglers of exotic animals. Suggestions to guide the adult in using the book with children are included. (20 pp, P, L)

**Elliott, David. *In the Sea*. Candlewick Press, 2012.**
Each page is beautifully illustrated to accompany a poem about a sea animal, such as the octopus, sea horse, sardine, and others. (32 pp, ILL)

**Esbaum, Jill. *Apples for Everyone*. National Geographic Society, 2009.**
Esbaum presents the progression from tree blooms with bees buzzing around to harvest to eating of apples. Photographs are delicious! (16 pp, P)

**Esbaum, Jill. *Everything Spring*. National Geographic Society, 2010.**
Beautiful photographs depict how plants and animals awaken in the spring to experience the spring rains and warm sunshine. (16 pp, P)

**Esbaum, Jill. *Seed, Sprout, Pumpkin, Pie*. National Geographic Society, 2009.**
Vivid photographs depict the life cycle of a pumpkin from seed to harvest. Examples of all the ways that grown pumpkins can be used are also included. (16 pp, P)

**Esbaum, Jill. *Winter Wonderland*. National Geographic, 2011.**
Esbaum shares some of the common characteristics of winter—the cold and snow, the storms, and the holidays. (16 pp, P)

**Feely, Jenny. *Stay Away!* Eleanor Curtain Publishing, 2003.**
Many animals are dangerous, and it is important for people to know to stay away. With close-up photographs Feely presents four animals to avoid. The book includes teacher version and literacy learning activities. (16 pp, TC, P, L, I, Series: Explorations)

**Fielding, Beth. *Animal Eyes*. Early Light Books, 2011.**
All kinds of animals' eyes, including humans', are portrayed in colorful photographs in this book. (36 pp, P, C, G, I)

---

*Legend:* pp = Number of pages; TC = Table of contents; P = Photos; ILL = Illustrated; C = Captioned; G = Glossary; I = Index; L = Leveled book; BB = Available in big book format

**Fischer, Kathleen.** *Counting at the Zoo.* **Abrams Learning Trends, 2005.**
Appealing photographs of zoo animals such as bears, giraffes, dolphins, and kangaroos provide readers the opportunity to count items up to 10. (14 pp, P, L, BB, Series: Big Book Math)

**Fischer, Kathleen.** *How Do We Tell Time?* **Abrams Learning Trends, 2005.**
Fischer provides examples of how readers can use the sun and moon to determine morning, afternoon, evening, and night. She then proceeds to discuss how observing the seasons is another way to tell time. (14 pp, P, L, BB, Series: Big Book Math)

**Flynn, Sarah Wassner.** *Baby Animal Pop!* **National Geographic Society, 2011.**
This adorable book includes giant cutouts of pop-up baby animals accompanied by interesting animal facts. (20 pp, P, C, Series: National Geographic Little Kids)

**Franco, Betsy, & Jenkins, Steve.** *Bees, Snails, & Peacock Tails: Patterns and Shapes . . . Naturally.* **Margaret K. McElderry Books, 2008.**
Jenkins's attractive collage illustrations and Franco's text present the many patterns and shapes found in the natural world. (40 pp, ILL)

**Frank, Matthew.** *Bird's-Eye View of a Neighborhood.* **Benchmark Education Company, 2009.**
Combing aerial photographs of locations with maps of those same locations, Frank demonstrates what a map is and how it can be used. (16 pp, TC, P and ILL, C, G, I, L, BB, Series: Social Studies Content Connections)

**Frank, Matthew.** *Children Past and Present.* **Benchmark Education Company, 2009.**
Pairing old photographs and illustrations with new colorful photographs, the book looks at how children today and those in the past are the same and different. (16 pp, TC, P, C, G, I, L, BB, Series: Social Studies Content Connections)

**Frank, Matthew.** *Map Skills.* **Benchmark Education Company, 2009.**
With clear and simple narrative this book explains maps, the compass rose, a map legend, and common map symbols. (16 pp, TC, P, C, G, I, L, BB, Series: Social Studies Content Connections)

**Frank, Matthew.** *Maps of My School.* **Benchmark Education Company, 2009.**
Using the familiar locale of a school, Frank illustrates how maps can depict rooms, buildings, playgrounds, and neighborhoods. (16 pp, TC, P, C, G, I, L, BB, Series: Social Studies Content Connections)

**Frank, Matthew.** *Needs Past and Present.* **Benchmark Education Company, 2009.**
Pairing illustrations depicting the past with modern photographs, this book looks at how people's needs have changed over the years as well as how the needs were and are met. (16 pp, TC, P and ILL, C, G, I, L, BB, Series: Social Studies Content Connections)

---

*Legend:* pp = Number of pages; TC = Table of contents; P = Photos; ILL = Illustrated; C = Captioned; G = Glossary; I = Index; L = Leveled book; BB = Available in big book format

**Frank, Matthew.** *Transportation Past and Present.* **Benchmark Education Company, 2009.**
Frank compares the modes of transportation that are used for waterways, railways, roadways, and airways today and in the past. (16 pp, TC, P, C, G, I, L, BB, Series: Social Studies Content Connections)

**Frost, Helen, & Gore, Leonid.** *Monarch and Milkweed.* **Atheneum Books for Young Readers, 2008.**
Soft, colorful illustrations follow the cycle of a monarch butterfly and the milkweed plant that is its "home." (40 pp, ILL)

**Frost, Helen, & Lieder, Rick.** *Step Gently Out.* **Candlewick Press, 2012.**
With few words on each page, Frost and Lieder use simple rhyming texts and unforgettable close-up photographs to introduce readers to the world of nature. (32 pp, P)

**Galvin, Laura Gates.** *Alphabet of Ocean Animals.* **Trudy Corporation and Smithsonian Institution, 2007.**
For each letter of the alphabet, an animal is introduced with a simple rhyme. The book also includes a pull-out poster and CD. (40 pp, ILL, G)

**Gibbons, Gail.** *Coral Reefs.* **Holiday House, 2007.**
Colorful illustrations of the many, many animals that make coral reefs their home accompany information about the location of coral reefs, the types of coral reefs, and how they are formed. (32 pp, ILL, C)

**Gibbons, Gail.** *Dinosaurs.* **Holiday House, 2008.**
With simple text and her distinctive illustrative style, Gibbons introduces the reader to paleontologists and many different dinosaurs. (32 pp, ILL, C)

**Gibbons, Gail.** *Elephants of Africa.* **Holiday House, 2010.**
What is special about the African elephant's trunk, ears, tusks, skin, eyes, and teeth are all addressed in this book that shares part of the information through text and part through Gibbons's illustrations. (32 pp, ILL, C)

**Gibbons, Gail.** *Galaxies, Galaxies!* **Holiday House, 2007.**
In this book Gibbons introduces the reader to the different types of galaxies and how astronomers are able to study them. (32 pp, ILL, C)

**Gibbons, Gail.** *Groundhog Day!* **Holiday House, 2007.**
Gibbons does more than just tell the history of Groundhog Day in this book. She also provides the reader information about this animal that has the country watching each February 2. (32 pp, ILL, C)

**Gibbons, Gail.** *Hurricanes.* **Holiday House, 2009.**
Gibbons shares through illustrations and text how hurricanes are formed, what each category means, some famous hurricanes, and how meteorologists try to predict the devastating storms. (32 pp, ILL, C)

---

*Legend:* pp = Number of pages; TC = Table of contents; P = Photos; ILL = Illustrated; C = Captioned; G = Glossary; I = Index; L = Leveled book; BB = Available in big book format

**Gibbons, Gail.** *It's Snowing*. **Holiday House, 2011.**

In her typical style, Gibbons uses illustrates and simple, clear text to explain snow to the young reader. (32 pp, ILL, C)

**Gibbons, Gail.** *Ladybug*. **Holiday House, 2012.**

From this book, written in Gibbons's typical simple and straightforward style, the reader learns about the ladybug, the common name for a red and black spotted beetle. Facts about the ladybug's body, life cycle, and enemies are included. (32 pp, ILL, C)

**Gibbons, Gail.** *Monarch Butterfly*. **Holiday House, 1989.**

With simple illustrations and text, Gibbons follows the life cycle of the monarch butterfly from egg to migration. (32 pp, ILL, C)

**Gibbons, Gail.** *My Baseball Book*. **HarperCollins Publishers, 2000.**

Colorful illustrations and very simple text explain the fundamentals of this American pastime. (22 pp, ILL, C, G)

**Gibbons, Gail.** *My Basketball Book*. **HarperCollins Publishers, 2000.**

The book is a beginner's guide to the game of basketball. Team makeup, scoring, and vocabulary are all addressed. (22 pp, ILL, C, G)

**Gibbons, Gail.** *My Soccer Book*. **HarperCollins Publishers, 2000.**

Gibbons's simple and colorful illustrations provide the reader with information about the game of soccer from what is needed to play to the rules governing the game. (22 pp, ILL, C, G)

**Gibbons, Gail.** *Snakes*. **Holiday House, 2007.**

Fascinating illustrations of many, many kinds of snakes as well as clear text share interesting facts about these creatures that move along the ground. (32 pp, ILL, C)

**Gibbons, Gail.** *Tell Me, Tree: All About Trees for Kids*. **Little, Brown and Company, 2002.**

Featuring Gibbons's trademark illustrations, this book describes how to plant seedlings and how to identify seeds and explores the different kinds of bark. This detailed book also provides pictures of how to clearly identify trees. (32 pp, ILL, C)

**Gibbons, Gail.** *Tornadoes*. **Holiday House, 2009.**

With simple text the books tells how tornadoes are formed, the different classifications for tornadoes, and what to do if one is coming. (32 pp, ILL, C)

**Gibbons, Gail.** *The Vegetables We Eat*. **Holiday House, 2007.**

With her colorful illustrations Gibbons introduces readers to eight different kinds of vegetables: leaf, tuber, stem, bulb, fruit, flower bud, seed, and root. (32 pp, ILL, C)

---

*Legend:* pp = Number of pages; TC = Table of contents; P = Photos; ILL = Illustrated; C = Captioned; G = Glossary; I = Index; L = Leveled book; BB = Available in big book format

**Glazer, Linda.** *Garbage Helps Our Garden Grow: A Compost Story.* **Millbrook Press, 2010.**
Accompanied by colorful photographs of real children at work, this book explains what compost is, how to make it, and how it can be used in the garden. (32 pp, P)

**Gordon, Sharon.** *Hearing.* **Scholastic, 2001.**
With a single sentence and colorful photograph on each page, this book tells the reader about the sense of hearing. (32 pp, P, G, I)

**Gordon, Sharon.** *Seeing.* **Scholastic, 2001.**
With no more than one sentence and one photograph per page, this book tells the reader about the sense of seeing. (32 pp, P, G, I)

**Gosman, Gillian.** *I Have Chicken Pox.* **PowerKids Press, 2013.**
Gosman presents the cause, symptoms, and treatment of chicken pox with photographs of young children to illustrate her points. (24 pp, TC, P, C, G, I, Series: Get Well Soon)

**Graham, Ian.** *Cars.* **QEB Publishing, 2008.**
From race cars to hybrid cars to cars so small they can be parked sideways, this books looks at the vehicle that is seen most on the road. (24 pp, TC, P, C, G, I, Series: Mighty Machines)

**Graham, Ian.** *Dump Trucks and Other Big Machines.* **QEB Publishing, 2008.**
Large photographs help convey the gigantic size of some very large trucks and other vehicles, such as tunnelers, cranes, and concrete mixers. 24 pp, TC, P, C, G, I, Series: Mighty Machines)

**Graham, Ian.** *Monster Trucks.* **QEB Publishing, 2008.**
Graham presents photographs of some of the fastest, biggest, more powerful trucks in the world. Some participate in monster truck shows; some have important jobs to do. (24 pp, TC, P, C, G, I, Series: Mighty Machines)

**Grant, Marsha.** *Let's Make Patterns!* **Abrams Learning Trends, 2005.**
Grant uses common items such as crayons, cookie cutters, buttons, and even children to demonstrate ABAB, ABC, AAB, and ABB patterns. (14 pp, P, L, BB, Series: Big Book Math)

**Grant, Marsha.** *Watch What Happens!* **Abrams Learning Trends, 2012.**
This book poses the question, "What will happen?" when colors are mixed, water gets cold, or other phenomena occur. Rebus problems are provided at the end for the reader to determine what will happen. (14 pp, TC, P, G, I, L, BB, Series: Big Book Science)

**Harper, Leslie.** *How Do Laws Get Passed?* **PowerKids Press, 2013.**
Accompanied by photographs of real lawmakers at work, the text in this book explains in simple terms the process of getting laws passed in our country. (24 pp, TC, P, C, G, I, Series: Civics Q&A)

---

*Legend:* pp = Number of pages; TC = Table of contents; P = Photos; ILL = Illustrated; C = Captioned; G = Glossary; I = Index; L = Leveled book; BB = Available in big book format

**Helfer, Ralph.** *The World's Greatest Lion: A True Story of Survival.* **Philomel Books, 2012.**
From the African grasslands to Hollywood, this book follows Zamba, a lion who appeared in many commercials, TV shows, and movies and was MGM Studios' mascot. (40 pp, ILL)

**Herold, Vickey.** *Clothes Then and Now.* **Benchmark Education, 2008.**
Herold compares the materials used to make clothes in the past and today as well as the differences in styles. (20 pp, TC, P and ILL, C, G, I, L, Series: Early Explorers Social Studies: Then and Now)

**High, Linda Oatman.** *The Cemetery Keepers of Gettysburg.* **Walker and Company, 2007.**
Told through the eyes of the son of the Gettysburg cemetery keeper, the events of summer of 1862—including the Battle of Gettysburg, the many burials afterward, and the address by Abraham Lincoln—are shared with the reader in this book. (32 pp, ILL)

**Hughes, Catherine D.** *First Big Book of Animals.* **National Geographic Society, 2010.**
Divided into geographic regions, this book includes vivid photographs and fascinating facts about many animals of the world. (128 pp, TC, P, C, G, I, Series: National Geographic Little Kids)

**Hughes, Catherine.** *First Big Book of Dinosaurs.* **National Geographic Society, 2011.**
This book shares facts about dinosaurs, from the smallest to the largest, such as their diet and why some may have had frills, crests, and long necks. (127 pp, TC, ILL, G, I)

**Hulbert, Laura.** *Who Has These Feet?* **Henry Holt and Company, 2011.**
On one page an animal foot is shown, and on the next page an illustration of the animal itself appears. Readers are asked to guess whose foot each is before turning the page. The final pages pull out to show all the animals and their feet. (40 pp, ILL)

**Hulbert, Laura.** *Who Has This Tail?* **Henry Holt and Company, 2012.**
Similar to *Who Has These Feet?*, this book includes several two-page spreads with illustrations of tails, and when the reader turns the page, the animal in its habitat is shown. The last pages are fold-outs with all the animals. (40 pp, ILL)

**Hutchinson, Caroline.** *Amazing Animal Senses.* **Newmark Learning, 2011.**
Examples of different animals with extraordinary senses of sight, hearing, smell, or taste are presented in this book. Suggestions for extension activities are provided. (16 pp, TC, P, Series: Rising Readers Leveled Books: Science)

---

*Legend:* pp = Number of pages; TC = Table of contents; P = Photos; ILL = Illustrated; C = Captioned; G = Glossary; I = Index; L = Leveled book; BB = Available in big book format

**Hutchinson, Caroline.** *How Do Baby Animals Grow?* **Newmark Learning, 2011.**
Brief text describes how polar bear, kangaroo, and penguin babies grow. Suggestions for extension activities are provided. (16 pp, P, L, Series: Rising Readers Leveled Books: Science)

**Hutchinson, Caroline.** *How Do You Stay Well?* **Newmark Learning, 2011.**
Simple text accompanies photographs of children doing the activities necessary to stay healthy. Suggestions for extension activities are provided. (16 pp, P, L, Series: Rising Readers Leveled Books: Science)

**Hutchinson, Caroline.** *I Can Move.* **Newmark Learning, 2011.**
Simple five-word sentences caption photographs of a child moving on different playground apparatus. Suggestions for extension activities are provided. (16 pp, P, L, Series: Rising Readers Leveled Books: Science)

**Hutchinson, Caroline.** *What Animal Am I?* **Newmark Learning, 2011.**
Riddles about squirrels, deer, birds, and spiders are accompanied by visual clues. Suggestions for extension activities are provided. (16 pp, P, L, Series: Rising Readers Leveled Books: Science)

**Hutchinson, Caroline.** *What Can We See in Nature?* **Newmark Learning, 2011.**
Examples of what can be seen at a garden, park, beach, and lake are given. Text is very simple—there is a five- to six-word sentence on each page. Suggestions for extension activities are provided. (16 pp, P, L, Series: Rising Readers Leveled Books: Science)

**Hutchinson, Caroline.** *What Do You See?* **Newmark Learning, 2011.**
Delicious photographs of red foods are presented alongside four-word sentences naming each. Suggestions for extension activities are provided. (16 pp, P, L, Series: Rising Readers Leveled Books: Science)

**Hutchinson, Caroline.** *What Lives at the Pond?* **Newmark Learning, 2011.**
A variety of animals that call a pond home are shown moving in different ways—flying, swimming, walking, et cetera. Suggestions for extension activities are provided. (16 pp, P, L, Series: Rising Readers Leveled Books: Science)

**Hutchinson, Caroline.** *What Season Is It?* **Newmark Learning, 2011.**
Hutchinson presents scenes of nature and activities associated with each of the four seasons in colorful photographs. Suggestions for extension activities are provided. (16 pp, P, L, Series: Rising Readers Leveled Books: Science)

**Hutchinson, Caroline.** *What Would You Eat in the Rain Forest?* **Newmark Learning, 2011.**
The book begins by showing what a monkey, a toucan, an anteater, a crocodile, a snake, and a jaguar would eat in the rain forest. It ends by asking readers what they would eat.

---

*Legend:* pp = Number of pages; TC = Table of contents; P = Photos; ILL = Illustrated; C = Captioned; G = Glossary; I = Index; L = Leveled book; BB = Available in big book format

Suggestions for extension activities are provided. (16 pp, P, L, Series: Rising Readers Leveled Books: Science)

**Hutchinson, Caroline. *Where Do Plants Live?* Newmark Learning, 2011.**
This book gives examples of plants that live on land and some that live in the water. Close-up photographs of the plants' leaves, fruit, or flower are also shown. Suggestions for extension activities are provided. (16 pp, P, L, Series: Rising Readers Leveled Books: Science)

**Hutchinson, Caroline. *Your Body Has Parts*. Newmark Learning, 2011.**
With simple text and photographs of children, the left-hand pages address different body parts, and the right-hand pages address what each body part does. Suggestions for extension activities are provided. (16 pp, P, L, Series: Rising Readers Leveled Books: Science)

**Iasevoli, Brenda. *Ants! They Are Hard Workers!* HarperCollins Publishers, 2005.**
This book is full of interesting facts about all different kinds of ants. The close-up, colorful photographs put the reader right in the ants' world. (32 pp, TC, P, C, G, Series: Time for Kids: Science Scoops)

**Jackson, Kay. *How Many Are Left?* Abrams Learning Trends, 2005.**
As a boy makes pancakes, the reader is asked to determine how many are left of each ingredient after some are added to the batter. In the end the young man makes it easy to determine how many pancakes are left as he eats them all! (14 pp, P, L, BB, Series: Big Book Math)

**James, Helen Frost. *S is for S'mores*. Thomson Gale, 2007.**
In simple rhyme, each letter of the alphabet is connected to an aspect of camping. Additional information is given in sidebars. The last page has a recipe for trail mix and some camping fun. (38 pp, ILL)

**Jenkins, Amanda. *Tornado!* Benchmark Learning, 2005.**
This is a reader's theater book with accompanying teacher's guide. It tells the story of five friends as a tornado approaches. (16 pp, G, L, Series: Reader's Theater: Science)

**Jenkins, Martin. *Ape*. Candlewick Press, 2007.**
This book presents the five different kinds of great apes in the world—orangutan, chimp, bonobo, gorilla, and human, comparing and contrasting each kind to the others. (48 pp, ILL, C, I)

**Jenkins, Martin. *Can We Save the Tiger?* Candlewick Press, 2011.**
Though the title implies the main topic of this book is the tiger, it actually examines a number of animals that are extinct or that are or have been threatened with extinction. These include the kakapo bird, the great auk penguin, and the American bison. Presented are the reasons for the threat of extinction and what is being done to prevent it from happening. (56 pp, ILL, C)

---

*Legend:* pp = Number of pages; TC = Table of contents; P = Photos; ILL = Illustrated; C = Captioned; G = Glossary; I = Index; L = Leveled book; BB = Available in big book format

**Jenkins, Steve.** *Actual Size.* **Houghton Mifflin Company, 2004.**
The colorful illustrations in this book show various body parts that belong to many animals, all in the actual size. Additional information on the animals is included in the last pages of the book. (28 pp, ILL)

**Jenkins, Steve.** *Almost Gone: The World's Rarest Animals.* **HarperCollins Publishers, 2006.**
Each page shows an animal that is quickly disappearing from our Earth. Listed is the geographic habitat of the animal as well as how many are left. The last pages present animals that are gone forever and those that are coming back from near extinction. (34 pp, ILL)

**Jenkins, Steve.** *The Beetle Book.* **Houghton Mifflin, 2012.**
Jenkins beautifully illustrates many different types of beetles with short descriptions of what makes each beetle unique. (40 pp, ILL, I)

**Jenkins, Steve.** *Bones.* **Scholastic, 2010.**
Human and animals bones are presented through paper collage with explanations of what each bone does. Some pages fold out for larger illustrations. (44 pp, I, C)

**Jenkins, Steve.** *Dogs and Cats.* **Houghton Mifflin Company, 2007.**
Start at the cover that says "Dogs and Cats," and the reader will learn about man's best friend. Flip the book and start at the cover that says "Cats and Dogs," and learn about this feline companion. (40 pp, ILL, C)

**Jenkins, Steve.** *Down, Down, Down: A Journey to the Bottom of the Sea.* **Houghton Mifflin, 2009.**
Beautiful, colorful collages set against the dark background of the deep sea introduce life down, down, down deep in the sea, creatures that glow, and marine snow. The last section gives more in-depth information on each animal in the book. (40 pp, ILL)

**Jenkins, Steve.** *Just a Second: A Different Way to Look at Time.* **Houghton Mifflin, 2011.**
Using animals and common occurrences, Jenkins illustrates what can be done in a second, a minute, an hour, et cetera. A timeline showing the average life span of many living things is included. (40 pp, ILL)

**Jenkins, Steve.** *Living Color.* **Houghton Mifflin, 2007.**
Beautiful illustrations provide the reader with information about animals that are yellow, blue, red, et cetera. The last section gives more in-depth information on each animal in the book. (32 pp, ILL, C)

**Jenkins, Steve, & Page, Robin.** *How Many Ways Can You Catch a Fly?* **Houghton Mifflin Company, 2008.**
This book presents the ways that different animals meet different challenges in their lives—getting food, raising young, finding shelter, et cetera. The last section gives more in-depth information on each animal in the book. (32 pp, ILL)

---

*Legend:* pp = Number of pages; TC = Table of contents; P = Photos; ILL = Illustrated; C = Captioned; G = Glossary; I = Index; L = Leveled book; BB = Available in big book format

**Jenkins, Steve, & Page, Robin.** *Move!* **Houghton Mifflin Company, 2006.**

This uniquely illustrated book shows many animal movements, such as slithering, swinging, walking, diving, and climbing. (32 pp, ILL)

**Jenkins, Steve, & Page, Robin.** *Sisters & Brothers: Sibling Relationships in the Animal World.* **Houghton Mifflin Harcourt, 2008.**

Jenkins and Page present information about the different types of sibling relationships that can be found in the animal world. The last section of the book contains additional facts about the animals presented earlier. (32 pp, ILL)

**Jenkins, Steve, & Page, Robin.** *Time for a Bath.* **Houghton Mifflin Harcourt, 2011.**

Each animal has its own way to keep clean, and Jenkins illustrates a wide variety of methods in this book. The last section gives additional information on animals mentioned earlier. (24 pp, ILL, Series: Time to)

**Jenkins, Steve, & Page, Robin.** *Time to Eat.* **Houghton Mifflin Harcourt, 2011.**

All animals must eat. This book presents how many do—from the large blue whale to the small black rat. The last section gives more in-depth information on each animal in the book. (24 pp, ILL, C, Series: Time to)

**Jenkins, Steve, & Page, Robin.** *What Do You Do With a Tail Like This?* **Houghton Mifflin Company, 2003.**

This creatively illustrated book describes what animals do with their eyes, noses, tails, and tongues. The last section of the book includes a detailed section on animal uses of the nose, ears, eyes, mouth, and feet. (32 pp, ILL)

**Jeunesse, Gallimard, & Valat, Pierre-Marie.** *Water.* **Moonlight Publishing, 2010.**

Using many plastic overlays, this book shares information about water. Jeunesse's text and Valat's illustrations present how much of the Earth is covered by water, the different forms of water, and how humans use water for survival and recreation. (34 pp, ILL, C, Series: My First Discoveries)

**Johnson, Claire.** *It All Adds Up.* **Abrams Learning Trends, 2005.**

At the beach, each child collects starfish, buckets of sand, or shells, among other things. The reader is asked to determine how many starfish two children collected all together as well as the combined totals for the other items. (14 pp, P, L, BB, Series: Big Book Math)

**Johnson, Etta.** *Local and State Government.* **Benchmark Learning, 2005.**

Johnson gives examples of why rules are needed, what services local and state governments provide, and the three branches of government on the state level. (24 pp, TC, P, C, G, I, Series: English Explorers Social Studies: Government and Citizenship)

---

*Legend:* pp = Number of pages; TC = Table of contents; P = Photos; ILL = Illustrated; C = Captioned; G = Glossary; I = Index; L = Leveled book; BB = Available in big book format

**Joubert, Beverly & Dereck.** *Little Kids' African Animal Book.* **National Geographic Society, 2011.**
Presented in alphabetical order, animals from Africa are shown in beautiful photographs with accompanying text. The book also includes an alphabetized list of animal facts. (48 pp, P, C, G)

**Judge, Lita.** *Bird Talk: What Birds Are Saying and Why.* **Roaring Book Press, 2012.**
With exquisite illustrations this book explains how various types of birds communicate. At the end of the book, many birds are described by their range and habitat. (48 pp, ILL)

**Judge, Lita.** *Born to Be Giants: How Baby Dinosaurs Grew to Rule the World.* **Roaring Book Press, 2011.**
Though many dinosaurs were large, they all started as babies. Judge tells the story of their lives as discovered by paleontologists in the digs. (48 pp, ILL)

**Judge, Lita.** *One Thousand Tracings: Healing the Wounds of World War II.* **Hyperion Books for Children, 2007.**
This true story begins in December 1946, when the author's father returned from World War II and then received a letter from a German friend who was suffering from a lack of everything. The American family collected items to send to them. This started a much larger effort to help those in 15 countries in Europe recover from the war. (40 pp, ILL)

**Judge, Lita.** *Yellowstone Moran: Painting the American West.* **Penguin Group, 2009.**
With beautiful watercolor illustrations, Judge presents the true story of Tom Moran, a painter from the city, who traveled out west to "the Yellowstone" to sketch and paint this wilderness. His sketches and paintings were presented to Congress and the president as evidence for the importance of protecting Yellowstone. As a result it was made the first American national park. (32 pp, ILL, C)

**Katz, Jon.** *Meet the Dogs of Bedlam Farm.* **Henry Holt and Company, 2011.**
Through photographs and text, four happy and hardworking dogs that live on Bedlam Farm in New York are introduced to the reader. Rose, Izzy, Frieda, and Lenore all help with farm chores. Rose herds the sheep out in the pasture. Izzy is a therapy dog who visits sick people. Frieda guards the farm and scares the cats. Lenore makes sure everyone is happy. Together, the dogs are a family. (32 pp, P, C)

**Keating, Frank.** *George: George Washington, Our Founding Father.* **Simon & Schuster, 2012.**
George Washington's life from the time he was born until he became the first US president is presented in first person. The book includes some of his Rules of Civility, a list that he wrote down as they were taught to him by his teachers. (32 pp, ILL)

---

*Legend:* pp = Number of pages; TC = Table of contents; P = Photos; ILL = Illustrated; C = Captioned; G = Glossary; I = Index; L = Leveled book; BB = Available in big book format

**Keating, Frank. *Theodore*. Paula Wiseman, 2006.**

Keating shares incidents in Theodore Roosevelt's life to bring to life this exciting personality who eventually became our 26th president. (32 pp, ILL)

**Keating, Frank. *Will Rogers: An American Legend*. Silver Whistle Harcourt, 2002.**

In text presented as typed notes pinned to a wall and drawings that look almost as clear as photographs, Keating and illustrator Mike Wimmer present the life of Will Rogers, his personality as well as his accomplishments. (32 pp, ILL)

**Kelly, Irene. *Even an Octopus Needs a Home*. Holiday House, 2011.**

From in the water, to up in the trees, to under the ground, Kelly explores how many animals make a home. (32 pp, ILL)

**Kelly, Irene. *Even an Ostrich Needs a Nest*. Holiday House, 2011.**

With engaging illustrations Kelly introduces some of the many types of nests made by birds. (20, ILL)

**Kelly, Irene. *It's a Butterfly's Life*. Holiday House, 2007.**

Step by step a butterfly's life is illustrated in this book by Irene Kelly. Soft-colored illustrations draw the reader into the action. (32 pp, ILL, C)

**Kelly, Irene. *It's a Hummingbird's Life*. Holiday House, 2003.**

In plain, straightforward text Kelly shares information about this jewel of a bird, from what it eats to how it migrates in the fall to warmer weather. (32 pp, ILL, C)

**Kenna, Kara, & Ostarch, Judy. *Dimes*. Judy O Productions, 2009.**

Shaped like a dime, this book tells the history and value of the coin as well as interesting facts about it. Sold as set with *Pennies, Nickels,* and *Quarters.* (24 pp, P, Series: All About Coins)

**Kenna, Kara, & Ostarch, Judy. *Nickels*. Judy O Productions, 2009.**

Shaped like a nickel, this book tells the history and value of the coin as well as interesting facts about it. Sold as set with *Pennies, Dimes,* and *Quarters.* (24 pp, P, Series: All About Coins)

**Kenna, Kara, & Ostarch, Judy. *Pennies*. Judy O Productions, 2009.**

Shaped like a penny, this book tells the history and value of the coin as well as interesting facts about it. Sold as set with *Nickels, Dimes* and *Quarters.* (24 pp, P, Series: All About Coins)

**Kenna, Kara, & Ostarch, Judy. *Quarters*. Judy O Productions, 2009.**

Shaped like a quarter, this book tells the history and value of the coin as well as interesting facts about it. Sold as set with *Pennies, Nickels,* and *Dimes.* (24 pp, P, Series: All About Coins)

**Kennedy, Jeannie. *Circus Performers*. Abrams Learning Trends, 2009.**

Kennedy depicts some of the different circus performers of today. Unlike in the past, when animals were a major part of circus entertainment, today it is the talents of these

---

*Legend:* pp = Number of pages; TC = Table of contents; P = Photos; ILL = Illustrated; C = Captioned; G = Glossary; I = Index; L = Leveled book; BB = Available in big book format

performers that fascinate crowds. They must work hard at their craft to stay safe while making the tricks look easy. Suggestions for using this book for reading and writing activities are included. (20 pp, TC, P, I, L)

**Kennedy, Jeannie. *On the Ball*. Abrams Learning Trends, 2009.**
Balls are used in soccer, baseball, basketball, and more. Some balls bounce; some have fuzz; some have holes; some have dimples. The football is not even round; it is an oval! Suggestions for using this book for reading and writing activities are included. (20 pp, TC, P, C, I, L)

**Kennedy, Jeannie. *Over the Bridge*. Abrams Learning Trends, 2009.**
This book provides the reader with a brief history of bridges and why they were built. Examples of some of the many different designs for bridges are also included. Suggestions for using this book for reading activities are included. (20 pp, TC, P, C, I, L)

**Kennedy, Jeannie. *A Trip to Space Camp*. Abrams Learning Trends, 2009.**
Kennedy shares how space camp provides a place where students can learn about space, math, and science. The book contains photographs of students' first-hand experiences with some of the training that astronauts must go through before going into space. Suggestions for using this book for reading and writing activities are included. (20 pp, TC, P, I, L)

**Kingfisher Editors. *Baby Animals at Night*. Kingfisher, 2012.**
Each photograph of a baby animal is accompanied by a brief description of what it does at night. Additional facts on the animals are found on the last pages. (14 pp, P, C, Series: Kingfisher: Baby Animals)

**Kingfisher Editors. *Baby Animals in the Forest*. Kingfisher, 2012.**
Interesting facts and adorable photographs depict what these animals do in the forest. Additional facts on the animals are found on the last pages. (14 pp, P, C, Series: Kingfisher: Baby Animals)

**Kingfisher Editors. *Baby Animals in the Sea*. Kingfisher, 2012.**
Baby animals that live by and in the sea are presented with brief narratives and simple photographs. (14 pp, P, C, Series: Kingfisher: Baby Animals)

**Kingfisher Editors. *Baby Animals in the Snow*. Kingfisher, 2012.**
This books presents, through photographs and brief text, baby animals as they deal with the snow in their environments. (14 pp, P, C, Series: Kingfisher: Baby Animals)

**Kingfisher Editors. *Baby Animals in the Wild*. Kingfisher, 2012.**
Close-up photographs of baby animals that live in the wild, along with simple text, give the reader a brief window into their world. Additional facts on the animals are found on the last pages. (14 pp, P, C, Series: Kingfisher: Baby Animals)

*Legend:* pp = Number of pages; TC = Table of contents; P = Photos; ILL = Illustrated; C = Captioned; G = Glossary; I = Index; L = Leveled book; BB = Available in big book format

**Kingfisher Editors.** *Pets.* **Kingfisher, 2012.**
Common household pets are portrayed in close-up photographs and brief descriptions. Additional facts on the animals are found on the last pages. (14 pp, P, C, Series: Kingfisher: Baby Animals)

**Kirk, Ellen.** *Human Footprint: Everything You Will Eat, Use, Wear, Buy, and Throw Out in Your Lifetime.* **National Geographic, 2011.**
Colorful photographs of everyday items illustrate how many items, such as cars, candy bars, clothes, et cetera, a person uses over a lifetime. Final pages give suggestions for reducing this footprint, the mark each person makes on the Earth's ecology. (32 pp, TC, P, Series: National Geographic Kids)

**Kottke, Jan.** *From Seed to Pumpkin.* **Scholastic, 2000.**
Clear photographs illustrate each step of a pumpkin's development. (23 pp, TC, P, G, I, L)

**Landau, Elaine.** *Corn.* **Children's Press, 1999.**
Landau introduces the reader to this staple crop, how it is grown, and for what it is used. (50 pp, TC, P, C, Series: A True Book)

**Lankford, Mary.** *Birthdays Around the World.* **HarperCollins, 2002.**
Lankford shares how birthdays are celebrated in seven countries outside the United States. Also included are some birthday superstitions. (32 pp, TC, ILL, I)

**Lappi, Megan.** *Decomposers.* **Weigl, 2012.**
Colorful close-up photographs show how natural items decompose. This book is part of a series that, when using the specially provided book code, connects with video, web links, et cetera. (24 pp, TC, P, C, G, I, L, Series: AV2: Food Chain)

**Layne, Steven, & Dover, Deborah.** *W Is for Windy City: A Chicago Alphabet.* **Sleeping Bear Press, 2011.**
From A to Z, this book describes great Chicago attractions, events, and people; it begins with the art institute and ends with the zoo. The history of Chicago is told through important people like Barack Obama, the Daleys, Oprah Winfrey, and Frank Lloyd Wright. (40 pp, ILL, C)

**Lee, Anna.** *Comparing Two Cities.* **Benchmark Learning, 2007.**
Lee compares and contrasts Beijing and Venice, their transportation systems, their foods, and their climates. (16 pp, P, C, G, L, Series: Early Explorers Social Studies: World Communities)

**Leedy, Loreen.** *Seeing Symmetry.* **Holiday House, 2012.**
In this book many, many examples of symmetry are presented, both in the natural world and in the human-made one. Even the front and back covers are symmetrical! (32 pp, ILL, G)

---

*Legend:* pp = Number of pages; TC = Table of contents; P = Photos; ILL = Illustrated; C = Captioned; G = Glossary; I = Index; L = Leveled book; BB = Available in big book format

**Lyon, G. E. *Mother to Tigers*. Atheneum/Richard Jackson Books, 2003.**
In this picture book biography, Lyon tells the remarkable story of Helen Martini, the founder of the Bronx Zoo's animal nursery and its first woman zookeeper. (32 pp, ILL)

**Markle, Sandra. *How Many Baby Pandas?* Walker & Company, 2009.**
Through photographs and text the reader learns about the Wolong Giant Panda Breeding Center in China. Here staff are trying to breed pandas to be released into the wild. (24 pp, P, C, G, I)

**Marsh, Laura. *Amazing Animal Journeys*. National Geographic Society, 2010.**
Beautiful photographs of animals in the wild document their migrations, from the zebra to the red crab to walruses. (48 pp, TC, P, C, G, I, Series: National Geographic Kids)

**Marsh, Laura. *Butterflies*. National Geographic Society, 2010.**
In fascinating photographs and descriptive text, Marsh depicts the monarch butterfly as it migrates south for the winter and then returns to begin its life cycle again in the spring. (48 pp, TC, P, C, G, I, Series: National Geographic Kids: Great Migrations)

**Marsh, Laura. *Caterpillar to Butterfly*. National Geographic Society, 2010.**
Each stage of the butterfly's life is presented in beautiful color photographs. Also included is an explanation of the difference between a butterfly and a moth. (32 pp, TC, P, C, G, Series: National Geographic Kids)

**Marsh, Laura. *Cheetahs*. National Geographic Society, 2010.**
Marsh presents many interesting facts about the fastest land animal on Earth. (32 pp, TC, P, C, G, Series: National Geographic Kids)

**Marsh, Laura. *Elephants*. National Geographic Society, 2010.**
This book depicts the annual migration the Mali elephant takes in search of food. Other interesting facts about this large land animal are also shared. (48 pp, TC, P, C, G, I, Series: National Geographic Kids: Great Migrations)

**Marsh, Laura. *Lizards*. National Geographic Society, 2010.**
This book brings the reader up close and personal with these sometimes terrifying, always captivating reptiles. (32 pp, TC, P, C, G, Series: National Geographic Kids)

**Marsh, Laura. *Ponies*. National Geographic Society, 2010.**
This book explains that one herd of wild ponies has been in existence for over 500 years but that nowadays ponies are used primarily for recreational riding. (32 pp, TC, P, C, G, Series: National Geographic Kids)

**Marsh, Laura. *Sea Turtles*. National Geographic Society, 2010.**
With colorful photographs Marsh tells of these intriguing creatures that are born on land but spend their lives in the ocean. (32 pp, TC, P, C, G, Series: National Geographic Kids)

---

*Legend:* pp = Number of pages; TC = Table of contents; P = Photos; ILL = Illustrated; C = Captioned; G = Glossary; I = Index; L = Leveled book; BB = Available in big book format

**Marsh, Laura. *Spiders*. National Geographic Society, 2011.**
Fascinating up-close photographs of spiders show readers what spiders do to survive. A gallery of "special spiders" is also included. (32 pp, TC, P, C, G)

**Marsh, Laura. *Tigers*. National Geographic Society, 2010.**
From an adorable cub to a fully grown adult busy surviving, Marsh portrays the life of a Bengal tiger. (32 pp, TC, P, C, G, Series: National Geographic Kids)

**Marsh, Laura. *Weird Sea Creatures*. National Geographic Society, 2010.**
Colorful photographs with interesting facts present some of the more unusual creatures found in the sea. (32 pp, TC, P, C, G, Series: National Geographic Kids)

**Matthews, John Thomas. *Our Earth*. Abrams Learning Trends, 2012.**
Matthews presents photographs and descriptions of different places on Earth, such as the Arctic, deserts, oceans, mountains, rain forests, and savannas. (14 pp, TC, P, G, I, L, BB, Series: Big Book Science)

**McNamara, Margaret. *Animals and the Seasons*. Benchmark Education Company, 2009.**
McNamara discusses how as temperatures change with the seasons, so do animals. The book provides photographs illustrating hibernation, migration, shedding, and changes in color. (16 pp, TC, P, C, G, I, L, BB, Series: Science Content Connections)

**McNamara, Margaret. *The Life Cycle of a Butterfly*. Benchmark Education Company, 2009.**
Clear, close-up photographs follow the progression from egg to larva to pupa to adult butterfly. (16 pp, TC, P, C, G, I, L, BB, Series: Science Content Connections)

**McNamara, Margaret. *The Life Cycle of a Frog*. Benchmark Education Company, 2009.**
Like all animals a frog has a life cycle. McNamara's book follows this cycle from egg to tadpole to adult frog and describes all the changes that take place during this fascinating cycle. (16 pp, TC, P, C, G, I, L, BB, Series: Science Content Connections)

**McNamara, Margaret. *Life in a Rural Community*. Benchmark Education Company, 2009.**
With colorful photographs McNamara depicts life in a rural community, its homes, jobs, and places for recreation. (16 pp, TC, P, C, G, I, L, BB, Series: Social Studies Content Connections)

**McNamara, Margaret. *Life in a Suburban Community*. Benchmark Education Company, 2009.**
McNamara discusses a suburban community's unique characteristics such as the types of homes there, where the residents work, and what types of recreation are available. (16 pp, TC, P, C, G, I, L, BB, Series: Social Studies Content Connections)

---

*Legend:* pp = Number of pages; TC = Table of contents; P = Photos; ILL = Illustrated; C = Captioned; G = Glossary; I = Index; L = Leveled book; BB = Available in big book format

**McNamara, Margaret.** *Life in an Urban Community.* **Benchmark Education Company, 2009.**

Large urban communities have homes much closer together than other types of communities. The variety of jobs is greater and the places for recreation more diverse. (16 pp, TC, P, C, G, I, L, BB, Series: Social Studies Content Connections)

**McNamara, Margaret.** *Plants and the Seasons.* **Benchmark Education Company, 2009.**

Using a variety of plants as examples, McNamara shows how plants change with each season. (16 pp, TC, P, C, G, I, L, BB, Series: Science Content Connections)

**McNamara, Margaret.** *Weather and the Seasons.* **Benchmark Education Company, 2009.**

This book shows the changes that take place over the four seasons and how those changes affect people and the activities they choose. (16 pp, TC, P, C, G, I, L, BB, Series: Science Content Connections)

**McNamara, Margaret.** *What Are Some Rules at Home?* **Benchmark Education Company, 2009.**

In this book McNamara explains how rules at home teach safety, responsibility, respect, and healthful habits. (16 pp, TC, P, C, G, I, L, BB, Series: Social Studies Content Connections)

**McNamara, Margaret.** *What Are Some Rules at School?* **Benchmark Education Company, 2009.**

This book shares the reasons for rules at school: to help you learn, to keep you safe, to teach respect, and to help you take care of your school. (16 pp, TC, P, C, G, I, L, BB, Series: Social Studies Content Connections)

**McNamara, Margaret.** *What Do Animals Need?* **Benchmark Education Company, 2009.**

From ermines to fish, ants, and ground agamas, McNamara illustrates why animals need food and water, oxygen, shelter, and space. (16 pp, TC, P, C, G, I, L, BB, Series: Science Content Connections)

**McNamara, Margaret.** *Why Do We Have Rules?* **Benchmark Education Company, 2009.**

In this book McNamara explains that rules and laws keep us safe and assure fairness and that obeying the rules and laws makes us good citizens of our communities. (16 pp, TC, P, C, G, I, L, BB, Series: Social Studies Content Connections)

**Merritt, Donna.** *Amazing Scientists.* **Abrams Learning Trends, 2009.**

This book tells of the important discoveries made by Galileo Galilei, Marie Curie, and George Washington Carver. (14 pp, TC, P, C, G, I, L, BB, Series: Big Book Science)

---

*Legend:* pp = Number of pages; TC = Table of contents; P = Photos; ILL = Illustrated; C = Captioned; G = Glossary; I = Index; L = Leveled book; BB = Available in big book format

**Merritt, Donna.** *Is It Likely to Happen?* **Abrams Learning Trends, 2005.**
Providing scenarios from everyday life, this book asks the reader to begin to apply the concept of probability to day-to-day occurrences. (14 pp, P, C, L, BB, Series: Big Book Math)

**Merritt, Donna.** *Let's Eat.* **Abrams Learning Trends, 2006.**
Focusing on eating healthy foods, Merritt walks the reader through how to make good choices. (14 pp, TC, P, G, I, L, BB, Series: Big Book Science)

**Merritt, Donna.** *Let's Figure It Out!* **Abrams Learning Trends, 2006.**
Providing problems from everyday life, Merritt asks the reader to decide whether to use subtraction or addition to figure out each answer. (14 pp, P, C, L, BB, Series: Big Book Math)

**Merritt, Donna.** *My Wonderful Body.* **Abrams Learning Trends, 2009.**
Using photographs of children overlaid with illustrations of organs, Merritt discusses the body's bones, muscles, brain, heart, stomach, and lungs and why each of these is important. (14 pp, TC, P, C, G, I, L, BB, Series: Big Book Science)

**Merritt, Donna.** *Playground Science.* **Abrams Learning Trends, 2006.**
A bicycle wheel, a seesaw, and a slide are all simple machines. Using photographs of children on the playground, this book shows how these simple machines make work and play easier. (14 pp, TC, P, G, I, L, BB, Series: Big Book Science)

**Merritt, Donna.** *The Water Cycle.* **Abrams Learning Trends, 2009.**
Through collection, evaporation, condensation, and precipitation, nature can recycle water. Merritt presents simple experiments children can do to see this water cycle in action. (14 pp, TC, P, C, G, I, L, BB, Series: Big Book Science)

**Mulcahy, Marie.** *How Scientists Observe.* **Abrams Learning Trends, 2006.**
Mulcahy shows how microscopes, binoculars, and telescopes help scientists observe objects. Even a camera can be an important tool for scientists. (14 pp, TC, P, C, G, I, L, BB, Series: Big Book Science)

**Mulcahy, Marie.** *Over, Under, In, and Out.* **Abrams Learning Trends, 2006.**
Delightful photographs of cats crawling all over the house looking for red yarn illustrate the concepts of *between, in front of, under, out,* and more. (14 pp, P, C, L, BB, Series: Big Book Math)

**Mulcahy, Marie.** *What Time Is It?* **Abrams Learning Trends, 2005.**
Various children are shown at different times of their school day, from waking up to going to sleep. Each photograph is accompanied by an analog clock that notes the time. (14 pp, P, C, L, BB, Series: Big Book Math)

**Murphy, Ann.** *How Do We Measure?* **Abrams Learning Trends, 2005.**
Pairs of animals, people, or items are presented and the reader is asked to compare the height, weight, length, et cetera. The final pages have additional pairs that the reader can compare. (14 pp, P, L, BB, Series: Big Book Math)

---

*Legend:* pp = Number of pages; TC = Table of contents; P = Photos; ILL = Illustrated; C = Captioned; G = Glossary; I = Index; L = Leveled book; BB = Available in big book format

**Murphy, Ann.** *The Life of a Butterfly.* **Abrams Learning Trends, 2012.**
Each stage of a butterfly's life from egg to caterpillar to pupa to adult butterfly to the migration south in the winter is depicted in beautiful photographs. (14 pp, TC, P, G, I, L, BB, Series: Big Book Science)

**Murphy, Ann.** *We Can Graph It!* **Abrams Learning Trends, 2005.**
A class was having a pizza party. They had to decide what kinds of pizza to get. They use a graph to show each child's favorite. Using the information, they ordered some pizzas for everyone. (14 pp, P, L, BB, Series: Big Book Math)

**National Geographic Kids.** *Count.* **National Geographic Society, 2011.**
This bright, colorful board book helps children learn to count while also learning fun facts about animals. (24 pp, P, Series: National Geographic Little Kids: Look and Learn)

**National Geographic Kids.** *Match!* **National Geographic Society, 2011.**
This National Geographic Society Little Kids Look and Learn book matches many little animals, things, or creatures with a big version of the same. (24 pp, P, C, Series: National Geographic Little Kids: Look and Learn)

**Nelson, Robin.** *Presidents' Day.* **Lerner Publications Company, 2003.**
Nelson gives readers the history of Presidents' Day, originally two separate days celebrating George Washington's and Abraham Lincoln's birthdays. (23 pp, P, G, I)

**Nelson, Robin.** *Staying Clean.* **Lerner Publications Company, 2006.**
Through photographs of real children and simple text, Nelson tells why it is important to stay clean and how to do it well. (32 pp, P, G, I, Series: Pull Ahead Books: Health)

**Newman, Mark.** *Polar Bears.* **Henry Holt and Company, 2011.**
Captivating photographs of this large, adorable yet fierce animal accompany interesting facts about the largest bear in the world. Information about how to help these animals whose population is quickly shrinking is also included. (32 pp, P, C)

**Nguyen, Linh.** *How Many Parts?* **Abrams Learning Trends, 2005.**
Brief story problems dealing with both sandwiches and cereal bars demonstrate the need for dividing the food into fractions so that everyone gets an equal portion. Explanation of the terms *whole* and *fraction* are also given. (14 pp, P, C, L, BB, Series: Big Book Math)

**Nunweek, Joseph.** *A Mammoth Eclipse.* **Abrams Learning Trends, 2009.**
An eclipse happens when the moon gets between the Earth and sun and hides the sun from us. A total solar eclipse, when day becomes night, seldom happens. Eclipses don't last long, and it may be many years before another one happens. This book shows a day when people in Asia experienced a total solar eclipse. Suggestions to guide the adult in using the book with children are included. (20 pp, TC, P, I, L)

---

*Legend:* pp = Number of pages; TC = Table of contents; P = Photos; ILL = Illustrated; C = Captioned; G = Glossary; I = Index; L = Leveled book; BB = Available in big book format

**Nunweek, Lynda.** *A Battle in the Deep Sea.* **Abrams Learning Trends, 2009.**

This book shows a sperm whale diving deep into the ocean looking for food. There it catches a giant squid that uses its tentacles to try to escape. As soon as the whale wins the battle, it must come to the surface for air. Suggestions to guide the adult in using the book with children are included. (16 pp, P, C, I, L)

**Nunweek, Lynda.** *The Battle to Breathe.* **Abrams Learning Trends, 2009.**

In this book a Weddell seal goes under the ice to catch food. While it can hold its breath for an hour, there is trouble. After catching its dinner, it must find a hole in the ice so it can get air, but other seals are also looking for a hole in the ice. Suggestions to guide the adult in using the book with children are included. (16 pp, P, I, L)

**Nunweek, Lynda.** *Bully Bugs.* **Abrams Learning Trends, 2009.**

Even though bugs are small, some of them can quickly catch and eat others. Some will fight other bugs too. Suggestions for using this book for reading activities are included. (16 pp, P, C, I, L)

**Nunweek, Lynda.** *The Hoatzin Bird.* **Abrams Learning Trends, 2009.**

The hoatzin birds of the South American rain forests have large wings, but they are not good flyers. They must use other ways to stay safe. Nests are built in trees over water to avoid snakes and monkeys, who like to eat the chicks. Claws on top of their wings, a bad smell, an awful noise, and the ability to swim under water also help them. Suggestions to guide the adult in using the book with children are included. (20 pp, TC, P, C, I, L)

**Nunweek, Lynda.** *Hunting for Treasure.* **Abrams Learning Trends, 2009.**

Small submarines and other special tools are used by treasure hunters to recover hidden treasures. Suggestions to guide the adult in using the book with children are included. (20 pp, TC, P, C, I, L)

**Nunweek, Lynda.** *Inside-Out Skeletons.* **Abrams Learning Trends, 2009.**

Skeletons support people on the inside, but skeletons support other animals on the outside. Shellfish and insects have these outside skeletons or *exoskeletons*. As these animals grow, they sometimes need to shed their old skeleton to grow a new, bigger one, and during the period the new skeleton is growing, they are very vulnerable. Some day people might also want artificial exoskeletons. Suggestions to guide the adult in using the book with children are included. (20 pp, TC, P, I, L)

**Nunweek, Lynda.** *The Junk Raft Journey.* **Abrams Learning Trends, 2009.**

This book tells of some people who made a raft out of the types of junk other people had been putting in the ocean. They went on a trip on the ocean to show others what the junk was doing. Suggestions to guide the adult in using the book with children are included. (16 pp, P, C, I, L)

**Nunweek, Lynda.** *Samso: The Green Dream.* **Abrams Learning Trends, 2009.**

The people who live on Samso, a small island in Denmark, use energy from plants, wind, water, and sunshine. None of these things will run out, and none pollute the Earth. The

---

*Legend:* pp = Number of pages; TC = Table of contents; P = Photos; ILL = Illustrated; C = Captioned; G = Glossary; I = Index; L = Leveled book; BB = Available in big book format

green dream of the people of Samso has come true! Suggestions to guide the adult in using the book with children are included. (20 pp, TC, P, C, I, L)

**Nunweek, Lynda.** *A Snake Wrangler.* **Abrams Learning Trends, 2009.**
When snakes come into the city, it is the snake wrangler's job to find them and take them away without hurting them. Snakes can be dangerous, so the wranglers need to be careful. Photographs document one snake wrangler's capture of a snake. Suggestions to guide the adult in using the book with children are included. (16 pp, P, C, I, L)

**Nuzzolo, Deborah.** *Tiger Shark.* **Capstone Press, 2008.**
Big colorful photos help the reader get up close and personal with these fierce predators that will eat just about anything. (32 pp, P, C, TC, G, I)

**Parot, Annelore.** *Kimonos.* **Chronicle Books, 2011.**
With flaps and cutouts, this book introduces many styles of Japanese clothing and hairdos. The colorful illustrations help show what the presented Japanese terms mean. (36 pp, ILL)

**Patent, Dorothy Hinshaw.** *Saving Audie: A Pit Bull Puppy Gets a Second Chance.* **Walker and Company, 2011.**
Heartwarming photographs tell the true story of Audie, a pit bull dog who was to be part of an illegal dog-fighting ring until he was rescued. (48 pp, P, C)

**Peterson, Brenda.** *Leopard and Silkie: One Boy's Quest to Save the Seal Pups.* **Christy Ottaviano Books, 2012.**
Six-year-old Miles is a seal-sitter who worked to protect the seals of the Pacific Northwest. This book tells his story. (32 pp, P)

**Pfeffer, Wendy.** *From Seed to Pumpkin.* **Scholastic, 2004.**
Colorful illustrations follow the progression of a pumpkin through the seasons from seed to pie. (33 pp, ILL, L)

**Pfeffer, Wendy.** *Life in a Coral Reef.* **HarperCollins Publishers, 2009.**
Beautiful collage illustrations tell the story of life in a coral reef from sun up to night. Additional information about coral reefs is given at the end of the book. (34 pp, ILL, Series: Let's-Read-And-Find-Out: Science)

**Ramirez, Mark.** *Energy All Around.* **Abrams Learning Trends, 2007.**
In colorful photographs Ramirez depicts energy in the forms of heat, light, and sound as it relates to everyday occurrences around us. (14 pp, TC, P, C, G, I, L, BB, Series: Big Book Science)

**Ramirez, Mark.** *Force and Motion.* **Abrams Learning Trends, 2007.**
Through photographs of children in motion, Ramirez shows that force can be pushing or pulling and that it can make an object move or even lift it. (14 pp, TC, P, C, G, I, L, BB, Series: Big Book Science)

---

*Legend:* pp = Number of pages; TC = Table of contents; P = Photos; ILL = Illustrated; C = Captioned; G = Glossary; I = Index; L = Leveled book; BB = Available in big book format

**Rappaport, Doreen.** *Eleanor, Quiet No More.* **Hyperion Books, 2009.**
With soft illustrations and direct quotes, this book tells the story of Eleanor Roosevelt, who went from a quiet, shy child to the First Lady of the United States and a leader in her own right. (48 pp, ILL)

**Raymond, Christopher.** *I Learn With My Senses.* **Abrams Learning Trends, 2012.**
In this book readers are asked to consider what they can learn using their senses of sight, hearing, touch, smell, and taste and what parts of their bodies they use to take in this information. (14 pp, TC, P, G, I, L, BB, Series: Big Book Science)

**Raymond, Christopher.** *The Mystery Seeds.* **Abrams Learning Trends, 2012.**
Raymond presents mystery seeds that are planted and observed. Roots, leaves, and a stem grow until finally a flower appears and the mystery is solved. (14 pp, TC, P, G, I, L, BB, Series: Big Book Science)

**Raymond, Christopher.** *Science Detectives.* **Abrams Learning Trends, 2009.**
In this book children take on the role of science detectives to look, record, and predict. Then they must experiment to see if their prediction comes true. (14 pp, TC, P, C, G, I, L, BB, Series: Big Book Science)

**Raymond, Christopher.** *Tell Me All About It.* **Abrams Learning Trends, 2012.**
Just as a scientist does, the reader of this book is asked to observe and predict size comparisons, sink/float outcomes, and magnet attraction. (14 pp, TC, P, G, I, L, BB, Series: Big Book Science)

**Reed, Hannah.** *Sea Otters in the Kelp Forest.* **Eleanor Curtain Publishing, 2009.**
Reed illustrates with photographs how sea otters contribute to life in the kelp forest and why these animals are protected. (16 pp, ILL, C, L, Series: Flying Start to Literacy)

**Reed, Hannah.** *Using Color.* **Eleanor Curtain Publishing, 2003.**
This book contains vivid photographs of animals using color to survive. This book includes a teacher version and literacy learning activities. (16 pp, TC, P, I, L, Series: Explorations)

**Reed, Hannah.** *What Am I?* **Eleanor Curtain Publishing, 2009.**
Reed presents a riddle describing one animal. Each page presents more information and comparisons to other animals. The last page has the answer to the riddle. (16 pp, P, L, Series: Flying Start to Literacy)

**Rees, Rod.** *Robots.* **Eleanor Curtain Publishing, 2003.**
Detailed descriptions of how robots can be used around the house and in the workplace accompany pictures of the robots at work. This book includes a teacher version and literacy learning activities. (24 pp, TC, P, C, L, Series: Explorations)

---

*Legend:* pp = Number of pages; TC = Table of contents; P = Photos; ILL = Illustrated; C = Captioned; G = Glossary; I = Index; L = Leveled book; BB = Available in big book format

**Reid, Margarette.** *Lots and Lots of Coins.* **Dutton Children's Books, 2011.**
Illustrations with speech "bubbles" share interesting facts about the history of money and in particular the coins used in the United States. (32 pp, ILL, C)

**Rizzo, Johanna.** *Oceans: Dolphins, Sharks, Penguins, and More!* **National Geographic Society, 2010.**
The colorful photographs in this book match the detailed descriptions of each sea animal. The book answers such questions as what makes a dolphin a dolphin and why penguins wear funny costumes. (64 pp, TC, P, C, G, I)

**Rodriguez, Miguel Ortega.** *How Else Can We Show It?* **Abrams Learning Trends, 2005.**
A class is picking their favorite pet. They use real objects, tally marks, a bar graph, and a pie chart to show how the class voted. (14 pp, P, L, BB, Series: Big Book Math)

**Romero, Libby.** *Discover Forensic Chemistry.* **Benchmark Education Company, 2006.**
Simple descriptions and photographs of the work done by forensic chemists present a first glimpse at this fascinating occupation. (24 pp, TC, P, C, G, I, Series: English Explorers: Chemistry)

**Romero, Libby.** *Discover Kitchen Chemistry.* **Benchmark Education Company, 2006.**
Photographs and simple descriptions show the chemistry that takes place in the kitchen. (24 pp, TC, P, C, G, I, Series: English Explorers: Chemistry)

**Romero, Libby.** *Discover Medical Chemistry.* **Benchmark Education Company, 2006.**
Pharmacists, doctors, scientists, nutritionists, and their work in medical chemistry are all portrayed in photographs and simple descriptions. (24 pp, TC, P, C, G, I, Series: English Explorers: Chemistry)

**Romero, Libby.** *Forensic Chemistry.* **Benchmark Education Company, 2006.**
This book has higher level text and builds on the information in *Discover Forensic Chemistry.* (32 pp, TC, P, C, G, I, Series: English Explorers: Chemistry)

**Romero, Libby.** *Kitchen Chemistry.* **Benchmark Education Company, 2006.**
This book has higher level text and builds on the information in *Discover Kitchen Chemistry.* (24 pp, TC, P, C, G, I, Series: English Explorers: Chemistry)

**Romero, Libby.** *Medical Chemistry.* **Benchmark Education Company, 2006.**
This book has higher level text and builds on the information in *Discover Medical Chemistry.* (24 pp, TC, P, C, G, I, Series: English Explorers: Chemistry)

---

*Legend:* pp = Number of pages; TC = Table of contents; P = Photos; ILL = Illustrated; C = Captioned; G = Glossary; I = Index; L = Leveled book; BB = Available in big book format

**Roth, Susan L., & Trumbore, Cindy. *The Mangrove Tree: Planting Trees to Feed Families*. Lee and Low Books, 2011.**
Beautiful textural collage pictures help tell the story of the mangroves that were planted by the Red Sea by Dr. Gordon Sato because of their tolerance of the salty climate. Everyone and everything benefited from the mangroves that provided food for animals and oxygen for all to breathe. (40 pp, ILL, C, G)

**Rotner, Shelley. *Senses in the City*. Millbrook Press, 2008.**
This book follows a group of children as they find all the things that can be seen, heard, smelled, tasted, and touched in the big city. (32 pp, P)

**Rotner, Shelley. *Senses on the Farm*. Millbrook Press, 2009.**
With large, wonderful photographs of children busy on a farm, Rotner shows how each sense is used through the many activities there. (32 pp, P)

**Rotner, Shelley, & Kelly, Sheila. *I'm Adopted*! Holiday House, 2011.**
Heart-warming photographs of children in their adoptive families provide the background for discussing the why and how of adoption as well as what it means to both the children and the families they join. (32 pp, P, C)

**Rotner, Shelley, & Kelly, Sheila. *Many Ways: How Families Practice Their Beliefs and Religions*. Millbrook Press, 2006.**
Rotner uses photographs of real families to show that while there may be many ways to practice religious beliefs, there are also similarities, and all should be respected. Information about the photographs and further readings are provided in the last section. (32 pp, P)

**Rotner, Shelley, & Kelly, Sheila. *Shades of People*. Holiday House, 2009.**
Rotner's photographs portray all the many shades of color seen on people's skin. Children in the photographs are shown doing everyday activities. (32 pp, P)

**Rotner, Shelley, & Woodhull, Anne. *The Buzz on Bees*. Holiday House, 2010.**
This book's colorful close-up photographs bring the reader into the world of bees. The important question, "Why are they disappearing?" is addressed, and suggestions are given for helping these busy creatures. (32 pp, P, C)

**Rotner, Shelley, & Woodhull, Anne. *Every Season*. Roaring Brook Press, 2007.**
With few words and beautiful photographs, the book shares the activities associated with each season. (32 pp, P)

**Rumsch, BreAnn. *Money Matters*. ABDO Publishing Company, 2013.**
The history of money is explained in this book as are concepts such as scarcity, credit, debt, and fiscal fitness. Also listed are all the different features of a US five-dollar bill

---

*Legend:* pp = Number of pages; TC = Table of contents; P = Photos; ILL = Illustrated; C = Captioned; G = Glossary; I = Index; L = Leveled book; BB = Available in big book format

and the names of some foreign coins and bills. A website is given for more information. (32 pp, TC, P, C, G, I, Series: Economy in Action)

**Rustad, Martha.** *Animals in Fall.* **Capstone Press, 2008.**
Simple text accompanies close-up photographs of many animals preparing for winter. (24 pp, TC, P, G, I, Series: Pebble Plus: All About Fall)

**Sanchez, Maria.** *Sun and Shadows, Sky and Space.* **Abrams Learning Trends, 2006.**
As the Earth spins creating night and day, it also rotates around the sun creating seasons and a year. The location of the sun in the sky also determines the length of shadows. (14 pp, TC, P, C, G, I, L, BB, Series: Big Book Science)

**Santiago, Rosario Ortiz.** *Amazing Plants.* **Abrams Learning Trends, 2006.**
Some plants smell bad; some plants hitch rides on animals. It is amazing how all the different plants survive! (14 pp, TC, P, G, I, L, BB, Series: Big Book Science)

**Sayre, April Pulley.** *Vulture View.* **Henry Holt, 2007.**
In simple rhyme the day of a vulture is revealed as it looks for food, cleans itself, and settles in for the night. (32 pp, ILL)

**Schmerler, Alison.** *Look for Shapes.* **Abrams Learning Trends, 2005.**
Using photographs of common everyday objects, Schmerler shows how squares, rectangles, triangles, and circles can be found in the world around us. (14 pp, P, L, BB, Series: Big Book Math)

**Schmerler, Alison.** *Solid Shapes.* **Abrams Learning Trends, 2005.**
Examples of spheres, cubes, cylinders, and rectangular prisms are presented in this book through photographs of common items. (14 pp, P, L, BB, Series: Big Book Math)

**Schreiber, Anne.** *Volcanoes!* **National Geographic, 2008.**
This book focuses on the "Ring of Fire," the eastern coast of Asia and the western coast of North and South America, to explain how volcanoes are formed and what happens during an eruption. (32 pp, TC, P, C, G, Series: National Geographic Kids)

**Schuetz, Kari.** *Giant Pandas.* **Bellwether Media, 2012.**
One to two sentences accompany each photograph, giving interesting facts about giant pandas. (24 pp, TC, P, G, I, L, Series: Blastoff Readers: Animal Safari)

**Schuh, Mari.** *Tools for the Garden.* **Capstone Press, 2010.**
Each photograph of a garden tool is accompanied by a simple explanation of its purpose. Also included is a list of additional readings and Internet resources. (24 pp, TC, P, G, I, Series: Pebble: Gardens)

---

*Legend:* pp = Number of pages; TC = Table of contents; P = Photos; ILL = Illustrated; C = Captioned; G = Glossary; I = Index; L = Leveled book; BB = Available in big book format

**Schuh, Mari. *Vegetables on My Plate*. Capstone Press, 2013.**
Using the MyPlate concept, this book explores the different ways vegetables can be part of a healthy diet. Photographs of young children enjoying these vegetables are included. (24 pp, TC, P, G, I, Series: Pebble Plus: What's on MyPlate?)

**Scott, Janine. *Climbing a Rock Wall*. Abrams Learning Trends, 2009.**
Rock climbing is hard work. For safety, climbers use special equipment and always climb with a partner. Getting down is much easier than getting up! Suggestions for using this book for reading and writing activities are included. (20 pp, TC, P, C, I, L)

**Scott, Janine. *Race to the Finish*. Abrams Learning Trends, 2009.**
Racing cars can take a lot of work. The cars and drivers spend days getting ready for the race. The drivers have special equipment to help them keep safe. What is done if there is a crash, what the different flags mean, and why some cars never finish a race are all explained in this book. Suggestions for using this book for reading and writing activities are included. (20 pp, TC, P, C, I, L)

**Serafini, Frank. *Looking Closely in the Rain Forest*. Kids Can Press, 2010.**
Every other page shows a small, close-up photograph of something in the rain forest and asks the reader to identify it. The next page shows a larger photograph accompanied by information about the plant or animal. (40 pp, P)

**Serrano, John. *Being a Good Citizen*. Newmark Learning, 2010.**
Serrano addresses what a good citizen should do at home, at school, and in the community. (16 pp, TC, P, C, L, Series: Rising Readers Leveled Books: Social Studies)

**Shanahan, Kerrie. *Animals That Store Food*. Eleanor Curtain Publishing Company, 2010.**
Detailed information how acorn woodpeckers, squirrels, beavers, pikas, honeypot ants, and bees store food accompany colorful photographs of each animal. (24 pp, TC, P, C, G, L, Series: Flying Start to Literacy)

**Shanahan, Kerrie. *Teach Me How*. Eleanor Curtain Publishing, 2009.**
Engaging photographs show parent animals teaching their young important survival skills. (16 pp, ILL, L, Series: Flying Start to Literacy)

**Shields, Amy. *First Big Book of Why*. National Geographic, 2011.**
From "Why do I have curly hair?" to "Why do bugs bite?" Shields provides easy to understand explanations for some of the many questions young children ask. Each answer has colorful and intriguing photographs to illustrate the information. (128 pp, TC, P, C. G, I, Series: National Geographic Little Kids)

**Shields, Amy. *Train*. National Geographic, 2011.**
This book presents the different types of trains, how trains helped built America, and other interesting facts about this mode of transportation. (32 pp, TC, P, G)

---

*Legend:* pp = Number of pages; TC = Table of contents; P = Photos; ILL = Illustrated; C = Captioned; G = Glossary; I = Index; L = Leveled book; BB = Available in big book format

**Simon, Seymour.** *Animals Nobody Loves.* **Chronicle Books, 2001.**
In Simon's book, beautiful close-up photographs accompany full-page descriptions of some of the more frightening animals on Earth. These include, among others, cobras, cockroaches, and piranhas. (48 pp, TC, P)

**Singer, Marilyn.** *Caterpillars.* **EarlyLight Books, 2011.**
With verse and simple text Singer shares the life of caterpillars—how they avoid predators, travel long distances, and go through metamorphosis. (40 pp, P, C, G, I)

**Smith, Jayne.** *Living Things Are Everywhere!* **Abrams Learning Trends, 2012.**
Living things grow. They need food, and they need to breathe. Plants make seeds to grow into new plants; animals make babies. The reader is asked to use these characteristics to determine whether something is living or nonliving. (14 pp, TC, P, G, I, L, BB, Series: Big Book Science)

**Sobol, Richard.** *The Story of Silk: From Worm Spit to Woven Scarves.* **Candlewick Press, 2012.**
Detailed text and illustrative photographs explain the process of producing silk, from the raising of the silk worms to the weaving of fabric. This book would best be read or paraphrased with children. (37 pp, P, C, G)

**Springett, Martin.** *Kate and Pippin: An Unlikely Love Story.* **Henry Holt and Company, 2012.**
This book uses photographs and simple text to tell the true story of how a rescued orphaned fawn and a family's Great Dane became the best of friends. (32 pp, P)

**St. George, Judith.** *Stand Tall, Abe Lincoln.* **Philomel Books, 2008.**
St. George's book focuses on Abraham Lincoln's life from his birth until he set off on his own. The importance of his mother, his stepmother, and school are all addressed. (48 pp, ILL)

**Stewart, Melissa.** *Deadliest Animals.* **National Geographic Society, 2011.**
With fascinating and often frightening photographs and complimentary text, Stewart shares information about some of the deadliest animals on Earth. (48 pp, TC, P, C, G, I, Series, National Geographic Kids)

**Stewart, Melissa.** *Snakes!* **National Geographic, 2009.**
Fascinating photographs depict the unique characteristics of snakes. (32 pp, TC, P, C, G, Series: National Geographic Kids)

**Stewart, Melissa.** *Titanic.* **National Geographic Society, 2012.**
The story of the tragic sinking of this great ship is told. Photographs of the past when the Titanic set sail and modern photographs of the sunken ship under water accompany the narrative. (48 pp, TC, P, C, G, I, Series: National Geographic Kids)

---

*Legend:* pp = Number of pages; TC = Table of contents; P = Photos; ILL = Illustrated; C = Captioned; G = Glossary; I = Index; L = Leveled book; BB = Available in big book format

**Stott, Carol.** *I Wonder Why Stars Twinkle and Other Questions About Space.* **Kingfisher, 2011.**

Each page addresses a different question about space. Answers are illustrated with drawings and comic pictures. (32 pp, TC, ILL, C, I, Series: I Wonder Why)

**Sutton, Sally.** *Demolition.* **Candlewick Press, 2012.**

Each set of pages depicts a different step in the process of demolition. Readers will enjoy the sound words used throughout the book. (32 pp, ILL)

**Swain, Cynthia.** *Schools Then and Now.* **Benchmark Learning, 2008.**

Alternating pages between depictions of then and now, Swain compares school buildings, furniture, and writing materials of the past with those of today. (16 pp, P and ILL, G, L, Series: Early Explorers: Social Studies: Then and Now)

**Sweet, Melissa.** *Balloons Over Broadway: The True Story of the Puppeteer of Macy's Parade.* **Houghton Mifflin Books for Children, 2011.**

Colorful illustrations accompany the story of Tony Sarg, a puppeteer in New York, whose puppets performed in Macy's store windows. When Macy's decided to have a parade on Thanksgiving Day in 1924, Tony was part of it. The wild animals that were part of the parade scared some children, so Macy's wanted Tony to replace the animals. Thinking of the Goodyear blimp, Tony designed the giant balloons that have become an iconic part of the parade. (40 pp, ILL, C, I)

**Swinburne, Stephen.** *Whose Shoes?* **Boyds Mills Press, 2010.**

Every other page depicts a pair of shoes with the question, "Whose shoes?" The next page shows the person who might wear them. (32 pp, P)

**Talia, James.** *At Lunchtime.* **Eleanor Curtain Publishing, 2003.**

Lunch is a young boy's favorite meal. He shares how he, his father, his mother, his grandma, and his grandpa spend their lunches. This book includes a teacher version and literacy learning activities. (20 pp, P, L, Series: Explorations)

**Thimmesh, Catherine.** *Friends: True Stories of Extraordinary Animal Friendships.* **Houghton Mifflin, 2011.**

This book of unlikely animal friendships tells the struggles of each animal and how each found companionship in an animal friend, in many cases one that most likely would have been a predator in the wild. (32 pp, P, C)

**Tomecek, Steve.** *Rocks and Minerals.* **National Geographic, 2010.**

With colorful photographs Tomecek introduces the reader to the many different types of rocks and minerals and identifies their origin. (32 pp, P, ILL, C, Series: National Geographic Kids: Jump Into Science)

---

*Legend:* pp = Number of pages; TC = Table of contents; P = Photos; ILL = Illustrated; C = Captioned; G = Glossary; I = Index; L = Leveled book; BB = Available in big book format

**Torrisi, Cathy.** *Before It Gets to the Store.* **Abrams and Company Publishers, 2009.**

Torrisi follows milk, apples, eggs, grains, and paper from their origins to the store. (14 pp, TC, P, G, I, L, BB, Series: Abrams Learning Trends)

**Torrisi, Cathy.** *Eat All Your Colors.* **Abrams Learning Trends, 2011.**

Pointing out that each color of fruit and vegetable does something to help your body grow and stay healthy, this book encourages readers to pick a colorful array of fruits and vegetables each day. (14 pp, TC, P, G, I L, BB, Series: Big Book Health & Safety)

**Torrisi, Cathy.** *Families Are Special.* **Abrams and Company Publishers, 2009.**

Celebrating the diversity of families found in our country, this book presents some of the many different family structures that can be found. (14 pp, TC, P, G, I, L, BB, Series: Abrams Learning Trends)

**Torrisi, Cathy.** *Get Up and Go!* **Abrams Learning Trends, 2011.**

The book points out the importance of exercise to having a healthy life. Suggestions of activities that can be done to get this exercise are given. (14 pp, TC, P, G, I, L, BB, Series: Big Book Health & Safety)

**Torrisi, Cathy.** *Getting Along.* **Abrams Learning Trends, 2009.**

Torrisi presents scenarios of conflict and asks the reader, "How would you like to be treated?" to illustrate the concept that getting along with others means treating them as you would want to be treated. (14 pp, TC, P, G, I, BB only, Series: Big Book Social Studies)

**Torrisi, Cathy.** *Healthy Day.* **Abrams Learning Trends, 2011.**

Illustrated with photographs of young children doing the various activities, Torrisi points out the many ways that a person can strive to lead a healthy lifestyle. (14 pp, TC, P, G, I, L, BB, Series: Big Book Health & Safety)

**Torrisi, Cathy.** *Hello, World!* **Abrams Learning Trends, 2009.**

This book presents many different ways to say "hello" in a variety of different languages. (14 pp, TC, P, G, I, L, BB, Series: Abrams Learning Trends)

**Torrisi, Cathy.** *I Keep Myself Safe.* **Abrams Learning Trends, 2012.**

Stressing the importance of keeping safe on a bike, in a car, in the sun, at home, and in the water, the book provides photographs of children doing just that. (14 pp, TC, P, G, I, L, BB, Series: Big Book Science)

**Torrisi, Cathy.** *I Know First Aid.* **Abrams Learning Trends, 2011.**

Torrisi models with photographs of children how young children can provide simple first aid when it is needed. (14 pp, TC, P, G, I, L, BB, Series: Big Book Health & Safety)

---

*Legend:* pp = Number of pages; TC = Table of contents; P = Photos; ILL = Illustrated; C = Captioned; G = Glossary; I = Index; L = Leveled book; BB = Available in big book format

**Torrisi, Cathy.** *Long Ago and Now.* **Abrams and Company Publishers, 2009.**

This book compares work, transportation, and city life in the past to what they are today. (14 pp, TC, P, G, I, L, BB, Series: Abrams Learning Trends)

**Torrisi, Cathy.** *Match-Up Fun.* **Abrams Learning Trends, 2005.**

Using instances of children at an amusement park, Torrisi provides examples of one-to-one correspondence. (14 pp, P, L, BB, Series: Big Book Math)

**Torrisi, Cathy.** *My Community.* **Abrams and Company Publishers, 2009.**

With simple text Torrisi presents what makes a community, such as its schools, post offices, police stations, libraries, markets, restaurants, hospitals, banks, and other places where people can work. (14 pp, TC, P, G, I, L, BB, Series: Abrams Learning Trends)

**Torrisi, Cathy.** *Our Country.* **Abrams Learning Trends, 2009.**

With photographs, illustrations, and simple text, this book introduces readers to basic facts about the United States of America. (14 pp, TC, P and ILL, G, I, BB only, Series: Big Book Social Studies)

**Torrisi, Cathy.** *Right Down the Middle.* **Abrams Learning Trends, 2006.**

Through simple illustrations and photographs of everyday items, the concept of symmetry is explored. (14 pp, P, L, Series: Big Book Math)

**Torrisi, Cathy.** *Take a Stand.* **Abrams Learning Trends, 2011.**

This book provides vignettes that give the reader the opportunity to make choices regarding taking a stand when injustices are being done. (14 pp, TC, P, G, I, BB only, Series: Big Book Health & Safety)

**Torrisi, Cathy.** *Tell Someone You Trust.* **Abrams Learning Trends, 2011.**

With each scenario, Torrisi asks, "Who would you tell?" so that readers can brainstorm people they can trust when they need help. (14 pp, TC, P, G, I, L, BB only, Series: Big Book Health & Safety)

**Torrisi, Cathy.** *We Need Rules.* **Abrams and Company Publishers, 2009.**

The book presents the case for why rules are important and needed so that schools can run smoothly. (14 pp, TC, P, G, I, L, BB, Series: Abrams Learning Trends)

**Torrisi, Cathy.** *What Should I Put on My Plate?* **Abrams Learning Trends, 2012.**

Appealing photographs of healthy food help the reader determine what is best to eat for a healthy lifestyle. (14 pp, TC, P, C, G, I, L, BB, Series: Big Book Science)

**Torrisi, Cathy.** *Where Are We?* **Abrams and Company Publishers, 2009.**

This book explains why people need maps, and how maps can help us to find places and things. Examples of this are provided. (14 pp, TC, P, G, I, L, BB, Series: Abrams Learning Trends)

---

*Legend:* pp = Number of pages; TC = Table of contents; P = Photos; ILL = Illustrated; C = Captioned; G = Glossary; I = Index; L = Leveled book; BB = Available in big book format

**Urbigkit, Cat.** *Brave Dogs, Gentle Dogs. Perros Guardianes, Perros Valientes.* **Boyds Mills Press, 2005.**
Adorable photographs help tell the story of sheep, the dogs who guard them, and their lasting friendship. (32 pp, P)

**Urbigkit, Cat.** *Cattle Kids: A Year on the Western Ranch.* **Boyds Mills Press, 2007.**
This book tells the true story of cattle kids, children who live on cattle ranches in the West and help with calving, branding, and vaccinating the cattle. (32 pp, P)

**Urbigkit, Cat.** *The Guardian Team: On the Job With Rena and Roo.* **Boyds Mills Press, 2011.**
Urbigkit tells the true story of Roo, a wild burro separated from her mother, and Rena, a small pup, who bonded on a farm in Wyoming. Together they became livestock guardians and protected lambs from predators. (32 pp, P)

**Urbigkit, Cat.** *Puppies, Puppies Everywhere!* **Boyds Mills Press, 2006.**
This book is filled with adorable pictures of puppies doing what puppies love to do. Accompanying simple verse shares additional information with the reader. (22 pp, P)

**Urbigkit, Cat.** *The Shepherd's Trail.* **Boyds Mills Press, 2008.**
In this book Urbigkit follows the life of a shepherd from breeding season to shearing season to lambing season. (32 pp, P)

**Urbigkit, Cat.** *A Young Shepherd.* **Boyds Mills Press, 2006.**
Cass, a 12-year-old boy who lives on a sheep ranch in Wyoming, has various duties he needs to perform to take care of his flock of sheep. (32 pp, P)

**Van Steenwyk, Elizabeth.** *First Dog Fala.* **Peachtree Publishers, 2008.**
This book tells the true story of Fala, President Franklin D. Roosevelt's dog, and how he and the president became fast companions. (32 pp, ILL)

**Wadsworth, Ginger.** *Camping With the President.* **Calkins Creek, 2009.**
Wadsworth tells the story of Teddy Roosevelt's four-day camping trip with John Muir, a world-famous naturalist, in Yosemite National Park. This was one of the inspirations for President Roosevelt setting aside public lands for national parks, a hallmark of his presidency. (32 pp, ILL)

**Wallner, Alexandra.** *Betsy Ross.* **Holiday House, 1994.**
While many know of Betsy Ross as the creator of the first American flag, many do not know the life story told in this book. With simple colorful illustrations Wallner tells the reader about this extraordinary woman. (32 pp, ILL)

**Wasp, Megan.** *All Kinds of Animals.* **Abrams Learning Trends, 2006.**
Colorful photographs of mammals, birds, fish, reptiles, amphibians, and insects accompany interesting facts about each. (14 pp, TC, P, C, G, I, L, BB, Series: Big Book Science)

---

*Legend:* pp = Number of pages; TC = Table of contents; P = Photos; ILL = Illustrated; C = Captioned; G = Glossary; I = Index; L = Leveled book; BB = Available in big book format

**Wasp, Megan.** *Amazing Animals.* **Abrams Learning Trends, 2006.**
Wasp discusses the amazing adaptations some species have made to survive. Some of these adaptations include camouflage, color, speed, shells, sprays, and quills. (14 pp, TC, P, C, G, I, L, BB, Series: Big Book Science)

**Wasp, Megan.** *Dinosaur Science.* **Abrams Learning Trends, 2006.**
The book introduces the science of paleontology and how it investigates these animals that have been gone for so many years. (14 pp, TC, P and ILL, C, G, I, L, BB, Series: Big Book Science)

**Wasp, Megan.** *Our Solar System.* **Abrams Learning Trends, 2006.**
This book presents the sun, the nine planets in our solar system, and the Earth's moon, sharing interesting facts about each. (14 pp, TC, P, C, G, I, L, BB, Series: Big Book Science)

**Wasp, Megan.** *Saving Our Planet.* **Abrams Learning Trends, 2006.**
Wasp both makes the case for why everyone needs to take care of our planet and suggests what children can do to help. (14 pp, TC, P, C, G, I, L, BB, Series: Big Book Science)

**Weatherford, Carole Boston.** *The Beatitudes: From Slavery to Civil Rights.* **Eerdmans Books for Young Readers, 2010.**
Based on each of the Beatitudes, moments in the struggle of African Americans to move from slavery to civil rights are presented in simple text. The last section of the book has short biographies on the people mentioned earlier. (36 pp, ILL)

**Weatherford, Carole Boston.** *Moses: When Harriet Tubman Led Her People to Freedom.* **Hyperion Books for Children, 2006.**
Beautiful illustrations and unique fonts tell the story of Harriet Tubman's first trip to freedom from slavery and her start as "the Moses of her people," leading others to freedom also. (48 pp, ILL)

**Weber, Belinda.** *Reptiles.* **Kingfisher, 2011.**
Captivating photographs invite the reader into the world of reptiles. Here the reader learns many interesting facts about these often-rejected animals. The book also includes projects that children can do in conjunction with the facts they have learned. (56 pp, TC, P, C, G, I, Series: Kingfisher Young Knowledge)

**White, Becky.** *Betsy Ross.* **Holiday House, 2011.**
Simple text tells the story of how Betsy Ross created the first American flag. The text is accompanied on each page by a different quilted scene. (32 pp, ILL)

---

*Legend:* pp = Number of pages; TC = Table of contents; P = Photos; ILL = Illustrated; C = Captioned; G = Glossary; I = Index; L = Leveled book; BB = Available in big book format

**Wood, Emily.** *Dogs.* **Eleanor Curtain Publishing, 2009.**
Appealing photographs of dogs and simple text depict all the many things they can do. Pairs with *Me* by Emily Wood. (16 pp, P, L, Series: Flying Start to Literacy)

**Wood, Emily.** *Me.* **Eleanor Curtain Publishing, 2009.**
Photographs of a young boy running, jumping, swimming, digging, eating, drinking, and sleeping each accompany a three-word sentence. This book pairs with *Dogs* by Emily Wood. (16 pp, P, G, L, Series: Flying Start to Literacy)

**Wood, Jenny.** *I Wonder Why Kangaroos Have Pouches and Other Questions About Baby Animals.* **Kingfisher, 2011.**
Presented as answers to questions a young child might ask, numerous facts are given about many different baby animals. (32 pp, TC, ILL, C, I, Series: I Wonder Why)

**Woolley, Marilyn.** *One Step, Two Step.* **Eleanor Curtain Publishing, 2003.**
This guided reading book follows friends as they stop at different colored doors to collect their playmates, counting the four steps between each. This book includes a teacher version and literacy learning activities. (12 pp, P, L, Series: Explorations)

**Woop Studios.** *A Zeal of Zebras: An Alphabet Collection of Nouns.* **Woop Studios, 2011.**
This book lists, in alphabetical order, collective nouns that refer to many different animal groupings. Each page has a unique print depicting the animals in their natural settings. (64 pp, ILL)

**Yezerski, Thomas.** *Meadowlands: A Wetlands Survival Story.* **Farrar Straus Giroux, 2011.**
Pen-and-ink watercolor pictures tell the story of The Meadowlands, an estuary in New Jersey. In the name of progress The Meadowlands became polluted by industries, people, and laboratories. Yezerski tells how this pollution was reversed so that The Meadowlands and its ecological system could survive. (40 pp, ILL, C)

**Yu, Nancy.** *Science is Everywhere!* **Abrams Learning Trends, 2006.**
Yu provides examples of how science can be found in the kitchen, the backyard, and even on the sidewalk. (14 pp, TC, P and ILL, C, G, I, L, BB, Series: Big Book Science)

**Zimmer, Tracie Vaughn.** *Cousins of Clouds: Elephant Poems.* **Clarion Books, 2011.**
The book describes elephants as inspiring poetry, and the poems contained therein describe the many attributes of elephants. (31 pp, ILL, C)

---

*Legend:* pp = Number of pages; TC = Table of contents; P = Photos; ILL = Illustrated; C = Captioned; G = Glossary; I = Index; L = Leveled book; BB = Available in big book format

**Zimmermann, Karl. *The Stourbridge Lion: America's First Locomotive*. Boyds Mills Press, 2012.**

The Stourbridge Lion, America's first steam locomotive, was built in the town of Stourbridge, England, and brought to the United States to carry coal. After traveling by boat to Honesdale, Pennsylvania, it made its history-making first run in 1829. (32 pp, ILL)

**Zoehfeld, Kathy Weidner. *Dinosaurs*. National Geographic, 2011.**

Zoehfeld presents interesting facts about both some large dinosaurs and some smaller ones. (32 pp, TC, ILL, C, G, Series: National Geographic Kids)

 Available for download at **www.corwin.com/theeverythingguide**

*Legend:* pp = Number of pages; TC = Table of contents; P = Photos; ILL = Illustrated; C = Captioned; G = Glossary; I = Index; L = Leveled book; BB = Available in big book format

# References

Afflerback, P., Pearson, P. D., & Paris, S. (2008). Clarifying differences between reading skills and reading strategies. *The Reading Teacher, 61*(5), 364–373.

Almasi, J. (2003). *Teaching strategic processes in reading.* New York, NY: Guilford Press.

Anderson, E., & Guthrie, J. T. (1999, April). *Motivating children to gain conceptual knowledge from text: The combination of science observation and interesting texts.* Paper presented at the annual meeting of the American Educational Research Association, Montreal, QC, Canada.

Anderson, N. A. (2013). *Elementary children's literature, infancy through age 11,* 4th ed. Upper Saddle River, NJ: Pearson.

Anderson, R. C., & Pearson, P. D. (1984). A schema-theoretic view of basic processes in reading. In P. D. Pearson, R. Barr, M. L. Kamil, & P. Mosenthal (Eds.), *Handbook of reading research,* 255–291. White Plains, NY: Longman.

Baines, B. (2008). *A den is a bed for a bear: A book about hibernation.* Washington, DC: National Geographic.

Baines, B. (2009). *What's in that egg? A book about life cycles.* Washington, DC: National Geographic.

Barth, A. (2009). *Heavier and Lighter.* Pelham, NY: Benchmark Education.

Baxter, M., & Mehigan, K. R. (1992, Summer). *Strategies for increasing the writing performance of identified Title I students.* National Urban Alliance (NUA) Symposium conducted for Title 1 Project, Prince George's County Public Schools, Maryland.

Berger, M., & Berger, G. (1999). *Do whales have belly buttons? Questions and answers about whales and dolphins.* New York, NY: Scholastic.

Biemiller, A. (1999). *Language and reading success.* Cambridge, MA: Brookline Books.

Brown, M. (2004). *My Name is Celia/Me llamo Celia, the life of Celia Cruz.* Flagstaff, AZ: Luna Rising Books.

Bullard, L. (2005). *Loud and quiet: An animal opposites book.* Brookstone, MD: Capstone Press.

Bunting, E. (2001). *Dandelions.* New York, NY: Sandpiper.

Caldwell, J., & Leslie, L. (2013). *Intervention strategies to follow informal reading inventory assessment: So what do I do now?* 3rd ed. Upper Saddle River, NJ: Pearson.

Callery, S. (2011). *Life cycles: Ocean.* New York, NY: Kingfisher.

Carle, E. (2007). *Eric Carle's ABC.* New York, NY: Grosset & Dunlap.

Carney, E. (2011). *National Geographic kids: Cats vs. dogs.* Des Moines, IA: National Geographic Children's Books.

Carter, B. (2000). A universe of information: The future of nonfiction. *The Horn Book, 76*(6), 697–707.

Caswell, L. J., & Duke, N. K. (1998). Non-narrative as a catalyst for literacy development. *Language Arts, 75*(2), 108–117.

Copple, C., & Bredekamp S. (Eds.). (2009). *Developmentally appropriate practice in early childhood programs serving children from birth through age 8,* 3rd ed. Washington, DC: National Association for the Education of Young Children.

Correia, M. P. (2011). Fiction vs. informational texts: Which will kindergartners choose? *Young Children, 66*(6), 100–104.

Dickmann, N. (2011). *Food from farms.* Chicago, IL: Heinemann Library.

Dr. Seuss. (1985). *The cat in the hat.* New York, NY: Random House. (Original work published 1957)

Duke, N. (2000). 3.6 minutes per day: The scarcity of informational texts in first grade. *Reading Research Quarterly, 35*(2), 202–224.

Duke, N. (2004). The case for informational text. *Educational Leadership, 61*(6), 40–44.

Duke, N., & Bennet-Armistead, S. (2003). *Reading and Writing Informational Text in the Primary Grades: Research-Based Practices.* New York, NY: Scholastic.

Duke, N., & Kays, J. (1998). "Can I say 'Once upon a time'?" Kindergarten children developing knowledge of information book language. *Early Childhood Research Quarterly, 132,* 295–318.

Duthie, C. (1994). Nonfiction: A genre study for the primary classroom. *Language Arts, 71,* 588–595.

Dyson, M. (2010). Reviews of kids' nonfiction. Marianne Dyson.com. Retrieved from http://www.mariannedyson.com/spacebooks.htm

Epstein, A. (2007). *The intentional teacher: Choosing the best strategies for young children's learning.* Washington, DC: National Association for the Education of Young Children.

Esbaum, J. (2009a). *National Geographic kids: Apples for everyone.* Washington DC: National Geographic.

Esbaum, J. (2009b). *Seed, sprout, pumpkin, pie.* Washington, DC: National Geographic.

Frank, M. (2009). *Transportation past and present.* Pelham, NY: Benchmark Education.

Freeman, Y. S., Freeman, D. E., & Mercuri, S. (2002). *Closing the achievement gap: How to reach limited-formal-schooling and long-term English learners.* Portsmouth, NH: Heinemann.

Galvin, L. (2007). *Alphabet of ocean animals.* Norfolk, CT: Soundprint.

Gambrell, L. B., & Jawitz, P. B. (1993). Mental imagery, text illustrations, and children's story comprehension and recall. *Reading Research Quarterly, 28*(3), 264–276.

Gibbons, G. (2002). *Tell me, tree.* Boston: Little, Brown.

Gill, S. (2009). What teachers need to know about the "new" nonfiction. *The Reading Teacher, 63*(4), 260–267.

Giorgis, C., & Glazer, J. (2012). *Literature for young children: Supporting emergent literacy, ages 0–8,* 7th ed. Boston, MA: Allyn & Bacon/Pearson.

Goldschmidt, P. (2010). *Evaluation of Seeds of Science/Roots of Reading: Effective tools for developing literacy through science in the early grades.* Los Angeles, CA: National Center for Research on Evaluation, Standards, and Student Testing and University of California. Retrieved from http://www.scienceandliteracy.org/sites/scienceandliteracy.org/files/biblio/seeds_eval_in_cresst_deliv_fm_060210_pdf_21403.pdf

Gough, P. B., & Tunmer, W. E. (1986). Decoding, reading, and reading disability. *Remedial and Special Education, 7,* 6–10.

Gustafson, S. (2007). *Favorite nursery rhymes from Mother Goose.* Seymour, CT: The Greenwich Workshop Press.

Halvorsen, A., Duke, N. K., Brugar, K. A., Block, M. K., Strachan, S. L., Berka, M. B., & Brown, J. M. (in press). Narrowing the achievement gap in second-grade social studies and content area literacy: The promise of a project-based approach. *Theory and Research in Social Education.*

Hart, B., & Risley, T. R. (1995). *Meaningful differences in the everyday experience of young American children.* Baltimore, MD: Paul Brookes.

Harvey, S., & Goudvis, A. (2007). *Strategies that work,* 2nd ed. Portland, ME: Stenhouse.

Hayes, D. P., & Ahrens, M. G. (1988). Vocabulary simplification for children: A special case of "motherese"? *Journal of Child Language, 15*(2), 395–410.

Heller, M. (2006). Telling stories and talking facts: First graders' engagement in a nonfiction book club. *The Reading Teacher, 60*(4), 358–369.

Hiebert, E. H., & Pearson, P. D. (2012–2013). What happens to the basics? *Educational Leadership, 70*(4), 48–53.

Hills, T. (2006). *Duck and goose.* New York, NY: Schwartz & Wade.

Hirsch, E. D. (2001). Overcoming the language gap. *American Educator, 25*(2), 4–7.

Hoffman, M. (1991). *Amazing Grace.* New York, NY: Dial.

Hopkinson, D. (2003). *Maria's comet.* New York, NY: Aladdin.

Hughes, C. (2010). *National Geographic little kids first big book of animals.* Washington DC: National Geographic.

Hulbert, L. (2011). *Who has these feet?* New York, NY: Henry Holt.

Hulbert, L. (2012). *Who has this tail?* New York, NY: Henry Holt.

Jenkins, S. (2004). *Actual size.* Boston, MA: Houghton Mifflin.

Jenkins, S., & Page, R. (2003). *What do you do with a tail like this?* Boston, MA: Houghton Mifflin.

Johnson, D. (2012). *The joy of children's literature,* 2nd ed. Mason, OH: Cengage Learning.

Joubert, B., & Joubert, D. (2011). *African animal alphabet.* Washington, DC: National Geographic.

Kamberelis, G. (1998). Relations between children's literacy diets and genre development: You write what you read. *Literacy Teaching and Learning, 3,* 7–53.

Kuhn, M. (2005). A comparative study of small group fluency instruction. *Reading Psychology, 26,* 127–146.

Kuhn, M. R., Schwanenflugel, P. J., Morris, R. D., Morrow, L. M., Woo, D. G., Meisinger, E. B., Sevcik, R. A., . . . Stahl, S. A. (2006). Teaching children to become fluent and automatic readers. *Journal of Literacy Research, 38*(4), 357–387.

Lyon, G. E. (2003). *Mother to tigers.* New York, NY: Atheneum/Richard Jackson Books.

MacDonald, S. (2009). *Shape by shape.* New York, NY: Little Simon.

Markle, S. (2009). *How many baby pandas?* New York, NY: Walker Books for Young Readers.

Marks, J. (2011). *How to make a bouncing egg.* North Mankato, MN: Capstone Press.

Marsh, L. (2010). *National Geographic kids: Great migrations: Elephants.* Washington, DC: National Geographic.

Marsh, L. (2011). *National Geographic kids: Spiders.* Washington, DC: National Geographic.

Martin, L. E., & Kragler, S. (2012). Early signs of self-regulating print: Kindergartners at work reading to understand fiction and nonfiction text. *Journal of Research in Childhood Education, 26*(2), 141–153.

Marzano, R. J. (2007). *The art and science of teaching.* Alexandria, VA: ASCD.

Marzano, R. J., Pickering, D. J., & Pollock, J. E. (2001). *Classroom instruction that works.* Alexandria, VA: ASCD.

Mavor, S. (2010). *Pocketful of posies, a treasury of nursery rhymes.* Boston, MA: Houghton Mifflin.

Mayer, M. (2003). *Frog goes to dinner.* New York, NY: Dial.

McMillan, B. (1993). Accuracy in books for young readers: From first to last check. *The New Advocate, 6*(2). Retrieved from http://www.brucemcmillan.com

Mehigan, K. R. (2005). The strategy toolbox: A ladder to strategic teaching. *The Reading Teacher, 58,* 552–556.

Metsala, J. L. (1999). Young children's phonological awareness and nonword repetition as a function of vocabulary development. *Journal of Educational Psychology, 91,* 3–19.

Moats, L. C. (1999). *Teaching reading is rocket science: What expert teachers of reading should know and be able to do.* Washington, DC: American Federation of Teachers.

Morgan, A., Wilcox, B. R., & Eldredge, J. L. (2000). Effect of difficulty levels on second-grade delayed readers using dyad reading. *Journal of Educational Research, 94*(2), 113–119.

Moss, B. (1997). A qualitative assessment of first graders' retelling of expository text. *Reading Research and Instruction, 37,* 1–13.

Moss, B., & Newton, E. (1998, December). *An examination of the informational text genre in recent basal readers.* Paper presented at the National Reading Conference, Austin, TX.

National Center for Education Statistics. (2011). *The nation's report card: Reading 2011* (NCES 2012–457). Washington, DC: National Center for Education Statistics, Institute of Education Sciences, US Department of Education.

National Council of Social Studies. (2010). *National curriculum standards for social studies: A framework for teaching, learning, and assessment.* Silver Spring, MD: NCSS.

National Geographic Kids. (2011). *National Geographic little kids look & learn: Match!* Washington, DC: National Geographic.

National Governors Association Center for Best Practices & Council of Chief State School Officers. (2010a). *Common core state standards, appendix A: Research supporting key elements of the standards.* Washington, DC: Author.

National Governors Association Center for Best Practices, Council of Chief State School Officers. (2010b). *Common core state standards for English/language arts & literacy in history/social studies, science and technical subjects.* Washington DC: Author.

National Reading Panel. (2000). *Report of the National Reading Panel: Teaching children to read: An evidence-based assessment of scientific-based literature on reading and its implication for reading instruction.* Washington, DC: National Institute of Child Health and Human Development.

National Research Council. (2012). *Framework for K–12 science education: Practices, crosscutting concepts and core ideas.* Committee on a Conceptual Framework for New K–12 Science Education Standards. Board on Science Education, Division of Behavioral and Social Sciences and Education. Washington, DC: The National Academies Press.

Nuzzolo, D. (2008). *Tiger shark.* Mankato, MN: Capstone Press.

Page, R., & Jenkins, S. (2006). *Move!* Boston, MA: Houghton Mifflin.

Palinscar, A. S., & Brown, A. L. (1984). Reciprocal teaching of comprehension-fostering and comprehension-monitoring activities. *Cognition and Instruction, 1,* 117–175.

Palmer, R. G., & Stewart, R. A. (2003). Nonfiction trade book use in primary grades. *The Reading Teacher, 58,* 426–434.

Pappas, C. C. (1993). Is narrative "primary"? Some insights from kindergarteners' pretend readings of stories and information books. *Journal of Reading Behavior, 25,* 97–129.

Pearson, P. D., & Fielding, L. (1991). Comprehension instruction. In R. Barr, M. L. Kamil, P. B. Mosenthal, & P. D. Pearson (Eds.), *Handbook of reading research* (Vol. II, pp. 815–860). White Plains, NY: Longman.

Pentimonti, J. M., Zucker, T. A., Justice, L. M., & Kaderavek, J. N. (2010). Information text use in preschool classroom read alouds. *The Reading Teacher, 63*(8), 656–665.

Pinkney, J. (2009). *The lion and the mouse.* New York, NY: Little Brown Books for Young Readers.

Piper, W. (1978). *The little engine that could.* New York, NY: Grosset & Dunlap.

Potter, J. (1995). *Nature in a nutshell for kids.* San Francisco, CA: Jossey-Bass.

Pressley, M. (2000). What should comprehension instruction be the instruction of? In M. Kamil, P. Mosenthal, P. D. Pearson, & R. Barr (Eds.), *Handbook of Reading Research* (Vol. III, pp. 545–561). Mahwah, NJ: Erlbaum.

Pressley, M. (2002). *Reading instruction that works: The case for balanced teaching,* 2nd ed. New York, NY: Guilford.

Price, L. H., Bradley, B. A., & Smith, J. (2012). A comparison of preschool teachers' talk during storybooks and information book read alouds. *Early Childhood Research Quarterly, 27,* 426–440.

Ringold, F. (1995). *Aunt Harriet's underground railroad in the sky*. Decorah, IA: Dragonfly.

Ringold, F. (2003). *If a bus could talk: The story of Rosa Parks*. New York, NY: Aladdin.

Rowland Reading Foundation. (2009a). The never-ending story. *SUPER Magazine, 7*, 8–11.

Rowland Reading Foundation. (2009b). Water, water everywhere. *SUPER Magazine, 7*, 6–7.

Rowland Reading Foundation. (2012). *Play ball!* Madison, WI: Author.

Schwake, S. (2012). *Art lab for kids: 52 creative adventures in drawing, painting, printmaking, paper, and mixed media*. Minneapolis, MN: Quarry Books.

Shanahan, T. (2013, April 23). *Learning from challenging text*. Paper presented at Plain Talk About Reading Institute, Center for Development and Learning, New Orleans, LA.

Shanahan, T., Fisher, D., & Frey, N. (2012). The challenge of challenging text. *Educational Leadership, 69*(6), 58–63.

Shields, A. (2011a). *The first big book of why*. Washington, DC: National Geographic.

Shields, A. (2011b). *Train*. Washington DC: National Geographic.

Shores, E. (2011). *How to make a bubble*. North Mankato, MN: Capstone Press.

Sidman, J. (2010). *Red sings from treetops, a year in colors*. Boston, MA: Houghton Mifflin.

Smolkin, L. B., & Donovan, C. A. (2001). The contexts of comprehension: The information book read aloud, comprehension acquisition, and comprehension instruction in a first-grade classroom. *The Elementary School Journal, 102*(2), 97–122.

Snow, C. E., Burns, S. M., & Griffin, P. (Eds.). (1998). *Preventing reading difficulties in young children*. Washington, DC: National Academy Press.

Stahl, S. A., & Nagy, W. E. (2006). *Teaching word meanings*. Mahwah, NJ: Lawrence Erlbaum.

Stanovich, K. E., & Cunningham, A. E. (1993). Where does knowledge come from? Specific associations between print exposure and information acquisition. *Journal of Educational Psychology, 85*(2), 211–229.

Stephens, K. (2008). A quick guide to selecting great informational books for young children. *The Reading Teacher, 61*(6), 488–490.

Taylor, B. M., Peterson D. S., Pearson, P. D., & Rodriguez, M. C. (2002). Looking inside classrooms: Reflecting on the "how" as well as the "what" in effective reading instruction. *The Reading Teacher, 56*, 270–279.

Viorst, J. (2009). *Alexander and the terrible, horrible, no good very bad day*. New York, NY: Atheneum.

Vitale, M. R., & Romance, N. R. (2011). Adaptation of knowledge-based instructional intervention to accelerate student learning in science and early literacy in grades 1 and 2. *Journal of Curriculum and Instruction, 5*(2), 79–93.

Wasp, M. (2006). *Amazing animals*. Waterbury, CT: Abrams.

Willems, M. (2004). *Knuffle Bunny: A cautionary tale*. New York, NY: Hyperion.

Winter, J. (2011). *The watcher: Jane Goodall's life with the chimps*. New York, NY: Schwartz & Wade.

Yopp, R. H., & Yopp, H. K. (2000). Sharing informational text with young children. *The Reading Teacher, 53*(5), 410–423.

Zimmer, T. (2011). *Cousins of clouds, elephant poems*. New York, NY: Clarion Books.

Zimmerman, K. (2012). *The Stourbridge Lion: America's first locomotive*. Honesdale, PA: Boyds Mills Press.

# Index

ABCs literature, 174
Aberg, Rebecca, 190, 203
Above-level readers:
    first grade guided reading lesson,
        103, 104*f*
    instructional strategies, 26
Accuracy/authenticity:
    text evaluation checklist, 39*f*, 161
    text selection criteria, 39–41
*Actual Size* (Jenkins), 34, 192, 229
Adams, Tom, 195, 203
*Adding Two-Digit Numbers* (Barth), 190, 205
*Addition and Subtraction* (Barth), 190, 205
*Addition Strategies* (Barth), 190, 205
*African Animal Alphabet* (Joubert & Joubert),
    31, 32*f*, 37–38, 46
*Alexander and the Terrible, Horrible, No Good,*
    *Very Bad Day* (Viorst), 150*f*
Aliki, 146*f*
*All About Scabs* (Yagu), 146*f*
Allen, Judy, 182, 203
Alliteration, 43–44
*All Kinds of Animals* (Wasp), 174, 251
*Almost Gone* (Jenkins), 177, 182, 229
*Alphabet of Ocean Animals* (Galvin), 45, 154*f*,
    174, 193, 223
*Amazing Animal Journeys* (Marsh), 174, 235
*Amazing Animal Senses* (Hutchinson), 174, 226
*Amazing Animals* (Wasp), 57, 174, 252
*Amazing Grace* (Hoffman), 150*f*
*Amazing Plants* (Santiago), 195, 245
*Amazing Scientists* (Merritt), 179, 198, 237
American Society for the Prevention of Cruelty to
    Animals (ASPCA), 52
Anderson, Laurie Halse, 180, 187, 188, 203
*Animal Baths* (Barner), 174, 205
*Animal Eyes* (Fielding), 174, 221
*Animal Fathers* (Eggleton), 174, 177, 213
Animal literature:
    general, 174–177
    life cycles, 190
    ocean, 193
    pets, 194
    wild/exotic, 177–178
    wild/native, 179

*Animals and the Seasons* (McNamara), 174, 198, 236
*Animals in the Fall* (Rustad), 174, 179, 198, 245
*Animals in their Habitats* (Castor), 184, 210
*Animals Nobody Loves* (Simon), 174, 247
*Animals That Store Food* (Shanahan), 174, 179, 246
*Ants! They Are Hard Workers!* (Iasevoli), 188, 228
*Ape* (Jenkins), 177, 228
*Apples for Everyone* (Esbaum), 54, 59, 195, 221
*Are They Equal?* (Cain), 191, 209
Arlon, Penelope, 178, 180, 199, 204
*Arthur* books (Brown), 152*f*
*Art Lab for Kids* (Schwake), 155*f*
Ask-and-answer questions, 55–56
Askew, Amanda, 200, 204
Assonance, 43–44
Aston, Dianna Hutts, 189, 204
*Astonishing Nervous System, The* (Crabtree
    Publishing), 147*f*
*A Tale of Two Cities* (Dickens), 1
*At Home With the Gopher Tortoise* (Dunphy),
    179, 182, 213
*At Lunchtime* (Talia), 183, 248
*Aunt Harriet's Underground Railroad in the*
    *Sky* (Ringold), 151*f*

*Baby Animal Pop!* (Flynn), 174, 222
*Baby Animals at Night* (Kingfisher Editors),
    174, 233
*Baby Animals in the Forest* (Kingfisher Editors),
    184, 233
*Baby Animals in the Sea* (Kingfisher Editors),
    184, 193, 233
*Baby Animals in the Snow* (Kingfisher Editors),
    177, 184, 233
*Baby Animals in the Wild* (Kingfisher Editors),
    177, 184, 233
*Baby Bonobos Alone* (Eggleton), 177, 213
Baines, Becky, 45, 47*f*, 154*f*, 178, 179, 188,
    190, 194, 198, 199, 204–205
*Balloons Over Broadway* (Sweet), 179, 187, 188, 248
Barile, Colleen, 187, 205
Barner, Bob, 174, 205
Barron, Rex, 146*f*
Barth, April, 54–55, 190, 191, 192, 199, 200,
    205–208

Bartholomew, Cathleen, 201, 208
*Battle in the Deep Sea, A* (Nunweek), 193, 240
*Battle to Breathe, The* (Nunweek), 193, 240
*Beautitudes, The* (Weatherford), 187, 252
*Bees, Snails, & Peacock Tails* (Franco & Jenkins), 194, 222
*Beetle Book, The* (Jenkins), 188, 229
*Before It Gets to the Store* (Torrisi), 189, 249
Behavioral modeling, 85–86
*Being a Good Citizen* (Serrano), 181, 246
Below-level readers:
    first grade guided reading lesson, 103, 104*f*
    instructional strategies, 24–25
    second grade guided reading lesson, 122–124
Bennett, Elizabeth Huff, 199, 208
Bennett-Armistead, Susan, 149
Berger, Gilda, 193, 208
Berger, Marilyn, 146*f*
Berger, Melvin, 193, 208
*Betsy Ross* (Wallner), 179, 187, 251
*Betsy Ross* (White), 180, 187, 252
Biden, Jill, 183, 208
*Big Earthquake, A* (Eggleton), 192, 213
*Big Gorilla* (Eggleton), 177, 213
Big-idea content, 23–24, 26–27
Bildner, Phil, 200, 208
Bingham, Caroline, 193, 209
Biographies literature, 179–180
*Bird's-Eye View of a Neighborhood* (Frank), 190, 222
Birds literature, 180
*Bird Talk* (Judge), 180, 231
*Birthdays Around the World* (Lankford), 181, 188, 234
*Bones* (Jenkins), 188, 229
*Bones* (Simon), 147*f*
*Bones You Own, The* (Baines), 188, 204
*Born to Be Giants* (Judge), 182, 231
Bourgeois, Paulette, 152*f*
Brannon, Barbara, 181, 209
*Brave Dogs, Gentle Dogs* (Urbigkit), 194, 197, 251
Brooks, Erik, 42
Brown, Marc, 152*f*
Brown, Margaret Wise, 118
Brown, Monica, 155*f*
*Brown Bear* (Eggleton), 179, 214
*Bug Hunters* (Eggleton), 188, 189, 214
*Building With Solid Shapes* (Barth), 199, 205
Bullard, Lisa, 42, 43*f*, 175, 209
*Bulldozers* (Askew), 200, 204
*Bully Bugs* (Nunweek), 188, 240
Bunting, Eve, 151*f*
Burne, David, 175, 209
*Busy Body Book, The* (Rockwell), 146*f*
*Butterflies* (Marsh), 188, 235
*Butterfly Is Patient, A* (Aston & Long), 189, 204
Butterworth, Chris, 189, 209
*Buzz on Bees, The* (Rotner & Woodhull), 189, 244

Cain, Brianna, 191, 209
Callery, Sean, 53, 178, 185, 193, 209
*Call of the Sea, The* (Eggleton), 181, 214
*Camping With the President* (Wadsworth), 196, 251

*Can We Save the Tiger?* (Jenkins), 177, 182, 228
Captions, 33–35
Carle, Eric, 154*f*
Carlson, Nancy, 146*f*
Carney, Elizabeth, 57, 58, 175, 194, 210
Carolan, Joanna, 180, 197, 210
Carolan, Terry, 180, 197, 210
*Cars* (Graham), 200, 225
Casteel, Christine, 192, 210
Castor, Debra, 184, 185, 196, 210–211
*Caterpillars* (Singer), 189, 247
*Caterpillar to Butterfly* (Marsh), 189, 190, 235
*Cat in the Hat, The* (Seuss), 157
*Cats vs. Dogs* (Carney), 57, 58, 194, 210
*Cattle Kids* (Urbigkit), 197, 251
Cause-and-effect structure, 45, 46*f*
Cella, Clara, 188, 211
*Cemetery Keepers of Gettysburg, The* (Oatman), 187, 226
*Centimeter and Meter* (Barth), 191, 192, 205
Chandler, Fiona, 146*f*
*Changing Colors* (Eggleton), 174, 214
Chapman, Todd, 174, 182, 211
*Cheetahs* (Marsh), 177, 235
Chen, Gloria, 194, 211
*Children Past and Present* (Frank), 187, 222
*Circus Performers* (Kennedy), 189, 232–233
Civics/citizenship literature, 181
Clark, Willow, 178, 211
Classroom management:
    first grade reading lesson, 105–107
    kindergarten reading lesson, 85–86
    second grade reading lesson, 124–125
*Climbing a Rock Wall* (Scott), 200, 246
*Clothes Then and Now* (Herold), 187, 226
College and Career Readiness Anchor Standards:
    Common Core State Standards (CCSS), 6–11
    craft and structure, 7*f*, 10*f*
    first grade, 9–11*f*
    grade-specific standards, 8, 9–11*f*
    informational text standards, 9–11*f*
    integration of knowledge and ideas, 7*f*, 11*f*
    key ideas and details, 7*f*, 9–10*f*
    kindergarten, 9–11*f*
    limitations of, 8
    range of reading/level of text complexity, 7*f*, 11*f*
    second grade, 9–11*f*
    Standard 1, 9*f*
    Standard 2, 9*f*
    Standard 3, 10*f*
    Standard 4, 10*f*
    Standard 5, 10*f*
    Standard 6, 10*f*
    Standard 7, 11*f*
    Standard 8, 11*f*
    Standard 9, 11*f*
    Standard 10, 11*f*
Common Core State Standards (CCSS):
    College and Career Readiness Anchor
        Standards, 6–11
    complex texts, 19
    cross-curriculum approach, 12

educational goals, 4
English Language Arts (ELA), 4
fiction text, 2, 12–16
first grade checklist, 165–167
first grade guided reading lesson, 102, 118–119
Foundational Skills Standards, 4, 8–9
fundamental shifts in, 4–6
informational text, 2, 4, 9–11f, 12
instructional goals, 2–3
instructional strategies, 19, 21–24
interdisciplinary learning, 4
Internet resources, 3
kindergarten checklist, 163–165
kindergarten read-aloud lesson, 82–83, 97–98
Language Standards, 4, 22–23
lesson plan template, 76–79
mission statement, 3
nonfiction text, 2, 12–16
organization of, 4
Range of Text Types (Standard 10), 2, 12
Reading Standards for Informational Text, 2, 4,
    9–11f, 12
Reading Standards for Literature, 4, 12
second grade checklist, 167–169
second grade guided reading lesson, 122–124,
    138, 139f
Speaking/Listening Standards, 4
Writing Standards, 4
Comparative structure, 45, 46f
Comparative thinking skills, 56–57
Compare and Order Numbers to 1,000 (Barth),
    191, 206
Compare Numbers to 100 (Barth), 206
Comparing Two Cities (Lee), 184, 234
Complex texts:
    Common Core State Standards (CCSS), 19
    instructional strategies, 19, 21–22
    qualitative factors, 19
    quantitative measures, 19
    reader/task considerations, 19
    value of, 19, 21
Comprehension strategies:
    ask-and-answer questions, 55–56
    comparative thinking skills, 56–57
    comprehension monitoring, 61–62
    fix-up tips, 61–62
    high-impact reading strategies, 51–62
    inferential reading, 53
    information interpretation, 58–59
    key ideas/details, 57–58
    prior knowledge utilization, 52
    reader strategy, 50–51
    references/resources, 59–60
    roadblocks, 61
    strategic instruction, 50, 51f
    strategy versus skill, 50
    summarize/synthesize, 60–61
    visualization techniques, 54–55
Consonance, 43–44
Content/curricular connection:
    text evaluation checklist, 47f, 162
    text selection criteria, 45–46

Coppendale, Jean, 200, 201, 211
Copyright date, 40
Coral Reefs (Gibbons), 185, 193, 223
Core instruction, 66
Corn (Landau), 195, 234
Council of Chief State School Officers (CCSSO), 3
Counting at the Zoo (Fischer), 177, 222
Counting to 10 and Beyond! (Bennett), 191, 208
Count (National Geographic Little Kids),
    175, 177, 239
Cousins of Clouds (Zimmer), 151f, 177, 253
Cover appeal, 31–32
Crabtree Publishing, 147f
Crocodile Mother, A (Eggleton), 177, 214
Cross-curriculum approach, 12
Culture literature, 181

Dandelions (Bunting), 151f
Davies, Nicola, 185, 193, 211–212
Day and Night in the Desert (Eggleton),
    179, 185, 214
Deadliest Animals (Stewart), 175, 247
De Capua, Sarah, 190, 212
Decomposers (Lappi), 175, 182, 234
Demolition (Sutton), 189, 248
Den Is a Bed for a Bear, A (Baines), 154f, 179,
    198, 204
Desalle, Nicole, 186, 198, 212
Descriptive structure, 45, 46f
Designing With Plane Shapes (Barth), 199, 206
Dickens, Charles, 1
Dickman, Nancy, 32–33, 197, 199, 212
Differentiated instruction:
    above-level readers, 26, 103, 104f
    below-level readers, 24–25, 103, 104f, 122–124
    first grade guided reading lesson, 102–103,
        104f, 105–107
    instructional strategies, 24–26
    on-level readers, 25–26, 103, 104f
    preparation for, 24
    second grade guided reading lesson, 122–124
Different or the Same? (Eggleton), 175, 214
Different Plants (Eggleton), 195, 214
Different Villages (Eggleton), 184, 215
Digestive System, The (Johnston), 146f
Digestive System, The (Petrie), 146f
Diggers (Askew), 200, 204
Dimes (Kenna & Ostarch), 192, 232
Dingo Fence, The (Eggleton), 197, 215
Dinosaurs (Allen), 182, 203
Dinosaur Science (Wasp), 182, 252
Dinosaurs (Gibbons), 182, 223
Dinosaurs literature, 182
Dinosaurs (Zoehfeld), 182, 254
Discover Forensic Chemistry (Romero), 194, 243
Discover Kitchen Chemistry (Romero), 194, 243
Discover Local and State Government
    (Brannon), 181, 209
Discover Medical Chemistry (Romero), 195, 243
D Is for Dinosaur (Chapman & Judge),
    174, 182, 211
Dogs and Cats (Jenkins), 194, 229

*Dogs* (Wood), 194, 253
*Dolphins to the Rescue* (Eggleton), 193, 215
Dominello, Brenda, 186, 195, 212–213
*Don't Forget, God Bless Our Troops* (Biden), 183, 208
Dorion, Christiane, 201, 213
Dover, Deborah, 174, 234
*Do Whales Have Belly Buttons?* (Berger & Berger), 193, 208
*Down, Down, Down* (Jenkins), 177, 185, 193, 229
*Down at the Waterhole* (Eggleton), 185, 215
Dowson, Nick, 176, 213
*Duck and Goose* (Hills), 152f
Duke, Nell, 149
*Dump Trucks and Other Big Machines* (Graham), 200, 225
Dunning, Joan, 179, 180, 213
Dunphy, Madeleine, 179, 182, 213
Dyson, Marianne J., 39

*Earth Day* (Cella), 188, 211
*Earth Rocks!* (Dominello), 195, 212
*Eat All Your Colors* (Torrisi), 186, 249
Ecology literature, 182–183
Eggleton, Jill, 174, 175, 176, 177, 178, 179, 180, 181, 182, 183, 184, 185, 186, 188, 189, 190, 192, 193, 194, 195, 196, 197, 199, 200, 201, 213–221
eHOW, 52
*Eleanor, Quiet No More* (Rappaport), 180, 196, 242
*Elephants* (Marsh), 35, 36f, 37, 38f, 177, 235
*Elephants of Africa* (Gibbons), 177, 223
Elliott, David, 193, 221
Endnotes, 37, 38f
*Energy All Around* (Ramirez), 195, 241
English Language Arts and Literacy in History/ Social Studies, Science, and Technical Subjects, 4
English Language Arts (ELA):
    literacy standards, 4
    student competency, 3–4
*Eric Carle's ABC* (Carle), 154f
Esbaum, Jill, 54, 59, 195, 196, 198, 199, 221
*Estimating Sums and Differences* (Barth), 191, 206
*Even an Octopus Needs a Home* (Kelly), 175, 180, 232
*Even an Ostrich Needs a Nest* (Kelly), 232
*Every Planet Has a Place* (Baines), 199, 204
*Every Season* (Rotner & Woodhull), 198, 244
*Everything Dogs* (Baines), 194, 204
*Everything Spring* (Esbaum), 198, 221
Explicit instruction:
    first grade guided reading lesson, 115f
    instructional strategies, 18–19, 26–27
    kindergarten read-aloud lesson, 84–85, 94f
    lesson plan template, 69, 70–71, 73f, 75f
    second grade guided reading lesson, 136f
Expository text:
    characteristics of, 12
    common structures, 45, 46f

Faction, 41
*Families Are Special* (Torrisi), 183, 249

Family literature, 183
Fantasy, 34
*Favorite Nursery Rhymes from Mother Goose* (Gustafson), 150f
*Feel the Force!* (Adams), 195, 203
Feely, Jenny, 176, 221
Fiction text:
    Common Core State Standards (CCSS), 2, 12–16
    cross-curriculum comprehension, 12
    influence of, 13
Fielding, Beth, 174, 221
*Finding Length* (Barth), 192, 206
*Fire Trucks and Rescue Vehicles* (Coppendale), 200, 211
*First Big Book of Animals* (Hughes), 34, 35, 55, 60, 175, 226
*First Big Book of Dinosaurs* (Hughes), 182, 226
*First Big Book of Why* (Shields), 198, 246
*First Dog Fala* (Van Steenwyk), 196, 251
*First Encyclopedia of the Human Body* (Chandler), 146f
First grade guided reading lesson:
    above-level readers, 103, 104f
    action steps, 107f, 109f, 115f, 117f
    below-level readers, 103, 104f
    challenges of, 119
    classroom management, 105–107
    classroom setting, 102–103, 104f
    Common Core State Standards (CCSS), 102, 118–119
    differentiated instruction, 102–103, 104f, 105–107
    explicit instruction (step three), 115f
    facilitate connections (step four), 117f, 118
    Foundational Skills Standards, 119
    grade-specific reading skills, 102
    grouping-without-tracking approach, 103
    guide reading (step two), 109f
    instructional strategies, 103, 104f, 106, 117, 119
    K-W-L (Know-Wonder-Learn) chart, 106, 108f, 117f
    Language Standards, 119
    lesson plan template, 107f, 109f, 115f, 117f
    on-level readers, 103, 104f
    pre-lesson information, 107
    reading preparation (step one), 107f
    reflection activity, 113–114, 120
    sample lesson, 108–112, 115–117
    skills-based groups, 101–102
    Speaking/Listening Standards, 119
First grade standards:
    College and Career Readiness Anchor Standards, 9–11f
    Common Core State Standards (CCSS), 102, 118–119, 165–167
    Foundational Skills Standards, 119, 165
    Language Standards, 119, 166
    lesson plan template, 76–77f
    Reading Standards for Informational Text, 9–11f, 165
    Speaking/Listening Standards, 119, 166
    Writing Standards, 166–167

Fischer, Kathleen, 177, 192, 222
Fisher, Douglas, 4
Five senses literature, 146*f*, 183
Fix-up tips, 61–62
Flynn, Sarah Wassner, 174, 222
Font, 32–33
*Food for Zebras* (Eggleton), 178, 215
*Force and Motion* (Ramirez), 195, 241
*Forensic Chemistry* (Romero), 195, 243
Format/visual appeal:
    text evaluation checklist, 32*f*, 161
    text selection criteria, 31–39
Foundational Skills Standards:
    Common Core State Standards (CCSS), 4, 8–9
    first grade, 119, 165
    first grade guided reading lesson, 119
    kindergarten, 163
    lesson plan template, 78–79
    second grade, 123–124, 167
    second grade guided reading lesson, 123–124
Franco, Betsy, 194, 222
Frank, Matthew, 57, 187, 190, 201, 222–223
*Franklin* books (Bourgeois), 152*f*
Fraser, Caitlin, 179
Frey, Nancy, 4
Friendship literature, 183
*Friends* (Thimmesh), 175, 183, 248
*Frog Goes to Dinner* (Mayer), 157
*From Seed to Pumpkin* (Kottke), 184, 195, 234
*From Seed to Pumpkin* (Pfeffer), 184, 195, 241
Frost, Helen, 185, 189, 190, 223
*Fuel the Body* (Tourville), 146*f*

*Galaxies* (Gibbons), 199, 223
Galvin, Laura Gates, 45, 154*f*, 174, 193, 223
*Garbage Helps Our Garden Grow* (Glazer),
    182, 184, 225
*Garbage in the River* (Eggleton), 182, 215
Garden literature, 184
Geography literature, 184
*George* (Keating), 180, 196, 231
*Germs Make Me Sick* (Berger), 146*f*
*Germ Stories* (Kornberg), 146*f*
*Getting Along* (Torrisi), 181, 183, 249
*Get Up and Go!* (Carlson), 146*f*
*Get Up and Go!* (Torrisi), 186, 249
*Giant Pandas* (Schuetz), 178, 245
Gibbons, Gail, 177, 182, 185, 188, 189, 190, 192,
    193, 196, 197, 199, 200, 201, 223–224
Glazer, Linda, 182, 184, 225
Glossary, 37–39
*Going Under* (Eggleton), 185, 215
*Going Up* (Eggleton), 185, 215
Goodall, Jane, 155*f*
*Good Enough to Eat* (Rockwell), 146*f*
Gordon, Sharon, 183, 225
Gore, Leonid, 189, 190, 223
Gosman, Gillian, 186, 225
*Go Wash Up* (Tourville), 146*f*
Graham, Ian, 200, 225
Grant, Marsha, 194, 195, 225
*Great Migrations* (Carney), 175, 210

*Griffin Vulture, The* (Eggleton), 178, 180, 216
*Groundhog Day!* (Gibbons), 188, 223
Grouping-without-tracking approach, 103
*Guardian Team, The* (Urbigkit), 183, 197, 251
Guided reading:
    focus, 18*f*, 20*f*, 67*f*, 68*f*
    format, 18*f*, 20*f*, 67*f*, 68*f*
    instructional strategies, 18*f*, 20*f*, 24–26
    lesson plan template, 67*f*, 68*f*
    text type, 18*f*, 20*f*, 67*f*, 68*f*
    *See also* First grade guided reading lesson;
        Second grade guided reading lesson
Gustafson, Scott, 150*f*

*Habitats Around the World* (Castor), 185, 210
Habitats literature, 184–186
*Hand of Nature, The* (Eggleton), 216
*Handy Horse, A* (Eggleton), 192, 194, 216
Harper, Leslie, 181, 225
*Harpy Eagle Chick* (Eggleton), 178, 180, 216
Headings, 35–36
*Healthy Day* (Torrisi), 186, 249
Healthy living literature, 146*f*, 186
*Hearing* (Gordon), 183, 225
*Hearing* (Rius), 146*f*
*Heavier and Lighter* (Barth), 54–55, 192, 206
Helfer, Ralph, 178, 226
*Helicopters Help* (Eggleton), 189, 200, 216
*Hello, World!* (Torrisi), 181, 249
Herold, Vickey, 187, 226
High, Linda Oatman, 187, 226
High-impact reading strategies:
    comprehension strategies, 51–62
    lesson plan template, 70*f*
Hills, Tad, 152*f*
History literature, 187
*Hoatzin Bird, The* (Nunweek), 180, 240
Hoffman, Mary, 150*f*
Holidays/special celebrations literature, 188
Hopkinson, Deborah, 155*f*
*How Did That Get in My Lunch Box?* (Butterworth),
    189, 209
*How Do Baby Animals Grow?* (Hutchinson),
    175, 178, 227
*How Do Laws Get Passed?* (Harper), 181, 225
*How Do We Measure?* (Murphy), 192, 238
*How Do We Tell Time?* (Fischer), 192, 222
*How Do You Stay Well?* (Hutchinson), 186, 227
*How Else Can We Show It?* (Rogriguez), 191, 243
*How Many Are Left?* (Jackson), 191, 228
*How Many Baby Pandas?* (Markle), 36, 37*f*,
    178, 182, 235
*How Many in All?* (Barth), 191, 206
*How Many Parts?* (Nguyen), 191, 239
*How Many Ways Can You Catch a Fly?* (Jenkins
    & Page), 175, 229
*How Scientists Observe* (Mulcahy), 198, 238
*How the Weather Works* (Dorion), 201, 213
*How to Make a Bouncing Egg* (Marks), 154*f*
*How to Make Bubbles* (Shores), 154*f*
Hughes, Catherine D., 34, 35, 55, 60, 175, 182, 226
Hulbert, Laura, 42–43, 154*f*, 177, 226

*Human Body, The* (Jeunesse), 146*f*
Human body literature, 146–147*f*, 188
*Human Footprint* (Kirk), 182, 234
*Hungry Fox* (Eggleton), 179, 216
*Hunting for Treasure* (Nunweek), 189, 240
*Hurricanes* (Gibbons), 192, 201, 223
Hutchinson, Caroline, 174, 175, 176, 178, 179,
    183, 186, 188, 196, 199, 226–228

*I Am Clean, I Am Healthy* (Desalle), 186, 212
Iasevoli, Brenda, 188, 228
*I Can Move* (Hutchinson), 188, 227
*If a Bus Could Talk* (Ringold), 155*f*
*I Have Chicken Pox* (Gosman), 186, 225
*I Keep Myself Healthy* (Dominello), 186, 198, 213
*I Keep Myself Safe* (Torrisi), 249
*I Know First Aid* (Torrisi), 186, 198, 249
*I Learn With My Senses* (Raymond), 183, 242
Illustrations, 33–35
*I'm Adopted!* (Rotner & Kelly), 183, 244
Imagery, 44, 45
*Important Book, The* (Brown), 118
*In a Nutshell* (Eggleton), 185, 216
*Inch, Foot, Yard* (Barth), 192, 206
Independent reading:
    focus, 18*f*, 67*f*
    format, 18*f*, 67*f*
    instructional strategies, 18*f*
    lesson plan template, 67*f*
    text type, 18*f*, 67*f*
Index, 37–39
Inferential reading strategy, 53
Informational text selection:
    accuracy/authenticity checklist, 39*f*, 161
    accuracy/authenticity evaluation, 39–41
    alliteration, 43–44
    assonance, 43–44
    captions, 33–35
    cause-and-effect structure, 45, 46*f*
    checklist guidelines, 161–162
    comparative structure, 45, 46*f*
    consonance, 43–44
    content/curricular connection checklist, 47*f*, 162
    content/curricular connection evaluation, 45–46
    copyright date, 40
    cover appeal, 31–32
    descriptive structure, 45, 46*f*
    endnotes, 37, 38*f*
    faction, 41
    font, 32–33
    format/visual appeal checklist, 32*f*, 161
    format/visual appeal evaluation, 31–39
    glossary, 37–39
    headings, 35–36
    illustrations, 33–35
    imagery, 44, 45
    index, 37–39
    instructional strategies, 30
    labels, 33–35
    letter size, 32–33
    meaning devices, 44, 45
    metaphor, 44

    *new* nonfiction, 30–31
    onomatopoeia, 43–44
    photographs, 33–35
    problem/solution structure, 45, 46*f*
    question/answer structure, 45, 46*f*
    realism versus fantasy, 34
    repetition, 43–44
    rhyme, 43–44, 45
    sequential structure, 45, 46*f*
    sidebars, 35–36, 37*f*
    simile, 44
    sound devices, 43–44, 45
    table of contents, 37–39
    text layout, 35–36
    text structure, 45, 46*f*, 47*f*
    type, 32–33
    writing style/appropriateness checklist, 42*f*, 162
    writing style/appropriateness evaluation, 42–45
Informational text standards. *See* Reading
    Standards for Informational Text
Informational text topics:
    ABCs, 174
    animals, general, 174–177
    animals, life cycle, 190
    animals, ocean, 193
    animals, pets, 194
    animals, wild/exotic, 177–178
    animals, wild/native, 179
    biographies, 179–180
    birds, 180
    civics/citizenship, 181
    culture, 181
    dinosaurs, 182
    ecology, 182–183
    family, 183
    five senses, 183
    friendship, 183
    garden, 184
    geography, 184
    habitats, 184–186
    healthy living, 186
    history, 187
    holidays/special celebrations, 188
    human body, 188
    insects, 188–189
    jobs, 189–190
    maps, 190
    math, 190–191
    measurement, 192
    money, 192
    natural disasters, 192
    patterns/symmetry, 194
    plants, 195–196
    presidents and families, 196–197
    ranch/farm life, 197
    reptiles, 197
    safety, 198
    science, 198
    science, physical, 194–195
    seasons, 198–199
    shapes, 199
    space, 199–200

sports/recreation, 200
transportation, 200–201
weather, 201
Insects literature, 188–189
*Inside-Out Skeletons* (Nunweek), 175, 240
Instructional strategies:
above-level readers, 26
below-level readers, 24–25
big-idea content, 23–24, 26–27
Common Core State Standards (CCSS),
19, 21–24
complex texts, 19, 21–22
differentiated instruction, 24–26
educational goals, 19, 21–27
explicit instruction, 18–19, 26–27
first grade guided reading lesson, 103, 104*f*, 106,
117, 119
guided reading, 18*f*, 20*f*, 24–26
independent reading, 18*f*
informational text selection, 30
informational text value, 21–22
intentional instruction, 23–24
interactive read-aloud, 18*f*, 20*f*, 23
kindergarten read-aloud lesson, 83, 84, 85, 96*f*
on-level readers, 25–26
oral language skills, 22–23
reading formats, 18*f*, 20*f*
scaffolded informational text reading, 18*f*, 20*f*
second grade guided reading lesson, 122, 124,
125, 132, 136, 138
shared reading, 18*f*, 20*f*
teaching preparation, 24
Intentional instruction, 23–24
Interactive read-aloud:
focus, 18*f*, 20*f*, 67*f*, 68*f*
format, 18*f*, 20*f*, 67*f*, 68*f*
instructional strategies, 18*f*, 20*f*, 23
lesson plan template, 67*f*, 68*f*
text type, 18*f*, 20*f*, 67*f*, 68*f*
*See also* Kindergarten read-aloud lesson
Interdisciplinary learning, 4, 79
Internet resources:
American Society for the Prevention of Cruelty
to Animals (ASPCA), 52
Common Core State Standards (CCSS), 3
eHOW, 52
lesson plan template, 75
National Geographic, 40
water cycle, 138
Interpretation strategy, 58–59
*In the Sea* (Elliott), 193, 221
*Inventions Change Our Lives* (Barile), 187, 205
*Is It Likely to Happen?* (Merritt), 191, 238
*It All Adds Up* (Johnson), 191, 230
*It's a Butterfly's Life* (Kelly), 189, 190, 232
*It's a Hummingbird's Life* (Kelly), 180, 190, 232
*It's Snowing* (Gibbons), 201, 224
*It Started With a Plant* (Eggleton), 195, 216
*I Wonder Why Kangaroos Have Pouches and Other
Questions About Baby Animals* (Wood), 175, 253
*I Wonder Why Stars Twinkle and Other Questions
About Space* (Stott), 199, 248

Jackson, Kay, 191, 228
James, Helen Frost, 174, 228
Jenkins, Amanda, 192, 201, 228
Jenkins, Martin, 177, 182, 228
Jenkins, Steve, 34, 44–45, 82, 175, 176, 177, 182,
185, 188, 192, 193, 194, 223, 229–230
Jeunesse, Gallimard, 146*f*, 195, 230
Jobs literature, 189–190
Johnson, Claire, 191, 230
Johnson, Etta, 181, 230
Johnston, Rebecca, 146*f*
Joubert, Beverly, 31, 32*f*, 37–38, 46, 178, 231
Joubert, Dereck, 31, 32*f*, 37–38, 46, 178, 231
Judge, Lita, 174, 180, 182, 187, 211, 231
*Junk Raft Journey, The* (Nunweek), 182, 240
*Just a Second* (Jenkins), 192, 229

*Kate and Pippin* (Springett), 175, 183, 247
Katz, Jon, 194, 197, 231
Keating, Frank, 180, 196, 197, 231–232
Kelly, Irene, 175, 180, 189, 190, 232
Kelly, Sheila, 181, 183, 244
Kenna, Kara, 192, 232
Kennedy, Jeannie, 187, 189, 200, 232–233
*Kimonos* (Parot), 181, 241
Kindergarten read-aloud lesson:
action steps, 86*f*, 87*f*, 94*f*, 95*f*
behavioral modeling, 85–86
classroom setting, 85
Common Core State Standards (CCSS), 82–83,
97–98
explicit instruction (step three), 84–85, 94*f*
facilitate connections (step four), 85, 95*f*
goals of, 96*f*
guide reading (step two), 84, 87*f*
informational text benefits, 82–83
instructional strategies, 83, 84, 85, 96*f*
Language Standards, 98
lesson plan template, 83–85
pre-lesson information, 86
reading framework, 96*f*
reading preparation (step one), 83–84, 86*f*
reflection activity, 92–93, 99
sample lesson plan, 87–91, 94–95
schedule/grouping, 96*f*
Speaking/Listening Standards, 98
Kindergarten standards:
College and Career Readiness Anchor
Standards, 9–11*f*
Common Core State Standards (CCSS),
82–83, 97–98, 163–165
Foundational Skills Standards, 163
Language Standards, 98, 164
lesson plan template, 76–77*f*
Reading Standards for Informational Text,
9–11*f*, 163
Speaking/Listening Standards, 97, 164
Writing Standards, 164–165
Kingfisher Editors, 174, 177, 184, 193,
194, 233–234
Kirk, Ellen, 182, 234
*Kitchen Chemistry* (Romero), 195, 243

*Knuffle Bunny* (Willems), 150*f*
*Knut, a Pet or Not?* (Eggleton), 178, 217
Kornberg, Arthur, 146*f*
Kottke, Jan, 184, 195, 234
K-W-L (Know-Wonder-Learn) chart,
    106, 108*f*, 117*f*

Labels, 33–35
*Ladybug* (Gibbons), 189, 224
Landau, Elaine, 195, 234
Language Standards:
    Common Core State Standards (CCSS), 4, 22–23
    first grade, 119, 166
    kindergarten, 98, 164
    second grade, 138, 168
Lankford, Mary, 181, 188, 234
Lapp, Diane, 4
Lappi, Megan, 175, 182, 234
Layne, Steven, 174, 234
Lee, Anna, 184, 234
Leedy, Loreen, 194, 234
*Leopard and Silkie* (Peterson), 182, 193, 241
Lesson plan template:
    action steps, 72–73*f*, 74–75*f*
    blank form, 74–75*f*, 171–172
    Common Core State Standards (CCSS), 76–79
    core instruction, 66
    explicit instruction (step three),
        69, 70–71, 73*f*, 75*f*
    facilitate connections (step four),
        69, 71–72, 73*f*, 75*f*, 77*f*
    first grade standards, 76–77*f*
    Foundational Skills Standards, 78–79
    guided reading, 67*f*, 68*f*
    guide reading (step two), 69, 70, 72*f*, 74*f*, 76–77*f*
    high-impact reading strategies, 70*f*
    independent reading, 67*f*
    instructional formats, 66, 67*f*, 68*f*
    interactive read-aloud, 67*f*, 68*f*
    interdisciplinary learning, 79
    Internet resources, 75
    kindergarten standards, 76–77*f*
    lesson goals, 66
    lesson planning, 67
    lesson steps, 69–72
    reading preparation (step one), 69, 72*f*, 74*f*, 76*f*
    scaffolded informational text reading, 67*f*, 68*f*
    second grade standards, 76–77*f*
    shared reading, 67*f*, 68*f*
    text-based responses, 76–78
    vocabulary, 70
    *See also* First grade guided reading lesson;
        Kindergarten read-aloud lesson; Second
        grade guided reading lesson
*Let's Eat* (Merritt), 186, 238
*Let's Figure It Out!* (Merritt), 191, 238
*Let's Make Patterns!* (Grant), 194, 225
*Let's Measure With Tools* (Casteel), 192, 210
Letter size, 32–33
Lieder, Rick, 185, 223
*Life Cycle of a Butterfly, The* (McNamara),
    189, 190, 236

*Life Cycle of a Frog, The* (McNamara), 190, 236
*Life Cycles: Ocean* (Callery), 53, 185, 209
*Life in a Coral Reef* (Pfeffer), 193, 241
*Life in an Urban Community* (McNamara), 184, 237
*Life in a Rural Community* (McNamara), 184, 236
*Life in a Suburban Community* (McNamara),
    184, 236
*Life of a Butterfly, The* (Murphy), 189, 190, 239
*Lion and the Mouse, The* (Pinkney), 157
Literacy in History/Social Studies, Science, and
    Technical Subjects, 4
*Little Cub* (Fraser), 179
*Little Engine That Could, The* (Piper), 152*f*
*Little Kids' African Animal Book* (Joubert &
    Joubert), 37–38, 178, 231
*Living Color* (Jenkins), 175, 229
*Living in a Cave* (Eggleton), 181, 217
*Living in Space* (Eggleton), 199, 217
*Living Things Are Everywhere!* (Smith),
    175, 195, 247
*Lizards* (Marsh), 197, 235
*Local and State Government* (Johnson), 181, 230
Long, Sylvia, 189, 204
*Long Ago and Now* (Torrisi), 187, 250
*Look for Shapes* (Schmerler), 199, 245
*Looking Closely in the Rain Forest* (Serafini),
    178, 185, 196, 246
*Look! No Tail!* (Eggleton), 175, 217
*Lots and Lots of Coins* (Reid), 192, 243
*Loud and Quiet* (Bullard), 42, 43*f*, 175, 209
*Lucky Seal* (Eggleton), 179, 217
*Lucky Water Buffalo Calf* (Eggleton), 178, 217
Lyon, George Ella, 52, 178, 235

MacDonald, Suse, 154*f*
*Mammals* (Burne), 175, 209
*Mammoth Eclipse, A* (Nunweek), 199, 239
*Mangrove Tree, The* (Roth & Trumbore),
    182, 196, 244
Manning, Mick, 146*f*
*Many Ways* (Rotner & Kelly), 183, 244
*Map Keys* (Aberg), 190, 203
*Map Skills* (Frank), 190, 222
Maps literature, 190
*Maps of My School* (Frank), 190, 222
*Maria's Comet* (Hopkinson), 155*f*
Markle, Sandra, 36, 37*f*, 178, 182, 235
Marks, Jennifer, 154*f*
Marsh, Laura, 35, 36*f*, 37, 38*f*, 108–112, 115–117,
    174, 177, 178, 179, 188, 189, 190, 193, 197,
    235–236
*Match!* (National Geographic Little Kids),
    43, 44*f*, 176, 239
*Match-Up Fun* (Torrisi), 191, 250
Math literature, 190–191
Matthews, John Thomas, 184, 236
Mavor, Salley, 150*f*
Mayer, M., 157
McMillan, Bruce, 40
McNamara, Margaret, 174, 176, 181, 184,
    189, 190, 196, 198, 201, 236–237
*Meadowlands* (Yezerski), 182, 253

*Me and My Amazing Body* (Sweeny), 146*f*

Meaning devices, 44, 45

Measurement literature, 192

*Medical Chemistry* (Romero), 195, 243

*Meet the Dogs of Bedlam Farm* (Katz), 194, 197, 231

Merritt, Donna, 179, 186, 188, 191, 195, 198, 237–238

Metaphor, 44

*Me* (Wood), 188, 253

*Mighty Muscular and Skeletal Systems, The* (Crabtree Publishing), 146*f*

*Monarch and Milkweed* (Frost & Gore), 189, 190, 223

*Monarch Butterfly* (Gibbons), 189, 190, 224

Money literature, 192

*Money Matters* (Rumsch), 192, 244–245

*Monsters of the Deep* (Davies), 193, 211

*Monster Trucks* (Graham), 200, 225

*Moses* (Weatherford), 180, 187, 252

*Mother to Tigers* (Lyon), 52, 178, 235

*Move!* (Jenkins & Page), 34, 176, 230

*Moving Elephants* (Eggleton), 178, 217

*Moving Seeds* (Eggleton), 196, 217–218

Mulcahy, Marie, 192, 194, 198, 238

Murphy, Ann, 189, 190, 191, 192, 238–239

*Muscles* (Simon), 146*f*

*My Amazing Body* (Thomas), 146*f*

*My Baseball Book* (Gibbons), 200, 224

*My Basketball Book* (Gibbons), 200, 224

*My Community* (Torrisi), 181, 184, 189, 250

*My Five Senses* (Aliki), 146*f*

*My Name Is Celia/Me Llamo Celia* (Brown), 155*f*

*My Soccer Book* (Gibbons), 200, 224

*Mystery Seeds, The* (Raymond), 196, 242

*My Wonderful Body* (Merritt), 188, 238

National Assessment of Educational Progress, 13, 22

National Geographic Little Kids, 43, 44*f*, 175, 176, 177, 239

National Geographic website, 40

National Governors Association (NGA), 3

Natural disasters literature, 192

*Nature in a Nutshell* (Potter), 155*f*

*Nature of Things, The* (Eggleton), 176, 218

*Needs Past and Present* (Frank), 187, 222

Nelson, Robin, 186, 188, 239

*Nervous System, The* (Riley), 147*f*

*Never-Ending Story, The*, 127, 130–132

Newman, Mark, 178, 239

*New* nonfiction, 30–31

Nguyen, Linh, 191, 239

*Nickels* (Kenna & Ostarch), 192, 232

*Night in the Garden* (Eggleton), 184, 185, 218

*No Bones* (Eggleton), 176, 218

Nonfiction text:
    Common Core State Standards (CCSS), 2, 12–16
    cross-curriculum comprehension, 12
    defined, 2
    disciplinary knowledge impact, 15
    expository text, 12
    for units of study, 15–16
        influence of, 13
        literacy development impact, 14
        *new* nonfiction, 30–31
        real-world applications, 13

*North* (Dowson), 176, 213

*Numbers to 100* (Barth), 191, 207

Nunweek, Joseph, 199, 239

Nunweek, Lynda, 175, 180, 182, 188, 189, 193, 197, 240–241

Nuzzolo, Deborah, 53, 193, 241

*Oak Tree Has a Life Cycle, An* (Castor), 196, 210

*Ocean* (Callery), 185, 193, 209

*Oceans and Seas* (Davies), 185, 193, 212

*Oceans* (Rizzo), 193, 243

*Octopus Mother* (Eggleton), 193, 218

*One More, One Less* (Barth), 191, 207

*One Step, Two Step* (Woolley), 183, 253

*One Thousand Tracings* (Judge), 187, 231

On-level readers:
    first grade guided reading lesson, 103, 104*f*
    instructional strategies, 25–26

Onomatopoeia, 43–44

*On the Ball* (Kennedy), 200, 233

Ostarch, Judy, 192, 232

*Our Country* (Torrisi), 181, 250

*Our Earth* (Matthews), 184, 236

*Our Solar System* (Wasp), 199, 252

*Over, Under, In, and Out* (Mulcahy), 194, 238

*Over the Bridge* (Kennedy), 187, 233

Page, Robin, 34, 82, 175, 176, 229–230

*Pandas* (Clark), 178, 211

Parot, Annelore, 181, 241

*Parts of a Plant, The* (Castor), 196, 210

Patent, Dorothy Hinshaw, 194, 241

Patterns/symmetry literature, 194

*Penguins* (Arlon), 178, 180, 204

*Pennies* (Kenna & Ostarch), 192, 232

Peterson, Brenda, 182, 193, 241

Petrie, Kristin, 146*f*

*Pets* (Kingfisher Editors), 194, 234

Pfeffer, Wendy, 184, 193, 195, 241

*Photographer's Diary, A* (Eggleton), 189, 197, 218

Photographs, 33–35

Pinkney, J., 157

Piper, Watty, 152*f*

*Place to Live, A* (Eggleton), 176, 218

*Plane Shapes* (Barth), 199, 207

*Planets* (Arlon), 199, 204

Plant literature, 195–196

*Plants and the Seasons* (McNamara), 196, 198, 237

*Plants in Their Habitats* (Castor), 185, 196, 211

*Play Ball!* (Rowland Reading Foundation), 85, 87–91, 94–95

*Playground Science* (Merritt), 195, 238

*Pocketful of Posies* (Mavor), 150*f*

*Polar Bears* (Newman), 178, 239

*Ponies* (Marsh), 179, 235

Potter, Jean, 155*f*

*President From Hawai'i, A* (Carolan & Carolan), 180, 197, 210

Presidents and families literature, 196–197
*President's Day* (Nelson), 188, 239
Prior knowledge utilization, 52
Problem/solution structure, 45, 46*f*
*Puppies, Puppies Everywhere!* (Urbigkit), 194, 251

*Quarters* (Kenna & Ostarch), 192, 232
Question/answer structure, 45, 46*f*

*Race to the Finish* (Scott), 200, 246
*Racing* (Eggleton), 200, 218
*Rainforest* (Callery), 178, 185, 209
Ramirez, Mark, 195, 241
Ranch/farm life literature, 197
Range of Text Types Standard (Standard 10), 2, 12
Rappaport, Doreen, 180, 196, 242
Raymond, Christopher, 183, 196, 198, 242
Read-alouds. *See* Interactive read-aloud; Kindergarten read-aloud lesson
*Reading and Writing Informational Text in the Primary Grades* (Duke & Bennett-Armistead), 149
Reading Standards for Informational Text:
     College and Career Readiness Anchor Standards, 9–11*f*
     Common Core State Standards (CCSS), 2, 4, 9–11*f*, 12
     craft and structure, 10*f*
     defined, 2
     first grade, 9–11*f*, 165
     integration of knowledge and ideas, 11*f*
     key ideas and details, 9–10*f*
     kindergarten, 9–11*f*, 163
     range of reading/level of text complexity, 11*f*
     second grade, 9–11*f*, 167
Reading Standards for Literature, 4, 12
*Real Tree House, A* (Eggleton), 181, 218
*Red Sings from Treetops* (Sidman), 151*f*
Reed, Hannah, 176, 179, 242
Rees, Rod, 195, 242
References/resources, 59–60
Reid, Margarette, 192, 243
Repetition, 43–44
Reptiles literature, 197
*Reptiles* (Weber), 197, 252
Rhyme, 43–44, 45
*Right Down the Middle* (Torrisi), 194, 250
Riley, Joelle, 147*f*
Ringold, Faith, 151*f*, 155*f*
Rius, Maria, 146*f*
Rizzo, Johanna, 193, 243
Roadblocks, 61
*Robot Crab* (Eggleton), 193, 219
*Robot Lander on Mars* (Eggleton), 199, 219
*Robots* (Rees), 195, 242
*Rocks and Minerals* (Tomecek), 195, 248
Rockwell, Lizzy, 146*f*
Rodriguez, Miguel Ortega, 191, 243

Romero, Libby, 194, 195, 243
Roth, Susan L., 182, 196, 244
Rotner, Shelley, 181, 183, 189, 197, 198, 244
Rowland Reading Foundation, 85, 87–91, 94–95, 125
Rumsch, BreAnn, 192, 244–245
Rustad, Martha, 174, 179, 198, 245

*Safe at Home* (Desalle), 198, 212
*Safe at Play* (Desalle), 198, 212
*Safe at School* (Desalle), 198, 212
Safety literature, 198
St. George, Judith, 180, 197, 247
*Same, More, or Less?* (Barth), 191, 200, 207
*Samso* (Nunweek), 182, 240–241
Sanchez, Maria, 200, 245
Santiago, Rosario Ortiz, 195, 245
*Saving Audie* (Patent), 194, 241
*Saving Our Planet* (Wasp), 183, 252
Sayre, April Pulley, 179, 245
Scaffolded informational text reading:
     focus, 18*f*, 20*f*, 67*f*, 68*f*
     format, 18*f*, 20*f*, 67*f*, 68*f*
     instructional strategies, 18*f*, 20*f*
     lesson plan template, 67*f*, 68*f*
     text type, 18*f*, 20*f*, 67*f*, 68*f*
Schmerler, Alison, 199, 245
*Schools Then and Now* (Swain), 187, 248
Schreiber, Anne, 192, 245
Schuetz, Kari, 178, 245
Schuh, Mari, 184, 186, 245
Schwake, Susan, 155*f*
*Science Detectives* (Raymond), 198, 242
*Science Is Everywhere!* (Yu), 198, 253
Science literature, 194–195, 198
Scott, Janine, 200, 246
*Seabird in the Forest* (Dunning), 179, 180, 213
*Sea Otters in the Kelp Forest* (Reed), 179, 242
Seasons literature, 198–199
*Sea Turtles* (Marsh), 193, 235
Second grade guided reading lesson:
     action steps, 126*f*, 127*f*, 136*f*
     below-level readers, 122–124
     classroom management, 124–125
     classroom setting, 124
     Common Core State Standards (CCSS), 122–124, 138, 139*f*
     differentiated instruction, 122–124
     explicit instruction (step three), 136*f*
     facilitate connections (step four), 136*f*, 138
     Foundational Skills Standards, 123–124
     guide reading (step two), 127*f*
     instructional strategies, 122, 124, 125, 132, 136, 138
     Language Standards, 138
     lesson plan template, 126*f*, 127*f*, 136*f*
     pre-lesson information, 125–126
     reading preparation (step one), 126*f*
     reflection activity, 133–134, 140–141
     sample lesson plan, 127–132, 135–138
     Speaking/Listening Standards, 138
     text complexity band, 122

Second grade standards:
  College and Career Readiness Anchor
    Standards, 9–11*f*
  Common Core State Standards (CCSS), 122–124,
    138, 139*f*, 167–169
  Foundational Skills Standards, 123–124, 167
  Language Standards, 138, 168
  lesson plan template, 76–77*f*
  Reading Standards for Informational Text,
    9–11*f*, 167
  Speaking/Listening Standards, 138, 168
  Writing Standards, 168–169
*Seed, Sprout, Pumpkin, Pie* (Esbaum), 196, 221
*Seeing* (Gordon), 183, 225
*Seeing Symmetry* (Leedy), 194, 234
*Senses in the City* (Rotner), 183, 244
*Senses on the Farm* (Rotner), 183, 197, 244
Sequential structure, 45, 46*f*
Serafini, Frank, 178, 185, 196, 246
Serrano, John, 181, 246
Seuss, Dr., 157
*Shades of People* (Rotner & Kelly), 181, 244
Shanahan, Kerrie, 174, 176, 178, 179, 246
*Shape by Shape* (MacDonald), 154*f*
Shapes literature, 199
Shared reading:
  focus, 18*f*, 20*f*, 67*f*, 68*f*
  format, 18*f*, 20*f*, 67*f*, 68*f*
  instructional strategies, 18*f*, 20*f*
  lesson plan template, 67*f*, 68*f*
  text type, 18*f*, 20*f*, 67*f*, 68*f*
*Shepherd's Trail, The* (Urbigkit), 197, 251
Shields, Amy, 57, 198, 201, 246
Shifts in standards, 4–6
Shores, Erika, 154*f*
*Showdown at the Food Pyramid* (Barron), 146*f*
Showers, Paul, 146*f*
Sidebars, 35–36, 37*f*
Sidman, Joyce, 151*f*
*Sight* (Rius), 146*f*
Simile, 44
Simon, Seymour, 147*f*, 174, 247
Singer, Marilyn, 247
*S Is for S'mores* (James), 174, 228
*Sisters & Brothers* (Jenkins & Page), 176, 230
Skills-based groups, 101–102
*Sleeping Animals* (Eggleton), 176, 219
*Sleep* (Showers), 146*f*
*Smell* (Rius), 146*f*
Smith, Jayne, 175, 195, 247
*Smoke Jumpers Help* (Eggleton), 189, 219
*Snakes* (Gibbons), 197, 224
*Snakes!* (Stewart), 197, 247
*Snake Wrangler, A* (Nunweek), 189, 197, 241
Sobol, Richard, 189, 247
*Solid Shapes* (Barth), 199, 207
*Solid Shapes* (Schmerler), 199, 245
Sound devices, 43–44, 45
Space literature, 199–200
Speaking/Listening Standards:
  Common Core State Standards (CCSS), 4
  first grade, 119, 166

  first grade guided reading lesson, 119
  kindergarten, 97, 164
  kindergarten read-aloud lesson, 98
  second grade, 138, 168
  second grade guided reading lesson, 138
*Spiders* (Marsh), 108–112, 115–117, 189, 236
*Splash* (Berger & Berger), 193, 208
*Splish Splash* (Rowland Reading Foundation), 125
Sports/recreation literature, 200
Springett, Martin, 175, 183, 247
*Stand Tall, Abe Lincoln* (St. George), 180, 197, 247
*Stars Above, The* (Eggleton), 199, 219
*Stay Away!* (Feely), 176, 221
*Staying Clean* (Nelson), 186, 239
*Step Gently Out* (Frost & Lieder), 185, 223
Stewart, Melissa, 175, 197, 247
*Story of Silk, The* (Sobol), 189, 247
Stott, Carol, 199, 248
*Stourbridge Lion, The* (Zimmerman), 57, 200, 254
*Subtracting Two-Digit Numbers* (Barth), 191, 207
*Subtraction Strategies* (Barth), 191, 207
*Suit for Spacewalking, A* (Eggleton), 199, 219
Summarize/synthesize strategy, 60–61
*Sun and Shadows, Sky and Space* (Sanchez), 200, 245
*Super Dog* (Eggleton), 194, 219
Sutton, Sally, 189, 248
Swain, Cynthia, 187, 248
Sweeny, Joan, 146*f*
Sweet, Melissa, 179, 187, 188, 248
Swinburne, Stephen, 190, 248

Table of contents, 37–39
*Take a Stand* (Torrisi), 181, 250
Talia, James, 183, 248
*Tall Tree, The* (Eggleton), 185, 196, 219
*Taste* (Rius), 146*f*
Taylor-Butler, Christine, 146*f*
*Teach Me How* (Shanahan), 176, 178, 246
*Tell Me, Tree* (Gibbons), 196, 224
*Tell Me All About It* (Raymond), 198, 242
*Tell Someone You Trust* (Torrisi), 198, 250
Text complexity band, 122
*Text Complexity* (Frey, Lapp, & Fisher), 4
Text layout, 35–36
Text structure, 45, 46*f*, 47*f*
*Thank You, Sarah* (Anderson), 180, 187, 188, 203
*Theodore* (Keating), 180, 197, 232
Thimmesh, Catherine, 175, 183, 248
Thomas, Pat, 146*f*
*Tiger Shark* (Nuzzolo), 53, 193, 241
*Tigers* (Marsh), 178, 236
*Time for a Bath* (Jenkins & Page), 176, 230
*Time to Eat* (Jenkins & Page), 176, 230
*Tiny Life on Your Body* (Taylor-Butler), 146*f*
*Titanic* (Stewart), 187, 247
Tomecek, Steve, 195, 248
*Tools for the Garden* (Schuh), 184, 245
*Tornadoes* (Gibbons), 192, 201, 224
*Tornado!* (Jenkins), 192, 201, 228
Torrisi, Cathy, 181, 183, 184, 186, 187, 189, 190,
  191, 194, 198, 249–250
*Touch* (Rius), 146*f*

Tourville, Doering, 146f
*Tractors and Farm Vehicles* (Coppendale), 200, 211
*Train* (Shields), 57, 201, 246
Transportation literature, 200–201
*Transportation Past and Present* (Frank), 57, 187, 201, 223
*Trip to Space Camp, A* (Kennedy), 200, 233
*Trucks* (Coppendale), 201, 211
Trumbore, Cindy, 182, 196, 244
*Turtle's Journey, The* (Eggleton), 193, 220
Type, 32–33

*Understanding Place Value* (Barth), 191, 207
*Understanding Tens and Ones* (Barth), 191, 207
*Under the Ice* (Eggleton), 185, 220
*Under Your Skin* (Manning), 146f
*Unforgettable Season* (Bildner), 200, 208
*Up Pops a Mushroom* (Eggleton), 196, 220
Urbigkit, Cat, 183, 194, 197, 251
*Using Color* (Reed), 176, 242

Valat, Pierre-Marie, 195, 230
Van Steenwyk, Elizabeth, 196, 251
*Vegetables on My Plate* (Schuh), 186, 246
*Vegetables We Eat, The* (Gibbons), 196, 224
Viorst, Judith, 150f
Visualization techniques, 54–55
Vocabulary, 70
*Volcanoes!* (Schreiber), 192, 245
*Vulture View* (Sayre), 179, 245

Wadsworth, Ginger, 196, 251
Wallner, Alexandra, 179, 187, 251
Wasp, Megan, 57, 174, 182, 183, 199, 251–252
*Watcher, The* (Goodall), 155f
*Watch What Happens!* (Grant), 195, 225
*Water, Water, Everywhere*, 127–132
*Water Cycle, The* (Merritt), 195, 238
*Water* (Jeunesse & Valat), 195, 230
*Weather and the Seasons* (McNamara), 198, 201, 237
Weatherford, Carole Boston, 180, 187, 252
Weather literature, 201
Weber, Belinda, 197, 252
*We Can Graph It!* (Murphy), 191, 239
*Weird Sea Creatures* (Marsh), 193, 236
*We Need Directions* (De Capua), 190, 212
*We Need Rules* (Torrisi), 181, 250
*Whales and Dolphins* (Bingham), 193, 209
*What Am I?* (Reed), 176, 242
*What Animal Am I?* (Hutchinson), 176, 227
*What Are Some Rules at Home?* (McNamara), 181, 237
*What Are Some Rules at School?* (McNamara), 181, 237
*What Can We See in Nature?* (Hutchinson), 186, 227
*What Did One Elephant Say to the Other* (Baines), 178, 205
*What Do Animals Need?* (McNamara), 176, 237

*What Do Plants Need?* (Castor), 196, 211
*What Do You Do With a Tail Like This?* (Jenkins & Page), 34, 82, 176, 230
*What Do You See?* (Hutchinson), 183, 227
*What Happens to a Hamburger* (Showers), 146f
*What Is in That Egg* (Baines), 45, 47f, 190, 205
*What Is Long?* (Eggleton), 176, 220
*What Is Longer? What Is Shorter?* (Barth), 192, 208
*What Is Next?* (Chen), 194, 211
*What Is Weather?* (Bartholomew), 201, 208
*What Lives at the Pond?* (Hutchinson), 179, 186, 227
*What Next?* (Eggleton), 220
*What Season Is It?* (Hutchinson), 199, 227
*What Should I Put on My Plate?* (Torrisi), 186, 250
*What's That?* (Eggleton), 176, 220
*What Time Is It?* (Mulcahy), 192, 238
*What Would You Eat in the Rain Forest?* (Hutchinson), 178, 186, 227–228
*Wheels* (Eggleton), 201, 220
*Where Are the Bats* (Eggleton), 179, 220
*Where Are the Solid Shapes?* (Barth), 199, 208
*Where Are We?* (Torrisi), 184, 190, 250
*Where Can They Live?* (Eggleton), 176, 186, 221
*Where Do Plants Live?* (Hutchinson), 186, 196, 228
*Whiskers* (Eggleton), 177, 221
White, Becky, 180, 187, 252
*Who Has These Feet?* (Hulbert), 42–43, 177, 226
*Who Has This Tail?* (Hulbert), 154f, 177, 226
*Whose Shoes?* (Swinburne), 190, 248
*Why Do We Have Rules?* (McNamara), 181, 237
*Wildlife Detective* (Eggleton), 178, 183, 190, 221
Willems, Mo, 150f
*Will Rogers* (Keating), 180, 232
*Winter Wonderland* (Esbaum), 199, 221
*W Is for Windy City* (Layne & Dover), 174, 234
Wood, Emily, 188, 194, 253
Wood, Jenny, 175, 253
Woodhull, Anne, 189, 198, 244
Woolley, Marilyn, 183, 253
Woop Studios, 174, 177, 253
*World of Farming: Food From Farms* (Dickman), 32–33, 197, 212
*World of Farming: Jobs on the Farm* (Dickman), 197, 212
*World of Farming: Seasons on a Farm* (Dickman), 197, 199, 212
*World's Greatest Lion, The* (Helfer), 178, 226
Writing Standards:
    first grade, 166–167
    kindergarten, 164–165
    second grade, 168–169
Writing style/appropriateness:
    text evaluation checklist, 42f, 162
    text selection criteria, 42–45

Yagu, Genichiro, 146f
*Yellowstone Moran* (Judge), 180, 231

Yezerski, Thomas, 182, 253
*Young Shepherd, A* (Urbigkit), 197, 251
*Your Body Has Parts* (Hutchinson), 188, 228
*Your Skin Holds You In* (Baines), 188, 205
Yu, Nancy, 198, 253

*Zeal of Zebras, A* (Woop Studios), 174, 177, 253
Zimmer, Tracie Vaughn, 151*f*, 177, 253
Zimmerman, Karl, 57, 200, 254
Zoehfeld, Kathy Weidner, 182, 254

# BECAUSE ALL TEACHERS ARE LEADERS

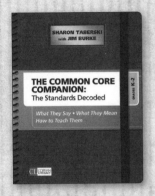

### Sharon Taberski

On that grades K–2 *Companion* teachers have been pleading for

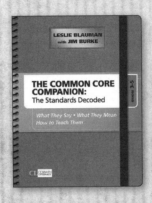

### Leslie Blauman

On the how-to's of putting the grades 3–5 standards into day-to-day practice

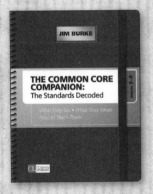

### Jim Burke

On what the 6–8 standards really say, really mean, and how to put them into practice

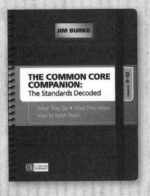

### Jim Burke

On that version of the 9–12 standards all high school teachers wish they had

### Michael Smith, Deborah Appleman & Jeffrey Wilhelm

On where the authors of the standards go wrong about instruction—and how to get it right

### ReLeah Lent & Barry Gilmore

On practical strategies for coaxing our most resistant learners into engagement and achievement